The Nature of the Farm

The Nature of the Farm

Contracts, Risk, and Organization in Agriculture

Douglas W. Allen and Dean Lueck

The MIT Press
Cambridge, Massachusetts
London, England

This book was set in Times Roman by Windfall Software (using ZzT_EX) and was printed and bound in the United States of America.

Library of Congress Cataloging-in-Publication Data

Allen, Douglas W.
  The nature of the farm : contracts, risk, and organization in agriculture / Douglas W. Allen and Dean Lueck.
    p. cm.
  Includes bibliographical references (p.).
  ISBN 0-262-12253-7 (hc. : alk. paper)
  1. Farm management. 2. Agriculture—Economic aspects. 3. Sharecropping. 4. Risk management.
5. Contracts, Agricultural. I. Lueck, Dean. II. Title.

S561 .A543   2003
640′.68—dc21   2002075125

Contents

Preface

Our career long interest in agriculture no doubt stems from the fact that both of us grew up on farms (big and small) and come from families with long histories of farming on the Canadian Prairies and the Great Plains of the United States. More than a decade ago, late in our graduate studies at the University of Washington, we realized our common background and began discussing farming and cropsharing and decided to reread Steven Cheung's classic, *The Theory of Share Tenancy*. Upon a second, more critical reading, we were surprised by the lack of farming details in Cheung's study and his casual empirical assertions. Although we still believe Cheung's work is a watershed in the economics of organization, we were surprised by Cheung's use of risk sharing to explain cropsharing. Risk-sharing arguments are often untestable and, more important, often divert attention from important incentive and enforcement issues in contracts and organization.

We then proceeded to examine the vast literature—mostly in the burgeoning area of principal-agent theory—spawned by Cheung's study. This literature, like Cheung's work, emphasized risk sharing as a rationale for contract and organizational forms. Furthermore, the theory focused on stylized facts that were at odds with our own understanding of modern North American agriculture. Most notable, the literature assumed that cropshare contracts had vanished from modern agriculture. Since we knew from our own experience that cropshare contracts were still widespread, we first set out to explain the existence and extent of these contracts in modern agriculture. We fondly recall when a senior professor of agricultural economics flat-out told us, "There are no cropshare contracts in American agriculture anymore." Now, of course, no one is surprised by the existence of share contracts, given the expansion of empirical work within and beyond agriculture.

In 1992 we published our first paper and subsequently began to direct our research toward developing an explanation of farm organization consistent with actual farming practices—especially those in modern developed agriculture—completely based on transaction costs and explicitly ignoring risk-sharing considerations. Since then we have published many more papers on contracts and organization in agriculture.

This book is a compilation, elaboration, and extension of our published work. We use new data to retest our original hypotheses. The book also elaborates on our past work by connecting and extending our earlier models. By linking studies together in a consistent theoretical framework and with consistent empirical evidence, the book allows the reader to easily see connections among a variety of topics, ranging from the choice of land contract to the determinants of vertical integration. In the process, the book makes a much stronger case for the transaction cost approach to agricultural organization than can be made by examining separate, focused studies one at a time. And, a decade after our first publication, we can say that our initial paradigm remains consistent with our most recent data and our most recent theoretical extensions.

Because of our focus on transaction costs and because of our empirical emphasis, our book might alternatively be titled "Ronald Coase Goes to the Farm." Instead, we shamelessly borrowed our title from Coase's famous article, originally published in 1937. The "nature" of the farm, however, has an interpretation that extends beyond Coase's use of "nature" for industrial firms. In agriculture, Mother Nature is the fundamental force that shapes the incentives and transaction costs that, in turn, ultimately shape agricultural organization.

We wish to express gratitude to those people who have helped us over the years. Foremost is our debt to Yoram Barzel, who not only guided our respective Ph.D. theses, but quietly and forcefully taught us about transaction cost economics. We also are grateful to those who helped us with data collection, particularly Bruce Johnson and Larry Jannsen who first supplied us (for free!) with the original Nebraska–South Dakota data from their own surveys of farmers and landowners. Various extension agents were instrumental in helping us design and collect the data for Louisiana and British Columbia, especially Howard Joynt of the British Columbia Ministry of Agriculture and Al Ortego, USDA extension economist at Louisiana State University. We also need to thank Ray Bollman of Statistics Canada for helping us fill in several blank spots on a number of tables. Four farmer-landowners—Henry Adolf, Gary Allen, Les Lueck, and Harold Munk—patiently answered questions and shared their farming experience, which greatly helped us understand general farming and contract practices. We also thank our friends and colleagues who never grew tired (or at least never told us) of reading about and discussing farming: Nabil Al-Najjar, Curt Eaton, Steve Ferris, D. Bruce Johnsen, Chuck Knoeber, James Meehan, Rulon Pope, Clyde Reed, Tom Ross, Randy Rucker, Zane Spindler, Wing Suen, Wally Thurman, and Jim Vercammen. Larry Boland deserves special mention for producing all of the graphs and for tolerating endless changes to them. There are thanks due to participants, too numerous to mention, in more than thirty presentations at seminars and conferences, although two conferences (thanks to David Martimort and Jacques Cremer) at the Institute for Industrial Economics at the University of Toulouse are worth noting. We also thank the four anonymous referees for The MIT Press who provided us with a wide range of important comments on the initial draft, and our editor John S. Covell for his encouragement from the very beginning of the publication process.

Finally, we would like to thank various institutions that have provided financial support during the past decade. Allen has been supported by the Social Sciences and Humanities Research Council of Canada. The National Science Foundation provided Lueck support from 1995–1998. The Center for Research on Contracts and the Organization of Enterprise (University of Pittsburgh) assisted in the collection and organization of data in 1995. Lueck was also supported as an Olin Faculty Fellow at the Yale Law School during 1994–1995. Penultimate drafts of the book were done while Allen was a visitor at the University of Canterbury in New Zealand, and while Lueck was a visitor at Universitat Pompeu Fabra in Spain.

1 Introduction

Despite their briefcase reputation, economists have shown a remarkable fascination with farming and its various economic details. This might be expected of the agricultural economists in the profession—after all, that's their job—but it also has been true of general economists. The economics literature is filled with discussions of farming, especially in the context of share contracting, specialization, and the division of labor on farms. This literature includes the classical economists Adam Smith, who noted the moral hazard incentives inherent in some farmland contracts, and John Stuart Mill, who identified the effect nature's seasons had on the ability to specialize in farm production. It also includes modern scholars such as recent Nobel Prize winner Joseph Stiglitz, who formally introduced the profession to the principal-agent paradigm in the context of farming, and Yoram Barzel, who first noted the multiple contracting problems that arise on both the farmer and landowner sides of the market. Economists have been especially enamored of share contracts, and the inquiry into their existence and efficiency has led, almost directly, to the modern theory of contracts.[1] Share contracts have been common worldwide for centuries, but perhaps more surprising, these "cropshare" contracts—as they are called by American farmers—remain common in modern developed agriculture as well.[2] Despite numerous theoretical inquiries into agricultural share contracts, however, and despite their common occurrence, surprisingly little is widely known about their details.

Although there is more to the "nature of the farm" than just share contracting for land, it is fair to say that our economic understanding of farm organization beyond share contracting is limited. For example, prior to the decision about the type of land lease, a landowner must decide whether to rent the land or farm the land for himself. What determines this choice? Furthermore, this decision of ownership versus contracting applies to the other major assets on the farm as well as to the land, and the patterns of owning are vastly different for equipment than for land. But what explains these different patterns of ownership? Although farming is one of the last industries in which the majority of firms are owned by families, over time the scope and depth of family ownership and production has eroded. What explains this dominance and partial erosion? Although it is impossible to analyze all organizational issues on the farm, we examine these questions in particular.

This book has several objectives. First, we wish to demonstrate the power of the transaction cost approach in understanding many organizational features of agriculture. Though we devote a great deal of attention to the issue of contract choice, we also examine the ownership structure of the farm and the question of vertical control. Though our specific models vary from chapter to chapter, the overriding theme is that contracts and other patterns of ownership are chosen to mitigate transaction costs (to be defined momentarily). In agriculture, transaction costs are heavily influenced by Mother Nature. Nature's uncertainty, via weather and pests, allows for suboptimal asset use, and through seasonal forces nature imposes constraints on production cycles that are not often found in the production of other commodities. We take pains to explore these constraints placed by nature and other farming details in order to understand the transaction costs that arise under different forms of organization. We then use this to derive testable propositions about contract and organization choice.

Second, we wish to contrast our transaction cost approach with theories based on, or including, risk-sharing motives. Virtually all economists who study the economics of organization recognize that incentives are important. The oldest, and most common, model of share tenancy is one in which there is a trade-off between the incentives of the farmer and his aversion to bear risk. Throughout the book we will refer to this model as the "principal-agent" model. In this model the contracts that provide the best incentives also generate the most risk. Risk is, in effect, the cost of incentives. Our model is also based on incentives, but incentives spread over many decisions made by the farmer, the landowner, or equipment owner depending on the problem at hand. As it turns out, many predictions from these two models are at odds with each other. We devote considerable space to empirically contrasting the two.

Third, we want to study organization (the ownership and the contracting) of modern agriculture in North America. That is, our book is a detailed study of the organization of a single industry—in both a historical and a contemporary context. Until quite recently, the economic analysis of farm contracts and organization has focused on historic and developing country cases.[3] As we mentioned in the preface, this has often led many to conclude that cropsharing does not exist in modern farming communities. Among modern agricultural economists who study North American farming, the focus has not been on contracts but on neoclassical analysis of costs, production, and commodity markets. A study of North American farming, where technology is advanced and where capital markets are well developed, provides an opportunity to test theories often applied to only Third World settings, and to explain a series of farming puzzles that have generally been ignored. Although our book relates to the literature that spans the fields of development, economic history, and agricultural economics, our book is not a literature survey. We make frequent references to such literature in order to provide context for our models and results; however, many excellent surveys already exist (for example, Otsuka and Hayami 1992), and we feel it unnecessary to repeat them.

Finally, our objective is to explain a variety of economic organizational puzzles in farming. Consider the following. Grain farmers use a large machine called a combine to harvest grain, and depending on the crops grown and the size of farm, this machine may only be used as little as two to three weeks per year. Combines are also one of the most expensive pieces of equipment a farmer might own, with larger models costing $150,000–$200,000. This is a classic case where economists would predict, based on the high cost and low utilization rate, that farmers should rent combines. Yet most farmers still own their combines and leave them idle for most of the year.

Our book examines many such puzzling observations, and while we develop numerous formal models within our basic transaction cost framework, the book is also an empirical analysis of testable predictions using contract and organization data. We use five separate data sources, supplemented with census data, to provide the bulk of our information. These data allow us to use standard econometric methods to test our predictions. In addition, we rely on historical case studies, on such topics as Bonanza farms and custom combining, to supplement our statistical analyses.

1.1   The Transaction Cost Approach to Contracting and Organization

Transaction Costs and Property Rights

At several places in this introduction we have mentioned the "transaction cost" approach, and the time has come to explain what we mean by this phrase and how we believe it differs from other economic approaches to organization. The transaction cost approach begins, of course, with Coase's classic works on the firm (1937) and social cost (1960).[4] In the latter paper Coase pointed out that when transaction costs are zero, the allocation of resources is independent of the distribution of property rights. Ironically, his most famous example is an agricultural application: the cattleman dealing with his crop farming neighbor over tresspassing cattle. When transaction costs are zero, the number of cattle tresspassing does not depend on whether the cattleman possesses the right to trespass or not. The outcome is determined by the joint wealth maximizing level of output on the two farms.

It remained for Cheung, in his pathbreaking book, to recognize the general implications of Coase's work to contracts. Cheung (1969) showed how, under the conditions of zero transaction costs, a cropshare contract could achieve the same outcome in terms of crop output as a cash rent contract could.[5] The result is completely general. When transaction costs are zero, it does not matter how the ownership of the inputs and outputs is distributed by the terms of a contract. Farmers can control land through cash leases, share contracts, or ownership; farms can be family run, sole proprietorships, or they can be large-scale corporations; and farms can be integrated completely from breaking ground to baking the bread, or disintegrated to the point of owning a wheat field for one day—it matters not one iota.

At this point many economists, and others, are ready to abandon Coase's idea. It cannot be stressed enough, however, that Coase's point was not that a model based on zero transaction costs had any relevance for understanding economic organization. Just the opposite. He argued that any analysis of economic organization must hinge on an examination of the transaction costs involved. His argument is as follows: If transaction costs equal zero, then property rights are perfect and organization does not matter; if these costs are not zero, then the explanation of organization lies in transaction costs. The grand hypothesis of the transaction cost approach is that contracts and organization are organized to maximize joint wealth net of transaction costs.

All of this, of course, begs the question "What are transaction costs?"—a question that is made more pressing given that Coase himself has never defined the term but instead just provided examples. Indeed, the transaction cost approach has been hindered at times by ambiguities in language and a general reluctance to define terms—especially the terms "transaction costs" and "property rights." In fact, there are two well-developed concepts of transaction costs in the economics literature. The first, developed by Demsetz (1968), defines transaction costs as the costs of transferring property rights in a market exchange. This is the definition found in the *The New Palgrave Dictionary of Economics*.[6] This approach typically posits some type of "transaction technology" that taxes the transaction and acts in many ways just like a tax. Because this notion of transaction costs was developed to analyze the volume of trade, its major drawback is that it is not useful for examining questions of contract and organizational choice. In another survey article, Allen (2000) calls this the "neoclassical" definition of transaction costs because of its emphasis on the volume of trade.[7]

We do not use the neoclassical concept of transaction cost. Instead, we use what has been called the "property rights approach" to transaction costs, where these costs are defined as *the costs of enforcing and maintaining property rights*—regardless of whether a market exchange takes place or not. Property rights, in turn, are defined as the ability to freely exercise choices over the asset in question. Transaction costs include the deadweight losses that result from enforcing property rights as well (Allen 1991, 2000; Barzel 1997).[8] As a result, transaction costs are more than the costs of a market exchange. That is, property rights may be required to be enforced in a private contract, through courts or other third party agencies, against thieves, or across market transactions. We employ this concept of transaction costs throughout our book because it is complete enough to explain organizational choices and because it more closely aligns with the modern literature on contracts and organization.

In order for transaction costs to exist, two conditions must be met. Information must be costly to obtain, and assets must be variable in their quality or characteristics, and alterable by man. That information must be costly is rather obvious. If everything is known, then enforcing and maintaining one's claim to property is redundant.[9] That assets must be both variable and alterable is perhaps less obvious. Essentially the only way someone can systematically infringe on another's property rights, and therefore make necessary efforts to enforce or maintain them, is for a confusion to exist over the effects of nature and the actions of people. The more uncertainty there is in nature and the more individuals are able to influence final outcomes, the larger the transaction costs. What makes farming such a rich field for a transaction cost approach is the obvious impact of Mother Nature, and the equally important impact of farming decisions on crop output.

Our approach to farming contracts and organization is a transaction cost approach because we develop a set of specific models that depend on the ability of contracting parties to police their interactions with each other. Although farmers enter into contracts with various parties (for example, custom combiners, laborers, landowners, pesticide applicators, storage firms), these contracts are never complete and problems arise in their enforcement due to nature's uncertainty and the complexity of the assets involved in production. Farmers can hide bales of hay that were intended to be shared with landowners, harvest crews can arrive late causing a reduction in crop value, and, of course, hired workers can generally shirk their duties. Transaction costs are the costs of engaging in and preventing these activities, along with any lost gains from trade that result. Both landowners and farmers seek to mitigate these costs. A theme throughout the book is that contracts have incentives that often substitute for direct monitoring. As a result, contracting problems are often solved by altering incentives given the constraints imposed by the particular farming technology, the role of nature, and the potential gains from specialization.[10]

Our transaction cost approach is in the tradition begun by Coase and Cheung, Alchion and Demsetz (1972), and most recently exposited by Barzel (1997). It is similar to Williamson's (2000) discussion of the New Institutional Economics, but differs from his (1979) view of transaction costs that emphasize the role of specific assets in determining organizational forms. Recently Hart (1995, chap. 2) developed what he calls a "property rights approach" to firm ownership. Our book has a similar spirit to that of Hart, but its method is broader. Hart's framework stresses the investments individuals make under different ownership structures. He notes that investments may become sunk, raising the costs of negotiating over the gains from trade in future periods, and that different asset ownership structures will influence investment and total value. Our model is more general and more relevant to farming where investment in such assets tends to play a minor role.

Five Important Ideas

Five important ideas define our framework and require discussion. First, we assume that all parties (farmers, landowners, other input owners) choose contracts and organizational forms because they *maximize the expected value of the relationship*, given the characteristics of all parties, the desired output, and the attributes of assets such as land and equipment. By focusing on joint wealth maximizing allocations, we ignore issues of bargaining and surplus division. In addition, the empirical implementation of bargaining strength seems impractical given the data available for our study. In the context of competitive farming where specific assets are minimal, this issue is relatively unimportant. Competition among farmers for land, and among landowners for renters, and competition between on- and off-farm opportunities generally determine the returns to individual factors of production within narrow bounds. This method assumes that "natural selection" has resulted in the most valuable contract or organization being chosen, and is based on the idea first proposed by Alchian (1950).[11] Farmers and landowners, like everyone else, are keenly aware of their incomes and just as aware of the effect of one type of contract over another on their bottom line. Given the general stability of farming communities, it seems only reasonable to assume that contracts and organization are fundamentally driven to maximize wealth.[12]

Second, while we abandon some aspects of typical contracting models, *uncertainty remains a crucial component*. Uncertainty allows individuals to exploit an exchange at the expense of the other party because it masks their actual effort. This factor is important in agriculture because weather, pests, and other natural phenomenon contribute so much to the final output. In a land lease, for example, uncertainty from weather and other natural forces means that the farmer has the opportunity to "exploit" the landowner in several ways: undersupplying effort, overusing soil quality attributes, and underreporting the shared crop, to name a few. The type of behavior we often focus on is moral hazard (or hidden action) where the farmer, landowner, or other asset user does not bear all of the costs of his actions. Moral hazard is just one type of transaction cost phenomenon, and like transaction costs in general, uncertainty is necessary for it to exist. Still moral hazard is not the only incentive effect we study; there are also measurement and enforcement costs arising from uncertainty.

Third, *all assets are complex in the sense that they are comprised of many attributes*. When assets are complex they create an opportunity for transaction costs to arise for every attribute, which subsequently allows for divided ownership over the various attributes because multidimensional assets are nontrivial to measure. A plot of land, for example, is characterized by its size, terrain, nutrients, moisture, soil type, and so on. Different ownership and contract types affect the various attributes in different ways, creating trade-offs. These trade-offs allow us to explain the choice of organization based on different transaction costs.[13]

Fourth, though nature has a random component in uncertainty, she has a *systematic component we call seasonality*. For contract choice we focus on the random aspect of nature. Poor harvests, soil erosion, and nutrient and moisture depletion can be blamed on acts of nature, even though land overuse may arise from improper tilling and pest control or other practices. Although random acts by nature are a common element in modern contract theory, our idea that nature also plays a systematic role is not found in the contracting literature.[14] Seasonality, instead, refers to crop cycles, the number and length of stages, and timeliness.

In part III of the book the predictable aspects of nature—its seasonality—become very important because they limit the degree to which farmers can specialize in production. Most types of farming are greatly restricted by nature. Both plant and animal crops have "growing seasons" that restrict the nature of farm production. As a result, farmers are seldom able to exploit many forms of economies of size and tend not to develop into large corporate farms.

Finally, throughout our book we attempt to explain farming contracts and organization in the context of *risk neutrality*. As we note below, this is a significant departure from most attempts to explain such matters. Risk aversion is an assumption about preferences that we do not make. There are several reasons for this. First, in modern agriculture, where the ability to avoid risk though insurance and asset markets is so well developed, it seems implausible that farmers and landowners would use their land contracts to further avoid risk. Second, as we show in chapter 6, empirical implementation of even the simplest risk-sharing hypotheses is difficult, and often impossible, because of the stringent data requirements. Third, by avoiding the complexity of preference and uncertainty modeling, we are able to develop models that yield clear and testable predictions. Ultimately, the importance of risk sharing is an empirical matter. Though we push our risk-neutral model in all directions, in part II we pause to compare our results with those based on risk sharing, where we find no compelling grounds to abandon our assumption of risk neutrality.

Modeling Transaction Costs

To summarize, we use a series of transaction cost models in which all parties are risk neutral, in which all assets are complex, and where nature is both an uncertain and seasonal force. These conditions make it costly for the contracting parties to identify exactly the input contributions of their counterparts and, similarly, make it costly to identify the quantity and quality of the output. In agriculture, nature's seasonal forces limit the gains from specialization and the ability of parties to monitor each other.

Although the specific models we use vary from chapter to chapter with the details of the questions we address, we outline the basic framework and its characteristics in this first chapter. In our models output takes the following general form:

$$Q = h(\text{land, labor, capital}) + \theta, \tag{1.1}$$

where Q is the observed harvested output that is assumed to have a unit price and $\theta \sim (0, \sigma^2)$ is the randomly distributed composite input of nature. Exactly how each input is defined depends on the question at hand. For example, when analyzing the choice of contract between cash rent and cropshare, the critical inputs are the unpriced land attributes supplied by the landowner (such as fertility and moisture content) and the labor effort of the farmer. When analyzing the decision to rent or buy an asset such as land, we make a distinction between the priced attributes of the land (such as size measured in acres) and the unpriced attributes (such as soil fertility). In other problems the various inputs may be seed, fertilizer, pesticide, or other nonland nonlabor inputs; labor time as opposed to effort; the number of tasks; and so on. The complexity of the models progresses throughout the book. The chapters on contract choice are simpler because they suppress issues of timing and specialization and focus on moral hazard and enforcement-monitoring costs. Later, these other aspects are introduced to discuss ownership types and vertical integration.

As these complications are added, the specific form of production function in equation (1.1) alters, but regardless of the specific form, our production function contains in it the basic structure necessary for the existence of transaction costs. Notably, output is determined by human action $h(\cdot)$ and nature θ. Inputs are not observable, and although the output Q is observable, it is a complex asset and cannot be perfectly measured. As a result, effort can be altered to suit the private interests of one party at the expense of the other. For example, low levels of output that result from low labor inputs could be blamed on poor weather conditions. Suboptimal level of inputs might also include applications of the inputs at an incorrect time. The simple additive uncertainty component also simplifies the analysis in models that maximize expected values.

In addition to this basic structure, we also make several assumptions regarding the function h. First we assume that h always has positive but diminishing marginal products. Second, we assume that all inputs are independent of one another. Both of these assumptions are intuitively appealing and create models that generate clear predictions. The assumption of independent inputs simplifies the model and increases the number of testable implications. Not only do we have no a priori theoretical grounds to assume which inputs are substitutes or complements, but there is empirical justification for their independence. First, were they not independent, contracts could adjust some input prices upward, others downward, to influence farmer behavior. This, however, is not observed for the cases we study.[15] Second, in chapter 5 we show that input cost sharing in cropshare contracts exhibits an all-or-nothing dichotomy; that is, input costs are either shared in the same proportion as output or are not shared at all. This result is consistent with independent inputs.

Price taking is another common feature of our models. For example, we always assume that the opportunity cost of the farmer's input is the competitive wage rate w per unit of farmer's effort, and the opportunity cost of the unpriced land inputs is r per unit. We also assume that farmers sell their output on world markets and that they cannot influence this output price. These assumptions seem reasonable in the context of modern agriculture with world trade, where individual farmers are small relative to both the input and output markets.

The logic of our models is straightforward. Once the precise production structure is constructed, we begin by deriving the first-best, zero transaction cost outcome for a specific problem. By "first-best" we mean not only that inputs are used in the optimal amounts, but also that inputs are fully specialized and applied at the appropriate time. We use this outcome as a benchmark to compare the actual contracts and organizations, because the presence of transaction costs makes this outcome unattainable. The second step is to examine the various contracts or organizations and determine the optimal value functions under each and to examine the comparative statics of these functions. Next, we assume in all cases that the joint wealth maximizing contract or organization is chosen. Finally, we test derived predictions using our data from North America.

1.2   The Role of Risk in Contract Economics

The transaction cost approach, with its trade-offs of one incentive against another, can be contrasted with the classic "principal-agent" approach to share contracting where it is assumed that contracts are designed to spread the risk of crop farming away from the farmer and partially on to the less risk averse landowner.[16] The fundamental idea that farmland contracts are designed around a trade-off between risks and incentives is commonplace among economists. Indeed, Stiglitz (1987) writes, "The sharecropping model has served as the basic paradigm for a wider class of relationships known as principal-agent relationships" (321), and Sappington (1991) notes, "The classic example of the principal-agent relationship has a landlord overseeing the activities of a tenant farmer" (46). In their important study Otsuka, Chuma, and Hayami (1992) claim that risk aversion "provides the most consistent explanation for the existence of a share contract" (2012). Relying on the standard risk-sharing framework, they further state: "As in typical agency models, the most obvious factor to be accounted for in considering the optimum contract choice is the presence of uncertainty coupled with the risk aversion of the contracting parties" (1987). The dominance of this approach in modeling the behavior of farmers and landowners is not limited to those studying developing countries or economic history (for example, Otsuka, Chuma, and Hayami 1992; Townsend 1994). It is routine among agricultural economists studying farm behavior—including acreage and crop choice studies as well as contract studies—to assume that farmers are risk averse and stress the role of risk sharing in determining behavior.[17]

Despite the prominence of the risk-sharing paradigm, the empirical evidence to support it is scarce.[18] In agriculture there has been little empirical work at the contract level and nearly all of this has been in developing economies (Otsuka, Chuma, and Hayami 1992). In one of the early studies to confront risk sharing and contract choice, Rao (1971) found that crops with high yield and profit variability were less likely to be sharecropped, directly refuting the anecdotal evidence originally provided by Cheung (1969). At the same time, studies by Rao and others (for example, Higgs 1973) tend to use rather small samples of highly aggregated data, making clear inferences difficult.[19] In chapters 6 and 7 we examine

Table 1.1
Crop riskiness and share contracting

Region	Yield coefficient of variation (% of share contracts)	
	Corn	Wheat
British Columbia	.27 (20%)	.18 (79%)
Louisiana	.29 (62%)	.21 (76%)
Nebraska	.12 (69%)	.11 (86%)
South Dakota	.14 (64%)	.25 (61%)

Sources: Appendix A and Allen and Lueck (1995, 1999a).

the risk-sharing hypothesis in detail, but even a glance at the facts suggests that this is not likely the case in modern farming. Table 1.1 shows the coefficient of variation for two major crops (corn and wheat) in our four distinct regions as well as the prevalence of share contracting for farming in those same regions. Contrary to the risk-sharing thesis, land used to grow high variance crops is not cropshared more often. Table 1.1 actually suggests the opposite: Crops with less yield variance are more often cropshared. As we show in chapter 6, this finding is consistent with transaction cost models that focus on measurement costs.

Our approach contrasts with the risk-sharing model.[20] In the classic risk-sharing model, a typical model assumes that a principal maximizes some objective function subject to an agent's incentive and individual rationality constraints. For sharecropping, most of these models postulate a risk-neutral landowner (principal) leasing land to a risk-averse farmer (agent). These models generate a trade-off between risk avoidance and imperfect incentives. A principal who cash rents to an agent has no incentive problem, but the agent "bears all the risk." By sharing with an agent, the principal suffers from agent moral hazard, but the agent no longer bears the full risk of the project and the payments can adjust accordingly. By using the transaction cost approach, we avoid the empirical difficulties of risk-sharing models while retaining other aspects (for example, uncertainty and moral hazard) of these models. We abandon both the principal-agent distinction and the assumption of risk aversion, and instead, we assume all parties are risk neutral.[21]

By treating both parties as risk neutral, we avoid the problem of defining which party is the principal and which is the agent, and also which party is more or less risk averse.[22] In modern farming it is especially difficult to establish such a dichotomy because farmers and

Table 1.2
Characteristics of farmers and landowners

Variable	British Columbia 1979	1992	Louisiana 1992	Nebraska–South Dakota 1986
Average age				
Landowners	52.8	57.0	63.9	≈50
Farmers	40.9	47.2	46.5	≈40
Average years of education				
Landowners	8.3	NA	NA	NA
Farmers	11.0	NA	NA	NA
Average acres of owned land				
Landowners	NA	499.5	748.5	661.2
Farmers	NA	439.4	122.7	435.5
Average acres of owned land				
Farmers with no leased land	NA	147.4	418.4	NA
Farmers with only share leases	NA	412.1	116.8	NA
Farmers with only cash leases	NA	241.3	185.4	NA
Percent of women				
Landowners	NA	NA	NA	34
Farmers	NA	NA	NA	6
Percent of landowners with farm experience	60	69.5	57.2	NA
Percent of farmers				
that rent and own land	NA	93	57	NA
that rent and rent out land	NA	6	6	6
that both share and cash lease	NA	10	24	23

Sources: Appendix A and Allen and Lueck (1995, 1999a).
Note: NA = not available.

landowners have nearly identical demographic characteristics and because farmers make virtually all the decisions, contrary to their oft-designated "agent" status. Table 1.2 points out a number of characteristics of the farmers and landowners that are common across all of our data sets. For example, the table shows that 60 percent of the landowners are or were at one time farmers. Furthermore, table 1.2 shows that renters are often landowners, and in some cases (6%) rent out land simultaneously as well as hold both share and cash rent contracts. The similar social-economic background and demographic features of farmers and landowners along with the coexistence of owning and leasing are inconsistent with a model that posits dichotomous preferences and risk sharing.

Another advantage of our risk-neutral approach is that we do not require data on exogenous risk to test the implications of our models. A significant difficulty in conducting tests of risk sharing lies in finding a reasonable empirical counterpart for the pure random variance in output caused by nature.[23] Obtaining such data is difficult because output data at the contract level are "contaminated" by inputs from nature and the farmer. Finding such measures in studies of franchising and other areas has proved difficult, and as a result scholars have either ignored them or relied on proxies that may seem reasonable, but are not often clearly linked to the underlying theoretical model and may be highly endogenous to the firm's behavior. To test explicitly for the negative relationship between risk and incentives, it is crucial to have such data, which are notoriously difficult to obtain. Such data are not necessary to test our model based on transaction costs and risk neutrality.

1.3   The Role of Government

Government intervention in agriculture in the United States and Canada is long-lived and prominent.[24] Yet, for the most part, we ignore the role of government in affecting the choice of contracts and organizations in agriculture. We have two primary reasons for doing this. First, and most important, these interventions generally do not affect the kinds of incentives we study and thus do not alter the relative costs and benefits of various contract and organizational choices. Second, to the extent there is an impact, our statistical data cannot readily isolate the effects of government. To illustrate these points, we first describe the basic features of agricultural policies and then link them to our study.

In the United States, large-scale intervention in agricultural production began with the New Deal legislation of the 1930s. This legislation established a set of policies providing for price supports and production controls, crop insurance and disaster payments, export subsidies, subsidized farm credit, land and water conservation, subsidized food distribution, and expanded research and extension activities.[25] These programs have varied over time but can be summarized as follows. Price supports (through target prices and nonrecourse loans) and acreage restrictions have been the basic policy for cotton, rice, wheat, and feed grains (barley, corn, grain sorghum, oats). Producers of these crops were entitled to government "deficiency payments" that cover the difference between the target price and the prevailing market price.[26] Soybean prices have been supported through loans and government purchases. Sugar prices have been supported by import restrictions and some price supports, and thus have impact on producers of sugarcane and sugar beets. Many other products, including milk and certain fruits, vegetables, and specialty crops (for example, almonds, oranges), are governed by marketing orders. These marketing orders typically limit the production of the governed commodities by specifying quality and other details of the product.[27] Milk marketing is different from other marketing orders in that price supports are explicitly used to limit output. The 1996 Farm Bill introduced some important changes in U.S. policy.[28] The target price system was replaced with a series of "transition payments" made directly to farmers. These payments, based on historical production, are in place for the years 1996–2002 and are thus "decoupled" from current production decisions. The 1996 bill did not alter the basic structure of the programs for dairy, peanuts, and sugar.

Several other policies are worth noting. Since the 1930s limits have existed on the amount of government payments any single farm(er) can receive, although there are methods of avoiding these restrictions (as we note in chapter 9). Farm capital is generally treated more favorably in the federal tax code than is nonfarm capital. And there have been conservation programs (Soil Bank, Conservation Reserve) since the 1950s, which pay farmers to take land out of production. There are other agricultural programs but these do not relate to the topics we study.[29]

In Canada government intervention has been less intrusive and of a slightly different form.[30] There have been no systems of target prices and government payments for grain. Wheat producers, however, must sell their crop through the Canadian Wheat Board (CWB).[31] Originally established in 1935, the CWB was given monopoly control over Canadian wheat in 1943. The rest of Canada's agriculture tends to be governed by what is called "supply management" (Schmitz, Furtans, and Baylis 2002). Products such as eggs, milk, and poultry are influenced by programs that limit imports with quotas and tariffs as well as domestic production quotas.

Agricultural programs in both countries are substantial in size and appear to be politically quite stable. In 2000, more than $29 billion in direct payments were made to farmers in the United States, including $11.6 billion for feed grains, $5.4 billion for wheat, $4 billion for cotton, and $1.5 billion for disaster assistance.[32] Nearly 34 million acres were enrolled in the Conservation Reserve Program, which pays farmers to keep formerly arable land out of production. This is roughly 7 percent of the 430 million acres of cropland (see table 1.1). According to the U.S. Census of Agriculture, net farm income was $46 billion (income = $196, expenses = $150) in 1997, which makes government payments the equivalent of more than half of net farm income. Programs in Canada tend to be less generous to producers than in the United States, yet they are still substantial.[33]

Among agricultural economists, the effects of government policies have been intensively studied with several areas of focus. One important area in this literature has been how farm policies affect crop production, including such issues as crop choice, acreage in production, farm prices, and crop yield. A second focus has been to estimate the deadweight losses of farm programs and the distribution of their benefits and costs. A third focus has been to study the political economy of farm programs in order to explain their form, their survival, and their variation across crops, regions and time. Despite this expansive literature, almost no analysis of the effects of farm programs on contracts and organization in agricultural production exists. For example, in the texts we cite here, there is almost no mention of such possible effects, with the exception of some discussion of the effects of limitations on farm payments (for example, Knutson, Penn, and Flinchbaugh 1998, 265–66; Pasour 1991, 140). This omission is, perhaps, not too surprising given the relatively limited attention of agricultural economists to contracts and organization.

In this study we focus on incentives arising from the transaction costs created when farmers, landowners, and other asset owners come together to produce agricultural output. Do these farm policies influence these incentives and thus influence the choices farmers make regarding contracts and organization? Generally we would say no: Farm programs do not differentially affect these incentives and thus do not substantively alter economic organization of farms. For example, there is no discernable gain from choosing a cash or a share land lease arrangement in order to increase the benefits derived from government policies.[34] Even if there were predictions, our large data sets all contain cross-section observations that are typically not suited to test potential prediction about the effects of farm policies. Because our cross section data are comprised of observation of farms producing program crops, we cannot capture changes in farm policy. Instead, we would need a panel that covered changes in regimes (for example, before and after the 1996 Farm Bill; before and after changes in crop insurance that might influence risk and thus alter benefits of cropsharing). For example, all of our data come from before passage of the 1996 Farm Bill, so we are unable to test for effects of this new regime.

Our treatment of government policy does not mean that government has no impact on contracts and organization, but that for the issues we examine, the implications are not readily forthcoming. Indeed, if one can discern how such programs have an impact on the incentives we find important, we would expect government to have predictable effects. At several points in the book, we consider some possible impacts of farm policies on contracts and organization. In the chapter 4 summary, we discuss how government programs might influence the choice between a cash contract or cropshare contract. In chapter 8, we consider how tax policies and subsidized credit influence the decision to own or contract for control of assets. And in chapter 9, we consider how limits on government payments and taxes influence farm ownership and organization.[35]

1.4   Other Literature

The agricultural economics literature has historically shown considerable interest in contracts and organization, although the focus has generally been different from what we examine in this book. In the first half of the twentieth century, many economists explored the differences between agriculture and other industries where large-scale production and corporate organization was dominant.[36] Agricultural economists have examined the structure of farm organization and farmland leasing, and those working at the various agricultural experiment stations at land grant universities have collected data on such issues.[37] Most of this work either predated Coase's work on the firm and social cost or was conducted without explicit recognition of it. Quite often the work is based on transaction cost ideas or has a subtext of costly information, but these issues are never directly mentioned.

Among modern agricultural economists who study North American agriculture, the focus has not generally been on contracts and economic organization, but on neoclassical analyses of costs, production, commodity markets, and the effects of agricultural policies. In the past decade, however, this began to change. For example, there have been analyses of contracts in poultry (Knoeber and Thurman 1994; Tsoulouhas and Vukina 1999), vegetables (Hueth and Ligon 1999), and vertical coordination (Frank and Henderson 1992; Hennessy 1996). This and related literatures are carefully summarized in Knoeber (2000); other less extensive summaries are found in Sexton and Lavoie (2001), Deininger and Feder (2001), and Vercammen and Schmitz (2001). To the extent that modern agricultural economists have examined issues of economic organization, they have relied more on risk-sharing arguments than on transaction costs. As a result this literature is quite distinct from the analysis in this book.[38]

In addition to agricultural economics, there is a considerable literature on farm contracts and organization in economic development and in economic history. In economic development, cropsharing has been a focus of analysis ever since Stiglitz's (1974) paper. This literature, like that in agricultural economics, has been dominated by risk-sharing models and an emphasis on theory over empirical work.[39] In recent years, however, there has been less emphasis on risk sharing and more discussion of multiple incentive margins (for example, Dubois 2002). In economic history, of course, agricultural topics are a mainstay, and discussions of contracts and farm organization are common. Transaction cost models have been much more prevalent in economic history than in other fields, perhaps because of the influence of Nobel Laureates Robert Fogel and Douglass North. Historical issues of slavery and serfdom obviously suggest the importance of property rights, and thus have led scholars to transaction cost economics.[40]

1.5 Organization of the Book

All substantive chapters (3–9) contain both a theoretical model and empirical analysis. Although there is a natural progression in the chapters, the book is analytically divided into three parts. Part I examines contract choice using the transaction cost paradigm, focusing on explaining the prevailing simplicity of contracts and the choice between cropshare and cash rent agreements. We show how land leases exist in a context where reputation and the common law are important. These factors allow farming contracts to be relatively simple arrangements even though the values of the transactions may be quite large. We also show that the ability of farmers to exploit soil, underreport output, and overreport inputs best explains choices between cash rent and cropshare and explains the details of cropshare contracts. Part II examines the implications of risk-sharing. Our data refute the common prediction of risk-sharing models—namely, that as the risk to farmers increases the incentives to farmers decreases. We also show that there is no evidence for the existence of ratchet contracts in our data, another prediction that is often found in contract theories based on risk. Finally, part III examines ownership and firm organization choices, such as why family farms have dominated farming and what determines the ownership pattern of assets. Here we return to our transaction cost framework for explanations. We generally find that assets are owned when gains from labor specialization are low and timeliness costs are high. We also find that family farming tends to dominate corporate farming for the same reasons. For those readers only interested in the transaction cost approach to farm contracts and organization, part II can be skipped without any loss of continuity.

2 Farming in North America

Before examining the economic forces that shape the organization of modern agriculture, one must have an understanding of some of its basic features. Modern agriculture is a complex business in which farmers use a combination of land, skilled and unskilled labor, expensive machinery, genetically engineered seed, chemical pesticides, and sophisticated cultivation and harvest techniques to produce a crop. Throughout the book we refer to a "farmer" as the individual with control over production. The farmer is likely to be a residual claimant, but not the only one.[1] Modern North American farms are large, capital-intensive enterprises compared to farms in less developed countries and compared to those just one-half century earlier.

2.1 Basic Farming Facts

Table 2.1 shows some summary statistics for the most recent census years for Canada and United States.[2] The table shows 1.9 million farms in the United States, averaging nearly 500 acres per farm.[3] The farms average over $100,000 in annual sales and have an average value of nearly $450,000. Table 2.1 also shows the numbers for Canada, which paints a similar picture.

Table 2.2 reports data on farm characteristics in 1920 and 1997, and clearly shows that changes in agriculture over the past century have been dramatic. As recently as 1920 there were over 6.5 million farms, averaging just 149 acres. At the same time, nearly one-third (30.1%) of the total U.S. population lived on farms. In 1920 most farmers still used draft horses to power their equipment, employing over 25 million draft horses and mules on farms.[4] By 1997 there were less than 2 million farms, and the average farm size had more than tripled to roughly 500 acres. Similarly, by 1997 less than 2 percent of the U.S. population resided on farms.[5] By 1997 large tractors had long dominated farming, with 3.9 million tractors in total and more than 15 percent of all farms having at least four tractors.[6] Use of chemical fertilizer and pesticides has also increased. In 1930 American farmers used just 16.5 pounds of commercial fertilizer per farmland acre. By 1985 that number had increased to 93.6 pounds per acre.[7]

Along with these dramatic changes in farming technology came equally dramatic increases in farm productivity.[8] In 1920 corn averaged 30.9 bushels per acre and wheat averaged 13.9 bushels per acre. By 1997 corn yields averaged 124.1 bushels per acre and wheat yields averaged 37.5 bushels per acre. The historical trend in North American farming has been toward fewer and larger farms, greater use of expensive equipment and chemicals (fertilizers and pesticides), and spectacular increases in crop yields. All of this change took place over the life span of a single farmer. Perhaps more dramatic, as we show later, the organization of farms has remained remarkably stable over this period of change.

Table 2.1
Features of modern North American agriculture: 1996–1997

Farm characteristics	United States (1997)	Canada (1996)
All farms		
Number of farms	1,911,859	276,548
Land in farms	931,795,255 acres	168,167,475 acres
Total cropland	431,144,896 acres	86,286,078 acres
Average farm size	487 acres	608 acres
Value of land and buildings	$859,854,761,532	$116,223,711,975
Average farm value	$449,748	$565,793
Market value of products	$196,864,649,000	$29,360,688,000
Average sales per farm	$102,970	$116,545
Land owned by farmers	59.4%	63.27%
Land leased by farmers	40.6%	36.73%
Land sold in 1988	12,509,000 acres (3.2%)	NA
Farms sold in 1988	37,590 farms (4.9%)	NA
Sales > $100,000		
Number of farms	345,988	83,140
Land in farms	526,974,339 acres	NA
Average farm size	1,523 acres	NA
Value of land and buildings	$471,892,687,212	NA
Average farm value	$1,363,899	NA
Market value of products	$172,124,601,000	NA
Average sales per farm	$497,487	NA
Land owned by farmers	53.9%	NA

Sources: USDA National Agricultural Statistics Service. *1997 Census of Agriculture*, United States Data, Chapter 1. Table 1. Historical Highlights: 1997 and earlier census years, p. 10. Land owned by farmers and land leased by farmers come from Table 46. Summary by Tenure of Operator: 1997, p. 57. 1988 dates from *1988 Agricultural Economics and Landownership Survey*, Table 1, p. 2-2. Data for Canada from Catalogue #93-356-XPB, Table 1.1, Table 2.1, Table 2.2, Table 10.1, and Table 25.1, Table Catalogue #93-359-XPB. Dollar figures are in their respective currencies. Farms > $100,000: USDA *1997 Census of Agriculture*, U.S. Data, Chapter 1, Table 50 (Summary by market value of agricultural products sold: 1997), pp. 1, 9, 11. Statistics Canada. *1996 Census of Agriculture.* 1996 Agricultural Operation National and Provincial Highlights Tables (Canada Highlights).
Note: Some farmers lease out land, so the sum of the percentages may exceed 100 percent. NA = not available.

There is considerable variation in these numbers for the specific areas that we study. In Nebraska and South Dakota where agriculture is still a dominant industry, over 80,000 farms remain. An average farmer uses approximately 1,200 acres of farmland and $80,000–$90,000 of farm equipment.[9] The average value of each farm's land and buildings is close to $500,00 in South Dakota and nearly $900,000 in Nebraska. Here the farmers grow such crops as barley, corn, hay, soybeans, and wheat, and sell an average of well over $100,000 in agricultural products each year.[10] Table 2.3 shows these figures for these two states as well as for British Columbia and Louisiana. Compared to the Great Plains, farms in Louisiana

Table 2.2
U.S. farming: 1920 and 1997

	1920	1997
FARMS	6,454,000	1,911,859
FARM SIZE (ACRES)	149	487
% OF U.S. POPULATION LIVING ON FARMS	30.1	1.9 [a]
DRAFT HORSES & MULES	25,199,000	almost none [b]
TRACTORS	246,000	3,936,014
GRAIN COMBINES	4,000	460,606 [c]
TRUCKS	139,000	3,497,735
CORN YIELD (bushels/acre)	30.9	124.1
WHEAT YIELD (bushels/acre)	13.8	37.5

Sources: USDA National Agricultural Statistics Service. *1997 Census of Agriculture*, United States Data, Chapter 1. Farms and farm size are in Table 1. Historical Highlights: 1997 and earlier census years, p. 10. The number of tractors, grain combines and trucks are in Table 13. Selected Machinery and Equipment on Place: 1997 and 1992, p. 22. Corn and wheat yield are in Table 41. Specified Crops Harvested-Yield per acre Irrigated and Non-irrigated: 1997, p. 38. The percent of Family farms is in Table 47. Summary by Type of Organization: 1997, p. 63. The farm population comes from USDA National Agricultural Statistics Service. *1998 Agricultural Statistics*. Table 9-17. The Farm Entrepreneurial Population and Farm Operators and Managers, 1993–1995, pp. 9–12. The U.S. population estimates comes from Population Estimates Program, Population Division, U.S. Census Bureau.
[a] Population for the year 1995.
[b] As of 1997 there are so few working animals on farms that the data is not collected in the *Census of Agriculture*.
[c] In 1960 there were over 1 million combines.

comprise less acreage but are more valuable per acre. In Louisiana crops such as cotton, rice, and sugarcane dominate, although there are also substantial acreages of corn and soybeans. Summary data for British Columbia farms are also shown in table 2.3. These farms tend to be smaller than those on the Great Plains or American Corn Belt, because there are numerous smaller farms specializing in fruit tree crops. Table 2.3 also shows summary statistics for those farms selling over $100,000 worth of products each year, for the state of Louisiana, Nebraska, and South Dakota.[11] These data are similar to the data from our farm surveys in these states.

2.2 Farm Contracting

Ever since Adam Smith's writings in the eighteenth century, economists have studied the choice among fixed rent (cash rent), fixed wage, and share (cropshare) contracts as possible ways of combining land and labor through contracts.[12] In North America, however, the relevant choice for combining land and farmers through contract is between cash rent and cropshare. The fixed wage contract is not a contract between a farmer and a landowner. Instead, it is a contract between a farmer and a relatively unskilled laborer for a specific

Table 2.3
Agriculture in British Columbia, Louisiana, Nebraska, and South Dakota

Farm characteristics	Louisiana (1997)	Nebraska (1997)	South Dakota (1997)	British Columbia (1996)
All farms				
Number of farms	23,823	51,454	31,284	21,835
Land in farms (acres)	7,867,528	45,525,414	44,354,880	6,249,444
Total cropland (acres)	5,331,411	22,092,954	19,355,256	1,297,539
Average farm size (acres)	331	885	1,418	286
Value per acre	$1,206	$645	$348	$2,213
Average value of equipment	$59,330	$84,535	$91,182	$33,502
Market value of products	$2,031,277,000	$9,831,519,000	$3,569,951,000	$1,839,216,758
Average sales per farm	$85,265	$191,074	$114,114	$84,233
Land owned by farmers (%)	46.2	56.9	61.8	61.7
Land leased by farmers (%)	53.8	43.1	38.2	38.3
% owned by family	86.6	82.2	86.7	NA
% owned by partners	7.8	8.8	8.3	NA
% family corporation	4.5	7.9	3.9	NA
% nonfamily corp.	0.4	0.4	0.3	NA
Farms with sales > $100,000				
Number of farms	4,192	18,205	9,447	NA
Land in farms (acres)	4,614,093	31,313,830	25,656,125	NA
Average farm size	1,101	1,720	2,716	NA
Market value of products	$1,810,559,000	$8,850,470,000	$2,904,208,000	NA
Average sales per farm	$431,908	$486,156	$307,421	NA

U.S. Sources: USDA National Agricultural Statistics Service. *1997 Census of Agriculture*, State Data. Table 1 and Table 11. Equipment value comes from Chapter 2, Table 9. *Canadian Sources:* Statistic Canada. Value included land and buildings. Dollar figures are in their respective currencies. Organization data: USDA National Agricultural Statistics Service, *1997 Census of Agriculture*, United States Data, Volume 1: Part 18, Chapter 1, Table 47.
Note: NA = not available.

task, such as apple picking or truck driving. In a fixed wage contract, a farmer (who controls the land and crop through ownership or contract) hires a "hand" to help with farming tasks. This hand typically has little human or physical capital and rarely plays a decision-making role on the farm.[13]

It is important to realize that in North America, landowners who lease their land have similar characteristics to the farmers they lease to. The landowners tend to be farmers themselves (or they once were), and the farmers usually own some farmland. Both nearly always own valuable equipment; they necessarily own specialized human capital; however, the farmer makes most of the farming decisions. Landowners who lease their land tend to be slightly older and slightly less educated than the farmers they lease to, but the differences are small. Drive into any coffee shop in a farming community and you would be hard pressed to distinguish the landowners from the farmers. During any given year, a "farmer" may cultivate his own land and lease the land of another landowner; a "landowner" may farm some of his own land and lease the rest of his land to another farmer. In 1997, only 60 percent of all American farms were operated by individuals who owned all their farmland and only 34 percent of all American farm acreage was cultivated by farmers who owned all of their land.[14] A specific contract will distinguish between a farmer and a landowner, but it is important to realize that in North America, unlike other parts of the world, no real class or economic difference exists between farmers and landowners.

Until recently, many economists have argued that share contracts tend to wither away as economies develop.[15] But share contracts have flourished in American agriculture through-out this century and continue to be widespread. In the first half of the twentieth century, some economists were aware of this. Gray et al. (1924) noted that in 1920 cropshare con-tracts were more common than cash rent in most states. Similarly, Johnson (1950) stated that "three-fourths of all rented agricultural land is leased under share contracts" (111). In fact, the cropshare contract is pervasive over the entire Great Plains, which is one of the world's most developed agricultural regions.[16] Our 1986 data show that over 75 per-cent of all landowner-farmer contracts in Nebraska and over 62 percent of all contracts in South Dakota were cropshare agreements. Our 1992 data show that 29 percent of contracts in British Columbia and 67 percent of contracts in Louisiana were cropshare contracts. Sotomayer, Ellinger, and Barry (2000) find that 70 percent of all contracts in Illinois are cropshare. Similarly, Tsoodle and Wilson (2000) find more than 70 percent of all contracts for nonirrigated land in Kansas are cropshare. Table 2.4 provides some information on mod-ern farmland contracts across the United States, and for the four areas we examine. It is clear from this table that leasing is important and that there is considerable variation in the use of the two different lease agreements.[17] The use of cash and share contracts also varies sub-stantially across regions of the United States. For example, in the Great Lakes region cash rent accounts for roughly 80 percent of all leases, while on the Great Plains they account for 50–55 percent of all leases (1999 AELOS, table 99).

In the past some economists have argued that landowners meticulously monitor the inputs of their cropshare farmers (for example, Eswaran and Kotwal 1985). But our evidence is to the contrary. Landowners seldom monitor farmer inputs, and then only in the most casual fashion—directly measuring farmer efforts and timing are unheard of. The fact that many landowners are absentee, living outside the county or state in which the rented land is located, supports our contention that direct monitoring of inputs by landowners is rare. In Nebraska, South Dakota, and Louisiana, over half of the landlords live in a different county from their leased farmland. Of these, close to half live in a different state. In British Columbia, 23 percent live in a different region or province.[18] Monitoring output, however,

Table 2.4
Some features of modern North American farmland contracts

Region	United States	Canada	British Columbia	Louisiana	Nebraska	South Dakota
General information (1996, 1997)						
% acres leased	41	37	19	54	43	38
ave. lease size (acres)	494	553	282	397	680	906
ave. land value/acre	$933	$848 [a]	$2,274 [b]	$1206	$645	$348
Cash leases (1999)						
% all leases	57	NA	71	47	42	57
% leased acreage	59	NA	72	45	52	55
Share leases (1999)						
% all leases	21	NA	29	35	42	29
% leased acreage	24	NA	28	43	30	27

Sources: (1) General information from *1997 Census of Agriculture* and *Statistics Canada 1996*. (2) For specific leases U.S information is from USDA National Agricultural Statistical Service. *1997 Census of Agriculture* and the *1999 Agricultural Economics and Landownership Survey* (Table 99). (3) The specific provincial lease data come from the 1992 (British Columbia) surveys described in the data appendix. (4) Leased acreage for Canada is per farm, not per plot leased.
Note: NA = not available.
[a] Calculated from 1,103 Canadian dollars.
[b] Calculated from 2,956 Canadian dollars.

either indirectly through the use of third parties (such as grain elevator reports) or directly, is not uncommon.

Economists have also argued that cropshare contracts necessarily divide the output between the farmer and the landowner equally.[19] The truth, however, is that cropshare contracts vary widely, and in most states in North America are more likely not to be 50-50 agreements. For modern agriculture, the farmer usually receives more than half of the harvested crop. On the Great Plains, only 4 percent of the cropshare contracts gave the farmer less than half the crop, while 66 percent gave the farmer more than half. Fifty-fifty sharing is much more common in the Corn Belt states of Iowa and Illinois (Sotomayer, Ellinger, and Barry, 2000; Young and Burke 2001), and in these cases it is also routine for farmers and landowners to also share input costs, again usually 50-50.[20]

Contracting in agriculture is not, of course, limited exclusively to agreements between farmers and landowners. There are contracts for equipment, labor, marketing, production, and services. These contracts use various methods of payment (for example, hours for tractors, revenue share for marketing) and impose various duties on both farmers and other contracting parties. These duties include sharing input costs, using specified techniques, and performing tasks at specified times. The contracts can be simple and short-term, or they can be complicated and long-term. Production contracts refer to arrangements in which the

Table 2.5
Features of typical agricultural contracts

Type	Features (parties, payment, duties)	Examples
Equipment	Farmer rents equipment on a time basis (day, month, year) or on an hourly rate of use.	Field implements, tractors
Farmland	Farmer rents land in return for a cash or share of the crop. Input costs are sometimes shared.	Small grains, pasture
Labor	Farmer hires labor for skilled and un-skilled work. Payment can be hourly, monthly, or based on piece rates.	Equipment operation, harvesting, fieldwork
Marketing	Farmer agrees to deliver crops of a specific quantity and quality to a processor. Farmer and marketing firm share the revenues. Farmer typically controls production and owns crop.	Apples, other fruit, dairy, sugar, cattle, vegetables
Production	Farmer agrees to produce a crop under the direction of another firm. Farmer will be required to use certain inputs and techniques and may share costs. Firm will generally control production and own the crop.	Seed, vegetables, poultry, swine
Service	Farmer hires firm to perform specific tasks. Typically the firms provides both the labor and the specialized equipment required.	Harvesting, pest control, cattle feeding

farmer does not control the production process or own the crop. Marketing contracts refer to arrangements in which the farmer maintains production control and crop ownership. Production contracts are common in the poultry and swine industries, while marketing contracts are common in corn, fruit, vegetables, and sugar.[21] Table 2.5 summarizes some of the features of these contracts and shows where they are most commonly found. Although our empirical focus is primarily on farmland contracts, we do examine contracts for equipment, production, and such services as harvesting and processing.

2.3   Farm Ownership and Organization

A key focus of our book is the determination of farm ownership, both over assets and across stages of production. One of the salient characteristics in the history of industry is the transition from family firms to large factory-style corporations. Large corporations dominate modern economies. In 1989 corporations made up 18.5 percent of all nonfarm businesses but generated 90 percent of all nonfarm business receipts.[22] Agriculture, however, has largely resisted the transition to large corporate ownership. The 1997 U.S. Census shows that approximately 86 percent of farms are organized as "family farms." Excluding small family-held corporations, farm corporations made up only 0.4 percent of all farms in 1997, 1.3 percent of all farm acreage, and generated only 5.3 percent of all sales receipts.[23] Especially

Table 2.6
Organization of farm business in North America

Type of organization	Acres	% Acres	Farms	% Farms	Receipts[a]	%Receipts
Canada (1996)						
Family	86,740,296	51.6%	168,007	60.8%	11,180,530	34.7%
Partnership	42,173,075	25.1%	74,8989	27.1%	7,756,586	24.1%
Family corporation	26,942,458	16.0%	27,082	9.8%	9,945,829	30.9%
Nonfamily corporation	4,917,049	2.9%	5,605	2.0%	3,203,293	9.9%
Other[b]	7,394,597	4.4%	956	0.4%	144,118	0.4%
United States (1997)						
Family	585,464,911	62.8	1,643,424	86.0	102,685,612	52.2%
Partnership	149,321,484	16.0	169,462	8.9	35,538,934	18.1%
Family corporation	119,559,203	12.8	76,103	4.0	45,889,331	23.3%
Nonfamily corporation	11,904,053	1.3	7,899	0.4	11,017,325	5.6%
Other[b]	65,545,604	7.0	14,971	0.8	1,753,447	0.9%

Sources: United States, *1997 Census of Agriculture*, Table 47, p. 63, and Canada, *1996 Census of Agriculture*.
[a] Receipts, in thousands of current dollars, are the market value of agricultural products sold.
[b] Includes trusts, municipalities, cooperatives, Indian reservations, and so on.

Table 2.7
Organization of nonfarm business in the United States

Type of organization	Number (1,000s)	Percent	Receipts ($billions)	Percent
Proprietorships	14,298	73	693	5.9
Partnerships	1,635	8.3	465	4.0
Corporations	3,628	18.5	10,440	90

Source: Statistical Abstract of the United States 1993, Table 848, p. 531.

in small grain production, farming continues to be dominated by small, family-based firms despite the tremendous changes that have taken place in agriculture over the past two centuries.[24] As shown in table 2.2, farm numbers have declined, farm size has increased, and technological changes have converted farms into capital-intensive enterprises, yet family farming still dominates in most farming sectors.

Tables 2.6 and 2.7 show data on organization for both farming and nonagricultural industries. Family-run operations dominate in farming, while nonfamily corporate ownership is trivial. This feature is exactly opposite what is found in the rest of the economy. The layman's notion of the family farmer fading away into history simply is not borne out by the evidence. The common sentiment over the disappearance of family farms no doubt reflects the reduction and loss of small farming communities. As farm sizes have increased, the number of families involved in farming has also fallen, making many small communities

Table 2.8
Vertical coordination in U.S. agriculture: 1980

Farm product	Percent vertical coordination	
	1960	1980
Citrus fruits	80.0%	100.0%
Sugar beets	100.0	100.0
Sugarcane	100.0	100.0
Vegetables for processing	75.0	98.1
Potatoes	70.0	95.0
Seed crops	80.3	90.0
Other fruits and tree nuts	35.0	60.0
Vegetables for fresh market	45.0	53.0
Dry beans and peas	36.0	3.0
Cotton	8.0	18.0
Oil-bearing crops	1.4	10.5
Food grains	1.3	8.5
Feed grains	0.5	7.5
Hay	0.3	0.5

Sources: Marion (1986), Table 2.7, p. 15, and Helmberger, Campbell, and Dobson (1981), pp. 616–618.

ghost towns. Of those left farming, however, they are still overwhelmingly organized as family farms.

Another important feature of agricultural organization is the extent to which producers are vertically coordinated into processing, storage, and distribution. In recent years, especially in the livestock industries, vertical coordination has increased. This coordination may be accomplished through joint ownership or through long-term contracting. Table 2.8 shows data on the extent of vertical coordination in various commodities using 1960 data from Helmberger, Campbell, and Dobson (1981) and 1980 data from Marion (1986). It is clear that the use of vertical coordination varies across products and is most important for such perishable crops as fruit and sugar. Although the level of vertical integration has increased over the time period, it is interesting to note how little the ranking has changed.[25]

In addition to the dominance of family farming, another interesting organizational feature is the distribution of ownership and contracting for assets, including such nonland assets as buildings and equipment. Farmers have the option to be the complete residual claimant of an asset through ownership, but they may also opt for incomplete ownership through lease contracts. While leasing of land is very common in modern agriculture, leasing of buildings and equipment is rare; although quite recently there has been an increase in equipment leasing. Table 2.9 shows this quite dramatically for British Columbia and Louisiana, where equipment and building ownership accounts for 98–100 percent of the assets examined. The

Table 2.9
Percent of farmer-owned assets: British Columbia and Louisiana (1992)

Asset	British Columbia	Louisiana
Land	82	38
Equipment		
Tractors	99	96
Harvestors	99	96
Cultivator	100	97
Planter	100	98
Trucks	99	98
Sprayer	100	98
Other	99	92
Buildings		
House	99	92
Shop	97	78
Barn	99	85
Storage	98	78
Other	99	94

Sources: Allen and Lueck (1992a) and *British Columbia and Louisiana Farmland Ownership and Leasing Survey* (1993).

puzzling feature of this observation is that much of this equipment has an extremely low utilization rate, often being used for only one or two weeks of the year.

2.4   Individual Contract Data

The data we use to test our models come from several sources and are supplemented with census data from the United States and Canada. Two data sets contain information on more than 3,000 contracts from Nebraska and South Dakota for the 1986 crop year. Two additional data sets contain information on more than 1,000 farms and nearly 2,500 plots of land (both owned and leased) from British Columbia and Louisiana during the 1992 crop year. In addition to information on land contracts, these data include information on the ownership of land, buildings, and equipment. We also use publicly available data from U.S. and Canadian censuses of agriculture. In each chapter we define and discuss the specific variables and samples that are used, but many of the details of these data are found in appendix A. Along with these statistical data sets, we use historical data on industries and case studies to further test our models. To our knowledge, this is one of the largest and most diverse collections of individual agricultural contract data in existence.

The data from Nebraska and South Dakota come from the *1986 Nebraska and South Dakota Leasing Survey*. To generate these data, questionnaires were sent to over 10,000 farmers and landowners in Nebraska and South Dakota, generating 1,615 usable responses for Nebraska and 1,155 for South Dakota, in which each observation represents a single farmer or landowner for the 1986 crop season. To conduct our tests for contract choice, in chapters 3–7 we reorganized the data so that each observation is a single farmland contract between a farmer and a landowner. Because many individuals had more than one contract this increased the sample size by 20 percent and resulted in 2,101 observations for Nebraska and 1,331 for South Dakota. These data contain information on the general characteristics of the farmer and landowner, the number of acres owned and leased, the type of contract, the type of crop grown, and so on. These data are used primarily in chapters 3–7 to examine the determinants of contract choice and design.[26]

The main data for British Columbia and Louisiana come from two surveys we conducted in January 1993, for the 1992 crop year. There were 460 usable responses for British Columbia and 530 for Louisiana. Unlike the Nebraska–South Dakota data, these data do not have detailed information on landowners who lease to farmers or information on input sharing within cropshare contracts. They do, however, have information on ownership of land and other assets. The 1,004 different farms that make up the British Columbia–Louisiana sample are often arranged in various ways to create different data sets. Because we use these data to examine several different questions, they are sometimes organized around a farm, a plot of land, equipment, or buildings. These data are used throughout the book. In chapters 3–7 they are used to examine the determinants of contract choice and design. In chapters 8 and 9 they are used to examine the determinants of ownership and organization. Table 2.10 shows the summary statistics for key variables in each of these four jurisdictions. As can be seen by comparing table 2.3 with table 2.10, our micro data are made up of the larger, more full-time farms.[27]

In addition to the statistical datasets described above, we make use of historical information on industries and regions, case studies of specific practices in industries, aggregate data, statistical findings from other studies, and information on law and legal decisions. For example, in chapter 3 we examine land contracts from the late 1800s in North Dakota and compare them to contemporary contracts. In chapter 8 we examine the organization of custom combining firms on the Great Plains. In chapter 9 we similarly examine the expansive, fully integrated "Bonanza farms" of the late 1800s, the transformation of the sugarcane industry after innovations in sugar processing, and the "industrialization" of much of the livestock industry in the last three decades. These additional data supplement the findings from our econometric estimates and also show the richness of the variation in contracts and organization over time and across regions.

Table 2.10
Summary statistics for individual contract data

Farm characteristics	British Columbia (1992)	Louisiana (1992)	Nebraska (1986)	South Dakota (1986)
Number of farms	462	542	1660	1772
Land in farms (acres)	158,190	390,147	2,241,332	1,011,812
Average farm size (acres)	343	719	1350	571
Average value of land, buildings, and equipment ($)	438,980	319,444	NA	NA
Average sales per farm ($)	100,448	254,328	NA	NA
Land owned by farmer (%)	81.4	37.8	NA	NA
Land leased by farmer (%)	18.6	62.2	NA	NA
Cash rent contracts (%)	26.7	32.5	32.4	26.5
Cropshare contracts (%)	73.3	67.5	67.6	73.5
Family farms (%)	75.9	71.5	NA	NA
Partnership farms (%)	11.2	13.4	NA	NA
Family corporations (%)	11.2	12.1	NA	NA
Nonfamily corporations (%)	0.01	0.02	NA	NA

Sources: Allen and Lueck (1992a; 1993b,c) and Johnson et al. (1988). *British Columbia and Louisiana Farmland Ownership and Leasing Survey* (1993) and *South Dakota and Nebraska Farmland Leasing Survey* (1986). *Note:* NA = not available.

Before we move on to the main analysis of the book, a comment should be made regarding endogeneity. Throughout the book we assume that crop choices are restricted and treated as exogenous to a contract. Although this simplifying assumption is never exactly true, it is a close and useful approximation for several reasons. First, soil and climate largely determine the choice of crop for the regions and crops we examine. This may not be true for areas such as California's Central Valley, where a wide range of crops are grown in a small region, but it is generally true in the regions we examine. For instance, in Louisiana, sugarcane is confined to roughly ten southern parishes, all having a similar climate and soil type. In British Columbia, commercial tree fruits are predominantly grown in the Okanagan region. Second, in areas where crops are rotated, these rotations are virtually fixed. For example, in the rice growing parishes of southwest Louisiana, rice and soybeans are switched every year. Finally, as shown in chapter 3, farmer's crop choices are severely constrained by reputation in the farmland lease market, so that farmers are not able to exploit a share contract by choosing a crop with a highly uncertain yield, such as sugarcane in Nebraska.

2.5 Summary

As one can see from the tables in this chapter, farming is a vast and varied business, organized in a myriad of ways. Over the past century farms have increased tremendously in physical size and in terms of output per acre. This has resulted in a dramatic reduction in the number of farmers. Over the middle eighty years of the twentieth century, the number of farmers fell from 30 percent of the population to under 2 percent. Still, it is most remarkable that the basic family organization of farming has remained in tact, with some notable exceptions. In addition to the variation in farm organization, considerable differences exist in terms of how farmers contract with one another. Both cropshare and cash rent contracts are prevalent in modern agriculture. Though the relative number of contracts has remained stable over the past century, very recently there have been trends toward more cash renting. When cropsharing exists, many shares are used with 50-50 being common, but not always the most dominant. Input sharing is also a very important part of cropshare contracts. The farm-level data that we use to test our model predictions come from across the North American continent and provide us with considerable variation in terms of crops grown and geographical conditions.

I CONTRACTS AND THE TRANSACTION COST FRAMEWORK

In part I (chapters 3–5) we examine contracting for land and focus on the classic question of what determines the optimal contract choice for the farmer and landowner. In chapter 3 we examine the form of these contracts and address the issue of why they are so simple. In doing so we put these contracts into their common law context and analyze the role reputation and specific assets play in policing behavior that is ultimately revealed. In chapter 4 we first develop the basic model that appears throughout the book. This model includes the trade-off between the incentive to overuse rented land and underreport the crop. In chapter 5 we extend this analysis to the case where many inputs other than land and labor are used and potentially shared. All three of these chapters provide evidence that support our transaction cost framework.

3 The Simplicity of Agricultural Contracts

It is a common scene in U.S. agriculture: A landowner and a tenant talk for a few minutes over a cup of coffee, then shake hands to clinch a one-year deal to rent a farm or piece of land. No fuss, no bother, no paperwork.
—Jonathan Knutson, *Ag Week*, Dec. 11, 1980

3.1 Introduction

In many settings, exchanges are governed by rather complicated contracts that explicitly denote dates, individuals, locations, prices, products, qualities, quantities, and contingencies for changing conditions. Contracts often extend for many years and may have complicated procedures in case of breach or dissolution. In agriculture, however, contracts are often surprisingly simple oral agreements lasting only a year. In this chapter, we examine why contracts should be so simple even though the value of the assets at stake is quite large.[1]

3.2 Contracts for Farmland

As noted in the introduction, farmers, large and small, routinely rent land. In stark contrast to the size and methods of modern farming, farmland leases are simple and informal. Rarely are they lengthy, detailed documents, and in many cases they are not even written. Using our Nebraska–South Dakota data we find that 58 percent of all contracts are oral. From the 1992 British Columbia–Louisiana data, we find that 54 percent of all contracts are oral.[2] Those leases that are written tend to be simple one- or two-page documents that specify only the names of the farmer and the landowner, the dates during which the contract is binding, the location of the land, the terms of the lease in dollars or shares, and possibly conditions for contract renewal.[3] Figure 3.1 shows a typical written Great Plains cash rent contract, this one from central North Dakota. In a few cases the contracts are more detailed and specify such responsibilities as paying land taxes, controlling noxious weeds, issuing penalties for defaulting, renewal conditions, and the fraction of the land that must lie fallow.

Notably, farmland contracts tend not to stipulate in detail how the land will be farmed; rather, they require the farmer use the land in a "thorough and farmer-like" or a "good and husband-like" manner. Farmland contracts are most often annual agreements subject to automatic renewal unless one party makes an early commitment not to renew. In our Nebraska–South Dakota data 65 percent of the contracts are annual, while for our Louisiana–British Columbia data 59 percent are annual. Sometimes the agreements are for several years, but rarely are they longer than five years. They are, however, typically renewed for extended periods, even up to thirty years. The markets that bring farmers and landowners together

---

FARMLAND LEASE

This agreement is between "landowner" of [residence] and "farmer" of [residence], April 1, 1982.

Southeast 1/4 of Section 17-140-63

"Farmer" agrees to pay "landowner" $30 per acre for 156 tillable acres for the crop year of 1982. Total payment of $4680.00, 10% due April 1, 1982—$468.00. 90% due October 1, 1982—$4212.00 for a total of $4680.00. This lease shall be renewed automatically year to year unless either party notifies the other party by September 15. If lease is not renewed, renter will be paid for the summer fallow with price per acre to be established at that time. All government payments go to the renter.

Signed by owner and renter.

Figure 3.1
Example of written farmland lease, North Dakota

are as informal as the contracts themselves, with the most common consummation taking place on the front porch or in the shop.

Costs of Farmland Contracting

In a farmland lease the farmer is not the full owner of the land and its valuable attributes. He owns many of the land's attributes for the contract period but does not own the future productivity of the land. His farming practices, however, can strongly influence the future value of the land. Likewise, the landowner has little financial interest (none if the contract is cash rent) in the actual harvest. The costs of contracting then, are the resource expenditures used to try to make both farmer and landowner act as though they were fully integrated farmer-landowners.

In principle, there is moral hazard on both sides of the contract, and this moral hazard can potentially be found in many dimensions. When assets (inputs or outputs) are shared, there are monitoring costs and theft to contend with. Poor harvests, soil erosion, and nutrient and moisture depletion can be blamed on acts of nature, even though these outcomes may arise from improper tilling and pest control or other practices. For example, on leased land farmers are not as careful with timing as they are on their own land. The timing of planting, cultivation, pesticide application, and harvest is crucial to successful farming. Harvesting too early or late can dramatically reduce crop yields, and applying pesticides at the wrong time can damage soil as well as reduce future crop yields.

Broadly speaking, there are two issues in contract enforcement. The first issue has to do with the *complexity* of the agreement. Contracts can specify, in great detail sometimes, the obligations and rights of the contracting parties. In principle, contracts can specify input levels, technologies, and various contingencies, but all of these dimensions will require resources to insure compliance. Contract length is related closely to complexity. Longer contracts align the incentives of both parties, especially for the maintenance and use of durable assets, but longer contracts necessarily require additional stipulations to handle conditions that change over time. In this chapter we examine the determinants of contract complexity and contract length.

The second contract enforcement issue has to do with the *structure or type* of contract, regardless of its complexity.[4] By contract structure we mean the method of payment (for example, cash, share) for the use of the asset and the allocation of duties among the contracting parties (for example, pest control, irrigation system maintenance). These structural features define the incentives of the contracting parties in their day-to-day activities. The determination of contract structures are examined in chapters 4 and 5.

3.3   Why Are Farmland Contracts So Simple?

To explain the simplicity of contracts, we focus on three economic factors: the presence of specific assets, the viability of market enforcement of contracts, and the viability of common law default terms that aid the enforcement of contracts.[5] Our general hypothesis is that contracts will be simple, short-term agreements (and often oral) when specific assets are lacking and when market and common law enforcement is inexpensive. Because these conditions are often met in the case of farmland contracts, such contracts are often simple and short as described by Knutson in this chapter's epigraph.

Specific Assets

Klein, Crawford, and Alchian (1978) and Williamson (1979) note that contracting parties with transaction-specific assets put themselves in a position of being held up at renegotiation when they use short-term contracts. The possibility of a holdup occurs because each party could potentially extract, during renegotiation, the other's quasi-rents once the investments were made.[6] For farmland contracts short-term leases are feasible because, in general, "appropriable quasi-rents" (rents tied to a specific asset) are absent.

Consider the assets involved in a farmland lease. Landowners bring just one asset to the exchange: land—an asset that typically is not specific to the exchange. Many other farmers could profitably use the land. This would, for example, easily include farmers located within five miles of the land, which would encompass an area over 50,000 acres (since one square mile or "section" has 640 acres.) If average farm size were 1,000 acres, this would mean that roughly fifty farmers could potentially use the land.

Farmers bring several assets to the exchange, most of which are not specific to the farmland transaction either. First, the farmer brings his human capital (farming skills), which are specific to the local area but are not specific to the contracted plot of land. The farmer could profitably farm other plots in the area with his present capital stock. Second, the farmer has his own land and buildings, but these can be sold and are not specific to a particular leased plot or leasing agreement.[7] Third, the farmer has equipment such as tractors, cultivators, and combines. Some of these implements are quite specific to a region. To take an extreme example, a sugarcane cutter has little use in Montana where no sugarcane is grown. Like buildings, these machines are not specific to the plot in the lease contract, in part because most of the equipment is transportable. Farming may not be unique in this regard, but it can hardly be characterized as a production process laced with specific assets.

In many cases irrigation assets are the only transaction-specific assets involved in a farmland contract. Irrigation investments include pumps, underground pipes, wells, and other equipment that are often fixed to the land as well as the farmer's skills in using a particular irrigation system on a specific plot of land. These investments are generally owned by the landowner. Because farmers run the system, pay for daily maintenance, and often share major repair costs, the possibility of contract holdup exists.

A more plausible potential holdup problem can occur with orchards.[8] Fruit trees are almost always owned by the landowner, while grain crops are not. However, as with irrigation, the farmer invests in specific capital in maintaining the trees. Although knowledge regarding pruning and general maintenance is transferable, the farmer's investment in maintaining the trees can be specific because individual orchards often have unique features. This is exacerbated by the fact that current maintenance has implications for future crops. This is less of a problem for annual small grains like wheat.

An extreme example of a holdup problem exists where a land contract is shorter than a given crop cycle, and requires renewal midway through a growing season. If a landowner were to renegotiate a lease just before harvest, the farmer would be in jeopardy. To our knowledge, however, land contracts always cover a crop cycle and so this issue is resolved easily. The bottom line is that many farmland contracts are not plagued by potential holdup problems that arise when an exchange is characterized by large specific assets.

Market Enforcement

It is well known that markets can self-enforce contracts. Punishment of cheaters, through lost future trade, encourages cooperation between contracting parties (Klein and Leffler 1981; Kreps 1990; Shapiro 1983; Williamson 1979). This market enforcement is most effective where information about cheating is good and a frequent and long-lived relationship is desired—conditions routinely met in farmland contracts. Farmers are often part of a small community of people who have known each other most of their lives. Farmers tend to have lived their entire lives at a single location and farm families have known each other for generations. Information travels fast in such a community, and people are quickly aware of anyone who cheats another and tend to avoid future dealings with that person. Thus, for both a landowner and a farmer, a long-term interest exists in maintaining a good relationship.[9]

The potential for market enforcement is greater when contracting parties have developed reputational capital that can be devalued when contracts are breached. Farmers and landowners develop reputations for honesty, fairness, producing high yields, and consistently demonstrating that they are good at what they do. In small, close-knit farming communities, reputations are well known. Over time landowners indirectly monitor farmers by observing the reported output, the general quality of the soil, and any unusual or extreme behavior.[10] Farmer and landowner reputations act as a bond. In any growing season a farmer can reduce effort, exploit soil, or underreport the crop. Similarly, a landowner can undermaintain fences, ditches, and irrigation systems. Accurate assessments of farmer and landowner behavior will be made over time, and those farmers and landowners who attempt to gain at each other's expense will find that others may refuse to deal with them in the future.[11]

The Common Law

A well-developed common law can also decrease the need for complex, long-term contracts by making it unnecessary to incorporate numerous and specific details of performance for the parties. For example, the prevalence of clauses or implied covenants of "good husbandry" point to the law as a contract enforcer, since violation of such a clause provides legal grounds to terminate the lease. Burkhart (1991) notes, "Every farm lease contains an implied covenant to work the farm in a farmer-like manner. If the tenant does not use good farming practices the covenant is breached and the landlord can recover damages. What constitutes a 'farmer-like manner' can be shown by custom, practices of area farmers, or county extension agents."[12] The well-known 1963 Iowa case of *McElwee v. DeVault* illustrates the law.[13] In this case the lease explicitly required the farmer to "farm said premises in a good farmer like manner," and the court upheld termination of the lease when the farmer failed to follow standard farming practices regarding cultivation, which led to soil degradation. The use of good husbandry clauses and the existence of implied covenants indicates that some farming practices are similar from plot to plot in the area and that *some* types of "bad" farming are easily identified, and thus need not be specified in the contract. In many regions, including those for which we have farmland contract data, farming is quite homogeneous within a locale. In such cases the law implicitly adds detail to contracts that appear to be simple.[14]

Although farmland contract disputes rarely end in court, there have been numerous cases of farming disputes, especially during the first half of the twentieth century, that established the meaning of good husbandry. These cases have involved such issues as overgrazing, destruction of trees, permitting noxious weeds to grow, plowing meadowlands, removing manure rather than spreading it, damage to buildings because of overloading storage areas with crops, and extracting minerals from the soil.[15] By now these practices are routinely held by courts to constitute poor husbandry, thus violating the terms of the farmland lease and allowing for very informal contracts, even when they are in writing.

3.4   Empirical Analysis: Variation in Contract Complexity

While it is true that, in general, farmland contracts are short and simple, they do vary: Some are oral rather than written, some are annual rather than multiyear agreements. Our previous discussion generates predictions about the determinants of oral versus written contracts and the determinants of annual versus multiyear contracts. These predictions are:

PREDICTION 3.1a   The greater the specific assets, the less likely a contract is oral rather than written.

PREDICTION 3.1b   The greater the reputational capital (or the lower the cost of market enforcement), the more likely a contract is oral rather than written.

PREDICTION 3.1c   The greater the development of the common law, the more likely a contract is oral rather than written.

PREDICTION 3.2a   The greater the specific assets, the less likely a contract is annual rather than multiyear.

PREDICTION 3.2b   The greater the reputational capital (or the lower the cost of market enforcement), the more likely a contract is annual rather than multiyear.

PREDICTION 3.2c   The greater the development of the common law, the more likely a contract is annual rather than multiyear.

Two types of data are used to test these enforcement cost predictions. The predictions about specific assets and reputation are tested against contract data using regression analysis. The predictions about the common law are tested against the historical record of farmland contracts around the turn of the twentieth century.

The regression analysis data come from the *1986 Nebraska and South Dakota Land Leasing Survey*, and the *1992 British Columbia and Louisiana Leasing and Ownership Survey*. These surveys collected data from farmers and landowners engaged in farmland leasing during the 1986 and 1992 crop seasons. Each observation is a single contract between a farmer and a landowner, where each contract is an exchange of rights to a tract of land. Before beginning the analysis, we find it useful to examine some features of the data used in this chapter. The definitions of the variables are provided in table 3.1. The definitions and summary statistics for all variables used in the book are found in appendix A. Our empirical focus is to explain whether a contract is oral or written and whether a contract is annual or multiyear. ORAL is a dummy variable that identifies oral contracts, and ANNUAL is a dummy variable that identifies annual contracts. They are used as dependent variables in the analysis that follows. Independent variables can be grouped into those that measure specific assets and those that measure reputation. IRRIGATION and TREES are dummy variables that indicate the presence of irrigation systems and tree crops, respectively, and both are used as specific asset variables. Several variables are used to measure reputation and the market enforcement of contracts: AGE (age of farmer), AGE^2, CHANGED PARTIES (dummy indicating new contracting party), and YEARS DURATION (duration of contract in years).[16] The size of the leased plot (ACRES), a dummy indicating parties knew each other (INFORMATION), a dummy for leases between family members (FAMILY), and the per acre value of the plot (VALUE) are used as control variables.

We use our contract data to estimate the determinants of contract structure (oral versus written, annual versus multiyear contracts) and test the previous predictions. We use the following empirical specification, where for any contract i the complete model is

$$C_i^* = X_i \beta_i + \epsilon_i \quad i = 1, \ldots, n; \quad \text{and} \tag{3.1}$$

$$C_i = \begin{cases} 1, & \text{if } C_i^* > 0 \\ 0, & \text{if } C_i^* \leq 0, \end{cases} \tag{3.2}$$

where C_i^* is an unobserved farmland contract response variable; C_i is the observed dichotomous choice of contract structure for plot i (in table 3.2 this is equal to 1 for oral contracts and equal to 0 for written contracts and in table 3.3 this is equal to 1 for annual contracts and equal to 0 for multiyear contracts); X_i is a row vector of exogenous variables including the constant; β_i is a column vector of unknown coefficients; and ϵ_i is a plot-specific error

Table 3.1
Definition of variables

Dependent variables	
ANNUAL	= 1 if annual contract; = 0 if multiyear contract.
ORAL	= 1 if oral contract; = 0 if written contract.
Independent variables	
ACRES	= number of acres covered by contract.
AGE	= farmer's age in years (for British Columbia and Louisiana).
AGE	= 1 if farmer is younger than 25,
	= 2 if 25–34 years old,
	= 3 if 35–44 years old,
	= 4 if 45–54 years old,
	= 5 if 55–64 years old,
	= 6 if older than 65 (for Nebraska and South Dakota).
CHANGED PARTIES	= 1 if parties have changed in past five years;
	= 0 if they have not changed.
FAMILY	= 1 if landowner and farmer were related; = 0 otherwise.
INFORMATION	= 1 if parties knew each other prior to lease; = 0 otherwise.
IRRIGATED	= 1 if land is irrigated; = 0 if dryland.
TREES	= 1 if fruit was grown (e.g., apples, pears, etc.); = 0 otherwise.
VALUE	= average per-acre value of farmland in county of lease.
YEARS DURATION	= number of years contract has been in place.

term. We use a logit model to generate maximum likelihood estimates of the model given by equations (3.1) and (3.2) for various contract samples.

Oral or Written?

The choice between oral and written contracts can be used to test predictions 3.1a and 3.1b and thus estimate the importance of specific assets and market enforcement in determining contract complexity. The primary benefit of using an oral contract is its simplicity. If a dispute arises, however, an oral agreement will be difficult for a third party to enforce. When market forces rather than a third party are the primary means of contract enforcement, an oral contract is more likely. There may be some circumstances, however, when disputes are more likely to occur, and in these cases a written contract is more likely. For example, if the farmer and the landowner wish to make a customized contract, it tends to be written.[17]

It is important to note that the Statute of Frauds—a common law contract rule— requires that contracts that cannot be performed in one year must be written to be legally enforceable.[18] For farmland contracts, the Statute of Frauds implies that all multiyear contracts must be written contracts in order for them to be enforced in a court. If the court were a routine mechanism of enforcement, we would expect all multiyear contracts to be written. Yet, our Nebraska–South Dakota data show that only 53 percent of multiyear contracts are written, and our British Columbia–Louisiana data show just 69 percent of the multiyear contracts are written. This, by itself, indicates that courts are often not used to enforce these contracts. Instead, farmers and landowners prefer to make oral agreements independent of the contract length and rely on the market to enforce the agreements.[19]

We test predictions 3.1a and 3.1b by using logit regression analysis to examine the effects of selected variables on the decision to use an oral or written lease. Table 3.2 shows the coefficient estimates for these equations. Because the data sets do not contain the same variables, we estimate different specifications for the Nebraska–South Dakota and British Columbia–Louisiana equations.

Irrigation assets and long-term crops like trees are specific assets in a land lease. In the presence of these assets, there is the potential for one party to hold up the other. A written contract is more likely to mitigate this possibility; thus prediction 3.1a implies that IRRIGATED and TREES (only available for the British Columbia and Louisiana data) will have negative coefficients. In both the equations the estimated coefficients for IRRIGATED are negative and statistically significant, indicating that contracts are more likely to be written when irrigation assets are present. In the British Columbia–Louisiana equation, the estimated coefficient for TREES is negative and statistically significant, also as predicted.

The better the reputation of the farmer or of the landowner, the more likely the contract will be oral, as implied by prediction 3.1b, because the simple oral contract can be relatively easily enforced. The age of the farmer (AGE) can be used to measure reputation, and we expect a quadratic relationship between a farmer's age and probability of an oral contract.[20] As the years go by, a farmer develops a reputation that increases the viability of an oral contract but this reputation effect should decline and become negative because of the well-known last period problem. If the farmer knows this will be the last period of a relationship, it becomes his interest to cheat since he cannot be punished by an end to the relationship (Klein and Leffler 1981). Thus, as the farmer reaches the end of his productive farm life, the reputation effect begins to weaken. In both equations we find, as expected, the estimated coefficients for AGE to be positive and for AGE^2 to be negative. All coefficients are statistically significant in a one-tailed test.

Other variables are also used to measure information about reputations. The estimated coefficients for YEARS DURATION is expected to be positive. As the duration of a contract increases (YEARS DURATION), the parties have more information about each other. If cheating or poor farming is detected, the contract would be terminated and so long-lived contracts reflect satisfied parties. Therefore the more often a contract has been renewed, the more likely it will be oral. We expect a negative coefficient for CHANGED PARTIES because this variable indicates a recent change in contracting parties, which is interpreted as a situation in which information is limited. New parties to a contract know less about each other and thus the contract is less likely to be oral. All the estimated coefficients have the

Table 3.2
Logit coefficient estimate of oral-written contract choice
(dependent variable = 1 if the contract is oral; = 0 if written)

Independent variables	Estimated coefficients		
Data sets	Nebraska–South Dakota (1986)	British Columbia–Louisiana (1992)	Predicted signs
CONSTANT	−1.094	−2.30	
	(−3.822)*	(−2.49)*	
Specific Assets			
IRRIGATED	−0.389	0.33	−
	(−5.165)*	(−2.23)*	
TREES		−0.75	−
		(−2.29)*	
Reputation			
AGE	0.147	0.108	+
	(1.562)	(2.77)*	
AGE^2	−0.019	−0.001	−
	(−1.543)	(−3.04)*	
CHANGED PARTIES	−0.226		−
	(−2.125)*		
YEARS DURATION	0.015	0.36	+
	(4.016)*	(4.57)*	
Controls			
ACRES	−0.0002	−0.001	−
	(−6.262)*	(−4.33)*	
INFORMATION	0.934		
	(4.270)*		
FAMILY	0.944	−1.66	
	(12.537)*	(−0.91)	
VALUE	−0.0004		−
	(−0.587)		
Log likelihood	−2,194.95	−692.6	
χ^2 (df)	303.8(9)	62.1(7)	
Observations	3,432	1,000	

Note: t-statistics are in parentheses.
* significant at the 5 percent level (one-tailed test for coefficients with predicted signs).

predicted signs and are statistically significant. Taken together with the AGE coefficients, the evidence in support of prediction 3.1b is strong in our data.

We use ACRES and VALUE as variables that control for the value of the contracted plot of land, and we use FAMILY and INFORMATION to control for information the parties have about each other. We expect that as assets becomes more valuable, the costs of damage, theft, and poor farming become higher and the contracts are less likely to be oral. Thus we expect the estimated coefficients for ACRES and VALUE to be negative. In both equations the estimated coefficient for ACRES is negative and statistically significant. VALUE is only available for the Nebraska–South Dakota data and has a negative and statistically significant coefficient as well.[21] We have no predictions for the coefficients on FAMILY and INFORMATION because it is not clear whether the information measured by these variables enhances or inhibits contracting. We find a positive coefficient for INFORMATION indicating more information leads to oral contracts. The coefficients for FAMILY, however, differ between the two data sets. For Nebraska–South Dakota the coefficient is positive (more likely to be oral) but the coefficient is insignificantly different from zero in the British Columbia–Louisiana data.

Annual or Multiyear?

The choice between annual and multiyear contracts can be used to test predictions 3.2a and 3.2b and thus estimate the importance of specific assets and market enforcement in determining contract complexity. This contract choice is more directly related to specific assets than to reputation, while the opposite is true of the choice between oral and written contracts. The primary benefit of multiyear farmland contracts is more likely to be the reduction of contract renewal costs. The primary cost of a multiyear contract is that it requires additional clauses so that it can be adjusted to changing conditions. These clauses also require additional enforcement effort.

We test predictions 3.2a and 3.2b by using logit regression analysis to examine the decision to use an annual or multiyear lease. Table 3.3 shows the coefficient estimates for these equations. Again, because the data sets do not contain the same variables, we estimate different specifications for the Nebraska–South Dakota and British Columbia–Louisiana equations.

IRRIGATED and TREES are again used as variables to indicate the presence of specific assets. An annual contract is less likely to mitigate this possibility; thus prediction 3.2a implies that IRRIGATED and TREES (only available for the British Columbia–Louisiana data) will have negative coefficients. Our findings are mixed for these predictions. The estimated coefficients for IRRIGATED is negative for the Nebraska–South Dakota equation but are positive for the British Columbia–Louisiana equation. One possible explanation for

Table 3.3
Logit coefficient estimates of annual-multiyear contract choice
(dependent variable = 1 if the contract is annual; = 0 if multiyear)

Independent variables	Estimated coefficients		
Data set	Nebraska–South Dakota (1986)	British Columbia–Louisiana (1992)	Predicted signs
CONSTANT	0.021	−1.34	
	(0.077)	(−1.42)	
Specific assets			
IRRIGATED	−0.068	.68	−
	(−0.889)	(4.22)*	
TREES		−.55	−
		(−1.56)	
Contract type			
CONTRACT	−0.126	−1.34	−
	(−1.532)	(−2.41)*	
Reputation			
AGE	0.292	.09	+
	(3.175)*	(2.38)*	
AGE^2	−0.042	−.001	−
	(−3.392)*	(−2.66)*	
CHANGED PARTIES	0.372		−
	(3.260)*		
YEARS DURATION	−0.003	−.012	−
	(−0.699)	(−1.58)	
Controls			
ACRES	0.000	−.001	
	(0.315)	(−2.88)*	
INFORMATION	−0.165		
	(−0.802)		
FAMILY	0.344	−.32	
	(4.642)*	(−1.75)	
VALUE	0.001		
	(3.918)*		
Log likelihood	−2,207.4	−651.1	
χ^2 (df)	61.589(10)	49.66(8)	
Observations	3,432	1,000	

Note: t-statistics are in parentheses.
* significant at the 5 percent level (one-tailed test for coefficients with predicted signs).

the positive finding in the second specification is the different type of irrigation present in this data. In Louisiana, flood irrigation is exclusively for rice, where it is used to control pests. This type of system is quite homogeneous across the rice growing region of south Louisiana and may not be a good measure of specific assets. In the British Columbia–Louisiana equation, the estimated coefficient for TREES is negative and statistically insignificant, as predicted.[22]

Because the type of contract (cropshare or cash rent) is likely to be a determinant of contract length we include a variable CONTRACT that indicates the presence of a cropshare arrangement. Cropshare contracts have a built-in adjustment mechanism, because the payment (from farmer to landowner) is in terms of the crop and not dollars. This means that changes in market prices do not require changes in the term of the contract, making adjustment clauses unnecessary and multiyear contracts less costly. This implies a negative coefficient for the variable CONTRACT, which we find in both equations. Both coefficients are statistically significant in a one-tailed test.

The better the reputation of the farmer or of the landowner, the more likely the contract will be annual, as implied by prediction 3.1b, because the simple annual contract can be relatively easily enforced. Again, the age of the farmer (AGE) can be used to measure reputation, and we expect a quadratic relationship between a farmer's age and probability of an annual contract. In both equations we find, as expected, the estimated coefficients for AGE to be positive and for AGE^2 to be negative. All coefficients are statistically significant in a one-tailed test. As with the oral-written contract estimates, we used several variables to measure information about reputations. The estimated coefficients for CHANGED PARTIES and YEARS DURATION are expected to be negative. YEARS DURATION is expected to be negative because an increase in contracting duration makes it more likely the parties will trust each other enough to enter into a longer term agreement. The estimated coefficients for YEARS DURATION are negative as predicted, but not statistically significant. The estimated coefficient for CHANGED PARTIES (only available for Nebraska–South Dakota) however, is positive and significant, refuting our prediction. Except for this anomaly, though, these estimates of the effects of reputation offer broad support for prediction 3.1b.

Finally, as in the logit estimates of ORAL, we use ACRES, FAMILY, INFORMATION, and VALUE as variables that control for the value of the contracted plot of land and the information among the parties. In this setting we have no predictions for the estimated coefficients. We do find that the estimated coefficient for ACRES is negative and statistically significant for British Columbia–Louisiana but is not significantly different from zero for Nebraska–South Dakota. VALUE, available only for the Nebraska–South Dakota data, is positive and statistically significant. The estimated coefficients for FAMILY and INFORMATION also vary from sample to sample.

Farmland Contracts during the Bonanza Era

Our discussion of the common law generated two predictions about the influence of common law default rules on the simplicity of contracts. The general idea—encompassed by predictions 3.1c and 3.2c—is that a well-developed common law will provide contracting parties with default rules that will reduce the need for complex agreements. We were unable to test these predictions because the cross-section data did not allow us to distinguish among various levels of common law development. The following discussion of farmland contract during a historical period in which the common law was ill-developed allows us an indirect test of these predictions.

In the late 1800s and early 1900s, large "Bonanza" farms arose on the plains bordering Minnesota and North Dakota. These farms ranged in size from 5,000 to 50,000 acres but ultimately were succeeded by smaller family farms.[23] In the beginning, these farms did not lease out land but were operated by hired labor. It soon became clear that the large size of the Bonanza farms limited their productive efficiency and the owners began to lease out the land in relatively small plots (for example, 100–200 acres). In sharp contrast to the simple (annual and oral) contracts that dominate modern farmland leases, these leases were remarkably detailed and always seem to have been written.[24] These contracts were several single-spaced typed pages detailing the often complicated terms of payment; the method, depth, and time of plowing; the amount of fallow land; and the time and type of seeding. For example, a 1894 contract between D. D. Dutton and the Amenia and Sharon Land Company specified, among other things, that

a tract not to exceed One Hundred and Twenty-Five (125) acres in area may be left unplowed to be summer fallowed during the season of 1895; also to plow before June 1st, 1894 all land now unplowed on said premises and to seed same to millet immediately after plowing, and to again plow said land seeded to millet after July 25th and before August 15th, 1894, said second plowing to be done at least Five (5) inches deep and all weeds and millet to be thoroughly turned under and entirely covered.[25]

There is a striking difference between this contract and the terse contract from 1982, also from North Dakota, shown in figure 3.1.

Why were these frontier-era contracts so complicated compared with the simple contracts that prevail today? The best answer—and one that is consistent with predictions 3.1c and 3.2c—seems to be that, in this young state, the common law was simply undeveloped, settlements were still being established, and a stable community did not yet exist.[26] There were no common law default rules, so that contracting parties needed to specify, in detail, the sort of things that would now simply fall under the category of good husbandry. Also, because communities had not yet developed, market enforcement via reputation was unlikely to have been important. The law, and reputations, take time to develop and until they are, contracting parties must specify the details in written agreements if they expect reliable enforcement.

3.5 Summary

Contract simplicity depends on the costs of enforcement. These costs vary from case to case and determine the detail of contracts. For farmland leases in the four North American juris-dictions we consider, contracts are usually short-term and lack all but the most rudimentary details. We have argued that this near universal simplicity reflects the comparative advan-tage of enforcing customary farming standards through the market and the common law, given the general absence of specific investments and the strength of market enforcement and common law default rules. This character of the farming economy—good information about reputations, desired long-term relationships, immobility of farmers and landowners, and few transaction-specific assets—lends itself to the pervasive use of what may seem to be rather naive contracts. We also used data on modern contracts to estimate the determi-nants of oral (versus written) contracts and annual (versus multiyear) contracts. Overall, we find that the presence of specific assets increases the probability a contract will be oral and annual, and that the lower the cost of market enforcement via reputation the greater the probability that a contract will be oral and annual. Our statistical findings are stronger for our estimates of oral contracts than for annual contracts. Finally, we find that the relative complexity of contracts on the frontier is explained by the lack of both a developed common law and a lack of farmer and landowner reputations. Market and common law enforcement does not work well, however, if infractions are difficult to detect. Though it may be easy to detect fundamental improper farming practices, detecting specific examples of improper tilling or output under reporting may be extremely difficult. For this, landowners and farm-ers choose specific structures of contracts to create proper incentives. We now turn to the choice and specific design of contracts in the next two chapters.

4 Choosing between Cropshare and Cash Rent Contracts

4.1 Introduction

In chapter 3, we showed how rather simple contracts persist in modern agriculture because of the absence of specific assets and because the common law and reputations substitute for explicit contractual details. In this way, even simple (and short-term) contracts can avoid gross breaches of contract that are relatively easy to observe. Other issues in contract structure, however, remain in need of explanation even when contract simplicity is accounted for. Prominent among these issues is the age-old question of the choice between cash rent contracts and cropshare contracts, which we examine in this chapter.[1]

Over the years economists have devoted an enormous effort examining the rationale for sharecropping. While considerable theoretical efforts have been made, it has only been in the last decade that numerous empirical studies have been undertaken, especially for modern Western agriculture.[2] Theoretical models often consider contracts that bear little resemblance to those found in the United States and Canada today and thus generally do not yield predictions relevant for the available data. The model of landowner-farmer contracting that we develop is consistent with modern farm contracts, and we test its implications against our data on individual contracts. This model serves as the basic framework for most of the subsequent chapters.

4.2 A Model of Contract Choice

Cheung (1969) demonstrated that when transaction costs are zero, contract choice will not influence the outcome of the contract; cash rent and cropshare contracts are equally efficient methods of coordinating landowners and farmers. This application of the Coase Theorem raises the obvious question: Why then, would farmers and landowners choose one type of contract over another? As we noted in chapter 1, the economist's response to this question was the development of transaction cost and risk-sharing theories of sharecropping. Historically most models within the theoretical literature on cropshare contracts contain elements of risk sharing, but in recent years theoretical work has shifted away somewhat from risk-sharing into double moral hazard, multitasking, and strategy.[3] Recent work includes, for example, Dubois (2002) on intertemporal incentives, Laffont and Matoussi (1995) and Sengupta (1997) on moral hazard and financial constraints, Ray (1999) on strategic delegation, and Arruñada, Garicano, and Vazquez (2001) on automobile franchising. This new theoretical literature mimics the recent change in emphasis in modern contract theory (for example, Gibbons 1998; Holmström and Roberts 1998), but like the old theory it is again rapidly outpacing empirical work (Chiappori and Salanié 2000). There also has been work in economic history on the choice of contracts which also has a transaction cost foundation.[4]

In this chapter we develop a model in the transaction cost tradition and ignore risk sharing by assuming both contracting parties to be risk neutral.[5] In our model we assume that a given tract of land is to be leased—owner cultivation is not an option—and the important choice is between a cash rent and cropshare contract. In developing a transaction cost model of contract choice, it is important to understand the incentives of each contract. In a cash rent contract, the farmer pays a fixed annual amount per acre of land and owns the entire crop. As a result, he supplies the optimal amount of his own inputs but overuses any inputs supplied by the landowner.[6] Farmers can increase their wealth by not planting crops in a proper rotation, overusing chemicals and fertilizers that damage the soil, and tilling in ways that increase current crop output but reduce the future productivity of the soil. By manipulating the timing of seeding, fertilizing, and harvest, the farmer can enhance his own return at the expense of the landowner's.[7] For example, if a hail- or rainstorm is expected, a farmer may harvest his own crop before a shared crop. In a cropshare contract the farmer shares the harvested crop with the landowner. Because the farmer receives less than the full amount of the crop, he uses fewer inputs and thus reduces the overall distortion from suboptimal input choices.[8] Hence, the benefit of the share contract is that it curbs the farmer's incentive to exploit the inputs supplied by the landowner, such as soil moisture and nutrients.

In principle, the landowner could also undersupply attributes of the land used by the farmer, but for the types of farming we consider, both farmers and landowners indicate that this is not likely. A landowner might be delinquent in road maintenance and fence upkeep, but we find little or no evidence that these are the duties of landowners for the cases we study. The large fraction of absentee landowners supports the view that landowners supply just land and no other services. Thus, we assume only the farmer chooses the inputs in these contracts, and our model features moral hazard only on the farmer's side.[9] Even though share contracts reduce total input distortions, they entail costs that are not present for cash rent contracts—the output has to be measured and divided.[10] For agriculture this requires physical measurement and division of the harvested crop. As a result, the farmer has an incentive to underreport the harvest to the landowner. Underreporting may take the form of crop quality as well as quantity. For example, a farmer may keep the best hay for himself, or he may keep the wheat with the fewest weeds, while not under-reporting quantity at all. Alternatively, land leased for pasture is most often cash rented because the costs of detecting quality and weight gain underreporting for live cattle is so high.[11] A cropshare contract also implies that both the farmer and the landowner must sell their share of the crop and incur the associated costs because cropshare contracts do not specify shares of the dollar value of the crop, but shares of the crop. The trade-off between input distortion costs and output division costs determines the contract choice, the joint wealth maximizing choice being the contract that yields the highest value of output net of all costs.

We use a two-stage contract choice model. First, we determine the input choices made by farmers in cash rent and cropshare contracts. Second, given the farmer's choices, we determine the contract that maximizes joint (farmer-landowner) wealth by comparing the net values of the two contracts as important parameters change. We assume there are just two inputs—farmland owned by landowners and farm capital (both human and physical) owned by farmers—and that both parties are risk neutral. As we stressed in the introduction, we also assume a random input to account for factors as weather and pests. Because of this uncertainty and because all of the attributes of the farmer and land inputs cannot be perfectly specified in a contract, there are opportunities for farmer moral hazard.

In all cases, we consider the use of a tract of farmland of fixed acreage that is contracted for use by a single farmer for a single growing season.[12] Following our general production discussion in chapter 1, let $Q = h(e, l) + \theta$, where Q is the harvested output (with unit price) per tract; e is a composite input of farmer inputs, including labor time and effort, equipment, and other farming materials; l is a composite input of land attributes, such as fertility and moisture content that are not specified in the contract; and $\theta \sim (0, \sigma^2)$ is a randomly distributed composite input that includes weather and pests. We assume that $h_e > 0$, $h_l > 0$, $h_{ee} < 0$, $h_{ll} < 0$, and $h_{el} = 0$, where the subscripts denote partial derivatives.[13] The opportunity cost of the farmer's input is the competitive wage rate w per unit of farmer's effort, and the opportunity cost of the unpriced land input (l) is r per unit. In a farmland contract the priced land attribute is acres, which for our purposes is ignored. Therefore it is worth stressing that r is not the price of land per acre, but the cost of the composite unpriced land input.

If contracts could be enforced without cost, there would be no input distortion and no output measurement. With risk-neutral landowners and farmers, the expected profit from the farming operation is maximized, resulting in the employment of e^* and l^* units of farmer and landowner inputs. These first-best, full-information input levels are identical for the cropshare and cash rent contracts and satisfy the standard conditions that marginal products equal marginal costs for both inputs.[14]

When contract enforcement is costly, however, the input choices will be second-best. In either contract, farmers have an incentive to exploit the land's unpriced attribute (l) because they do not face the full costs, r. In addition, farmers have an incentive to underreport the output in the cropshare contract. We examine the differential outcomes of the cash rent and cropshare contracts by modeling these incentives. For both contracts, the farmer chooses the inputs, which depend on the type of contract. Once the input levels are determined, the net value of each contract can be evaluated.

Cash Rent Contracts

For the cash rent contract, the farmer hires a tract of farmland for a lump-sum fee paid just prior to the growing season.[15] He owns the entire crop and chooses his inputs to maximize expected profit. Because the farmer does not have indefinite tenure of the land, he does not face the true opportunity cost of using the attributes of the land. We denote the reduced costs he faces as $r' < r$, so the farmer's objective is

$$\max_{e,l} \Pi^r = h(e,l) - we - r'l. \tag{4.1}$$

The second-best solutions e^r and l^r satisfy: $h_e(e^r) \equiv w$ and $h_l(l^r) \equiv r'$. Given that $h_{el} = 0$, we note that the farmer's input level is identical to the first-best optimum; that is, $e^r = e^*$. It is also clear, however, that since $r' < r$, $l^r > l^*$, implying that the land is overworked because the farmer does not face the full cost of using the land's attributes.[16]

Cropshare Contracts

In a cropshare contract, the farmer has exclusive use of the plot of land without paying the landowner prior to production. At harvest time, the crop is divided between the farmer and landowner, with the farmer receiving sQ and the landowner receiving $(1-s)Q$, where $0 < s < 1$.[17] The farmer bears all costs of the variable inputs except the differential cost of the land's unpriced attributes. The farmer's objective is

$$\max_{e,l} \Pi^s = s[h(e,l)] - we - r'l. \tag{4.2}$$

Now the second-best solutions e^s and l^s satisfy: $sh_e(e^s) \equiv w$ and $sh_l(l^s) \equiv r'$. These solutions indicate that the farmer supplies too few of his inputs because he must share the output with the landowner; that is, $e^s < e^*$. As with cash rent, the farmer overuses the land attributes, or $l^s > l^*$; however, since $l^r > l^s > l^*$, the use of the land is less excessive than it is with cash rent. This means that although a share contract still provides the farmer with an incentive to overuse the land, this incentive is not as powerful as it is with the cash rent contract.

Figure 4.1 demonstrates the equilibrium of the model. For simplicity of presentation, the graphs use identical and linear marginal product curves for each input. When contracts are enforced without cost, the first-best input levels e^* and l^* are chosen. In a cash rent contract the farmer faces reduced costs of using land attributes and chooses l^r, resulting in a deadweight cost of DFG. In a share contract the perceived marginal products to the farmer are lower, and therefore, he reduces the amount of both inputs used to e^s and l^s, resulting in two deadweight costs, ABC and DEH. In order to understand the differential effects of the contract, consider a switch from cash rent to cropshare. In a cropshare contract the farmer chooses less of both inputs, which has two offsetting effects: the reduction in the use of land attributes (l) increases the value of the contract, while the decrease in effort (e) lowers it. The optimal share will be the one that just equates the marginal loss (AB) due to reducing effort to the marginal gain (EH) due to reducing the level of the land attributes. One obvious implication of the model is that l^s is always greater than l^* since $r' < r$.[18] If

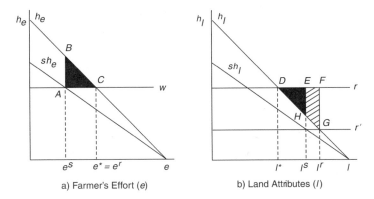

Figure 4.1
How share contracts minimize total input distortion.

there were no output division costs, the cropshare contract would always be superior to cash rent because of the reduction in total input distortion. Cropshare contracts, however, do not always dominate cash rent contracts, since they do create an incentive to underreport the quality and quantity of crop.[19]

Comparative Statics of Contract Choice

Farmers and landowners choose the contract that maximizes the joint expected return to the tract of land.[20] Analytically, this requires comparing the expected net return to the land in both contracts, where the net return is given by the appropriate indirect objective function. For the cash rent contract,

$$V^r(w, r, r') = h(e^r, l^r) - we^r - rl^r. \tag{4.3}$$

With the cropshare contract, there are additional costs of measuring and dividing the harvested crop. These costs are given by μ so that the net value function is

$$V^s(w, r, r', \mu) = h(e^s, l^s) - we^s - rl^s - \mu. \tag{4.4}$$

The joint maximization problem is to choose the larger of V^r and V^s.

The trade-off between the two contracts is straightforward, as shown in table 4.1. The benefit of cash rent is the avoidance of the costs of dividing output μ. The benefit of cropsharing is the reduction in the total distortion of input levels. Hence cropsharing should be observed when output measurement costs are low and when soil attributes are easy to exploit. Cash rent contracts should be observed under the opposite conditions. The effect of

Table 4.1
Summary of incentives for contract choice

	Effort moral hazard	Land moral hazard	Output underreporting
Cropshare contract	Less	Yes	Yes
Cash rent contract	More	No	No

parameter changes on the net value of each contract can illuminate this trade-off and lead to hypotheses about contract choice. We consider changes in output division costs, μ, and the opportunity cost of land attributes, r.

Consider first how changes in μ affect V^r and V^s. The net value of the cash rent contract, V^r, does not depend on output division costs. The net value of the cropshare contract, V^s, however, declines as these costs increase. By the Envelope Theorem, $\partial V^s / \partial \mu < 0$. For low costs, the cropshare contract maximizes net value; for high costs, the cash rent contract maximizes net value. This implies that

PREDICTION 4.1   As the costs of output division increase, it is less likely that the cropshare contract will be chosen.

The comparative statics for r are similar. By the Envelope Theorem, $\partial V^s / \partial r = -l^s$ and $\partial V^r / \partial r = -l^r$, where $l^r > l^s$. Because neither l^s nor l^r depend on r, the second derivatives of V^s and V^r with respect to r are zero. Therefore, V^s and V^r are linear functions of r. Thus, an increase in the cost of land attributes will lower the value of either contract (holding r' constant), but it will lower the value of the cash rent contract more because land inputs are used more intensively in a cash rent contract than in a cropshare contract ($l^r > l^s$). This implies that

PREDICTION 4.2a   As the unpriced attribute of the land becomes more easily damaged, it is more likely a cropshare contract will be chosen.

PREDICTION 4.2b   As land value increases, it is more likely a cropshare contract will be chosen.

These predictions—regarding the choice of contract for different levels of crop division costs μ, and a farmer's incentive to exploit the soil ($r - r'$)—can be tested by using data on contracts and the characteristics of crops, farmers, and landowners that allow us to measure output division costs and soil exploitation.

Our model also has implications about the level of input use under both types of contracts. However, the data available in our surveys of contracts from British Columbia, Louisiana, Nebraska, and South Dakota only allow a test of the contract choice implications. These data have no information on the use of any farm inputs. A study by Shaban (1987), however, offers support for our implications for input choices. Using data from Indian villages, Shaban found that input use was significantly lower (from 19 to 55%) on shared land compared to owned land. He concludes that the data refute the idea that land owners are able to stipulate and perfectly monitor input uses in a share contract. More recently, Canjels (1996) finds heavier input use (for example, fertilizer, pesticides) in cash rent contracts compared to cropshare contracts using data from the United States in the late 1980s.

4.3 Empirical Analysis: The Choice of Contract

To test the above predictions we use data from the same leasing surveys used in chapter 3. Again, each observation is a single contract between a farmer and a landowner, and the variables used in this chapter are listed in table 4.2. Though the appendix describes the data in more detail, it is again useful to examine some features of the data used in this chapter. CONTRACT is a dummy variable that identifies cropshare contracts, and ADJUSTMENT is a dummy variable that identifies the presence of an adjustment clause in a cash contract. These are used as dependent variables in the analysis that follows. For the Nebraska–South Dakota data we have over 3,400 contracts, and for the British Columbia–Louisiana data we have over 1,000 contracts. Information on ADJUSTMENT is only available for the Great Plains data. For some estimates we divide the Nebraska–South Dakota data into two subsamples: one for which farmers provided data (1,261 contracts) and one for which landowners provided data (2,171 contracts). Some information is only available for farmers or for landowners.[21] These anomalies are discussed as they arise.

Independent variables can be grouped into those that measure output division costs and soil exploitation. HAY and INSTITUTION are dummy variables that indicate the presence of hay and institutional landowners, respectively, are used as output division variables. IRRIGATED, RICE, ROW CROP, and TREES are dummy variables that indicate the presence of irrigation systems, rice, row crops, and tree crops, respectively, and are also used as soil exploitation variables. DENSITY is the population density for the county in which the plot lies and is also a soil exploitation variable.[22] A number of variables are used as controls, and depending on the data set these include the age of the farmer (AGE), the size of the leased plot (ACRES), a dummy for leases between family members (FAMILY), the total farm sales (FARM SALES), and the fraction of income derived from the farm (FARM INCOME). ROW*HAY is an interaction variable also used as a control.[23] ABSENT is a dummy identifying absentee landowners and ACRES OWNED measures percent of farm acres owned by the farmer. These last two variables are used to test hypotheses from other sources than our model.

Table 4.2
Definition of variables

Dependent variables

CONTRACT   = 1 if contract was a cropshare contract; = 0 if a cash rent contract.

Independent variables

ABSENT   = 1 if landowner lived in county different than contracted land; = 0 otherwise.
ACRES   = number of acres covered by contract.
ACRES OWNED   = percentage of farmed acres that are owned by the farmer.
AGE   = farmer's age in years (for British Columbia and Louisiana).
AGE   = 1 if farmer is younger than 25,
                             = 2 if 25–34 years old,
                             = 3 if 35–44 years old,
                             = 4 if 45–54 years old,
                             = 5 if 55–64 years old,
                             = 6 if older than 65 (for Nebraska and South Dakota).
DENSITY   = population per square mile in the county of farm operation.
FAMILY   = 1 if landowner and farmer were related; = 0 otherwise.
FARM INCOME   = 1 if less than 30% of total income comes from farming.
                             = 2 if between 30% and 49%.
                             = 3 if between 50% and 80%.
                             = 4 if more than 80%.
FARM SALES   = total farm sales for 1992.
HAY   = 1 if hay and other grass crops were the major income-producing crops;
                             = 0 otherwise.
INSTITUTION   = 1 if the landowner is an institution (available for Nebraska and South Dakota farmer sample);
                             = 0 if the owner is an individual.
IRRIGATED   = 1 if land is irrigated; = 0 if dryland.
RICE   = 1 if the crop was rice; = 0 otherwise.
ROW CROP   = 1 if a row crop (corn, sugar beets, sugarcane soybeans, sorghum);
                             = 0 if not a row crop (wheat, oats, barley).
TREES   = 1 if fruit was grown (e.g., apples, pears, etc.);
                             = 0 if no fruit was grown.

Prediction 4.1 says that a cropshare contract is most likely to occur when the costs of dividing the crop are relatively low. Crops can be divided into two categories to identify changes in output division costs: crops sold through public markets and crops sold through private sales. Most cash crops (grains typically) grown in our jurisdictions are sold at local elevators, probably within a thirty-mile drive, where the crop is independently weighed, graded, and, if there is a cropshare contract, divided. Most farm towns, especially on the Great Plains, have very few elevators, and it is usually well known where farmers take their crops.[24] Crops that must go to an elevator are relatively easy to measure. Alfalfa, brome, and native hay are crops in our sample that are not weighed and sold at an elevator or other third-party location. Because these hay crops are more difficult to measure at the time of harvest, we expect cash rent contracts are more likely to be chosen.[25] Similarly, a cash rent contract is more likely to be chosen when the costs of on-farm storage is high, rendering crop storage in a public elevator more likely.

Although we have no data on the extent of on-farm storage, we have other information on landowners that can be used. Not all farmland owners are private individuals. In some cases, farmers lease land from city or state governments, Indian tribes, banks, or other "institutional" landowners. For these landowners, crop division costs are likely to be relatively large. Agents of the institution would have little a priori knowledge or interest in the yield or possibilities for underreporting. Thus, we expect institutional landowners to be more likely than private landowners to cash rent their land. To summarize, we expect negative coefficients for HAY and INSTITUTION.

Predictions 4.2a and 4.2b state that cropshare contracts are more likely when soil exploitation costs are high. Our data can be used to identify situations in which this is likely to be true. For example, if farmland is soon to be used for purposes other than agriculture, then soil quality becomes less important. In the extreme case, where the land is to be converted at the end of the current contract, the incentives of the landowner and the farmer toward soil extraction would be identical ($r' = r$). In this case, a cash rent contract would approximate the first-best solution and would be chosen over cropshare. Thus, we expect cash rent farming to be more common for farmland near urban populations, because the value of the land for nonfarm uses is relatively high. The variable DENSITY approximates the urbanization of an area and indicates the extent to which farmland may have alternative uses.

Other situations can also be used to identify cases where soil exploitation is relatively unimportant. Irrigated land is less likely to suffer from soil exploitation because irrigated land does not require fallowing, which is a method of conserving soil moisture.[26] Thus, cropshare contracts are expected to be less likely for irrigated land than for land that is not irrigated. Tilling, cultivating, and other physical manipulations of the soil present the same incentive conflict between the landowner and the farmer as fallowing does. The farmer does not have the incentive to take the long view regarding tilling. In certain cases, excessive tilling can lead to wind and water erosion, nutrient depletion, and loss of moisture, which may not be problematic in the immediate period but will lead to reduced crops in the future. For example, in the relatively dry climate on the Great Plains, the evaporation of surface moisture draws subsurface moisture upward and reduces the total amount available for current and future crops. Cropsharing is more likely to be chosen when tillage becomes more important because the potential for land exploitation is greater. When one is considering the incentives for different tillage practices, it is useful to distinguish between row crops (such as corn, potatoes, soybeans, and sugar beets), where the land is tilled more intensively and other crops (such as barley, hay, and wheat) where the land is tilled less intensively.

Thus, cropshare contracts are more likely to be chosen for row crops where tillage is important.[27] To summarize, we expect negative coefficients for DENSITY and IRRIGATED and a positive coefficient for ROW CROP.

Cash Rent versus Cropshare Estimates

We use our contract data to estimate the determinants of cropshare contracts (versus cash rent contracts) and test the predictions from our model. We use the same general empirical specification from chapter 3, so that for any farmland contract i the complete model is

$$C_i^* = X_i \beta_i + \epsilon_i \quad i = 1, \ldots, n; \quad \text{and} \tag{4.5}$$

$$C_i = \begin{cases} 1, & \text{if } C_i^* > 0 \\ 0, & \text{if } C_i^* \leq 0, \end{cases} \tag{4.6}$$

where C_i^* is an unobserved farmland contract response variable; C_i is the observed dichotomous choice of land contract for plot i, which is equal to 1 for cropshare contracts and equal to 0 for cash rent contracts; X_i is a row vector of exogenous variables including the constant; β_i is a column vector of unknown coefficients; and ϵ_i is a plot-specific error term. We use a logit model to generate maximum likelihood estimates of the model given by equations (4.5) and (4.6) for various contract samples.

Table 4.3 shows the logit coefficients estimates of the influence of selected variables on the choice of contract for the Nebraska–South Dakota sample. The first equation includes all contracts (3,432). The coefficient estimates for the output division variables—HAY and INSTITUTION—are both negative and statistically significant as predicted. The coefficient estimates for the soil exploitation variables—DENSITY, IRRIGATED, and ROW CROP— also have the expected signs and are statistically significant. This implies that when soil exploitation is of less concern, a cropshare contract is less likely.[28] In the second and third equations in table 4.3, all of the coefficient estimates for these variables still fulfill the predictions, although in a few cases the t-statistics fall. These estimates offer support for our theory of contract choice and are also consistent with the observation of Gray et al. (1924, 589) that "especially in the Corn Belt it is frequently customary to cash rent the hay land while sharing the grain crop." Dubois (2002) finds that in the Philippines, corn—a crop that is hard on the land—is more likely to be cropshared than are the main alternatives of rice and sugar.

While we do not have data on soil quality directly, two recent empirical studies support our model. Using data from a special U.S. Census survey, Canjels (1996) finds that erodible land is more often cropshared. Similarly, Sotomayer, Ellinger, and Barry (2000) use a set

Table 4.3
Logit regression estimates: Cropshare vs. cash rent, Nebraska and South Dakota (1986)
(dependent variable = 1 if cropshare contract; = 0 if cash rent)

Independent variables	Full sample	Farmer sample	Landowner sample	Predicted sign
CONSTANT	−0.94	−0.30	0.28	
	(−0.61)	(−1.07)	(1.48)	
Output division				
HAY	−0.38	−0.18	−0.55	−
	(−2.71)*	(−0.79)	(−2.99)*	
INSTITUTION		−0.73		−
		(−3.26)*		
Soil exploitation				
DENSITY	−0.001	−0.001	−0.052	−
	(−2.00)*	(−1.31)	(−1.93)*	
IRRIGATED	−0.97	−0.73	−1.12	−
	(−8.37)*	(−4.24)*	(−6.86)*	
ROW CROP	2.76	2.10	3.44	+
	(23.97)*	(11.78)*	(20.36)*	
Other models				
ABSENT			−0.23	−
			(−1.71)*	
AGE		0.07		−
		(1.29)		
ACRES OWNED		−0.003		−
		(−0.93)		
FAMILY	−0.07	−0.046	0.30	+
	(−0.77)	(−0.32)	(2.16)*	
Controls				
ACRES	0.00002	0.0004	−0.00005	
	(0.28)	(2.92)*	(−1.11)	
FARM INCOME		−0.09	−0.18	
		(−1.77)	(−2.76)*	
ROW*HAY	0.039	0.16	−0.03	
	(0.19)	(0.56)	(−0.10)	
Observations	3,432	1,261	2,171	
χ^2 (df)	1,141.37(7)	300.83(11)	941.03(9)	
Log likelihood	−1,507.17	663.29	780.38	

Note: t-statistics in parentheses.
* significant at the 5 percent level (one-tailed test for coefficient with predicted signs).

of contracts from Illinois and find that land with higher quality soil is less likely to be cash rented. Both of these findings are consistent with predictions 4.2a and 4.2b.

Two control variables—ACRES and ROW*HAY—are included in all equations. ROW*HAY was included because of the data overlap we mentioned earlier. In all cases the coefficient for this variable was insignificantly different from zero. ACRES was included to control for the possibility that the size of the farm influences contract choice. The estimated coefficients for ACRES vary across the sample but show no statistically significantly effect in the full sample. FARM INCOME is also included as a control in the smaller samples.[29] The negative and statistically significant coefficients indicate that contracting parties (farmer or landowner) with larger fractions of income from farming are less likely to choose a cropshare contract.

Table 4.4 shows the estimated coefficients from a logit regression using the British Columbia–Louisiana data. The table shows estimates for the full sample and for British Columbia (155 contracts) and Louisiana (414 contracts) separately. The British Columbia–Louisiana data sample sizes are sensitive to the inclusion of variables because those variables relating to farm capital and wealth contain a number of missing observations. We estimated the equations in table 4.4 without these variables and obtained results for the remaining ones that were similar to those presented.

The estimates are similar to those found in table 4.3. For instance, as expected the estimated coefficients for HAY are negative and (usually) statistically significant. The coefficients for INSTITUTION are always negative and statistically significant. The estimated coefficients for IRRIGATED, however, are less supportive than in the Nebraska–South Dakota data. Only in the full and British Columbia samples are the estimates negative and they are not statistically significant. For the Louisiana sample, the estimates are actually positive. A plausible explanation is that for these data the IRRIGATED variable is dominated by flood irrigated rice that does not capture the soil exploitation phenomenon the same way it does for the Great Plains. The estimates for ROW CROP are, as expected, positive and statistically significant, except for the British Columbia sample.[30] Two additional variables, RICE and TREES, are used to measure the potential for soil exploitation. Rice, though not a row crop, is a crop for which soil degradation can be severe because of weed and disease problems; hence, it is expected to be shared.

Fruit trees, however, provide a novel test of our hypothesis, because the source of exploitation are the trees themselves, and farmers can extract more fruit in a given year at the expense of crops two or three years down the road by improper pruning. The share contract dampens this incentive and encourages proper tree maintenance.[31] Thus, we predict, and find, that the coefficients are positive (and statistically significant) for RICE and TREES. Orchards are found in British Columbia, but not in our Louisiana data. Hence the variable TREES is left out of the Louisiana regression.

Table 4.4
Logit regression estimates: Cropshare vs. cash rent, British Columbia and Louisiana (1992)
(dependent variable = 1 if cropshare contract; = 0 if cash rent)

Independent variables	Full sample	British Columbia sample	Louisiana sample	Predicted sign
CONSTANT	−0.86	−2.59	0.08	
	(−1.57)	(−2.16)*	(0.13)	
Output division				
HAY	−0.31	−0.78	−1.40	−
	(−0.77)	(−1.41)	(−1.05)	
INSTITUTION	−1.25	−2.11	−0.94	−
	(−3.24)*	(−1.91)*	(−1.99)*	
Soil exploitation				
DENSITY			−0.005	−
			(−0.94)	
IRRIGATED	−0.31	−0.89	0.002	−
	(−0.87)	(−1.07)	(0.00)	
RICE	2.27		1.59	+
	(5.05)*		(3.21)*	
ROW CROP	1.60	1.49	1.21	+
	(5.75)*	(1.39)	(3.66)*	
TREES	2.44	3.51		+
	(3.77)*	(3.58)*		
Other models				
ABSENT	9.01	10.30	8.41	−
	(0.88)	(0.53)	(0.75)	
AGE	0.008	0.031	−0.004	−
	(0.86)	(1.47)	(−0.37)	
ACRES OWNED	−1.29	−.51)	−1.17	−
	(−3.23)*	(−0.62)	(−2.36)*	
FAMILY	0.49	−0.105	0.47	+
	(1.70)	(−1.39)	(1.41)	
Controls				
ACRES	0.0001	0.0001	0.0002	
	(0.28)	(0.00)	(0.00)	
FARM SALES	0.02	−0.12	0.015	
	(0.47)	(−0.81)	(0.29)	
Observations	569	155	414	
χ^2 (df)	222.31(12)	57.15(11)	90.51(13)	
Log likelihood	−433.37	−114.59	−297.72	

Note: t-statistics in parentheses.
* significant at the 5 percent level (one-tailed test for coefficients with predicted signs).

ACRES is again used as a control variable in all equations. In each case the estimated coefficient in not statistically significant, indicating that the size of the land plot does not affect contract terms.

Absentee Owners, Agricultural Ladders, Capital Constraints, and Families

We use additional variables to test our model against predictions—about absentee landowners, the agricultural ladder, capital constraints, and families—made elsewhere in the literature.[32] The Nebraska–South Dakota data are most amenable because we have extra information depending on whether or not farmers or landowners were surveyed. The British Columbia–Louisiana data do not have a detailed landowner component, so some of these tests can be conducted only against the Great Plains contract data.

In the landowner sample, ABSENT is included to test a common prediction of landowner behavior. In many models, landowners are assumed to provide valuable farming information and policing along with the land; therefore, the "absentee landowner" faces higher costs of participating in farming activities. This implies that absentee landowners will be less likely to cropshare, so the estimated coefficient for ABSENT should be negative.[33] The negative coefficient in the landowner sample supports this prediction. The prediction is, however, not consistent with the estimates in table 4.4 using the British Columbia–Louisiana data. Our model has no explicit prediction because the landowner does not monitor the farmer.

In the traditional theory of the agricultural ladder, a farmer "climbs" from wage farmer sharecropper to cash renter to, ultimately, landowning farmer. In Spillman's (1919) words: "The first rung of the agricultural ladder is represented by the period during which the embryo farmer is learning the rudiments of his trade. In a majority of cases this period is spent as an unpaid laborer on the family farm. The hired man stands on the second rung, the tenant on the third, while the farm owners has attained the fourth or final rung of this ladder" (171).

Although the ladder hypothesis is not derived from a well-defined economic model, it has had a strong following among agriculturalists and it does have a clear prediction regarding the choice between cash rent and cropshare. This implication is simply that older farmers, or those with more farming experience, are more likely to cash rent. Thus, the variable AGE is predicted to be negative. The evidence in the second equation in table 4.3, however, rejects this hypothesis, because the coefficient is small, positive, and statistically insignificant. The data in table 4.4 also reject this hypothesis using the British Columbia–Louisiana data.

In a cash rent contract, a farmer must pay the landowner prior to harvest; in a cropshare contract, the payment comes after harvest. Thus, there is a long history in economics, from Gray et al. (1924) to Laffont and Matoussi (1995), who argue that farmers facing capital constraints will be more likely to choose a cropshare contract. We use the variable ACRES OWNED—which measures the amount of land owned by a farmer—to measure such a financial constraint. The farmer who owns more of his land base should have more collateral and be able to secure loans more cheaply. Thus, the capital constraint theory implies a negative coefficient for ACRES OWNED.[34] We find some support for this prediction, especially in the British Columbia–Louisiana data (table 4.4) where all coefficient estimates are negative and two are statistically significant. There is weaker support in the Nebraska–South Dakota data (table 4.3).[35]

The variable FAMILY is included—in all specifications and for both data sets—to examine how family relationships influence the choice of contract. Otsuka and Hayami (1988) argue that contracts between family members will generally be easier to enforce, so that most contracts will be between related individuals rather than "strangers." The aggregate evidence, however, refutes their hypothesis: Most contracts are not between family members. In our Nebraska–South Dakota data, 66 percent of the contracts are between nonfamily members. Furthermore, Otsuka and Hayami claim that sharecropping should be more common among family members, implying a positive coefficient on FAMILY in all specifications. The Nebraska–South Dakota data (table 4.3) reveals that only one of the three coefficients in positive and statistically significant. The British Columbia–Louisiana data (table 4.4), however, shows that all coefficients are positive and two are statistically significant. Overall, then we find modest support for the prediction that cropshare contracts will be more likely among family members.[36]

Adjustment Clauses in Cash Rent Contracts

In the typical cash rent contract, the farmer is the complete residual claimant of the crop. In our Nebraska–South Dakota data, however, roughly 10 percent of the cash rent contracts (100 out of 1,008) have provisions to vary the amount of cash rent due to changes in actual yields. We examine these cash rent adjustment clauses in order to further test our model, which implies that farmer-landowner contracts are organized to reduce the losses from input distortions and output division costs.

Because these adjustments are always upward—when crop yield meets a prespecified level, the cash rent is increased—these clauses convert the cash rent contract into a partial cropshare contract. A higher-than-expected yield may indicate that the farmer has overused the soil contrary to the landowner's long-term desires. An adjustment clause may, in part, serve as a deterrent to a farmer's excessive use of the land, because his marginal share is reduced at the point at which the clause takes affect. Because an adjustment clause is a partial share contract, predictions 4.1, 4.2a, and 4.2b are applicable. This implies that the adjustments will be more common for land where the farmer's ability to exploit the soil is high. In addition, since the adjustment clause requires a measurement of the crop, crops where the division costs are high should be less likely to have adjustment clauses. Thus, we expect that adjustment clauses will be less likely for hay land or irrigated land, because the ability of the farmer to overuse the land is limited in these cases, and hay crops are easier to underreport at harvest. With row crops, where the ability to exploit the soil is greater and where the relative cost of division is lower, adjustment clauses are more likely.

We test our predictions by using the sample of cash rent contracts from the Nebraska–South Dakota data using the empirical specification in equations (4.5) and (4.6). Table 4.5 presents the results of a logit regression equation that estimates the effects of several variables on the decision to include an adjustment clause in the cash rent contract. Our model predicts that all variables should have the same sign as in the previous test since the presence of an adjustment clause with a cash rent contract approximates a cropshare contract. Except for DENSITY, all estimated coefficients support our predictions. For the variables HAY and IRRIGATED we expect—and find—a negative relationship, although the coefficient for IRRIGATED is not statistically significant. The variable ROW CROP is positive and significant, as predicted, since the adjustment clause will discourage exploiting the soil to increase the current crop. DENSITY is predicted negative because alternative uses for the land reduce the cost of soil exploitation; however, this prediction is refuted by the data.

Like the estimates in table 4.3, we include ACRES, FAMILY, and ROW*HAY as control variables. ACRES and ROW*HAY have no statistically significant effect on the presence of an adjustment clause. FAMILY, however, has a positive and statistically significant effect on the probability that an adjustment clause will be chosen. This indicates that family members are more likely to exploit the soil under a pure cash rent contract than are nonfamily members. This finding is consistent with the majority of our estimates in tables 4.3 and 4.4 and supports the prediction that family members are more likely to use share contracts.

We also estimated this equation with the farmer sample to test our prediction about institutional landlords. The estimates for this equation are also shown in table 4.5. The coefficient for INSTITUTION was negative as predicted, and significant at the 10 percent level. The other coefficients were similar in size and statistical significance levels to the full sample coefficients.

4.4   Farmland Contracts in Historical Europe

Adam Smith was not a fan of cropsharing. His major discussion of the topic appears in chapter II of book III of *The Wealth of Nations*, under the general heading of "Discouragement of Agriculture." There Smith provides a brief history of agricultural contractual arrangements, beginning with the Roman Empire and continuing to his day. A major theme for Smith was that historical agriculture often involved slavery, and given the disincentives of slaves to work, innovate, and look after farm capital, these types of farms were eventually

Table 4.5
Logit regression estimates: Cash rent adjustment clauses, Nebraska and South Dakota (1986)
(dependent variable = 1 if adjustment clause is present)

Independent variables	Full sample	Farmer sample	Predicted sign
CONSTANT	−2.44	−1.96	
	(−9.19)*	(−4.83)*	
Output division			
HAY	−0.75	−1.18	−
	(−1.95)*	(−1.92)*	
INSTITUTION		−1.15	−
		(−1.85)*	
Soil exploitation			
DENSITY	0.001	0.002	−
	(2.37)*	(1.59)	
IRRIGATED	−0.06	−0.16	−
	(−0.22)	(−0.46)	
ROW CROP	0.90	0.72	+
	(3.67)*	(2.10)*	
Controls			
ACRES	−0.0001	0.0001	
	(−1.04)	(0.46)	
FAMILY	0.46	−0.066	
	(2.07)*	(−0.20)	
ROW*HAY	−1.08	−0.22	
	(-1.52)	(0.25)	
Observations	1,008	437	
Chi-square (df)	45.76(7)	22.21(8)	
Log likelihood	−300.88	−144.31	

Note: t-statistics in parentheses.
* significant at the 5 percent level (one-tailed t-test for coefficient with predicted signs).

replaced by owned farms that often rented out land. Smith takes pains to point out that he viewed cropsharing as little better than slavery. For example, Smith stated (1992 [1776]):

To the slave cultivators of ancient times, gradually succeeded a species of farmers known at present in France by the name of metayers. They have been so long in disuse in England that at present I know no English name for them. The proprietor furnished them with the seed, cattle, and instruments of husbandry, the whole stock, in short necessary for cultivating the farm. The produce was divided equally between the proprietor and the farmer. (P. 366)

Adam Smith was not particularly interested in explaining why a cropsharing system survived in most of France while it failed to exist in England. Possibly influenced by the near continuous wars with France during the time, Smith made certain to argue the inferiorities of the French system. One of Smith's (1992 [1776]) important contributions to the analysis of cropsharing is his introduction of the notion of the share acting as a tax on behavior: "The tithe, which is but a tenth of the produce, is found to be a very great hindrance to improvement. A tax, therefore, which amounted to one-half, must have been an effectual bar to it" (376).

Interestingly, Smith (1992 [1776]) also was keen to point out the issue of the problem of measurement with cropsharing and noted that "in France, where five parts out of six of the whole kingdom are said to be still occupied by this species of cultivators, the proprietors complain that their metayers take every opportunity of employing the master's cattle rather in carriage than in cultivation; because in the one case they get the whole profits to themselves, in the other they share them with their landlord" (367).

In contrast to Smith, John Stuart Mill in his *Principles of Political Economy* (book II, chapter VIII) offered a much more balanced, and surprisingly modern, approach to cropsharing and cash renting. Writing roughly a century later than Smith, Mill agreed with Smith that France and Italy had a great deal of cropsharing and that this share acts as a tax on effort. Mill, however, surveyed several contemporary writers at the time, noting that these contracts had been in existence a long time, that the level of cultivation was not suffering, and that there was a great deal of variation in the contracts across the region. Mill (1965 [1871]), in great contrast to Smith, thus concluded: "I do not offer these quotations as evidence of the intrinsic excellence of the metayer system; but they surely suffice to prove that neither 'land miserably cultivated' nor a people in 'the most abject poverty' have any necessary connexion (*sic*) with it, and that the unmeasured vituperation lavished upon the system by English writers is grounded on an extremely narrow view of the subject" (315).

While the difference between Smith and Mill is of interest for those who follow the history of economics, our point here is more narrowly related to our own predictions about the determinants of farmland contracts. Both Smith and Mill acknowledged that cash rent and cropsharing existed in Europe, and that France, Italy, and Spain tended to be dominated by cropsharing while the northern European countries tended to be dominated by cash rent contracts. Many other writers since Smith and Mill, including modern economic historians, would agree with this general characterization of the distribution of farmland contracts across historical Europe. For instance, Kohn (2001) states: "Both fixed rent and share leases were to be found wherever the limited term lease appeared, but in most regions one or the other eventually came to predominate. The fixed-rent lease was the more common form in Northern France, the Low Countries, Western Germany, and the Po Valley. The share lease predominated in Western and Southern France and in Tuscany" (3). Similarly, when discussing France, Hoffman (1984) notes: "Sharecropping flourished both during the inflation of the sixteenth century and during the declining prices of the 1600s . . . despite overall similarities in European population trends, sharecropping took root only in particular areas, such as parts of Italy and France" (310–311). Many other recent studies also confirm this generalization, including Carmona and Simpson (1999) and Galassi (1992).

Although there are no detailed historical statistics on the precise distribution of these lease arrangements, the general facts appear consistent with our model. In northern Europe the most common type of farming would have been for small grains and grass crops. In southern France, Italy, and Spain grapes, olives, and fruit were much more important.[37] As we mentioned earlier in the context of fruit trees in British Columbia, the share contract mitigates the farmer exploiting the tree or vine asset. With grapes and fruit, pruning can be done in certain ways that increase the short-run volume of fruit, but that over time kill the tree or drastically reduce the long-term productivity of the tree. Sharing lowers the incentive of the farmer to do this in the same manner it lowers the incentive to exploit soil attributes.[38] The observations about European land leasing, first made by Adam Smith and John Stuart Mill, thus suggest that land contracts were chosen in response to the costs of enforcing contracts over assets with many attributes. The dominance of cash rent contracts in England and northern Europe was the result of the relative dominance of small grain and grass farming. Similarly, the dominance of cropsharing in France, Italy and Spain was the result of the relative dominance of orchard crops.

4.5 Summary

In this chapter we have shown the transaction cost approach to be a useful tool for understanding the choice of contracts for farmers and landowners in modern and historical agriculture. It is an unfortunate reality that transaction cost models often hinge on unobservable parameters. If economists could directly and cheaply measure the ability of farmers to exploit soil moisture and nutrients or the number and quality of hay bales taken, then so could landowners and farmers and there would be no contract incentive issues. Despite the problems with identifying output division costs and the cost of exploiting soil attributes faced by the farmer, we feel that our variables are reasonable and accurate. The ability to obtain detailed knowledge of farming practices helps exploit the theoretical model, and our evidence indicates that the choice of cash rent and cropshare contracts lies primarily in their ability to create proper incentives.

As we note in chapter 1, government programs might influence contract choice. For example, farm commodity programs are another factor that could potentially influence farmland contracts. For some crops (for example, barley and wheat) farmers get direct payments; for some crops (for example, soybeans and sugar beets) farmers do not receive direct payments but receive indirect subsidies through tariffs; and for other crops (for example, cattle, hay) there are no programs. It is not clear what a model based on government programs would imply, since the payments do not depend on the allocation of input costs. Furthermore, in the context of our model, it is not at all clear how government programs would influence measurement costs or soil exploitability. These programs reduce income variability, so—assuming risk aversion—one might argue that nonprogram crops be treated differently from program crops. But, for the Nebraska–South Dakota data, virtually all crops are program crops, so there is no way to test for effects even if implications were available. Interestingly, the only nonprogram crop is hay, and it is virtually never cropshared, contrary to the risk-sharing hypothesis.

Our data show that cropshare contracts are more likely when crop division costs are low and where the ability of farmers to adversely affect the soil is high, and that cash rent contracts often contain clauses that discourage exploitation of the soil. Our coefficient estimates support our general theory that the variation in contracts is largely determined by the costs of enforcing the contracts in various situations. Not only are the signs of our estimated coefficients consistent with our predictions, but the magnitude of the coefficients dwarf the coefficients for both the control variables and the variables testing other theories. The next chapter extends our model to the case of input sharing and provides more evidence in favor of the transaction cost framework.

5 Sharing Inputs and Outputs

5.1 Introduction

The model and evidence in chapter 4 showed that moral hazard and enforcement costs (over land quality and output sharing) determined the choice between a cash rent and a cropshare contract. In this chapter we extend the model developed in chapter 4 to focus solely on cropshare contracts and, in particular, to determine the optimal sharing rule for both the crop output and the variable input costs. Though cropshare contracts are common, they differ from one another in that some include the provision for some or all of the inputs to be shared, while others contain no such provision. Heady (1947) was one of the first to point out that sharing input costs in the same proportion as the output share offsets the taxing effect of the share on that input. His result almost exhausts what economists have had to say regarding input sharing, save Braverman and Stiglitz (1982). In this chapter we derive explicit predictions about the relationship between input and output shares. In particular, our model makes the rather strong prediction that inputs are either shared in the same proportion as the output or they are not shared at all.[1]

5.2 Optimal Cropshare Contracts

The model is developed in three stages. First, we examine the incentives of the farmer to choose inputs given exogenous input and output shares. Second, we derive the optimal cropshare and input shares that maximize the expected net value of the contract, taking the farmer's input choices as constraints in a joint wealth maximization problem. Third, we derive the comparative statics of various share contract forms by examining the effects of parameter changes on the joint wealth of a contract. Testable implications are derived at each stage.

Production and Input Use

We extend the previous analysis by assuming that there are three types of inputs rather than just two: farmland owned by landowners; farm labor owned by farmers; and other variable inputs, such as fertilizer and seed, that may be owned by both farmers or landowners. All other model assumptions remain the same.[2] Hence, output is now $Q = h(e, l, k_i) + \theta$, where all variables are as defined in chapter 4, and k_i is one of several (n) inputs such as fertilizer, pesticide, or seed. The opportunity cost of the ith variable input is c_i per unit. In general, we ignore the subscripts on the k_i inputs and examine one such input at a time. Because the inputs are assumed to be independent, this causes no problem and clarifies the notation. In the empirical section, however, we consider many inputs.

Assuming risk neutrality and zero contract enforcement costs, the farmer and landowner jointly maximize expected profit by employing the first-best, full-information input levels e^*, l^*, and k^*. These input choices do not depend on the contracted input and output shares and satisfy the standard conditions that marginal products equal marginal costs.

It is not surprising that the nature of the solution here is similar to the one found in chapter 4. When contract enforcement is costly, the chosen input levels will be second best. Because farmers do not have indefinite tenure of the land, they face lower opportunity costs of the land attributes, $r' < r$. As a result, they exploit the land's unpriced attributes, l, just as they did in chapter 4. When the crop is shared the farmer owns sQ and the landowner owns $(1-s)Q$, and the farmer supplies less of his own labor and capital than he would if he owned the entire crop—again, as they did in chapter 4. For each shared input, however, the farmer pays $q(ck)$ and the landowner pays $(1-q)(ck)$, where $q \in [0, 1]$ is the farmer's share of input costs. If $q < 1$, the farmer overuses the shared inputs because he bears less than their full marginal cost.

Extending the analysis of the last chapter, we find that there are costs of measuring and dividing both the shared output and each shared input. However, two crucial inputs—the farmer's effort and the landowner's land—are not shared because the division costs are prohibitively high. Thus, for a single tract of farmland under a cropshare contract, the farmer's objective is[3]

$$\max_{e,l,k} \Pi^s = s[h(e, l, k)] - we - r'l - qck. \tag{5.1}$$

The second-best optimal input levels e^s, l^s, and k^s satisfy $sh_e(e^s) \equiv w$, $sh_l(l^s) \equiv r'$, and $sh_k(k^s) \equiv qc$. From the first-order conditions and the assumption of independent inputs, it is clear that the optimal input choices differ from the first-best, or zero transaction cost, case. It follows that the farmer supplies too few of his inputs because he must share the output with the landowner; that is, $e^s < e^*$. Similarly, the farmer overworks the land because he does not face the full cost of using the land's attributes; that is, $l^s > l^*$.[4] Finally, it is evident that, depending on the relative size of q and s, the farmer may use too much, too little, or the optimal amount of the other inputs. For these inputs, if $q = s$, then $k^s = k^*$; if $q > s$, then $k^s < k^*$; and if $q < s$, then $k^s > k^*$.

Measurement Costs and Input Sharing

The farmer's optimal input choices—e^s, l^s, and k^s—effectively constrain the potential value of the cropshare contract. To maximize joint wealth, the farmer and landowner contract for the optimal output share (s^*) and input share (q^*) in recognition of these constraints. Their joint problem is

$$\max_{s,q} V = h(e^s, l^s, k^s) - we^s - rl^s - ck^s - m, \tag{5.2}$$

where m is the cost of measuring and dividing each input. Without considering these measurement costs, s^* and q^* satisfy[5]

$$e_s(h_e - w) + l_s(h_l - r) + k_s(h_k - c) = 0, \quad \text{and} \tag{5.3}$$

$$e_q(h_e - w) + l_q(h_l - r) + k_q(h_k - c) = 0. \tag{5.4}$$

If input measurement costs are ignored, the solutions to equations (5.3) and (5.4) determine the optimal sharing rules, s^* and q^*. If, however, there are costs of measuring and dividing the input, they must be considered in order for s^* and q^* to be derived. If these costs (m) are lump-sum expenditures and the inputs are unrelated, then the solution to equations (5.3) and (5.4) is dichotomous and the choice of the optimal cropshare is made after the decision about input cost sharing is made.[6]

As long as these measurement costs are worth incurring, the model implies that input-sharing and output-sharing rules will be identical; that is, $q^* = s^*$. If these costs are not worth incurring, however, then input costs will not be shared and the farmer will bear all costs; that is, $s^* < q^* = 1$. This is proved by examining (5.4) and considering the case for which measurement costs are small and worth incurring. Because inputs are independent, $e_q = l_q = 0$. Also, because $k_q < 0$, a drop in the farmer's cost of input k leads him to choose an increased amount of the input. Thus, equation (5.4) implies that $h_k = c$. The first-order condition in the farmer's problem, $sh_k(k^s) \equiv qc$, must also hold, implying that $q^* = s^*$. Therefore, when inputs are shared the optimal sharing rules must satisfy

$$e_s(h_e - w) + l_s(h_l - r) = 0, \quad \text{and} \tag{5.5}$$

$$q^* = s^*. \tag{5.6}$$

The optimal use of inputs is illustrated by figure 5.1, which considers the case where input shares equal output shares.[7] For clarity the marginal product curves for each input are again drawn as identical and linear. Each panel shows the marginal product curve for each input; it also shows the farmer's share of the marginal product that depends on the optimal share s^*. Because the farmer shares the crop, he applies less capital and labor, which results in a marginal distortion equal to AB. The landowner's inability to fully price the land's attributes results in overuse by the farmer and a marginal distortion equal to CD. For the other variable inputs, sharing rules yield no marginal distortion, because input and output shares are identical. For the value of the contract to be maximized, the optimal output share s^* must be chosen so that the marginal distortions on inputs e and l exactly offset (AB= CD).[8]

When measurement costs are large and not worth incurring, the farmer must bear all of the input costs; that is, $q = 1$. The assumption of independent inputs still implies that $e_q = l_q = 0$; but now $h_k \neq c$, because $s \neq q$ and $s < 1$ in any cropshare contract, which also

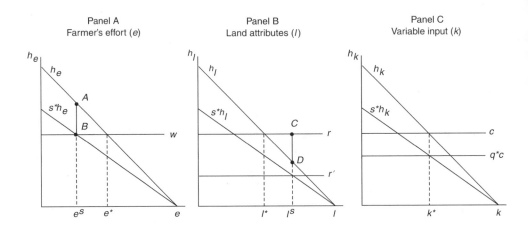

Note: *s** is chosen so that *AB = CD*.

Figure 5.1
Output shares and input use: $q^* = s^*$

implies $k_q = 0$. Thus, if inputs are not shared, the optimal sharing rules must satisfy

$$e_s(h_e - w) + l_s(h_l - r) + k_s(h_k - c) = 0, \quad \text{and} \tag{5.7}$$

$$q^* = 1. \tag{5.8}$$

The optimal use of inputs is illustrated by figure 5.2, which considers the case where the farmer pays all of the input costs. For e and l, the incentives for input use are the same as when the inputs are shared, resulting in the marginal distortions AB and CD. For each of the other k inputs, however, the lack of input sharing results in lower use and a marginal distortion equal to EF per input. The optimal output share s^* is chosen so that the marginal negative distortions (AB and EF) are exactly offset by the marginal positive distortion (CD); that is, AB + EF = CD. If there are many (n) other k inputs, then $AB + \sum_{i=1}^{n}(EF) = CD$.

This analysis indicates a dichotomy in the choice of the optimal input share: Either input and output shares are equal, or the farmer pays the entire input cost. Under our assumptions, an optimal cropshare contract has no middle ground: $q^* = s^*$ or $q^* = 1$.

PREDICTION 5.1   Parties to cropshare contracts will either (i) only share output, the pure cropshare contract where $q^* = 1$, and $s^* < 1$ or (ii) share both inputs and output in the same proportion, the input-output cropshare contract where $q^* = s^* < 1$.

Two more predictions immediately follow from this analysis.

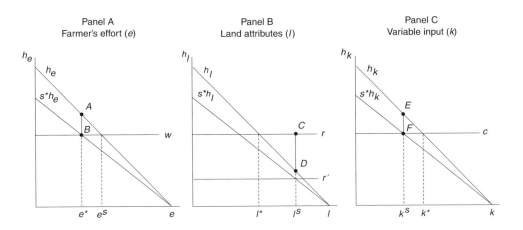

Note: s^* is chosen so that $AB + EF = CD$.

Figure 5.2
Output shares and input use: $q^* = 1$

PREDICTION 5.2   The optimal output share (s^*) will be higher when inputs are not shared ($q^* = 1$) than when inputs are shared ($q^* = s^*$).[9]

PREDICTION 5.3   When inputs are not shared ($q^* = 1$), the optimal output share s^* will rise as the number of other k inputs increase.

Prediction 5.2 holds because the distortions are spread over more inputs when inputs are not shared. This can be seen by comparing figures 5.1 and 5.2. Prediction 5.3 holds because the distortions will be spread across more margins. Furthermore, this analysis refutes the argument that proportional input sharing is required for efficient cropshare contracts. The model also implies a relationship between the fraction of contracts for which input costs are shared and the farmer's share of the output.

PREDICTION 5.4   The fraction of input costs that are shared will increase as the farmer's share of the output decreases.

Prediction 5.4 holds because, for any input k, the input distortion increases as the output share to the farmer falls. This occurs because the farmer's incentives are increasingly at odds with those of a complete owner of the crop. This distortion can be viewed as an increase in the potential benefit of having the farmer pay the same portion of the input costs as his share of the output. Sharing input costs creates incentives that move the contract toward the first-best input use, but requires that inputs be measured. The model implies that the costs of dividing inputs are more likely to be worth overcoming as the share of the farmer's harvest decreases because the costs are lump sum.

Pure Cropshare Contracts and Input-Output Cropshare Contracts

The choice between a pure cropshare contract ($q^* = 1, s^* < 1$) and an input-output cropshare contract ($q^* = s^* < 1$) is a dichotomous one that can be examined by comparing the expected net return to the land in both contracts.[10] The trade-off between the two contracts is straightforward. The pure cropshare contract has the advantage of avoiding the input division costs, m. The input-output share contract further reduces the input distortion that arises in any share contract. With the input-output cropshare contract, each input k is used at its first-best level, allowing for a further reduction in the output share in order to abate soil exploitation. The effect of parameter changes (m, r) on the net value of each contract can illuminate this trade-off and lead to hypotheses about contract choice.

Consider exogenous changes in m. The net value of the pure cropshare contract does not depend on input division costs, but the net value of the input-output cropshare contract declines as these costs increase. Let V^{IO} and V^P be the indirect objective functions for input-output sharing and pure cropsharing contracts, respectively. Then for any input k, the Envelope Theorem yields $\partial V^{IO}/\partial m = 0$ and $\partial V^P/\partial m < 0$. For low costs, the input-output cropshare contract maximizes net value; for high costs, the pure cropshare contract maximizes net value. This analysis parallels that in chapter 4 and implies the following:

PREDICTION 5.5   As input division costs (m) increase, it is more likely that the pure cropshare contract will be chosen ($q^* = 1$).

The comparative statics for r are similar. For any input k, the Envelope Theorem yields $\partial V^{IO}/\partial r = -l^1$ and $\partial V^P/\partial r = -l^2$, where $l^1 > l^2$, l^1 is derived when $q = 1$, and l^2 is derived when $0 < q < 1$. Because neither l^1 or l^2 depends on r, the second derivatives of V^{IO} and V^P with respect to r are zero. Thus, V^{IO} and V^P are declining linear functions of r. An increase in the costs of land attributes will lower the value of the input-output cropshare contracts, but it will lower the value of the pure cropshare contract even more because the land is used more intensively in the pure cropshare contract ($l^1 > l^2$) as a result of a larger cropshare. This implies the following:

PREDICTION 5.6   As the costs of land attributes increase or as land exploitation becomes more costly ($r - r'$ increases), the chosen contract will more likely be an input-output cropshare contract ($q^* = s^*$).

By recognizing how land attributes may be exploited in various situations, we derive specific implications. The problem of land exploitation tends to be less serious for irrigated land than for dry-farming land because tilling is not as important and soil moisture storage

Table 5.1
Summary of incentives for input sharing

	Effort moral hazard	Land moral hazard	Other input moral hazard	Output underreporting
Inputs shared	More	More	No	Yes
Inputs not shared	Less	Less	Yes	No

is not important. For row crops (such as corn, potatoes, soybeans, and sorghum), tilling during the growing season is much more important than it is for such small grain crops as barley and wheat. For these crops, excessive tilling can lead to soil exploitation, which can be curtailed by reducing the output share to the farmer. As a result, we expect the farmer's share of output to be lower for row crops and higher for irrigated land. These implications are consistent with the findings from chapter 4 that, ceteris paribus, irrigated land and hay land tend to be governed by cash rent contracts (where the farmer's share is 100%) and that row crops tend to be governed by cropshare contracts. We summarize the model trade-offs in table 5.1.

5.3 Empirical Analysis: Dichotomous Input and Output Sharing

To test these predictions we use the Nebraska–South Dakota contract data, where the variables used in the chapter are defined in table 5.2. The British Columbia–Louisiana data do not contain enough information on input sharing to test these predictions. Our model allows two sets of empirical tests. First, there are predictions about the relationship between input shares and output shares, including implications about the choice between pure ($q = 1$) and input-output ($q = s$) cropshare contracts. Second, there are predictions about the size of the optimal share (s). Both of these tests result from our model in which the ability of the farmer to exploit soil ($r - r'$) and the costs of measuring inputs (m) are determining parameters. Even though these parameters are not directly observable, there are distinct situations in which measurement costs are high and the farmer's ability to exploit the soil is great, allowing us to test the model's implications. In addition, we are able to observe directly input and output shares and identify situations—farmer, landowner, and land characteristics—in which we can expect soil exploitation or input measurement to be problematic.

The division of input costs between farmers and landowners varies across contracts (see table 5.3). The input shares tend to take one of two forms: Either the farmer bears all input costs other than the land costs, making his input share 100 percent, or the farmer and the landowner share the input costs in the same proportion as the output. In other words, if the

Table 5.2
Definition of variables

Dependent variables

CHEMICAL APPLICATION	= 1 if farmer pays 100% of chemical application cost;
	= 0 if the farmer pays the same portion as his cropshare.
DRYING	= 1 if farmer pays 100% of crop drying cost;
	= 0 if the farmer pays the same portion as his cropshare.
ENERGY	= 1 if farmer pays 100% of the irrigation energy cost;
	= 0 if the farmer pays the same portion as his cropshare.
FERTILIZER	= 1 if farmer pays 100% of the fertilizer cost;
	= 0 if the farmer pays the same portion as his cropshare.
HARVEST	= 1 if farmer pays 100% of the harvesting cost;
	= 0 if the farmer pays the same portion as his cropshare.
HERBICIDE	= 1 if farmer pays 100% of the herbicide cost;
	= 0 if the farmer pays the same portion as his cropshare.
INSECTICIDE	= 1 if farmer pays 100% of the insecticide cost;
	= 0 if the farmer pays the same portion as his cropshare.
QSHARE	= 1 if farmer pays all input costs;
	= 0 if farmer pays input costs proportional to his output share.

Independent variables

ABSENT	= 1 if landowner lived in county different than contracted land; = 0 otherwise.
ACRES	= number of acres covered by contract.
CORN, OATS, SOYBEANS, WHEAT	= 1 if corn (oats, soybeans, wheat) was the major income-producing crop;
	= 0 if not.
INPUTS	= the number of inputs where the farmer pays all costs.
IRRIGATED	= 1 if land is irrigated; = 0 if dryland.
ROW CROP	= 1 if row crop (corn, sugar beets, sugarcane soybeans, sorghum);
	= 0 if not a row crop (e.g., wheat, oats, barley).
YEARS DURATION	= number of years contract has been in place.

farmer's output share is 50 percent, then his input cost share is 50 percent. Heady, (1947) argued that output shares must be equal to input shares for a cropshare contract to be efficient. Prediction 5.1 contradicts Heady's contention and so do our data.

Dichotomous Rules for Input Shares

The Nebraska–South Dakota evidence is remarkably consistent with prediction 5.1. For the three most common cropshare rules (50-50, 60-40, and 67-33), $q = 100$ percent or $q = s$ in nearly all contracts (see table 5.4).[11] It is rare to find cases where $q \neq s$ if $q < 100$ percent. For instance, in 83 percent of 67-33 cropshare contracts, farmers and landowners share equally in the cost of fertilizer; 13 percent of the contracts have the farmer pay all such costs. Thus, these two input-sharing rules account for 96 percent of all cases. In general, as table 5.4 shows, these two rules ($q = s$ or $q = 100$ percent) combine for well over 90

Table 5.3
Distribution of cropshare and input share terms: Nebraska and South Dakota (1986)

Cropshare to farmer	Number of contracts	Percent of contracts
20	1	0.1
25	10	0.6
30	1	0.1
33	30	1.8
40	27	1.6
43	2	0.1
50	389	23.7
55	3	0.2
60	590	36.0
65	5	0.3
67	530	32.3
69	2	0.1
70	3	0.2
75	29	1.8
80	1	0.1
90	3	0.2
99	11	0.7

Farmer's input share	Number of contracts (%)		
	Fertilizer	Harvest	Seed
0	6 (0.4)	15 (0.9)	30 (1.8)
25	5 (0.3)	0 (0.0)	2 (0.1)
33	13 (0.8)	0 (0.0)	0 (0.0)
40	16 (1.0)	2 (0.1)	2 (0.1)
43	2 (0.1)	2 (0.1)	0 (0.0)
50	363 (22.4)	91 (5.6)	298 (18.3)
55	2 (0.1)	1 (0.1)	2 (0.1)
60	531 (32.7)	25 (1.5)	51 (3.1)
65	0 (0.0)	1 (0.1)	1 (0.1)
67	397 (22.6)	25 (1.5)	38 (2.3)
70	3 (0.2)	0 (0.0)	2 (0.1)
75	17 (1.0)	3 (0.2)	1 (0.1)
80	1 (0.1)	0 (0.0)	0 (0.0)
85	0 (0.0)	2 (0.1)	0 (0.0)
100	268 (16.5)	1,461 (89.6)	1,199 (73.7)

Table 5.4
Input and output sharing: Percentage of cropshare contracts for which input share equals output share ($q = s$), or equals 100 percent ($q = 1$)

Input	$s = 50\%$			$s = 60\%$			$s = 67\%$		
	$q = 50\%$	$q = 100\%$	Both	$q = 60\%$	$q = 100\%$	Both	$q = 67\%$	$q = 100\%$	Both
FERTILIZER	92%	1%	93%	94%	1%	95%	83%	13%	96%
HERBICIDE	92	3	95	81	16	97	57	38	95
INSECTICIDE	92	3	95	83	13	96	57	39	96
SEED	80	16	96	11	85	96	8	90	98
HARVESTING	30	66	96	6	93	99	7	93	100
CHEMICAL APPLICATION	48	47	95	41	57	98	39	58	97
DRYING	86	10	96	77	18	95	58	39	97
ENERGY	92	5	97	60	32	92	34	51	85

Percentage of cropshare contracts for which output share (s) equals input shares (q) when inputs are shared

Input	$q = 50\%$	$q = 60\%$	$q = 67\%$
CHEMICAL APPLICATION	91%	94%	90%
DRYING	94	95	96
FERTILIZER	90	95	90
HARVESTING	90	92	96
HERBICIDE	93	96	93
ENERGY	87	96	89
INSECTICIDE	93	96	93
SEED	95	96	84

percent of all input-share policies. The only exception is energy costs, for which these rules combine for 85 percent of the policies.

In addition, for contracts with input shares of 50 percent, 60 percent, and 67 percent, the bottom section of table 5.4 shows the percentage of contracts for which the output share is the same as the input share. For example, for cropshare contracts that require the farmer to bear 50 percent of the costs of chemical application (row 1), 91 percent also have an output share of 50 percent. The evidence presented offers strong support for our prediction that either input costs will be shared by the farmer and landowner in the same proportion as output or the farmer will bear all costs. This dichotomy refutes the implications of a model that relies on interlinkage of inputs by manipulating input prices (Braverman and Stiglitz 1982). Furthermore, this evidence refutes the prediction that output shares always equal input shares. Finally, our explicit consideration of contract enforcement costs—here, input measurement costs—neatly explains the dichotomy in contract structure.

Table 5.5
The relationship between cropshare rules and input share rules

Input	Rule	Cropshare mean	t-value (df)	Two-tailed probability
CHEMICAL APPLICATION	$q = s$	0.5800	4.45	0.0001
	$q = 1$	0.6013	(1577)	
DRYING	$q = s$	0.5764	6.52	0.0001
	$q = 1$	0.6061	(1582)	
FERTILIZER	$q = s$	0.5908	7.33	0.0001
	$q = 1$	0.6311	(1501)	
HARVEST	$q = s$	0.5364	8.46	0.0001
	$q = 1$	0.6006	(1611)	
HERBICIDE	$q = s$	0.5771	10.36	0.0001
	$q = 1$	0.6215	(1554)	
INSECTICIDE	$q = s$	0.5766	9.52	0.0001
	$q = 1$	0.6181	(1561)	
ENERGY	$q = s$	0.5505	10.03	0.0001
	$q = 1$	0.6062	(1595)	
SEED	$q = s$	0.5240	20.15	0.0001
	$q = 1$	0.6179	(1600)	

Determinants of Input Shares

Prediction 5.2 says that output shares will be higher for pure cropshare contracts ($q = 1$) than for input-output cropshare contracts ($q = s$). The input-output cropshare contract results in the use of variable inputs at the "optimal" level ($s = q$ implies that $k = k^*$). We test this prediction by comparing the farmer's mean output share for pure cropshare contracts with the mean share for input-output cropshare contracts. Table 5.5 shows the mean output share to the farmer for each input according to whether input costs were shared ($q = s$) or fully borne by the farmer ($q = 1$). For each input, the farmer's mean output share is significantly higher (averaging 61% versus 56%) when the farmer bears all the input costs ($q = 1$) than when he shares them with the landowner ($q = s$). This evidence further supports the general idea that input measurement costs are an important determinant of the details of agricultural contracts. If there were no such costs ($m = 0$), input sharing would always occur and in the same proportion as output sharing ($q = s$).[12]

Prediction 5.5 says that when input measurement costs are low, the input-output cropshare contract is more likely to be chosen because it comes closer to the first-best level of input use. One can distinguish cases in which input division costs are expected to be low, and one can distinguish between various inputs. Inputs such as fertilizer and seed are purchased in the market. Other inputs, such as harvesting, are not as routinely purchased, but more often provided by the farmer. Measurement costs are likely to be much lower for inputs purchased directly in the market than for those provided by the farmer. Inputs purchased in the market will necessarily be measured and sold by a noninterested third party, making it difficult for the farmer to cheat the landowner by overbilling the landowner or simply carelessly wasting the inputs.

Thus, we expect that market inputs (fertilizer, herbicide, insecticide, and seed) are more likely to be shared by the farmer and landowner in the same proportion as the output, while nonmarket inputs (chemical application, drying, irrigation energy, and harvesting) are more likely to be the complete responsibility of the farmer.[13] In other words, we expect $q = s$ for market inputs and $q = 1$ for nonmarket inputs. The data support this prediction. For all three major cropshare rules represented in table 5.4 (50-50, 60-40, and 67-33), the percentage of contracts for which the farmer pays all costs tends to be greatest for market inputs.[14] For example, in 67-33 cropshare contracts the farmer pays for all harvest costs 93 percent of the time; he pays for all fertilizer costs only 13 percent of the time.

Prediction 5.4 implies that the fraction of contracts where $q = s$ will be greater for 60-40 contracts than for 67-33 contracts, and that it will be even greater for 50-50 contracts. This prediction is supported by the data in table 5.4. For instance, drying costs are proportionally shared ($q = s$) in 58 percent of the 67-33 contracts, in 77 percent of the 60-40 contracts, and in 86 percent of the 50-50 contracts. With a few minor exceptions, this relationship holds for all inputs. Furthermore, it is expected that input shares (q) and output share (s) will be positively correlated for all crop inputs. We calculated correlation coefficients for all inputs and found them to be positive in all cases; the null hypothesis of zero correlation was rejected at less than the 1 percent level.

Input Sharing within Contracts

Thus far, we have examined the data for variation in input-sharing rules across contracts. Our model, however, has implications for the structure of input sharing within each cropshare contract. Within each contract, market inputs should be treated the same, and likewise for any nonmarket inputs. For instance, if seed is shared at 60-40, then so should fertilizer, pesticide, and herbicide be shared at 60-40, and the cropshare should also be 60-40. Nonmarket inputs (chemical application, drying, irrigation energy, and harvesting) are predicted to be the responsibility of the farmer. Tables 5.6 and 5.7 show the distribution of inputs shared within contracts and strongly support the implications of our model. The data expose the dominance of the sharing rule dichotomy ($q = s$ or $q = 1$) and make clear the distinction between sharing rules for market and nonmarket inputs, thus supporting predictions 5.1 and 5.5.

Table 5.6 shows the input-sharing rules breakdown for the entire sample of 1,628 contracts. The upper section of the table shows all eight inputs, while the lower part distinguishes between market and nonmarket inputs. The entry in each cell shows the number of contracts (out of the 1,628 total) that satisfy the respective numbers of inputs that are shared in the same proportion as the crop (horizontal axis) and those that are fully the responsibility of the farmer (vertical axis). For instance, the entry "220" at the intersection of row 5 and column 3 indicates that 220 of the 1,628 contracts have five input shares equal to the cropshare, with the remaining three inputs fully the farmer's burden. The entry in row 0, column 8 shows that 209 contracts stipulated that all eight inputs were paid fully by the farmer; by contrast, the entry in row 8, column 0 shows that 24 contracts required all inputs to be shared exactly the same as the crop.

Prediction 5.1 implies that the contract entries should lie on the diagonal. As is evident from the table, this is the overwhelming outcome. In fact, 1,405 (86%) of the contracts meet this test. The diagonal just to the left of the main diagonal (the 7-7 diagonal) is also supportive. The 7-7 diagonal shows the number of contracts for which seven of the eight inputs fit the predicted dichotomy. If these contracts are included, the dichotomy covers 1,525 (94%) of the contracts. Again, the dichotomy is self-evident from the lower section of the table, which separates market from nonmarket inputs. For market inputs, 1,456 (89%) contracts are on the main diagonal; for nonmarket inputs, 1,432 (88%) of the contracts are on the main diagonal. If contracts on the 3-3 diagonal are added, then the numbers are 1,540 (95%) for market inputs and 1,552 (95%) for nonmarket inputs. Table 5.7 breaks down the contracts even further into contract groups that have identical cropshares (50-50, 60-40, and 67-33, respectively). In all cases the main diagonal accounts for between 91 percent and 96 percent of the contracts. Including the 3-3 diagonal accounts for between 96 percent and 99 percent of all contracts.

Tables 5.6 and 5.7 also confirm prediction 5.5 about market versus nonmarket input-sharing rules. Market inputs are easier to measure, so we expect their sharing to be equal more often than nonmarket inputs to the output share ($q = s$). Nonmarket inputs are more likely to be the full responsibility of the farmer ($q = 100\%$). All four tables support this prediction, which can be tested by examining the main diagonal of the tables. For market inputs we expect to see a greater portion of the contracts on the lower left portion of the diagonal (where $q = s$ dominates); for nonmarket inputs we expect a greater portion on the upper right section (where $q = 100$ dominates). Inspection shows this to be true. For example, when all contracts are considered, the lower part of table 5.6 shows that 233 contracts (14%) have all four market input shares equal to 100 percent, whereas 723 contracts (44%) have all four nonmarket shares equal to 100 percent. Similarly, 310 contracts (19%) have all four market input shares equal to the cropshare, whereas only 22

Table 5.6
Distribution of input-sharing rules within contracts

		All inputs $q = 100\%$								
		0	1	2	3	4	5	6	7	8
	0	1	7	5	21	11	24	9	49	209
	1	1	0	0	1	3	3	11	186	
	2	0	1	0	1	1	5	144		
	3	0	0	0	12	162				
$q = s$	4	0	1	0	21	231				
	5	0	3	18	220					
	6	0	10	158						
	7	4	71							
	8	24								

Market vs. nonmarket inputs

		Market inputs $q = 100\%$				
		0	1	2	3	4
	0	16	47	17	59	233
	1	2	5	6	262	
$q = s$	2	1	8	153		
	3	11	498			
	4	310				

		Nonmarket inputs $q = 100\%$				
		0	1	2	3	4
	0	9	19	30	77	723
	1	2	6	26	372	
$q = s$	2	10	12	233		
	3	5	82			
	4	22				

Note: Total contracts = 1,628.

contracts (1%) have all four nonmarket shares equal to the cropshare. As table 5.6 shows, the pattern is consistent even when cropshare is held constant.

Additional support for the model comes from comparing market and nonmarket sharing rules while letting cropshare vary as shown in table 5.7. As noted in section 5.2, the model suggests that the fraction of contracts for which input costs are shared in proportion to output will increase as the farmer's share of the output decreases. Again, inspection of the tables shows that the fraction of contracts where the number of inputs shared like output shares (or borne fully by the farmer) falls as cropshare rises. To illustrate, track the row 4, column 0 entry for market inputs in table 5.7. For 50-50 contracts the percentage of all four input

Table 5.7
Distribution of input-sharing rules for market and nonmarket inputs

50-50 cropshare ($N = 389$)

		Market inputs $q = 100\%$								Nonmarket inputs $q = 100\%$				
		0	1	2	3	4			0	1	2	3	4
	0	2	12	3	8	33		0	0	0	3	12	93
	1	1	1	0	5			1	0	1	10	90	
$q = s$	2	0	2	17			$q = s$	2	2	5	106		
	3	5	49					3	2	50			
	4	251						4	15				

60-40 cropshare ($N = 580$)

		Market inputs $q = 100\%$								Nonmarket inputs $q = 100\%$				
		0	1	2	3	4			0	1	2	3	4
	0	6	11	2	8	40		0	1	2	4	23	242
	1	0	2	0	95			1	0	1	14	157	
$q = s$	2	0	2	63			$q = s$	2	0	3	100		
	3	3	311					3	0	27			
	4	37						4	6				

67-33 cropshare ($N = 530$)

		Market inputs $q = 100\%$								Nonmarket inputs $q = 100\%$				
		0	1	2	3	4			0	1	2	3	4
	0	3	6	2	23	125		0	0	1	2	15	353
	1	0	2	2	154			1	0	0	2	124	
$q = s$	2	0	2	66			$q = s$	2	0	1	27		
	3	1	131					3	0	5			
	4	13						4	0				

shares equaling the cropshare is 65 (25 out of 389), for 60-40 it is 6 (37 out of 580), and for 67-33 (13 out of 530) it is 2. This trend is robust for market and nonmarket inputs and for all cropshare rules.

Estimation of Contract Choice

To estimate the choice between pure cropshare and input-output cropshare contracts, the contract data are reorganized so that input shares are dichotomous; that is, input costs are either fully borne by the farmer or shared proportionally. Thus, for any contract i the complete model is

$$q_i^* = X\beta + \epsilon_i \tag{5.9}$$

$$q_i = \begin{cases} 1, & \text{if } q_i^* = 1 \\ 0, & \text{if } q_i^* = s^*, \end{cases} \tag{5.10}$$

where X is a row vector of explanatory variables including the constant, β is a column vector of unknown coefficients, and ϵ_i is an error term. In equation 5.9, q_i^* denotes the true underlying input share that is observed as either shared or not shared. The equality $q_i = 0$ means that the farmer's share of input costs equals his output share; the similarly observable equality $q_i = 1$ means that the farmer pays all the input costs. Tables 5.8 and 5.9 show the results of logit estimation of the model given by equations 5.9 and 5.10. In all estimates the focus is on testing predictions 5.5 and 5.6. In the pooled sample used in table 5.8, the dependent variable (QSHARE) equals one if the contract is a pure cropshare arrangement and zero if the contract shares input costs and output in the same proportion. In table 5.9 the dependent variable is also dichotomous but is specific to each of the eight inputs, so that the variable equals one if the specific input (for example, fertilizer) is paid for by the farmer. It equals zero if the costs are shared in the same proportion as output.

For table 5.8, a new pooled data set was created in which each input for each contract became an observation. This resulted in 12,485 observations on input-sharing rules. Two logit equations estimate the probability that the cost of any input will be fully borne by the farmer rather than shared with the landowner. Prediction 5.6 is tested using the variable HIGH VALUE, which equals 1 if the crop is either irrigated or a row crop, and is intended to measure the value of the land attributes. The estimated coefficient is predicted to be negative. The problem of land exploitation is more serious for highly valued land than for poor land. By sharing input costs, the farmer's share of the output can be reduced (l^s gets closer to l^*), thus reducing the farmer's incentive to exploit the soil. In both specifications in table 5.8, the estimated coefficient is negative and statistically significant, supporting prediction 5.6.

Prediction 5.5 is confronted using the variable MARKET, which is a dummy indicating whether or not an input is purchased in the market. Inputs purchased in the market are

Table 5.8
Logit regression coefficient estimates on pooled data: Nebraska and South Dakota (1986)
(dependent variable = 1 if farmer pays all input costs; = 0 if farmer pays input costs proportional to his output share)

Independent variables	Full sample	Farmer sample	Predicted sign
CONSTANT	2.962	2.205	
	(30.07)*	(16.69)*	
MARKET	−1.648	−1.241	−
	(−35.43)*	(−20.46)*	
HIGH VALUE	−1.661	−1.149	−
	(−17.49)*	(−9.62)*	
LEASED ACRES		−0.415	−
		(−4.12)*	
Observations	12,485	3,940	
Model χ^2	1,693.41	562.21	
Degrees of freedom	(2)	(3)	

Note: t-statistics in parentheses.
* significant at the 5 percent level (one-tailed test for coefficients with predicted signs).

less expensive to measure and to divide, so the estimated coefficient for MARKET is expected to have a negative coefficient.[15] The estimated coefficients, in both specifications, are negative and statistically significant, supporting prediction 5.5. We also estimated these equations by modifying the MARKET dummy to include irrigation energy as a market input. This specification slightly decreased the size of the MARKET coefficients, but it did not appreciably alter the other estimates or their standard errors.

Prediction 5.5 can also be confronted using the variable LEASED ACRES, which measures the fraction of farm acres that the farmer leases in the observed contract. If the farmer leases all of his acres from one landowner, then his ability to shirk on shared input use is severely curtailed. However, if a farmer has other farm acres, either owned outright or leased from another landowner, it is possible for him to divert shared inputs from one plot of land to another and bill the landowner for the extra costs. LEASED ACRES is used only in a sample in which farmers responded to the survey. As prediction 5.5 implies, we found the estimated coefficient for LEASED ACRES to be negative and statistically significant. This finding indicates that farmers who lease from different landowners or also own some land are less likely to use a contract in which input costs are shared.

Predictions 5.5 and 5.6 are tested again in table 5.9 which shows separate logit estimation for each of the eight crop inputs. As in the pooled data set, we estimated two equations for each input. Again, the estimated coefficients for HIGH VALUE and LEASED ACRES are all predicted to be negative. Since the dummy variable MARKET cannot be defined in the

Table 5.9
Logit regression estimates for eight crop inputs
(dependent variable = 1 if farmer pays all input costs; = 0 if farmer pays input costs proportional to his output share)

Input (sample size)	HIGH VALUE	LEASED ACRES	χ^2	(df)
	Independent variables			
SEED	−1.458			
(full, n=1572)	(−4.766)*		32.92	1
(farmer, n=500)	−1.590	−0.981		
	(−2.915)*	(−2.892)*	20.07	2
FERTILIZER	−1.520			
(full, n=1497)	(−8.345)*		64.22	1
(farmer, n=467)	−1.204	−0.338		
	(−3.451)*	(−0.749)	10.96	2
HERBICIDE	−1.833			
(full, n=1544)	(−8.989)*		100.50	1
(farmer n=487)	−1.543	−0.385		
	(−4.631)*	(−1.178)	24.97	2
INSECTICIDE	−1.960			
(full, n=1558)	(−9.126)		111.04	1
(farmer, n=493)	−1.795	−0.533		
	(−5.039)	(−1.637)*	33.13	2
CHEMICAL APPLICATION	−0.585			
(full, n=1563)	(−2.770)*		8.45	1
(farmer, n=497)	−0.785	−0.158		
	(−1.860)*	(−.400)	4.14	2
ENERGY	−3.025			
(full, n=1576)	(−4.256)*		54.85	1
(farmer, n=495)	−2.481	−0.681		
	(−2.442)*	(−1.902)*	22.92	2
DRYING	−2.492			
(full, n=1577)	(−7.182)*		102.03	1
(farmer, n=496)	−2.702	−0.178		
	(−4.485)*	(−.568)	1.21	2
HARVEST	−0.638			
(full, n=1598)	(−1.712)*		3.49	1
(farmer, n=505)	−0.136	−1.638		
	(−0.245)	(−3.515)*	11.79	2

Note: t-statistics in parentheses.
* significant at the 5 percent level in a one-tailed test.

unpooled sample, it is left out of the logit estimates in tables 5.9. As table 5.9 illustrates, the estimated coefficients for individual inputs add further support to the model. In all cases the coefficients have the predicted sign, and in the majority of the cases they are statistically significant. Although the magnitude and significance of the coefficient estimates vary from input to input, this evidence shows that the relationships found in table 5.8 are robust and generally hold across many different crop inputs.

Estimation of Cropshare Rules

As the two sets of first-order conditions (equations 5.5, 5.6, 5.7, and 5.8) imply, once the decision about input cost sharing has been made, the optimal cropshare rule can be chosen. The optimal input share ($q^* = 1$ or $q^* = s$) and the potential for soil exploitation will both influence the optimal cropshare, s^*. Prediction 5.3 states that when inputs are not shared, output share will rise as the number of other k inputs increases, because the distortions will be spread across more margins. Predictions 5.2 and 5.6 imply that as the potential for soil exploitation increases, the more likely the contract will be an input-output contract and thus the lower will be the output share to the farmer. For each contract i the model is

$$\ln(s_i/(1 - s_i)) = Z\eta + Q_i\theta + \epsilon_i, \tag{5.11}$$

where Z is a row vector of explanatory variables, η is a column vector of unknown coefficients, Q_i is the number of inputs paid fully by the farmer, θ is the corresponding coefficient, and ϵ_i is an error term. The natural logarithm of the output share ratio, $\ln(s/(1 - s))$, is used instead of the output share because s is a limited-dependent variable, where $0 < s < 1$. Table 5.10 shows the results of ordinary least squares (OLS) estimation of equation 5.11 using three different specifications.[16]

Prediction 5.3 is tested using the variable INPUTS, which measures the number of inputs for which the farmer pays all costs (Q) and is expected to be correlated positively to the farmer's share of the crop. In all specifications we find the estimated coefficient to be positive and statistically significant.

We test prediction 5.2 using several variables to measure the potential for soil exploitation. In the first two specifications, the variables IRRIGATED and ROW CROP measure the potential for the farmer to exploit the soil. As discussed in chapter 4, IRRIGATED indicates land that is less subject to soil exploitation and ROW CROP indicates the opposite. Thus, the estimated coefficients are expected to be negative for ROW CROP and positive for IRRIGATED. In both specifications the estimated coefficients have the expected sign and are statistically significant. In the last equation, dummy variables for specific crops—CORN, OATS, SOYBEANS, and WHEAT—are included instead of ROW CROP. Because CORN and SOYBEANS are row crops, we expect their coefficients to be negative. OATS and

WHEAT are not row crops, and we expect their coefficients to be positive. All of these crop coefficients have the predicted sign, and all are statistically significant but CORN.

We also include two control variables in the last two equations. YEARS DURATION measures the number of years of continuous contracting and ACRES measures the size of the contracted plot of land. In both equations the estimated coefficient on ACRES is not significantly different from zero, indicating that the size of the contracted land parcel does not influence the terms of the cropshare rule. The estimated coefficient for YEARS DURATION is positive and statistically significant, indicating that the farmer's share will be higher the greater the duration of the relationship. While we include YEARS DURATION as a control, this variable has a plausible economic interpretation. If the number of years of past contracting can be taken as a proxy for a farmer's reputation for good husbandry, then as the number of years increases the farmer is expected to act more as if he were an integrated landowner-farmer.[17] As a result, soil exploitation is reduced compared to a situation in which the landowner contracts with a farmer for the first time (r' is closer to r for long-term contractors), and there is less need for the farmer's share of the crop to be low to mitigate that problem. In turn, a higher share of the crop to the farmer assures a more ideal use of the farmer's inputs.

5.4 Custom versus Incentives

Our analysis of cropshare contracts would not be complete without mentioning a curious feature of these data—cropshares take on relatively few discrete values. Table 5.3 shows that 50-50, 60-40, and 67-33 are by far the most common divisions. Less common are 25-75, 33-67, 40-60, and 75-25. Completely absent are such divisions as 58.5-41.5 or 62-38.[18] Recently, Young and Burke (2001) attempt to explain the extent to which custom determines this feature of share contracts. They use recent data from Illinois and an argument based on custom to claim that these contracts are rigid around a few focal shares. Focalness and frequency of use are valuable, according to them, because they reduce the costs of bargaining. Over time, contracts within a given region become homogeneous and focused on a few discrete shares, while large differences in land quality lead to variations in focal shares across different regions.

The notion that share contracts are focal around 50-50, as we have mentioned in chapter 2, is commonly held by economists. Unfortunately, it often stems from examining specific crops in isolation. For example, Young and Burke (2001) examine farmland contracts in Illinois, where two crops—corn and soybeans—account for 92 percent of the harvested cropland acreage in the state. Since these contracts tend to share output 50-50, their sheer dominance in that region lends the appearance of focalness. Had Young and Burke examined

Table 5.10
OLS cropshare regression coefficient estimates
(dependent variable = ln(SHARE/(1−SHARE)))

Independent variables	Full sample	Full sample	Full sample	Predicted sign
CONSTANT	0.1556	0.1102	0.0435	
	(3.076)*	(1.998)*	(0.881)	
Measurement costs				
INPUTS	0.0652	0.0653	0.0581	+
	(10.953)*	(10.972)*	(9.920)*	
Soil exploitation				
ROW CROP	−0.12020	−0.11691		−
	(−3.471)*	(−3.313)*		
IRRIGATED	0.0985	0.0993	0.1169	+
	(4.025)*	(4.058)*	(4.545)*	
CORN			−0.04282	−
			(−1.364)	
OATS			0.1338	+
			(4.149)*	
SOYBEANS			−0.0822	−
			(−3.180)*	
WHEAT			0.1123	+
			(4.554)*	
Controls				
YEARS DURATION		0.0031	0.0029	
		(2.787)*	(2.675)*	
ACRES		1.284 E − 05	−3.372 E − 05	
		(0.305)	(−0.805)	
Observations	1,628	1,628	1,628	
F-value	58.84	37.03	31.22	
Adjusted R^2	0.096	0.099	0.129	

Notes: t-statistics in parentheses.
* significant at the 5 percent level (one-tailed test for coefficients with predicted signs).

different crops in different regions, they would have found dominant equilibrium shares different from 50-50. Indeed, sometimes they can be substantially different. The dominant share for apples in British Columbia is 85 percent, for sugarcane in Louisiana is 80 percent, and for wheat in Nebraska is 67 percent.

Focalness often appears when no consideration is given to sharing input costs. Table 5.11 shows frequency distributions for share terms, controlling for crops and for the allocation of input costs for corn and soybeans from the Nebraska–South Dakota data. When the inputs are shared, the 50-50 contract dominates in a manner similar to what Young and Burke

Table 5.11
Cropshare frequencies by crop type and input cost allocation

| | Nebraska–South Dakota | | Northern Illinois | Nebraska–South Dakota | | Southern Illinois |
	Corn	Soybeans	All crops	Corn	Soybeans	All crops
Inputs shared?	Yes	Yes	Uncertain	No	No	Uncertain
Farmers' share (%)						
3/4 (75)	0	0	0	1.2	0.6	0
2/3 (67)	8.3	3.6	1.7	28.3	15.7	53.5
3/5 (60)	16.6	17.4	2.3	60.1	73.7	31
1/2 (50)	69.7	74.6	94.8	6.8	6.1	14

Sources: Illinois data from Young and Burke (2001), Figure 3, p. 562. The Nebraska–South Dakota data does not include irrigated cropland.

find in Illinois. Table 5.11 also shows the frequency distribution of cropshare terms for these same crops when inputs are not shared. The distinction between contracts with and without input sharing is striking. When inputs are not shared, the 50-50 contract falls from the dominant type to third place after 3/5 and 2/3.

The distinction between contracts with and without input sharing is remarkably similar to the distinction Young and Burke find when comparing northern to southern Illinois. Young and Burke find that over 90 percent of the shares are 50-50 in northern region but both 3/5 and 2/3 contracts easily dominate 50-50 in the southern region of the state. They attribute the difference to "regional custom" based on soil differences. However, their data seem to show a correlation between input and output sharing. In fact, in an unpublished companion paper, Burke and Young (2000) state: "In the north, over 86% of the contracts are (1/2, 1/2) [that is, the output share is 1/2 and the input share is also 1.2]. In the south, about 39% of the contracts are of the form (3/5, 1) or (2/3, 1); fully 79% of the contracts use either 3/5 or 2/3 as the tenant's share of output and 3/5, 2/3, or 1 as the tenant's share of input" (7). We consulted the source of the Illinois data used by Young and Burke and found that the northern regions share inputs 96 percent of the time, while in the southern region this occurs only 33 percent of the time.[19] Hence, it seems that the difference attributed to regional custom based on soil quality actually reflects differences in input sharing.

As we point out in this chapter, input sharing terms are crucial in understanding the structure of cropshare contracts. Depending on the input sharing rule, one might find common shares, but the shares vary with the degree of input sharing. In fact, we would predict that the contracts in the northern region of Illinois are nearly all contracts in which the input costs are shared, and in particular the input shares are 50-50.

Though share contracts are not focal around 50 percent there is no denying their discreteness and the fact that they take on simple fraction values. This puzzle, however, begins to disappear when one considers the method and history in which a crop is produced and shared on rented land. Among farmers and landowners, 50-50 contracts are called "halves," 60-40 contracts are called "fifths," 67-33 contracts are called "thirds," and so on. It seems that these simple fractions hark back to the days when crop division was split as follows: In a two-thirds–one-third contract the farmer would keep for himself two truckloads of wheat for every one delivered to the landowner. In fact, this type of load-by-load division is sometimes still found. Corn, for instance, is planted and harvested in well-defined rows and is often governed by 50-50 share agreements when the land is rented. In these cases a farmer's harvester may cut two rows at a time, and during harvest he cuts two rows, leaves the next two, and then cuts the following two until the field has been covered. On this first pass, all of the corn is kept by the farmer. Within days, the farmer cuts the remaining corn, which goes to the landowner. During the interim, it is a trivial matter for the landowner to drive by the field to see that he's getting a random 50 percent of the crop. This practice is impractical with most crops, but it demonstrates how incentives can result in standard sharing practices.[20]

The use of discrete sharing rules that mimic simple fractions can be viewed as rules that economize on measurement costs when measurement technology is imprecise. The simple fact is that inputs are not exactly known, and increases in knowledge come from increased measurement. Through experience landowners have rough ideas of what a yield should be; rough ideas of how much effort, seed, fertilizer, and chemicals are being used; and rough ideas of the crop, weather, and pest conditions. For a given crop and locale there is likely to be one cropshare rule that provides a rough approximation to the ex ante second-best equilibrium based on the general knowledge of the landowner and farmer. Finer divisions are possible, but they require large costs of monitoring. Given the large and variable role of nature, this monitoring must be done every year. Thus, although it is possible to have cropshares with such terms as 52-48, it simply makes no sense to split this way or some other marginal difference, when the landowner is incapable of knowing the exact relative contributions without incurring enormous costs.

Discreteness has benefits and costs, and this explains why there are so few equilibrium shares compared to cash rents. As developed in this and earlier chapters, a major cost of the cropshare contract is underreporting of the output. Having finer divisions of output is meaningless when output cannot also be economically measured more finely. This, of course, is not the case with a cash rent contract where underreporting output does not arise and the monitoring of cash payments is trivial. On the other hand, the benefits of having payments fine-tuned are higher with cash rent contracts. Changes in economic fundamentals, such as land productivity or input costs, will have first-order effects with cash rent contracts, since the farmer is the complete residual claimant of the crop, and changes in the cash rent do not alter any marginal incentives. Cropshare contracts, however, are less sensitive to such changes. Thus, it is natural that cash rent contracts are more finely tuned than cropshare contracts. In fact, the Nebraska–South Dakota data show rather smooth terms in cash rent contracts. The model term ($15 per share in 1986) accounts for just 7 percent of all cash contracts. Given the lack of focalness in cash contracts and the near equal division of contracts between cash and share, it would seem that a contract theory based on custom is not supported by the data.

5.5   Summary

In this chapter we have focused on the differential incentives of various contract provisions and derived implications about the fraction of the crop that is owned by the farmer as well as the fraction of the input costs borne by both the farmer and the landowner. In particular, we expect that with cropsharing the farmer either bears the entire cost of inputs or shares the costs with the landowner in the same proportion as he shares the output. With striking clarity, these Nebraska–South Dakota data show the input-sharing dichotomy predicted by the model. In these two Great Plains states, farmers either pay all input costs or share them in the same proportion as their share of the crop.[21] These data also show that proportional input sharing is more likely as the farmer's share of the output decreases. This is expected because the distortions from output sharing are greater as the farmer's share of the harvest falls. Input sharing is a method of reducing these distortions. We also found that inputs readily purchased in the market were more likely to be shared than other inputs, and farmers who had land in addition to the observed cropshare plot were less likely to share inputs than were farmers who leased all their land in a single cropshare contract. Farmers and landowners may routinely share the costs of fertilizer and seed, but they rarely jointly own and share the use of buildings, combines, and tractors. In light of our model, this finding is not surprising.

Chapters 3, 4, and 5 contain transaction cost models of contract choice in modern agriculture. We have shown that they are consistent with the observed characteristics of farming in the four locations we examine. Our models have been based on a trade-off between different transaction cost incentives. Before we apply this framework to questions of ownership patterns and vertical integration, we turn our attention to an analysis of the well-known trade-off between risk sharing and effort moral hazard, in the context of the basic principal-agent model. It is common to find risk sharing at the heart of economic models of contract choice. In the next two chapters we show that to the extent this idea is testable, it has virtually no support from our data.

II RISK SHARING AS AN ALTERNATIVE FRAMEWORK

In part II (chapters 6 and 7), we examine two topics borne of models that include risk sharing as well as incentives. This basic framework is often called the principal-agent model. In chapter 6 we test several predictions derived from a classic risk-sharing model of contracts against our data on individual farmland contracts, focusing on the classic prediction that the more risky a crop, the more likely it is cropshared. Even though the idea that contracts are often structured to share risk is a time-honored feature of contract theory, overall we find almost no evidence to support this prediction, or many related predictions.

Within modern contract theory, this basic framework has also been used to analyze contract relationships over time. When an agent (farmer) deals with a principal (landowner) over time, he reveals information about his true productivity. As a result, landowners have an incentive to exploit this. In anticipation of exploitation, the farmer shirks even more to avoid revealing information. Landowners and farmers who contract over a long period of time should commit themselves to contract terms to avoid this type of behavior. When farmers are more itinerant, landowners use their experience with other farmers to *ratchet* up the terms of the contract in their favor. In chapter 7 we use the Great Plains contract data to addresses this issue. Like our findings in chapter 6, we do not find support for this implication of the risk-sharing framework.

6 Risk Sharing and the Choice of Contract

6.1 Introduction

Although Cheung's (1969) model of contract choice for cropsharing includes transaction costs, it also depends on risk aversion on the part of the farmer.[1] Cheung essentially asserts that cropshare contracts entailed higher transaction costs but allows the risk to be shared between the farmer and landowner. In his words (1969), "the choice of contractual arrangement is made so as to maximize the gain from risk dispersion subject to the constraint of transaction costs" (64). From this somewhat simple beginning, modern contract theory subsequently emerged with a focus on sharecropping that postulated a trade-off between risk sharing and moral hazard incentives.[2] The risk-sharing foundation remains more or less intact today and has been used to explain various contractual arrangements including executive compensation (Garen 1994), franchising (Martin 1988), insurance (Townsend 1994), leasing (Leland 1978), partnerships (Gaynor and Gertler 1995), and sharecropping. Milgrom and Roberts (1992) summarize the dominant result: "Efficient contracts balance the costs of risk bearing against the incentive gains that result" (207). For economists studying agriculture, in both developed and undeveloped economies, this risk-sharing framework in the context of a classic principal-agent model was adopted quickly and still retains its primacy.

Before developing and testing the model, it is important to distinguish the critical difference between the "standard" principal-agent approach to contracts and the transaction cost approach. Both are fundamentally concerned with the incentives created by different contract structures and the costs of making the incentives compatible with wealth maximization. The critical difference is in the costs of aligning incentives. With the standard principal-agent approach, risk bearing is the cost of having the farmer bear more responsibility for his actions. Under our transaction cost approach, the costs of better incentives on one margin are offset by monitoring costs or moral hazard on another margin. There are other minor differences as well, but our focus in this chapter is on the critical component of risk sharing. Although we raise several arguments against using risk sharing to explain contract choice, our main focus is empirical.

We take this approach because despite the prominence of the risk-sharing paradigm, the empirical evidence to support its implications is scarce.[3] Moreover, when compared to an alternative transaction cost model, risk-sharing models do rather poorly. Table 6.1 summarizes the literature in which competing predictions have been tested against contract data. In studies examining everything from farm contracts to franchises, the evidence in support of transaction cost models outperforms the predictions based on risk sharing.[4]

Table 6.1
Summary of previous empirical contracting studies that consider risk sharing and transaction costs

Study	Topic	Risk sharing	Transaction cost
Cheung (1969)	Farmland	Limited	Limited
Rao (1971)	Farmland	No	Yes
Allen and Lueck (1992a)	Farmland	No	Yes
Umbeck (1977)	Gold mining	No	Limited
Hallagan (1978)	Gold mining	Ambiguous	Ambiguous
Martin (1988)	Franchising	No	Yes
Lafontaine (1992)	Franchising	No	Yes
Leffler and Rucker (1991)	Timber sales	Ambiguous	Yes
Mulherin (1986)	Natural gas	No	Yes
Lyon and Hackett (1993)	Natural gas	No	Yes

Most empirical land contracting studies have examined the effects of contract choice on input use rather than estimating the factors that determine contract choice (Hayami and Otsuka 1993).[5]

In this chapter we test a standard risk-sharing model of contracts against our data on individual farmland contracts. The chapter begins with a principal-agent model of share contracting that generates predictions that are testable with our data. Unlike our earlier transaction cost models that allowed for more than one unobservable margin of behavior, the model we present only allows farmer effort to be unobservable. Next, we test the risk-sharing implications of this model against our contract data, by linking the contract data to reasonable measures of exogenous risk by using data on crop yield variability.

Modern North American agriculture is a particularly good test bed for the risk-sharing theory compared to undeveloped agricultural economies. First, the property rights to land are well defined and enforced, unencumbered by political land reforms. Second, the behavior of farmers and landowners is not severely constrained by caste systems or other potentially dominating cultural forces.[6] Third, asset values are relatively large, making the gains from optimal contract design relatively large as well. Finally, there are reliable data on regional crop yield variability that can be used to approximate exogenous risk. In general, we find no support for predictions motivated by risk sharing. We finish the chapter by contrasting the risk-sharing predictions with those derived from our earlier model where both parties were risk neutral.

6.2 A Model with Risk-Averse Agents

With sharecropping, the typical risk-sharing model makes several routine assumptions: the principal is a risk-neutral landowner and the agent is a risk-averse farmer;[7] the effort of the farmer is not observable; the landowner is unable to shirk and the land cannot be exploited by the farmer; and finally, farm production is variable, depending on both the effort of the farmer and random forces. Relying on these assumptions, we derive predictions about the structure of share contracts and the choice between cropshare and cash rent contracts.[8]

We begin by assuming that for a given plot of land, crop production is $Q = (e + \theta)$, where e is the unobservable effort of the farmer, and θ is a random variable with mean 0 and variance σ^2. This production function is routine in principal-agent analyses applied to agriculture and to business.[9] The farmer's income from the land contract is Y, and $U(Y) = E(Y) - (R/2)Var(Y)$ is the farmer's utility function where $R \in [0, \infty]$ is the farmer's coefficient of absolute risk aversion.[10] Following Pratt (1964), we assume decreasing absolute risk aversion (DARA), so that $R'(W) < 0$ where W is total individual wealth. In share contracts only the crop is shared, with both parties selling their shares independently in competitive markets. As a result, $s \in [0, 1]$ is the contracted share of output owned by the farmer and $\beta \in [-\infty, \infty]$ is the value of any fixed (cash) payments made by the farmer to the landowner. Farmer income is $Y = s(e + \theta) - [c_0 + c_1 e + (c_2/2)e^2] - \beta$, where c_i for $i = 0, 1, 2$ are parameters of the effort cost function, and the farmer's expected utility (EU) is $EU = se - [c_0 + c_1 e + (c_2/2)e^2] - (R/2)s^2\sigma^2 - \beta$.

The landowner maximizes expected profits subject to the farmer's incentive compatibility (IC) and individual rationality (IR) constraints, solving

$$\max_{s,\beta} = E[(1 - s)(\hat{e} + \theta) + \beta]$$

subject to (IC) $\hat{e}(s) = \dfrac{s - c_1}{c_2} = \text{argmax EU},$ and   (6.1)

(IR) $U(\hat{e}) \geq U^0,$

where U^0 is the farmer's reservation utility. The optimal contract parameters (s^*, β^*) are[11]

$$s^* = \frac{1}{(1 + Rc_2\sigma^2)}$$ (6.2)

$\beta^* \in [-\infty, \infty].$ (6.3)

Predictions

The equilibrium contract that solves this model also trades off the incentive effects of greater output shares to the agent against the risk aversion of the agent and generates two predictions immediately.

PREDICTION 6.1   If a share contract is chosen, it will be normally accompanied by a cash payment.[12]

PREDICTION 6.2   Share contracts will not be chosen unless farmers are risk averse.

Prediction 6.1 is implied because the model predicts a continuum of contracts ranging from a fixed wage contract ($s = 0$ and $\beta < 0$) in which the farmer is paid a wage by the landowner to a fixed rent contract ($s = 1$ and $\beta > 0$) in which the farmer retains the crop and pays rent to the landowner. In between these poles are an infinite number of share contracts in which crop ownership is split and fixed payments allocate rents ($s \in (0, 1)$ and $\beta \in [-\infty, \infty]$). Prediction 6.2 is implied because if the farmer were risk neutral, then the optimal contract would be a fixed rent contract in which the farmer was the complete residual claimant of the output. Farmer effort would be first-best since there would be no moral hazard. Thus, by incorporating risk-averse preferences into the model, a rationale for share contracts emerges. This is because a risk-averse farmer prefers a contract in which he is not compensated solely on the basis of variable output, as in a fixed rent contract. The greater the risk aversion of the farmer the more likely a contract will share output.

By examining the comparative statics of the optimal sharing rule, two more predictions are implied:

PREDICTION 6.3   As output variability (σ^2) increases the farmer's share of output will decrease.

PREDICTION 6.4   Under declining absolute risk aversion, as farmer wealth increases the farmer's share of output will increase.

Prediction 6.3 follows directly from equation (6.2), since $\partial s / \partial \sigma^2 = (Rc_2)/(1 + Rc_2\sigma^2)^2 < 0$. We can see from the same equation that if the crop has zero risk ($\sigma^2 = 0$), then the optimal share is $s^* = 1$; that is, a cash rent contract emerges. Prediction 6.4 also follows from equation (6.2), since $\partial s^* / \partial R = -(c_2\sigma^2)/(1 + Rc_2\sigma^2)^2 < 0$. If the farmer is not risk averse ($R = 0$), then the optimal share is $s^* = 1$, implying a cash rent contract. Since $R'(W) < 0$, there is also a positive relationship between s^* and W.

In this standard model, changes in contract form are continuous because changes in parameters (R, σ^2, W), which lead to marginal increases (decreases) in crop shares to the farmer, are offset by marginal increases (decreases) in payments to the landowner. In the contract setting we observe in North America and elsewhere, these incremental adjustments are not always realized. Instead, changes in parameters ultimately lead to discrete changes in contract choice, as from cropsharing to cash renting or vice versa. As the model stands, the farmer and landowner would always share the crop ($0 < s < 1$) because sharing always has some benefit of spreading risk when farmers are risk averse.

Evidence from earlier chapters and from around the world (Hayami and Otsuka 1993) shows that the actual range of contracts is much more limited. In particular, farm contracts tend to not have fixed fee components, although there is often sharing of input costs. Also, as mentioned earlier, one extreme contract form—fixed wage farmers—is generally not present in modern North American farming. As a result, the relevant choice of farmland contract is between a fixed cash rent contract ($s = 1$ and $\beta > 0$) and pure cropsharing contract ($0 < s < 1$ and, $\beta = 0$).

Although it is not crucial to the empirical tests we perform, it is useful to make a slight modification to the standard risk-sharing model to generate predictions about discrete contract choices.[13] To do this, the model of contract choice between cash rent and cropshare requires differential costs of the two contract regimes. We assume that each contract entails a fixed "contract cost" (C^c and C^s), which is largest for share contracts; that is, $C^s > C^c$. Share contracts are likely to have higher costs because they require division and monitoring of both the shared output that is susceptible to theft and the inputs that are provided under moral hazard incentives.[14] In a cash rent contract $s^c = 1$ and the farmer chooses the first-best effort level, $e^* = (1 - c_1)/c_2$, so the total expected contract value is

$$V^c = e^* - [c_0 + c_1 e^* + (c_2/2)(e^*)^2] - (R/2)\sigma^2 - C^c. \tag{6.4}$$

In a share contract, $0 < s^s < 1$ and $e = \hat{e}(s) = (s - c_1)/c_2 < e^*$, so the expected contract value is

$$V^s = \hat{e}(s^s) - [c_0 + c_1\hat{e}(s) + (c_2/2)(\hat{e}(s))^2] - (R/2)(s^s)^2\sigma^2 - C^s. \tag{6.5}$$

For our purposes, the parameters of interest are the variance of the random input, σ^2, the farmer's risk preferences, R, and the farmer's wealth, W. Two predictions follow:

PREDICTION 6.5   As output variability (σ^2) increases, it is more likely that a share contract will be chosen over a cash rent contract.

PREDICTION 6.6   Under declining absolute risk aversion, as farmer wealth increases, it is more likely that a cash rent contract will be chosen over a cropshare contract.

Prediction 6.5 is the classic risk-sharing prediction, and the one to which we devote much of our attention. It is proven by examining the comparative statics of these indirect objective functions. The ratio V^c/V^s is decreasing in σ^2. This follows from $\partial V^c/\partial\sigma^2 = -(R/2)$ and $\partial V^s/\partial\sigma^2 = -(R/2)s^2$, so both V^c and V^s are decreasing in σ^2. For $s^* \in (0, 1)$ it follows that V^c declines more rapidly than V^s. Prediction 6.6 can be proven in a similar manner. The ratio V^c/V^s is decreasing in R. This follows from $\partial V^c/\partial R = -(\sigma^2/2)$ and $\partial V^s/\partial R = -(s^2\sigma^2)/2$, so both V^c and V^s are decreasing in R. For $s^* \in (0, 1)$, it follows that V^R declines more rapidly than V^s. The ratio V^c/V^s is increasing in W. This follows from $R'(W) < O$ and the direct effect of changes in R just shown.[15] The general incentive structure of this risk-sharing model is laid out in table 6.2.

Table 6.2
Summary of incentives for risk sharing

	Effort moral hazard	Land moral hazard	Risk sharing	Contract costs
Cropshare contracts	Yes	No	Yes	High
Cash rent contracts	No	No	No	Low

Implementing the Predictions

In the standard principal-agent model, the farmer's utility depends on the level and variance of income derived from the land contract. The farmer's income, in turn, depends on the price of the crop (P) times the crop quantity (Y). In principle, the variance in income (PY) will influence the choice of contract, yet the above predictions ignore income variability (because we normalized the output price to unity) and focus exclusively on output (crop yield) variability. In practice, we are able to ignore price and income variability in the tests we perform because of the way we develop our contract data sample.[16]

In our tests of predictions 6.3 and 6.5, we use contract data in which all farmers grow the same crop. Moreover, all of these crops are sold in world markets in which individual farmers are price takers. This means that there is no variance in price across farmers and that income variance is equivalent to yield variance. Generally if P and Y are independent then $Var(PY) = \sigma_P^2\sigma_Y^2 + \sigma_P^2\mu_Y^2 + \sigma_Y^2\mu_P^2$, where σ^2 is the variance and μ is the mean. This implies that data on the mean and variance of output prices would be needed to test the standard risk-sharing model. When price is constant, $Var(PY) = P^2\sigma_Y^2$, and price data are still required to measure the variance in income. However, if price has no variability across the observations because of price-taking markets, then two possibilities emerge. First, if price is literally constant then $Var(PY) = k\sigma_Y^2$, where k is a scale parameter and incorporating price data in a regression would simply rescale the estimated coefficients on yield variability. Second, if price is random, but the same for all observations, then the regression constant incorporates the price data.

Even when the test conditions are so controlled that price variability can be ignored, other issues for the appropriate measure of yield variability remain. Testing predictions 6.3 and 6.5 requires data on the variance in the random input, σ^2. We measure this exogenous variability by using data on crop yields.[17] Still, successfully conducting these tests has potential problems because production (crop yield) variability has two sources: 1) exogenous variability that cannot be influenced by the contracting parties (variability of θ or σ^2), and (2) endogenous variability that is influenced by the actions of any contracting party (variability of e). The impediment to performing tests of risk sharing lie in the difficulty of finding a reasonable empirical counterpart for σ^2 at the contract level, one that is not contaminated with endogenous variability.[18] Finding such measures in studies of franchising and other areas has proved difficult (Lafontaine and Bhattacharyya 1995), so most scholars have either ignored them or relied on proxies that seem reasonable, but are not often clearly linked to the underlying theoretical model and may be highly endogenous to the firm's behavior.[19]

In order to purge completely the endogenous variability in farm production, a true measure of variability in the random input would require daily time series data on a composite variable for each crop that included all natural factors from rainfall and temperature to sunlight and insect populations. Such a composite variable would be a proxy for θ and would require measures of the quantities of these natural parameters. More important, it would also require measures of the timeliness of these parameters. Such data are simply not available on a crop-by-crop basis. Timeliness is of particular importance for weather variables such as rainfall.[20] Simple measures of rainfall would not, for example, provide information about hail- or rainstorms during the middle of a harvest. It is entirely possible, for instance, that a late August rainfall in South Dakota can severely harm a swathed wheat crop ready to be combined and simultaneously aid a standing crop of corn or sunflowers to be harvested later.

In lieu of this measurement problem, we use data on crop yield variability for the region in which a plot of farmland is located, to approximate this ideal measure of exogenous variability when there are large numbers of farmers in a relatively homogeneous region. To illustrate, define a "region" as an area where n farmers produce the same crop and face the same exogenous forces of nature and use the same technology each year. For any individual farmer producing crop j, the output or yield (per acre) for period t will be

$$Y_{ijt} = e_{ijt} + \theta_{jt} \quad i = 1, \ldots, n; \ j = 1, \ldots, k; \ \text{and } t = 1, \ldots, T; \tag{6.6}$$

where θ_{jt} is distributed with mean 0 and intertemporal variance σ_j^2 as in the theoretical model. The random input θ_{jt} varies across time and crops but not across farms within a region. Aggregating across n farmers, average per-period regional yield is $\bar{Y}_{jt} = (\sum_{i=1}^{n} Y_{ijt})/n$, which simplifies to

$$\bar{Y}_{jt} = \left[\sum_{i=1}^{n} \frac{e_{ijt}}{n} \right] + \theta_{jt} \tag{6.7}$$

The first term on the right-hand side of equation (6.7) approaches a time-independent constant as n gets "large," so the variance of average regional yield for crop j becomes[21]

$$Var(\bar{Y}_{jt}) = Var(\theta_{jt}) = \sigma_j^2. \tag{6.8}$$

The counties and parishes in our data set closely approximate the conditions described by the model in equations (6.6)–(6.8). First, each county or parish has several hundred or more farmers using nearly identical technology. The mean number of farms per county or parish is 456 for Louisiana, 650 for Nebraska, and 551 for South Dakota. Second, these crops are sold in competitive world markets, so individual farmer output does not have price effects and farmers face the same price variation. Third, the regions for which data are available are reasonably homogeneous areas where idiosyncratic risks are not important.[22] As a result, for the crops and regions we examine, variability in average regional yields (measured as the standard deviation or coefficient of variation) is a strong, though not perfect, measure of variability in the random input.

To implement this approach, we collected ten to fifteen years of time series data on the variability in crop yields for thirteen different crops for the region of each observed contract. Crop yield is calculated as total crop output in a region divided by total acres of the crop in the region. By doing this we measure exogenous variability for each contract choice observation in our data set. We calculate yield variability, which approximates exogenous variability (σ^2), in two ways: (1) STD ($\bar{Y}_t$), the standard deviation of yield over time; and (2) CV($\bar{Y}_t$), the coefficient of variation of yield over time. For the Nebraska–South Dakota contract data, we calculate these measures at the county level and for larger, relatively homogeneous regions that include several counties. For Louisiana, we use only parish (county) yield data, and for British Columbia we use only yield data from rather large and less homogeneous geographic regions. The definitions for these data are found in appendix A, along with their means (and standard errors) for each crop.[23] The calculations and sources for these data are explained in appendix A.

6.3   Empirical Analysis: Risk Sharing and Contract Choice

To test these predictions we must couple data on exogenous variability with microlevel data on individual farm contracts. We begin this section by describing the data and examining some preliminary findings. We then examine the extent to which risk parameters (derived previously) explain contact features by estimating their effects on contract choice. We also examine related risk predictions based on wealth, institutions, and the extent of futures markets. All variables used in this chapter are defined in table 6.3.

Farm-Level Contract Data

In addition to the data used in earlier chapters, some of the information here comes from an additional survey, the *1979 British Columbia Farming Lease Survey*. As before, appendix

Table 6.3
Definition of variables

Dependent variables	
CONTRACT	= 1 if contract was a cropshare contract.
	= 0 if contracts was cash rent.
Independent variables	
BUILDING VALUE	= total value in $1,000s of all owned buildings multiplied by the equity in the farm.
CORN, OATS,	
SOYBEANS, WHEAT	= 1 if corn (oats, soybeans, wheat) was the major income-producing crop; = 0 if not.
COUNTY CV	= coefficient of variation for crop yield in a county.
COUNTY MEAN	= mean crop yield in a county.
COUNTY STD	= standard deviation of crop yield in a county.
EQUIPMENT VALUE	= total value in $1,000s of all owned equipment multiplied by the equity in the farm.
FUTURES MARKET	= 1 if there is an organized futures market for the crop (barley, canola, cotton, corn, oats, rice, soybeans, sugar, wheat);
	= 0 if there is no futures market.
INSTITUTION	= 1 if the landowner is an institution (available only for Nebraska and South Dakota farmer samples);
	= 0 if landowner is an individual.
REGIONAL CV	= coefficient of variation for crop yield in a region.
REGIONAL MEAN	= mean crop yield in a region.
REGIONAL STD	= standard deviation of crop yield in a region.
ROW CROP	= 1 if row crop (corn, sugar beets, sugarcane, soybeans, sorghum);
	= 0 if not a row crop (wheat, oats, barley).
STATE CV	= coefficient of variation for crop yield in a state or province.
TREES	= 1 if fruit was grown (e.g., apples, pears, etc.);
	= 0 if no fruit was grown.
WEALTH	= total value of all owned buildings, equipment, and land multiplied by the equity in the farm.

A describes the data sources, shows summary statistics, explains calculations, and shows that these samples compare favorably to state- and province-wide averages.

Preliminary Findings: Crop Yield Variability and Contract Type

The most famous risk-sharing prediction (6.5) is that share contracts are more likely to be chosen in settings where uncertainty is high. A simple, preliminary way to identify a risky setting is to classify crops by their yield variability. We examine this prediction by considering, first, state- and province-wide measures of risky crops, and, second, how risky crops influence contract choice at the farm level.

Table 6.4 presents the region-wide coefficient of variation (CV) in yield for the major crops in British Columbia, Louisiana, Nebraska, and South Dakota. The coefficient of variation is preferred to standard deviation for this test for two reasons. First, the coefficient of variation has no units and many of the crops we examine are measured in different units. For example, hay is measured in tons while wheat is measured in bushels. Second, using the coefficient of variation controls for differences in means even for those crops that are measured in the same units. This is important when comparing dryland and irrigated crops, where irrigation always increases average yields.

Using this measure, one finds that a greater CV indicates a more variable crop and thus is predicted to be a crop that is more often governed by share contracts rather than cash leases. For each state or province the crop CVs are listed in ascending order, from top to bottom. Table 6.4, however, shows there is no clear relationship between the use of share contracts and crops with inherently high CVs. In particular, table 6.4 shows the state-wide and province-wide CVs and the prevalence of share contracts as fraction of all contracts, as a fraction of leased acreage, and as a fraction of all farmland. Simple inspection of the data shows no obvious positive correlation: Moving down each column of crops for a given region shows no monotonic increase in the fraction of cropshare contracts. In appendix A (tables A.9 and A.10) we present OLS estimates of the effect of CV on the extent of cropsharing and confirm the intuition gained from simply visually inspecting table 6.4. Although these numbers are crude and preliminary, they do not support the risk-sharing thesis.[24]

Consider, for example, the case of sugarcane in Louisiana. Sugarcane has one of the least variable crop yields of any crop in our data set (CV = 0.099), yet sugarcane land is overwhelmingly cropshared (78% of all leases and 81% of all leased acres). By the risk-sharing thesis, sugarcane is expected to be a crop that should be cash rented relatively more often than other crops. Throughout the rest of this chapter we conduct more sophisticated and exhaustive tests of the risk-sharing model; however, the results never differ from the simple observations of table 6.4. There is no systematic evidence that contract choice depends on risk sharing.

The Effect of Risk on Contract Choice

Although the previous analysis does not support the risk-sharing predictions, these inferences are limited because of the level of data aggregation. In particular, because these states and provinces are large geographic areas, heterogeneity could bias the estimates using crop dummies. A more precise test is to examine the extent of share contracts for a single crop across regions where natural parameters such as weather and pests directly influence the yield variability of the crop. By selecting a sample of land contracts for which crops are the same, we can examine how natural variability affects contract choice. Where the data allow it, we separate irrigated plots from dryland plots even for the same crops because irrigation uses different technology and reduces the yield variance. Natural variability for a homogeneous locale is measured using both CV and STD for two sizes of geographic regions.

Table 6.4
Yield variability and contract choice

Region/crop	South Dakota 1975–1991		Nebraska 1975–1991	
	Crop yield coefficient of variation	Fraction of cropshare contracts	Crop yield coefficient of variation	Fraction of cropshare contracts
ALFALFA (Irrigated)			0.035	0.51
BARLEY	0.139	0.91		
CORN (Irrigated)	0.023	0.58	0.112	0.69
CORN (Dryland) [a]	0.140	0.64	0.235	0.74
SOYBEANS	0.143	0.72		
SOYBEANS (Irrigated)			0.085	0.67
SOYBEANS (Dryland)			0.168	0.76
OATS	0.191	0.59	0.155	0.80
SORGHUM	0.195	0.59		
SORGHUM (Irrigated)			0.081	0.71
SORGHUM (Dryland)			0.145	0.83
BARLEY	0.238	0.53		
WHEAT	0.247	0.61	0.114	0.86

Region/crop	Crop yield [a] coefficient of variation	Fraction of cropshare contracts	Fraction of acres cropshared	
			Leased	All
Louisiana (1992)				
MILO (Sorghum)	0.057	0.76	0.77	0.56
SUGARCANE	0.099	0.78	0.81	0.70
SOYBEANS	0.121	0.75	0.76	0.58
HAY	0.121	0.67	0.94	0.29
COTTON	0.197	0.53	0.52	0.30
WHEAT	0.207	0.76	0.78	0.59
RICE	0.278	0.68	0.76	0.61
CORN	0.293	0.62	0.41	0.37
British Columbia (1992)				
ALFALFA	0.126	0.15	0.01	0.004
HAY	0.149	0.23	0.13	0.03
WHEAT	0.175	0.79	0.68	0.38
APPLES	0.184	0.66	0.77	0.16
OATS	0.212	0.43	0.38	0.05
BARLEY	0.216	0.58	0.85	0.17
CANOLA	0.250	0.25	0.05	0.00
CORN	0.270	0.20	0.36	0.04

[a] For Louisiana, the data came from 1975–1991. For British Columbia, the data came from 1980–1991.

REGIONAL CV and REGIONAL STD measure the coefficient of variation and standard deviation, respectively, for each crop for regions within the states. Similarly, COUNTY CV and COUNTY STD measure exogenous risk at the county or parish (for Louisiana) level.

We combine the Nebraska and South Dakota samples because they are contiguous states from south to north and because the contract data for both come from the same survey during the same year. In both states the eastern reaches are comprised of better soils, greater precipitation, and a more predictable climate than their western counterparts. It is worth noting that the far eastern portions of these two states border Iowa and are effectively part of the Corn Belt, while the far western portions border Wyoming and are effectively part of the High Plains. The general consequence is that crops in western counties tend to have lower and more variable yields compared to eastern counties.[25] Louisiana exhibits a similar variability, although it runs mainly from south to north instead. South Louisiana tends to have a more stable, subtropical climate that makes crop yields higher and less variable than those grown in the north. British Columbia, which is larger than all three states combined, exhibits greater heterogeneity than do any of these three states. In many cases the heterogeneity is so strong that crops are strictly limited to certain regions.[26]

The variation in crop yield CVs (and STDs) across these jurisdictions is substantial.[27] For example, in Nebraska the minimum COUNTY CV for corn is 0.21, the maximum COUNTY CV is 0.75, and the mean COUNTY CV is 0.28. For South Dakota, the same measures are 0.10, 0.40, and 0.23, respectively. In Louisiana, the measures are 0.14, 0.76, and 0.30, respectively. Table A.4 shows these statistics for other crops and for COUNTY STD. This variability in natural conditions within the jurisdictions we study allows us to conduct tests of risk sharing under favorable conditions.

The Choice of Contract: Cropshare vs. Cash Rent. To test prediction 6.5 with crop-specific contract data we use the following empirical specification, where for any contract i and crop j the complete model is

$$C_{ij}^* = \sigma_{ij}^2 \Delta_j + X_j \Pi_j + \epsilon_{ij} \quad i = 1, \ldots, n_j; \ j = 1, \ldots, 15; \quad \text{and} \tag{6.9}$$

$$C_{ij} = \begin{cases} 1 & \text{if } C_{ij}^* > 0 \\ 0 & \text{if } C_{ij}^* \le 0, \end{cases} \tag{6.10}$$

where C_{ij}^* is an unobserved contract response variable; C_{ij} is the observed dichotomous choice of farmland contracts for crop j, which is equal to 1 for cropshare contracts and equal to 0 for cash rent contracts; n_j is the number of contracts for a crop-specific sample; σ_{ij}^2 is the crop-specific variability of the random input for a given plot of land (as measured by CV or STD); Δ_j is the corresponding coefficient for crop j; X_j is a row vector of control variables including the constant; Π_j is a column vector of unknown coefficients; and e_{ij} is a crop-specific error term. The control variables—which include measures of plot size, family relationships, and farmer and land characteristics—are similar but not identical across the data sets (see appendix A). We use a logit model to generate maximum likelihood estimates of the model given by equations (6.9) and (6.10) for fifteen crop-specific contract samples ($j = 15$), nine on the Great Plains and six in Louisiana.

Table 6.5 presents the logit coefficient estimates from forty-eight separate estimated equations for the Great Plains (36 equations) and Louisiana (12 equations) data for the two exogenous variability measures at both the county and regional level. Each entry in table 6.3 is an estimated CV or STD coefficient—that is, an estimate of Δ_j and its associated t-statistic, derived from a separate estimated equation.[28] For example, the entry in the upper left cell (-12.59) is the estimated coefficient for REGIONAL CV from the equation using a sample of dryland corn contracts ($n_j = 539$) in Nebraska and South Dakota. The remaining entries in the first column use the same contract sample but replace REGIONAL CV with the other three measures of σ_j^2. The remaining columns represent the same exercise using contract samples for other crops. For the Nebraska–South Dakota data, we estimate these equations with nine crop samples using four measures of σ_j^2 (REGIONAL CV, REGIONAL STD, COUNTY CV, and COUNTY STD). This results in thirty-six coefficient estimates presented in the top half of table 6.5. For Louisiana the number of estimated equations and coefficient estimates for Δ_j is twelve because we have data on only six crops and because the state of Louisiana collects data only for parishes, eliminating the use of REGIONAL CV and REGIONAL STD.[29] Prediction 6.5 from the risk-sharing model predicts a *positive coefficient* for σ_j^2—the more variable is the yield for crop j in a region, the more likely the land contract will be a cropshare—that is, the model implies $\Delta_j > 0$ for all j crops.

Overall, the estimates fail to support the risk-sharing model. The estimates consistently show that increases in exogenous crop yield variability do not increase the probability of cropsharing. In forty-eight estimated equations there is not a single significant and positive coefficient estimate of Δ_j. In fact, more than one-half of the coefficient estimates are negative. Moreover, eleven of these negative estimates are statistically significant, showing that increases in exogenous risk actually reduces the probability of share contracting. We also estimate equations (6.9) and (6.10) without control variables (using only CV or STD), and with a smaller set of control variables than used in table 6.5. Neither of these alternative specifications change the findings reported in table 6.5 although the specification reported in table 6.3 consistently gave more precise estimates.

The Choice of the Farmer's Cropshare. In this section we restrict our analysis to the set of cropshare contracts in order to test prediction 6.3, which states that higher variability crops result in a lower share to the farmer. For this exercise we use the farmer's contracted

Table 6.5
CV and STD coefficient estimates from forty-eight logit regressions of contract choice
(dependent variable = 1 if cropshare contract; 0 if cash rent contract)

Nebraska and South Dakota crop samples

Variable	Dryland corn	Irrigated corn	Dryland soybeans	Irrigated soybeans	Dryland sorghum	Irrigated sorghum	Barley	Oats	Wheat
REGIONAL CV	−12.59	−1.50	−31.62	12.08	1.46	9.83	−1.51	−6.80	−2.49
	(−2.62)*	(−3.24)*	(−2.79)*	(1.61)	(0.26)	(0.68)	(0.21)	(−2.09)*	(−1.55)
REGIONAL STD	−0.16	−0.02	−0.24	0.30	−0.10	0.18	−0.85	−0.12	−0.03
	(−2.22)*	(−0.78)	(−0.48)	(1.58)	(−0.47)	(0.95)	(−2.24)*	(−1.69)*	(−0.36)
Observations (n_j)	539	1,378	479	524	341	276	234	540	1,250
COUNTY CV	−1.95	−5.33	−6.99	1.90	2.57	1.13	−0.52	−8.40	−1.94
	(−0.54)	(−1.88)*	(−0.94)	(0.27)	(0.30)	(0.12)	(−0.11)	(−2.45)*	(−1.19)
COUNTY STD	0.01	−0.04	0.09	0.07	0.17	0.03	−0.16	−0.19	0.01
	(0.15)	(−1.91)*	(0.93)	(0.39)	(0.99)	(0.23)	(−0.97)	(−2.35)*	(0.15)
Observations (n_j)	521	1,257	477	522	321	269	226	540	1,248

Louisiana crop samples

	Corn	Soybeans	Cotton	Rice	Sugarcane	Wheat
COUNTY CV	−11.98	−3.00	14.16	5.21	9.75	972.17
	(−1.26)	(−0.83)	(1.63)	(0.56)	(0.73)	(0.04)
COUNTY STD	−0.98	0.42	0.01	−0.34	−0.01	115.99
	(−1.32)	(1.29)	(0.51)	(−1.03)	(−0.02)	(0.04)
Observations (n_j)	18	92	61	79	52	8

Note: t-statistics in parentheses. The corn and wheat equations in the Louisiana crop samples use fewer control variables because of the small samples.
* significant at the 5 percent level for a one-tailed test.

share of output as our dependent variable. Because this variable ranges from zero to one, the model for each share contract i for crop j is

$$s_{ij} = \sigma_{ij}^2 \gamma_j + Z_j \xi_j + \epsilon_{ij}; \quad \text{if } s_{ij} < 0; \quad \text{and}$$

$$s_{ij} = 1 \quad \text{otherwise} \quad i = 1, \ldots, n_j; j = 1, \ldots, 14, \tag{6.11}$$

where s_{ij} is the farmer's share of the crop for the ith contract governing the jth crop; σ_{ij}^2 is the crop-specific variability of the random input for a given plot of land (again measured by CV or STD); γ_j is the corresponding crop-specific coefficient; Z_j is a row vector of explanatory variables including the constant; ξ_j is a column vector of unknown coefficients; and ϵ_{ij} is a crop-specific error term. The control variables are nearly identical to those used in the estimation of equations (6.9) and (6.10) and are explained in appendix A.

We use a right-censored tobit model to generate maximum likelihood estimates of the model given by equation (6.11) for the same fourteen crop-specific samples of cropshare contracts from the Great Plains (9 crops) and Louisiana (5 crops) data.[30] Table 6.6 presents the tobit estimates of 6.11 and shows the estimates of γ_j from forty-six estimated equations, thirty-six using Great Plains crop samples and ten using Louisiana crop samples. Like table 6.5, each entry in table 6.6 is an estimated CV or STD coefficient—that is, an estimate of γ_j, derived from a separate estimated equation. Accordingly, the entry in the upper left cell (21.96) is the estimated tobit coefficient for REGIONAL CV from equation 6.11 using a sample of cropshare contracts for dryland corn ($n_j = 521$) in Nebraska and South Dakota. The rest of the table is organized like table 6.5. Prediction 6.3 implies a *negative* coefficient for the CV and STD variables; that is $\gamma_j < 0$ for all j crops. Of the forty-six estimates, twenty-eight are not significantly different from zero, thus failing to support the risk-sharing prediction. More than half (30) of the estimated coefficients actually have a positive coefficient, and fourteen are significant. Only four estimates are negative and significant.[31]

Wealth, Risk, and Contract Choice

It is often assumed that as wealth increases, individuals become less risk averse in absolute terms. The assumption of declining absolute risk aversion (DARA) for farmers is so routine among agricultural economists that Pope and Just (1991) note, "Decreasing absolute risk aversion has emerged as a 'stylized' fact or belief" (743). In our model, DARA implies that wealthier farmers should cash rent more often than poor farmers (prediction 6.6). This follows, because as wealth increases, the amount of exogenous risk the farmer is willing to bear should rise. A corollary to this prediction is that the share the farmer receives should also rise with his wealth (prediction 6.4). Larger output shares mean that the farmer is bearing more of the exogenous variability.

Table 6.6
CV and STD coefficient estimates from forty-six tobit regressions of output shares in cropshare contracts (dependent variable = SHARE

Nebraska and South Dakota crop samples

Variable	Dryland corn	Irrigated corn	Dryland soybeans	Irrigated soybeans	Dryland sorghum	Irrigated sorghum	Barley	Oats	Wheat
REGIONAL CV	21.96	−57.75	84.81	−82.64	23.65	−32.46	64.70	53.96	19.90
	(1.14)	(−3.69)*	(2.01)*	(−1.24)	(0.63)	(−0.36)	(1.89)*	(4.33)*	(2.88)*
REGIONAL STD	0.10	−0.40	−3.53	−2.25	0.52	−0.29	4.77	1.16	−0.38
	(0.39)	(−3.27)*	−(2.19)*	−(1.25)	(0.32)	(−0.24)	(3.20)*	(4.12)*	(−1.09)
Observations (n_j)	539	1,378	479	524	341	276	234	540	1,250
COUNTY CV	−5.31	−15.03	33.75	−7.30	7.32	44.64	16.56	68.21	22.53
	(−0.32)	(−0.88)	(1.57)	(−0.11)	(0.41)	(0.68)	(0.88)	(5.26)*	(3.20)*
COUNTY STD	−0.32	−0.12	−0.90	−0.02	−0.96	0.78	0.43	1.51	0.20
	(−1.49)	(−0.89)	(−1.13)	−(0.01)	(−2.62)*	(0.99)	(0.69)	(4.89)*	(0.57)
Observations (n_j)	521	1,257	477	522	321	269	226	540	1,248

Louisiana crop samples

	Corn	Cottons	Rice	Soybeans	Sugarcane
COUNTY CV	5.30	2.11	7.81	6.51	12.70
	(0.80)	(0.85)	(2.73)*	(4.73)*	(3.99)*
COUNTY STD	0.17	0.37E-02	0.12	0.34	0.27
	(1.02)	(0.79)	(2.20)*	(3.73)*	(1.57)
Observations (n_j)	18	61	79	92	52

Note: t-statistics in parentheses.
* significant at the 5 percent level in a one-tailed test.

Only the British Columbia–Louisiana data have adequate information on farmer wealth levels to conduct appropriate tests. These surveys have information on the value of all owned land, buildings, and equipment and on the amount of equity the farmer has in the farm. The value of total assets in these samples ranges from $0 to over $3 million. Although these data do not perfectly measure wealth, they are close approximations because farmers in the regions we examine tend to derive most of their income from farm activities. In our Louisiana sample 93 percent of the farmers are full time operators and in our British Columbia sample 75 percent are full-time farmers (see table A.1). Furthermore, because farmers generate wealth from many parcels of land (owned and leased) over their careers, each of these variables measure wealth that is exogenous to the farmland contracts we examine.

Table 6.7 reports two sets of estimates for both British Columbia and Louisiana. These equations use the same sample as did the equations reported in tables 6.5 and 6.6, simply adding the additional wealth variables. The control variables include the crop dummies and the variables that measure various characteristics of farmers, land, and landowners (see appendix A). The upper panel shows logit parameter estimates of contract choice, and the lower panel shows tobit parameter estimates of the farmer's contracted share of output under cropsharing. For both logit and tobit estimation we use either (1) the aggregate level of wealth (WEALTH), or (2) the component parts (BUILDINGS, EQUIPMENT, and LAND) of total wealth. Under DARA the coefficient signs for WEALTH and other variables measuring wealth should be negative for the logit estimates, but positive for the tobit estimates.

Overall, as table 6.7 shows, the estimates give only limited support to the predictions based on DARA. The logit estimates of the WEALTH coefficient are insignificantly different from zero for both British Columbia and Louisiana, failing to support DARA. When the wealth measure is broken into its component parts, the estimates become less consistent. For British Columbia none of the estimates are significantly different from zero, although the signs are not the same. For Louisiana all coefficient estimates are significant, but the results are mixed with negative effects for BUILDINGS and LAND and a positive effect for EQUIPMENT. Many of these estimates are consistent with effects of capital constraints discussed in chapter 4, where we found evidence that as wealth increased (making capital constraints less binding) contracts were less likely to be share arrangements.

The estimates from the tobit share equations in the lower panel of table 6.7 give similarly mixed results. Like the logit estimates, the tobit estimates of the WEALTH coefficient are not significantly different from zero for both British Columbia and Louisiana, failing to support DARA. When WEALTH is broken into its three components, the results remain unfavorable to DARA. Of the six estimated coefficients, only one is positive and statistically significant, while four are insignificantly different from zero. To summarize, we find no consistent evidence supporting the effect of wealth on contract choice under a model of risk sharing.

Further Tests: Futures Markets, Large Landowners, and Off-Farm Income

The risk-sharing predictions examined thus far have all been explicitly derived from the principal-agent model presented at the beginning of this chapter. There are, however, additional predictions consistent with this model that can be tested with our data, using the variables FUTURES MARKET, INSTITUTION, and FARM INCOME. The tests that we perform using these variables are scattered across many of the estimated equations in this chapter and are sometimes, but not always, presented in the tables connected with the previous tests. In this section we discuss this final set of risk-sharing tests.

Table 6.7
Estimated coefficients for wealth effects

Independent variables	British Columbia		Louisiana		Predicted sign
Logit regressions: $Y = 1$ if share contract					
WEALTH	9.2 E − 05		−4.0 E − 04		−
	(0.15)		(−0.93)		
BUILDINGS		−2.1 E − 07		−3.4 E − 06	−
		(−0.14)		(−1.91)*	
EQUIPMENT		−5.4 E − 07		3.13 E − 06	−
		(−0.18)		(3.28)*	
LAND		3.8 E − 08		−1.6 E − 06	−
		(0.07)		(−2.96)*	
FUTURES MARKET	0.98	1.00	1.11	1.54	−
	(1.94)*	(1.86)*	(2.10)*	(2.71)*	
INSTITUTION	−1.04	−0.96	0.07	−0.48	+
	(−1.48)	(−1.32)	(0.14)	(−0.86)	
Model χ^2 (df)	20.56 (9)	20.62 (9)	24.62 (9)	55.55 (11)	
Correct prediction	70%	70%	69%	72%	
Observations	176	176	355	355	

Independent variables	British Columbia		Louisiana		Predicted sign
Tobit regressions: $Y =$ farmer's share					
WEALTH	0.28 E − 04		0.27 E − 03		+
	(0.82)		(1.31)		
BUILDINGS		0.14 E − 06		−0.78 E − 07	+
		(1.46)		(−0.09)	
EQUIPMENT		−0.28 E − 06		−0.78 E − 06	+
		−(0.16)		(−1.94)*	
LAND		0.54 E − 07		0.41 E − 06	+
		(0.17)		(1.83)*	
FUTURES MARKET	−0.38	−0.36	0.19	−1.77	+
	(−1.36)	(−1.17)	(0.80)	(−5.96)*	
INSTITUTION	0.55	0.41	0.31	0.34	−
	(1.52)	(1.10)	(1.16)	(1.15)	
Log likelihood	−351.37	−350.35	−1204.75	−2377.03	
Observations	176	176	355	355	

Note: t-statistics in parentheses.
* significant at the 5 percent level in a one-tailed test.

First, consider tests using FUTURES MARKET. This dummy variable equals one when a crop is traded in a futures market. Because futures markets are an alternative method of sharing risk, when they are present the farmer is, ceteris paribus, less likely to choose a share contract.[32] In all six of the equations in table 6.7 we included FUTURES MARKET, which should be negatively correlated with share contracts. The predicted coefficient estimate for FUTURES MARKET is, once again, negative for the logit equations but is positive for the tobit equations. The top panel of the table shows that none of the four logit estimates support this version of risk sharing—all four estimates are positive and significantly different from zero. The bottom panel in table 6.7 is also unfavorable to this prediction, with only one of the four estimates to be positive, but statistically insignificant.[33]

Next, consider the variable INSTITUTION, which is used to isolate the effects of landowner wealth on contract choice. By definition, INSTITUTION identifies large, wealthy landowners, thus isolating the cases when, by all traditional measures, the landowner should be less risk averse than the farmer. These landowners should be more likely than smaller landowners to share contract with farmers. Risk sharing thus predicts positive INSTITUTION coefficients for the logit estimation of contract choice and negative INSTITUTION coefficients for the tobit estimation of the farmer's cropshare. The coefficient estimates for INSTITUTION are reported in table 6.7, along with the wealth and futures market variables, and do not support the risk-sharing prediction. In the logit estimates in the upper panel, only one estimated coefficient is positive but still statistically insignificant, while the other three coefficients are statistically insignificantly different from zero. In the tobit estimates in the lower panel, all of the four coefficients are positive but none are significantly different from zero.

Other estimates of INSTITUTION coefficients using the equations in tables 6.5 and 6.6 further undermine support for this risk-sharing hypothesis.[34] INSTITUTION was included in the crop-specific logit equations used to estimate the coefficients for CV and STD in table 6.5. For each crop sample we estimated four equations, corresponding to the four different measures of exogenous variability. For Louisiana, we estimated these equations for only three crops (soybeans, rice, sugarcane) resulting in just six estimated coefficients. We find that four of the six are insignificantly different from zero, but that both rice coefficients are positive.[35] In order to estimate these equations for the Nebraska–South Dakota data, we used a smaller sample for which the variable INSTITUTION was available (see appendix A). Because there were no institutional landowners for sorghum (dryland and irrigated), we estimated the crop-specific contract choice equations for only seven crops. This resulted in a total of twenty-eight estimated coefficients (7 crops times 4 risk measures). None of the estimated coefficients are significantly different from zero, indicating that INSTITUTION does not affect contract choice as predicted by the risk-sharing model.

Similarly, INSTITUTION was included in the crop-specific tobit equations used to estimate the coefficients for CV and STD in table 6.6. For Louisiana we estimated these equations for the same three crops resulting in six estimated coefficients. None of the coefficient estimates are insignificantly different from zero. Again, for the Nebraska–South Dakota data, we use a smaller sample to estimate the crop-specific output share equations, resulting in a total of twenty-eight estimated coefficients. None of these coefficient estimates were significantly different from zero.

Finally, we used FARM INCOME to test the related hypothesis that farmers with little or no outside or "off-farm" sources of income will be more likely to share contract in order to share risk with the landowner. FARM INCOME measures the amount of a farmer's income derived from farming in four categories ranging from a small to high fraction. As a result, the estimated FARM INCOME coefficients are expected to be positive for logit estimates of contract choice and negative for tobit estimates of the farmer's share. FARM INCOME was included in the crop-specific logit equations used for table 6.5 and in the crop-specific tobit equations used for table 6.6. For Louisiana, we estimate these equations for four crops (cotton, rice, soybeans, sugarcane) resulting in sixteen (8 logit and 8 tobit) estimated coefficients.

Consider the estimates derived from the logit equations specified in table 6.5. For Louisiana, we find that all eight estimated coefficients are negative, rather than positive, and six of these are significant. None are positive and significant. Conducting the same exercise for the Nebraska–South Dakota data results in twenty-eight estimated coefficients. All estimated coefficients for FARM INCOME are negative and nine are significant. Contrary to the risk-sharing prediction, none of the estimated coefficients are positive and significantly different from zero.

FARM INCOME was also included in the crop-specific tobit equations used to estimate the coefficients for CV and STD in table 6.5. For Louisiana, we estimated these equations for the same four crops resulting in eight estimated coefficients. Again, we found that none of the coefficient estimates are significantly different from zero. For the Nebraska-South Dakota data, we obtain twenty-eight estimated coefficients and find that none are negative and significantly different from zero. Furthermore, six estimated coefficients are positive and significant. Overall, like the estimates of coefficients for FUTURES MARKET and INSTITUTION, the estimates for FARM INCOME do not support risk sharing.

6.4   Back to Risk Neutrality

The evidence presented in this chapter fails to support the standard risk-sharing model, which has dominated the study of contracts in agriculture and beyond. In particular, the predictions based on changing risk parameters are consistently refuted. In this section we consider the results in this chapter from the perspective of our transaction cost framework that assumed risk-neutral contracting parties.

Risk-Neutral Approaches to Share Contracts

In the traditional principal-agent model, risk aversion is a necessary condition for share contracting because the only behavioral margin is the farmer's (unobservable) effort, providing the well-known trade-off between farmer shirking and risk avoidance. As we have seen, in chapters 4 and 5, risk aversion need not be required to explain share contracting as long as other behavioral margins besides farmer effort are considered. With risk neutral parties, and contrary to prediction 6.2, share contracts can still be optimal when there are additional incentive problems, such as double-sided moral hazard, multitask agency, or measurement costs. As argued earlier, for farming there is good reason to believe that the single margin moral hazard model is an inappropriate model of farmer and landowner incentives. Land, like farmer effort, is also a variable input that often allows for landowner moral hazard. Landowners, for instance, may not properly maintain fences or irrigation equipment. At the same time, farmers can damage the land because lease contracts for land do not, and cannot, specify all the characteristics of the land. In addition, there are costs of measuring and dividing shared output and input costs. In part III we consider the organizational issues of asset ownership and vertical integration, and we see that the number of margins under which transaction costs of one type or another can arise becomes very large indeed. Extending the transaction cost framework in these circumstances is straightforward, whereas extending a model incorporating risk sharing verges on intractable.

In our risk-neutral transaction cost model of share contracting, the trade-offs are distinct from the risk-sharing versus farmer-shirking trade-off. First, share contracts distribute the deadweight losses from moral hazard over many margins. Second, share contracts create incentives for overuse and underreporting of those assets (inputs and the output) that are shared. As shown in earlier chapters, share contracts are chosen when the costs of dividing and measuring shared assets are low and the margins for moral hazard are large and many. On the other hand, fixed payment contracts may emerge when measurement costs are high and moral hazard margins are small and few.

The Risk-Sharing Evidence Revisited

The most important principal-agent prediction (prediction 6.5)—as output variability increases, sharecropping should be more common—was not supported by the data from Louisiana, Nebraska, and South Dakota in tables 6.5 and 6.6. Our risk-neutral approach,

however, generally implies the opposite prediction. Under risk neutrality, avoiding exogenous variability through sharing offers no benefits. At the same time, as output becomes
more variable, the opportunities for the farmer to underreport (in effect, steal) the crop
increase. Greater exogenous yield variability allows the farmer to hide his actions behind
Mother Nature. Increases in output variability increase the cost of share contracts, so we
would expect a decrease in the use of cropshare contracts, or a negative coefficient on CV
and STD. This prediction is generally supported by our data, both at the aggregate level
(table 6.4) and at the contract level (table 6.5).[36]

Table 6.4 shows that land contracts for low-variability crops are often dominated by the
sharing arrangement.[37] In Louisiana this is especially true for sugarcane, which has one of
the lowest CVs (0.099) in our sample, yet is predominantly shared (80% of all leased acres).
In the Great Plains share contracting for corn is important (60%–70% of contracts) even
though it has a relatively low CV (roughly 0.100). At the contract level, table 6.5 shows
considerable support for this implication. Table 6.5 shows that twenty-seven of forty-eight
estimated coefficients are negative and eleven of these are significant at the five percent
level, generating substantially more support than the standard principal-agent model.

Crop underreporting, however, is only part of the risk-neutral transaction cost story.
Row crops like corn, soybeans, and sorghum tend to be shared because of soil exploitation
problems (see chapter 4). Soil exploitation problems also increase with increased variance
in the random input, so these crops are predicted to have lower farmer shares when output
variability increases. Grain crops, on the other hand, do not experience as severe a soil
exploitation threat as row crops, and therefore the farmer's share rises with output variability
to counter underreporting.

The Distribution of Contracts across Assets.   In agricultural applications, the risk-
sharing framework has focused on the land lease contract. Yet land is only one of many
important farm inputs governed by contracts. Many other assets besides land—buildings,
equipment, skilled and unskilled labor—are important, and contracts routinely govern their
use. A risk-sharing rationale for land sharing should also imply share contracts for other
important assets like buildings and equipment. Data from British Columbia and Louisiana,
however, offer no indication that other assets are shared frequently like land. Table 6.8 shows
the distribution of sole ownership, shared ownership, and leasing for buildings, equipment,
and land. Sole ownership is, by far, the dominant regime for buildings and equipment, but
not for land. Buildings are not often leased apart from land and in these cases they are never
leased on a cropshare basis. Equipment leasing, too, is never based on output shares and is
far less common than for land leasing. When farmers lease equipment they usually pay a
daily rate or a rate based on hours of engine use, which is measured with gauges in tractors
and combines. This variation across different assets is inconsistent with the risk-sharing

Table 6.8
Ownership and leasing of agricultural assets

Asset	British Columbia		Louisiana	
	Owned	Leased	Owned	Leased
EQUIPMENT				
Tractors	99%	1%	96%	4%
Harvest equipment	99	1	96	4
Cultivator	100	0	97	3
Trucks	99	1	98	2
Sprayer	100	0	98	2
BUILDINGS				
House	99%	1%	92%	8%
Shop	97	3	78	22
Barn	99	1	85	15
Storage	98	2	78	22
LAND				
Crops	76%	24 (15)[a]%	30%	70 (22)%
Grass	74	26 (20)	71	29 (21)
Pasture	70	30 (30)	74	26 (23)
Fruit	81	19 (12)	83	17 (17)

Sources: 1992 Louisiana Farmland Leasing and Ownership Survey and *1992 British Columbia Farmland Leasing and Ownership Survey.*
[a] The number in the parentheses is the percentage of cash rent leases. For example, for cropland in British Columbia 24 percent of the land is leased. This is made up of 15 percent cash rent leases and 9 percent cropshare leases.

approach to contract choice and offers one more example of its shortcomings. In chapter 8 we extend our earlier risk-neutral model to explain this variation.

A Risk Preference Reversal in North American Farming?

The standard risk-sharing approach routinely assumes that landowners are risk neutral and farmers are risk averse. If the landowner were more risk averse, however, the model predicts cash rent contracts.[38] Could our empirical findings in tables 6.5 and 6.6 be explained by simply reversing the risk preferences of some farmers and landowners? There are many reasons to think the answer is no. Preference reversal does not explain the coefficient estimates on the FUTURES MARKET or INSTITUTION variables. Nor is preference reversal consistent with the wealth effects examined in table 6.7. Moreover, two additional sets of facts grind against this explanation of our findings. First, farmers and landowners in North America have remarkably similar demographic characteristics, so it is not obvious how to assign risk preferences. Second, farmers simultaneously hold more than one type of contract and play both sides of the farmland lease market. In the introduction to the book, table 1.2 points out a number of characteristics of the farmers and landowners that are common across all of our data sets. Table 1.2 shows that 60 percent of the landowners are or were at one time farmers. The similar social-economic background and demographic features of farmers and landowners are inconsistent with a model that posits dichotomous preferences and risk sharing. But there is even more. Table 1.2 shows that renters are often landowners and in some cases (6%) rent out land simultaneously, as well as hold both share and cash rent contracts. It is difficult to explain the coexistence of an individual being on both sides of a market with a simple incentive versus risk-sharing trade-off. It is also difficult to explain why a farmer would hold both types of contracts, without imposing unrealistic assumptions on farmer preferences.

6.5   Summary

The trade-off between risk and incentives has become a mantra among economists working on agency issues, despite the lukewarm evidence in its favor.
—Canice Prendergast, "What Trade-off of Risk and Incentives?"

We have used our data on individual contracts in modern North American agriculture—where cropshare contracts remain an important part of farming—to test some well-known predictions derived from the standard risk-sharing model that includes an incentive trade-off. On a case-by-case basis, using many different empirical specifications, we find that our evidence consistently fails to support the predictions of the traditional risk-sharing model. Cropshare contracts are not more likely when crop riskiness increases, when landowners are institutions, or when farmers derive more of their income from farming. Furthermore, cropshare contracts are not less likely when farmer wealth increases, or when futures markets exist. Risk sharing cannot explain the pattern of leasing for other assets, nor can it easily explain simultaneous cash rent and cropshare contracting by the same farmer. Collectively, our tests provide robust evidence that forces besides risk sharing are more important in shaping agricultural land contracts. At the same time, we find more support for our model that assumes risk-neutral contracting parties and stresses multiple margins for moral hazard and enforcement costs, supporting long-time critics of risk aversion such as Goldberg (1990) and recent critics such as Prendergast (2000).[39]

While our results show almost no support for predictions derived from a classic risk-sharing model, this does not, of course, rule out the possibility that other risk-based models could explain farmland contracts. For example, recently there have been a number of attempts to explain why we have, along with others, found a positive or insignificant relationship between risk and incentives. Some of these attempts include models of preference matching (for example, Ackerberg and Botticini 2002; Serfes 2001). In these models there is heterogeneity in both the leased asset (land, in our case) and the risk preferences of the agent. Landowners and risk-averse farmers compete for one another and match in ways that either create a positive relationship between risk and incentives, or other nonmonotonic relationships, depending on various assumptions. It is certainly possible that risk preference matching and other new ideas may indeed be able to resurrect risk sharing as a basis for understanding contracting. The idea of matching is worthy of further exploration, but there are two problems. First, empirically identifying differences in risk preferences is likely impossible. Second, there is no reason that the effects of matching should be restricted to risk preferences. Matching might take place in terms of land types, reputations, asset types, and so on. Still what we have shown here is that the classic risk-sharing model is not a useful empirical paradigm and that transaction cost economics offers an empirically supported alternative.[40]

In the next chapter we analyze a relatively new development in the theoretical analysis of contracts—the possibility of so-called ratchet effects. This phenomenon is also developed from a principal-agent model with risk averse agents to be consistent with the literature that gave birth to it. As with this chapter, we find no evidence for complicated ratchet effects existing in modern agriculture.

7 Ratchet Effects in Agricultural Contracts

The tendency for performance standards to increase after a period of good performance is called the ratchet effect.
—Paul Milgrom and John Roberts, *Economics, Organization and Management*

7.1 Introduction

In chapter 3 we argued that farmers and landowners, though their contracts were short and simple, often contract with one another for long periods of time. We also argued that the nature of farming communities allowed reputations to develop, and that these policed many of the gross opportunities for misbehavior that might otherwise occur with such seemingly simple contracts. It turns out, however, that with the principal-agent model analyzed in chapter 6, we get distinct implications for behavior when the farmer and landowner deal with each other over time. This chapter continues to explore the model presented in chapter 6 by examining one of its most famous dynamic predictions—the ratchet effect. As with the common predictions of risk sharing, we find little evidence supporting this exotic implication.[1]

In classic risk-sharing models in agriculture, where farmer performance is measured with error, landowners design optimal contracts that are both incentive compatible and profit maximizing. In general, the optimal contract provides incentives for the farmer, so that higher levels of output lead to higher levels of pay. If the landowner and the farmer engage in a series of contracts over time, information is collected on past performance, and this information could be used to set new standards of farmer behavior in order to increase the wealth of the landowner when he cannot otherwise commit to constant contract terms. It is well known, however, that using past performance to define standards creates incorrect incentives in the absence of long-term commitments by the contracting parties. Farmers who shirked in the past, and whose poor performance is partially attributed to nature, are rewarded with contracts based on low expectations of output. On the other hand, farmers who performed well in the past, and provided information on how productive they are, are penalized with high future standards. A landowner's incentive to increase standards over time in light of past performance is known as the *ratchet effect*.

The term ratchet effect comes from early studies of the Soviet Union where planners would often penalize plant managers for the increased output under new incentive schemes, claiming that the higher output proved shirking in the earlier period.[2] From these earlier studies, and from the theoretical literature, it is well known that using past performance to define future standards creates imperfect incentives for the agent. Thus in order for optimal contracts to emerge, it is important that the landowner be able to commit himself to a stable multiperiod contract. Although we examine the ratchet effect in a model with moral hazard, many studies examine the effect in models with adverse selection where the ratchet effect leads to excessive pooling equilibria (for example, Freixas, Guesnerie, and Tirole 1985; Kanemoto and MacLeod 1992). The general issue in either case is whether or not there is commitment by the contracting parties in a multiperiod relationship.

Commitment to contract terms is critical because when farmers anticipate the ratchet effect, they lower their efforts in the current period given that they expect to be punished in the future. This lower level of effort reduces the joint value of the contract and, as a result, provides the incentive for landowners to commit themselves to the terms of a contract when dealing with the same farmer over time.[3] If information is produced by one farmer who then leaves, and then a new farmer leases the land, the landowner may exploit what was learned with the past employee by increasing the new farmer's incentives within the contract.[4] In this case there is no reduction in effort in the first period because there is a different farmer in the following period. This change in contract terms in the second period reflects the better information about the relative contributions of the new farmer and the random inputs of nature. More specifically, the better information results in a lower estimated variance of performance in the second period. A lower estimated variance implies that the landowner makes fewer mistakes in separating the farmer's contribution to output from nature's contribution.

Principal-agent models that incorporate a ratchet effect lead to a strong prediction regarding the dynamic structure of contracts.[5] When there is a new farmer, and past performance reveals useful information about the current period, then contract incentives should strengthen over time, with the fixed payment to the landowner also increasing over time.[6] When the landowner continually contracts with the same farmer, however, then the contract incentives and effort levels should remain constant. Milgrom and Roberts (1992) put it this way:

The theory thus predicts that when the parties write contracts for one period at a time and when past performance embodies useful information for evaluating future performance, incentives will become more intense over time, as the parties utilize past experience to incorporate more accurate performance expectations in their contracts. . . . the actual effort levels elicited from the worker will also rise over time. . . . The argument . . . is only correct, however, if there is a new occupant in the job in each period. (P. 234)

Despite the recent theoretical attention given to the ratchet effect, models that include them have not been empirically tested against contract data.[7] In this chapter we use our farm-level data to test for the presence of ratchet effects.

7.2 A Two-Period Model of Farmland Contracts with Ratchet Effects

We slightly modify the principal-agent model from chapter 6 to create a two-period principal-agent model of farmland contracting to clarify the ratchet effect and demonstrate its testable implications.[8] We assume that the landowner is risk neutral and the farmer is risk averse, all cost and revenue functions are the same each period, there are no wealth effects, there is no discounting, and nature draws from the same distribution in both periods. These are the standard assumptions made in a dynamic principal-agent model in order to focus on the ratchet effect. The no wealth effect assumption implies that the coefficient of risk aversion is constant and that the optimal contract maximizes the total certainty equivalent income, subject to any incentive constraints. We make these assumptions to focus on the ratchet effect.[9]

Furthermore, we assume there is a pool of homogeneous (equal ability) farmers, which rules out adverse selection and leaves only moral hazard.[10] Farmer moral hazard, as always, exists because nature plays a large role in agricultural production and because farmer effort is costly to observe. Over time, however, landowners become more knowledgeable about nature, and they use this information to alter the contract in their favor.

Since two forms of incentive contracts dominate—cropshare and cash rent contracts, a ratchet effect might manifest itself in two potential ways. First, there may be a ratchet effect in the choice of one type of contract versus another. Second, the ratchet effect might arise within share contracts. We search for ratchet effects in both contexts and begin with the choice between cash rent and cropshare contracts, and then examine the ratchet effect within cropshare contracts alone.

Cash Rent versus Cropshare Contracts

In agricultural land leasing where farmers and landowners contract over the use of land and where the choice is between share contracts and cash rent contracts, the principal-agent model with ratchet effects suggests that new farmers are more likely to lease land with cash rent contracts, since cash rent contracts have stronger farmer incentives or are "higher-powered." When cash rent contracts are used with new farmers, landowners can exploit the information obtained over past seasons with previous renters and still maintain the reservation income of those who currently work the land.[11]

To show this, assume the contract between the farmer and landowner generates the following income for the farmer in each period:

$$Y = sQ - \beta - C(e) \geq \bar{Y}, \tag{7.1}$$

Table 7.1
Summary of dynamic contracting incentives

	Landowner committed to consistent contract?	Constant effort and incentives in each period?	Ratchet effect?	Empirical implementation
Case I	Yes	Yes	No	Same farmer in both periods.
Case II	No	No	Yes	Different farmer in each period.

where Y is the income to the farmer, $\bar{Y}$ is the farmer's reservation income from another plot of land, s is the farmer's share of output Q, β is a side payment to the landowner, $C(e)$ is the farmer's effort cost function, and the price of output is normalized to one. In each period $i \in \{1, 2\}$, observed output is $Q_i = e_i + \theta_i$, where e_i is the unobservable effort of the farmer, and $\theta_i \sim (0, \sigma^2)$ is a random input.[12] A cash rent contract implies $s = 1$ and $\beta > 0$, while a share contract implies $s \in [0, 1]$ and $\beta \in (-\infty, \infty)$. A cash rent contract is a pure high-powered contract, because the farmer is the complete residual claimant. A share contract has lower-powered incentives since $s < 1$.

We examine two moral hazard cases that generate the second-best outcomes summarized in table 7.1. In case I the landowner commits to maintaining the contract over two periods, while in case II there is no such commitment. Case I corresponds to the situation of an ongoing landowner-farmer relationship, while case II corresponds to a new farmer dealing with an established landowner in period 2. In both cases farmers exert less than the first-best level of effort, and the optimal share is less than one. Compared to the first-best optimum, there is less effort because the farmer does not own the entire output and there is moral hazard.

Case I: Dynamic Commitment. First, consider the case where the landowner ignores any new information when deciding what incentives to set in period 2 so there is no possibility of a ratchet effect. This is equivalent to having (dynamic) commitment to the terms of the contract over the two periods. Given the assumption of no wealth effects, the optimal contract maximizes the total certainty equivalent income of the farmer and the landowner, subject to the incentive compatibility constraints for each period. The value of the contract is the certainty equivalent that is equal to total output, minus the farmer's risk premium and cost of effort. As a result the optimal contract follows from:

$$\max_{e_1, e_2} V = Q(e_1) + Q(e_2) - C(e_1) - C(e_2) - (R/2) \, Var(s_1\theta_1 + s_2\theta_2), \tag{7.2}$$

subject to $\quad s_1 = C'(e_1), \; s_2 = C'(e_2),$

where R is the constant coefficient of absolute risk aversion. Since the problem is symmetric across periods, and since by assumption $Var(\theta_1) = Var(\theta_2)$, the optimal solution requires $s_1 = s_2$, and $e_1 = e_2$. This means that the contract has identical incentives (s) and work effort (e) in each period.

Case II: No Commitment over Time. Now consider the case in which two one-period contracts are made sequentially, and the landowner learns about the relative contribution of nature by observing the output in the first period. In this case there is no commitment to the terms of the contract over the two periods. Following Milgrom and Roberts (1992), we assume there is a positive correlation between the values of the random inputs (θ_1 and θ_2) in the two periods; that is, a high value of θ_1 means a high value of θ_2 is likely. This means that the landowner can use observed performance in the first period to get an estimate $\hat{\theta}_2$ of the random input in the second period, (θ_2). In turn, this estimate ($\hat{\theta}_2$) can be used to obtain a better estimate of the farmer's actual effort in the second period, (e_2).[13]

Let the landowner's estimate of θ_2 be given by $\hat{\theta}_2 = \gamma(e_1 + \theta_1)$, where γ is an adaptive expectation of the landowner, used to estimate nature's contribution to farm output in the second period.[14] The output that the landowner uses to pay the farmer is now adjusted by the estimate of nature from the first period, and becomes $\hat{Q}_2 = Q_2 - \hat{\theta}_2 = e_2 + \theta_2 - \hat{\theta}_2$. The landowner now uses this information to adjust the contract so that the farmer's compensation (gross income) over the two periods becomes[15]

$$Y = [\beta_1 + s_1 Q_1] + [\beta_2 + s_2 \hat{Q}_2]. \tag{7.3}$$

After substituting—$Q_1 = e_1 + \theta_1$, $\hat{Q}_2 = e_2 + \theta_2 - \hat{\theta}_2$, and $\hat{\theta}_2 = \gamma(e_1 + \theta_1)$—and collecting terms, the compensation function can be rewritten as

$$Y = [\beta_1 + (s_1 - \gamma s_2)(e_1 + \theta_1)] + [\beta_2 + s_2(e_2 + \theta_2)]. \tag{7.4}$$

It is clear that the effective share coefficient on first-period output (Q_1) is not the nominal contract amount (s_1) paid under the case of commitment, but a smaller net amount ($s_1 - \gamma s_2$). In terms of first-period compensation, the direct return to additional effort is s_1, but greater effort in the first period leads to a reduction in compensation for second-period effort by γs_2. This means the share in the first period ($s_1 - \gamma s_2$) is lower than the share in the second period (s_2). This model does not imply the contract would have a complicated formula whereby the share in the first period would be, for instance, 60 percent minus some fraction of the share in the second period. We would simply observe two sequential share contracts that might give the first farmer 50 percent of the crop in the first year, and then observe a second farmer getting 60 percent of the crop in the second year.

This upward adjustment is the *ratchet effect*. The incentives for farmer effort are increased—or become more high-powered—from period 1 to period 2. In other words, the farmer's share of output is "ratcheted up" over time as long as there is no commitment to contract terms and the landowner can learn about the value of the random input.[16] In the case where the farmer's incentive increases to the point where $s_2 = 100$ percent, the contract has switched from a share contract to a cash rent contract.

Thus far the model has been specified in terms of the landowner's ability to commit to a contract or not. When there is commitment, there are constant incentives or shares across periods. When there is no commitment, there is the ratchet effect or rising shares over time. In order to operationalize this model we follow (Milgrom and Roberts 1992) and consider commitment as equivalent to an ongoing relationship between a farmer and a landowner . When a farmer and landowner have an ongoing relationship, they have an incentive to avoid the ratchet effect, and we expect that they will commit to consistent contract terms over time. On the other hand, if there is a new farmer, there is no commitment, and the landowner will fully exploit his knowledge, based on past information. In this case, incentives should be higher than with the past farmer. An additional implication of this reasoning is that if a new landowner is involved in the second period contract, then constant incentives should be used because he will be unable to measure accurately the past performance on the farm. Over the two periods the ratchet effect will be absent because a change in landowners means that the landowner is not able to acquire information about the farmer's past performance. This leads to two predictions about the choice of a contract.

PREDICTION 7.1   New farmers contracting with established landowners are more likely to cash rent land.

PREDICTION 7.2   New landowners contracting with either new or established farmers are more likely to cropshare.

The Terms of Share Contracts

A ratchet effect might also lead to changes in the terms of a cropshare contract, without causing a switch to cash rent contracts. Because the formal analysis in this context is similar to the contract choice model, we only explicitly analyze case II (no commitment). To begin, we simplify by replacing the side payment with an input cost share. Even though modern share contracts do not often have side payments, they routinely share nonlabor input costs as we showed in chapter 5. As a result the income for a farmer with a share contract becomes

$$Y = sQ - qk - C(e) \geq \bar{Y}, \tag{7.5}$$

where $q \in (0, 1)$ is the share of input costs borne by the farmer, k represents aggregate nonlabor input costs (for example, fertilizer, seed), and $Q_i = e_i + k_i + \theta_i$ in each period to include noneffort inputs.[17]

The farmer's two-period compensation without commitment is now

$$Y = [s_1 Q_1 - q_1 k_1] + [s_2 \hat{Q}_2 - q_2 k_2], \tag{7.6}$$

where qk replaces the side payment β. As above, a series of substitutions—$Q_1 = e_1 + k_1 + \theta_1$, $\hat{Q}_2 = e_2 + k_2 + \theta_2 - \hat{\theta}_2$, and $\hat{\theta}_2 = \gamma(e_1 + k_1) + \theta_1$—allow us to rewrite the compensation function as

$$Y = [(s_1 - \gamma s_2)(e_1 + k_1 + \theta_1) - q_1 k_1] + [s_2(e_2 + k_2 + \theta_2) - q_2 k_2]. \tag{7.7}$$

Since the structure of this problem is identical to the contract choice problem, the structure of the solution is also identical. As before, it is clear that the effective share coefficient on first-period output is not the nominal contract amount (s_1) but a smaller amount ($s_1 - \gamma s_2$). This implies that effort and the actual shares increase over time. This is the ratchet effect, again. When there is no commitment, output shares (s) will be higher for new farmers. Notice that equation (7.7) also implies that the input cost shares remain constant over time. In contrast, if a new landowner is involved in the contract, he has no knowledge of past performance, and, consequently, he should not provide the farmer with higher powered incentives. The ratchet effect therefore plays a similar role within share contracts in terms of incentives increasing over time, which leads to the second set of predictions.

PREDICTION 7.3 New farmers should receive a higher output share than farmers with ongoing contracts; however, input cost shares should remain constant.

PREDICTION 7.4 New landowners should not change the output shares to their farmers compared to established landowners.

7.3 Empirical Analysis: Testing for Ratchet Effects

To test these predictions, we again use the contract data from the 1986 Nebraska and South Dakota Leasing Survey.[18] Recall there are 3,432 contracts in total, of which 2,424 are cropshare and 1,008 are cash rent. Of these, 264 cropshare contracts and 29 cash rent contracts had new farmers within five years of the survey. In addition, 115 cropshare and 38 cash rent contracts had new landowners within five years of the survey. The data set has information on whether input and output shares changed and on the direction of the change for output shares. The definition of the variables used in this chapter are found in table 7.2.

Ideally, to test the ratchet effect we would like a panel data set containing information on contract terms as well as farmers and landowners. However, because our cross-section data includes retroactive information, they are still well suited to test the predictions from

Table 7.2
Definition of variables

Dependent variables

CONTRACT	=	1 if contract was a cropshare contract; = 0 if a cash rent contract.
SHARE-UP	=	1 if share term was increased in the last five years; = 0 if not.

Independent variables

ACRES	=	number of acres covered by contract.
AGE	=	1 if farmer is younger than 25,
	=	2 if 25–34 years old,
	=	3 if 35–44 years old,
	=	4 if 45–54 years old,
	=	5 if 55–64 years old,
	=	6 if older than 65 (for Nebraska and South Dakota).
DENSITY	=	population per square mile in the county of farm operation.
FAMILY	=	1 if landowner and farmer were related; = 0 otherwise.
HAY	=	1 if hay or other grass crops were the major income producing crops;
	=	0 otherwise.
INPUTS CHANGED	=	1 if share of inputs changed in past five years;
	=	0 if there was no change.
IRRIGATED	=	1 if land is irrigated; = 0 if dryland.
NEW FARMER	=	1 if farmer is new within five years;
	=	0 if farmer has not changed.
NEW LAND OWNER	=	1 if land owner is new within five years;
	=	0 if landowner has not changed.
ROW CROP	=	1 if row crop (corn, sugar beets, sugarcane, soybeans, sorghum);
	=	0 if not a row crop (wheat, oats, barley).
YEARS DURATION	=	number of years contract has been in place.

---

the ratchet effect model. In particular, the data contain information on the history of tenant farmers over the five years prior to the survey. This is the critical piece of information that allows us to test the predictions from a model with ratchet effects because we know whether or not there has been a change in the tenant farmer or the landowner. In our empirical analysis the two periods in our theoretical model correspond to the periods with the old (period 1) and new farmer (period 2).

We use these data to test the predictions of our model by estimating the effect of new farmers and landowners on contract choices and on the terms of cropshare leases. Once again, we use the following empirical specification:

$$C_i^* = X_i\beta_i + \epsilon_i \quad i = 1, \ldots, n; \quad \text{and} \tag{7.8}$$

$$C_i = \begin{cases} 1, & \text{if } C_i^* > 0 \\ 0, & \text{if } C_i^* \leq 0, \end{cases} \tag{7.9}$$

where C_i^* is an unobserved farmland contract response variable; C_i is the observed dichotomous choice of land contract for plot i, which is equal to 1 for cropshare contracts and equal to 0 for cash rent contracts; X_i is a row vector of exogenous variables including the constant; β_i is a column vector of unknown coefficients; and ϵ_i is a plot-specific error term. We use a logit model to generate maximum likelihood estimates of the model given by equations (7.8) and (7.9) for a various contract samples.

In general, the model predicts that cash rent contracts should be more common and output shares should be higher in the second period. For this estimation we also use the same variables (ACRES, AGE, FAMILY, HAY, INPUTS CHANGED, IRRIGATED, DENSITY, ROW CROP, and YEARS DURATION) in our previous estimates to control for farm size, age, whether or not contracts are between family members, whether the number of inputs changed, the presence of irrigation, local population density, the type of crop, and the number of years the landowner and farmer have contracted with each other.

In particular, including AGE allows us to control for the effects of farming experience and assures that our NEW FARMER variable is representing farmers who are new to the contracted plot of land. We test these predictions using the entire contract sample, as well as several subsamples.

Cropshare versus Cash Rent

To test predictions 7.1 and 7.2 we use a sample that contains both cropshare and cash rent contracts.[19] Table 7.3 presents the coefficient estimates for several logit regressions on the choice of contract. The dependent variable in all cases is one if the contract is cropshare and zero if the contract is cash rent. The first column presents the results using the entire contract sample. The other estimates come from three additional subsamples: contracts for which the farmer and landowner are unrelated (column 2), only oral contracts (column 3), and annual or short-term contracts (column 4). Each of these subsamples allows us to control for various factors that might influence the magnitude of the potential ratchet effects. In each case the ratchet effect is expected to be larger than the full sample case. For example, it might be expected that the ratchet effect is stronger with unrelated individuals because more information is known about family members to begin with and ratcheting up incentives on relatives may be frowned on within a family. On the other hand, oral contracts involve less commitment, and as a result, ratchet effects should be more common. Likewise, shorter annual contracts may imply less commitment and a higher likelihood of ratchet effects.

We directly test for the presence of ratchet effects by including the variables NEW FARMER and NEW LANDOWNER in all the logit regressions. Prediction 7.1 implies a negative coefficient for the NEW FARMER variable, but the estimated coefficients for NEW FARMER are all positive and none are statistically significant, so we cannot reject

Table 7.3
Logit regression estimates of contract choice: Nebraska and South Dakota, 1986
(dependent variable = 1 if share contracts; 0 if cash rent contract)

Independent variables	All contracts	Nonfamily contracts	Oral contracts	Annual contracts	Predicted signs
CONSTANT	−0.50	−0.92	−0.57	−0.41	
	(−4.14)	(−4.06)	(−2.39)	(−1.18)	
Ratchet effect variables					
NEW FARMER	0.24	0.25	0.23	0.23	−
	(1.48)	(1.12)	(0.98)	(0.65)	
NEW LANDOWNER	0.06	−0.14	−0.16	−0.44	+
	(0.30)	(−0.47)	(−0.58)	(−1.06)	
Control variables					
ACRES	0.42	0.75	0.80	1.00	
	(0.45)	(1.42)	(4.39)*	(0.74)	
AGE	0.10	0.09	0.13	0.14	
	(3.60)*	(2.31)*	(3.52)*	(2.49)*	
FAMILY	−0.02		−0.33	−0.003	
	(−0.26)		(−2.65)*	(−0.03)	
HAY	−0.36	−0.40	−0.54	−0.65	
	(−3.01)*	(−2.41)*	(−3.36)*	(−2.57)*	
INPUTS CHANGED	−0.26	0.20	−0.08	0.83	
	(−1.03)	(0.49)	(−0.20)	(0.76)	
IRRIGATED	−0.96	−1.16	−1.00	−1.35	
	(−8.22)*	(−6.89)*	(−6.44)*	(−5.26)*	
DENSITY	−0.001	−0.001	−0.001	−0.001	
	(−1.98)	(−0.91)	(−1.94)	(−1.56)	
ROW CROP	2.76	3.20	2.54	2.86	
	(28.30)*	(22.4)*	(19.42)*	(13.67)*	
YEARS DURATION	0.03	0.03	0.02	0.02	
	(6.50)*	(4.23)*	(2.53)*	(2.07)*	
Log likeliood	−2,077.5	−1,79	−1,109	−493	
% correct	81.56	83.58	81.81	83.42	
Model χ^2 (df)	1202 (11)	862.2 (10)	528.6 (11)	308.2 (11)	
Observations	3,432	1,912	2,067	947	

Note: t-statistics in parentheses.
* significant at 5 percent (one-tailed test for coefficients with predicted signs).

Table 7.4
Summary statistics for new farmers and landowners: Share contracts

Variables	Only a new farmer	Only a new landowner
Number of contracts (%)	264 (100)	115 (100)
Share of inputs changed (%)	47 (17.8)	18 (15.6)
Number of shared inputs changed (%)	37 (14)	8 (6.9)
Lease changed to cropshare (%)	36 (13.6)	10 (8.6)
Farmer's share dropped (%)	15 (5.7)	10 (8.7)
Farmer's share increased (%)	20 (7.5)	5 (4.3)

the null hypothesis of no ratchet effect. Prediction 7.2 implies that the presence of a new landowner should increase the probability of a share contract; the estimated coefficient for NEW LANDOWNER is expected to be positive. In three cases the estimated coefficients are negative and in all four specifications the standard errors are too large to allow statistical significance. Overall then, the estimates shown in table 7.2 fail to reject the null hypothesis of no ratchet effects and suggest that ratchet effects are not present in the choice of land leasing contract.

Changes in Share Contracts

The second set of empirical tests examines the determinants of particular sharing rules within cropshare contracts in order to test predictions 7.3 and 7.4. Table 7.4 reports some summary statistics for cases in which a new landowner or farmer is involved in the cropshare contract. The data in table 7.4 are generally inconsistent with ratchet effects existing within the set of all share contracts. When there is a new farmer, both input cost shares and the number of inputs change, which refutes prediction 7.3 that states they should remain constant. The output share to the farmer increased more often than it decreased, which is consistent with prediction 7.3. Furthermore, when there is a new landowner input cost shares change less often and output shares decrease more often than they increase. However, the difference in proportions between the two samples is not statistically significant.[20]

In order to further test predictions 7.3 and 7.4, we use several samples containing only share contracts to estimate the following model:

$$ln(s_i/(1 - s_i)) = Z_i\phi_i + \epsilon_i, \tag{7.10}$$

where s_i is the farmer's share of the output for the ith contract, Z is a row vector of explanatory variables, ϕ is a column vector of unknown coefficients, and ϵ is an error term.[21]

Table 7.5 presents the results from four OLS estimations of equation (7.10). As in the logit estimates, the variables NEW FARMER and NEW LANDOWNER are used.

Prediction 7.3 implies a positive sign for the estimated coefficient of NEW FARMER, since a higher share means the contract has higher power. Only the sample of nonfamily members provides an estimated coefficients that is positive and statistically significant; the rest are either negative or statistically insignificant. Prediction 7.4 implies a negative sign for the estimated coefficient of NEW LANDOWNER. Even though all four estimated coefficients are negative, none are close to being statistically significant. As with the regression estimates from table 7.3, there is no consistent support for the ratchet effect within share contracts.

Predictions 7.3 and 7.4 can also be tested by estimating the probability that a farmer's cropshare changed in the recent past. Table 7.6 shows the estimated coefficients from a logit regression in which the dependent variable is one if the farmer's share increased within the last five years. These estimates do show some support for the presence of ratchet effects. First, the estimated equation shows that NEW FARMER is positively related to rising farmer shares, consistent with prediction 7.3. Second, the estimated equation also show that NEW LANDOWNER is positively related to rising farmer shares. Although this result is statistically insignificant, it is inconsistent with prediction 7.4.[22]

Economic Significance and Other Variables

Two separate tests of ratchet effects have been conducted. The first examined whether contracts would be switched from low-powered share contracts to high-powered cash rent contracts, and the other looked at whether shares would be increased when a new farmer started farming the land. In both cases we found limited evidence consistent with ratchet effects. Furthermore, the magnitude of the estimated coefficients for the two variables NEW LANDOWNER and NEW FARMER were dwarfed by the size of the estimated coefficients of the other variables in the regression, suggesting that, unlike our results in chapters 3–5, ratchet effects have little economic significance. Table 7.3 shows that several nonratchet variables have much larger coefficients. In particular, the coefficient on the dummy variable ROW CROP is almost eleven times larger than the coefficients for the binary ratchet variables. From table 7.3, even in the full sample case where output shares do rise with the presence of new farmers, the effects of NEW FARMER and NEW LANDOWNER are not as large as those associated with the choice of crop.[23] Thus, in addition to the lack of statistical significance, the small coefficient size also suggests that these two variables (NEW FARMER, NEW LANDOWNER) have a small economic impact and that the ratchet effect is unimportant in the context of this contracting example.

Although the two variables for new farmers and landowners offer the most direct test for the presence of ratchet effects, the positive estimated coefficient on the YEARS DURA-TION variable in table 7.3 could be interpreted as consistent with the ratchet effect. This positive relationship shows that long-term contracting parties are more likely to choose share

Table 7.5
OLS regression estimates of output share in share contract sample: Nebraska and South Dakota (1986)
(dependent variable = ln(SHARE/(1−SHARE)))

Independent variables	All contracts	Nonfamily contracts	Oral contracts	Annual contracts	Predicted signs
CONSTANT	0.48	0.49	0.50	0.47	
	(8.96)*	(8.00)*	(7.68)*	(6.67)*	
Ratchet effect variables					
NEW FARMER	0.05	0.07	−0.02	−0.006	+
	(1.19)	(1.69)*	(−0.38)	(−1.32)	
NEW LANDOWNER	−0.02	−0.04	−0.05	−0.04	−
	(−0.42)	(−0.68)	(−0.82)	(−0.56)	
Control variables					
ACRES	−0.00001	−0.00002	−0.00004	0.00003	
	(−1.04)	(−1.43)	(−1.13)	(−1.57)	
AGE	0.01	0.01	0.004	0.007	
	(1.57)	(0.79)	(0.025)	(0.77)	
FAMILY	0.03		−0.04	0.02	
	(1.20)		(−1.44)	(0.65)	
HAY	0.05	0.05	0.06	0.04	
	(1.74)	(1.40)	(1.83)	(1.11)	
INPUTS CHANGED	0.002	−0.05	−0.02	0.07	
	(0.004)	(−0.73)	(−0.23)	(0.93)	
IRRIGATED	0.04	−.002	0.02	0.04	
	(1.34)	(−0.06)	(0.62)	(1.12)	
DENSITY	−0.0003	−0.0004	−0.0003	−0.0005	
	(−2.39)*	(−2.39)*	(−1.73)	(−2.10)*	
ROW CROP	−0.23	−0.19	−0.13	−0.20	
	(−6.70)*	(−4.67)*	(−3.25)*	(−4.27)*	
YEARS DURATION	0.004	0.003	0.004	0.005	
	(2.86)*	(2.36)*	(3.14)*	(3.34)*	
Adjusted R^2	0.025	0.027	0.014	0.021	
F-value	6.71	4.71	3.01	4.11	
(df)	(11, 2,412)	(10, 1,314)	(11, 1,584)	(11, 1,606)	
Observations	2,423	1,324	1,595	1,617	

Note: t-statistics in parentheses.
* significant at 5 percent (one-tailed test for coefficients with predicted signs).

Table 7.6
Logit regression estimates of changes in share contracts: Nebraska and South Dakota (1986)
(dependent variable = 1 if farmer's share increased in past 5 years; = 0 if not)

Independent variables		Predicted signs
CONSTANT	−3.15	
	(−8.03)*	
Ratchet effect variables		
NEW FARMER	0.55	+
	(1.77)*	
NEW LANDOWNER	(0.16)	−
	(0.33)	
Control variables		
ACRES	0.00	
	(0.46)	
FAMILY	0.00	
	(0.02)	
HAY	−0.18	
	(−0.58)	
INPUTS CHANGED	2.91	
	(9.50)*	
IRRIGATED	−0.25	
	(−0.75)	
DENSITY	0.00	
	(0.69)	
ROW CROP	−0.84	
	(−2.59)*	
YEARS DURATION	−0.01	
	(−1.13)	
Log likelihood	−307.59	
% correct	97.19	
Observations	2,424	

Note: t-statistics in parentheses.
* significant at 5 percent (one-tailed test for coefficients with predicted signs).

contracts over cash rent contracts, and as such, the variable YEARS DURATION could be considered a proxy ratchet variable. The longer two parties contract with each other, the more likely the contract involves commitment and lower powered incentives, despite the learning done over time by the landowner. Again, the effect is small both in absolute size and relative to other variables. The estimates in table 7.3 imply that an additional year to the relationship, calculated around the mean of the dependent variable, leads to a 0.61 percent increase in the probability of a share contract. Compared to the effect of having a row crop, which increases the probability of a share contract by 56 percent at the mean, this effect is economically unimportant.

In the context of tables 7.4 and 7.5, one might consider the YEARS DURATION coefficient along the same lines. In these cases, however, the estimated coefficients for YEARS DURATION are not consistent with the ratchet effect. In table 7.5 the coefficient is positive and statistically significant, indicating that longer term relationships have greater share terms. This is inconsistent with prediction 7.3 and suggests that landowners do not commit to terms with ongoing farmers. Finally, in table 7.6, the estimated coefficient for YEARS DURATION is not significantly different from zero. Taken together the effect of YEARS DURATION on contract design offers little support for the existence of economically important ratchet effects in agricultural contracts.

7.4 Summary

In chapter 4 we saw that the choice between cropshare and cash rent contracts, at least for our regions, is best explained by efforts to mitigate soil exploitation and crop underreporting. Farmers have an incentive to overuse rented land under a cash rent contract, and a cropshare contract curbs this incentive. At the same time, cropshare contracts create an incentive to underreport part of the crop because the contract taxes reported output. Efforts to measure underreporting are costly and prevent share contracts from dominating cash rent contracts everywhere. Depending on which incentive problem is more serious, one contract or another emerges as a second-best outcome.

Evidence to test a hypothesis like the ratchet effect is not easy to come by. Data on both sides of the contract, as well as contract history, are required. Because agriculture and share contracting are important theoretical applications of the principal-agent model, and because our data meet the conditions laid out in the theoretical literature, this chapter provides an important test. Our evidence suggests that the ratchet effect is generally unimportant in modern agricultural land contracts. We did find that within cropshare contracts, limited evidence exists that input and output shares move in ways consistent with ratchet effects, although the effects are relatively small. We find virtually no evidence to support the ratchet effect in the determination of contract choice compared to other explanatory variables. Overall, our estimates show that even in the limited cases in which there is support for a ratchet effect in private agricultural share contracts, they tend not to be economically significant.

Our findings do raise the question of why ratchet effects are so limited in these data. Several possibilities exits. First, if farmer heterogeneity is important, then adverse selection incentives in the absence of commitment could lead to other behavior that would not generate the ratchet effects in predictions 7.1 to 7.4. This seems unlikely in the context of farming where farmers and landowners are relatively homogeneous. Second, if information about farmers and landowners is sufficiently cheap to produce, then the landowner may face reputation costs, even across farmers, which would limit his ability to change contracts when dealing with a new farmer. Third, chapters 4 and 5 showed that multiple task moral hazard is important in determining contract choice. This explains the dominance of row crops in our estimates. Row crops require large amounts of soil manipulation and share contracts are used to limit over exploitation. It may be the case that soil manipulation is so important that adjusting the shares for a ratchet effect leads to serious soil depletion. Unfortunately, our data do not allow us to separate out these different explanations.[24]

The general absence of ratchet effects may be unique to agriculture, or it may be quite common. Ratchet effects can only occur when contract commitment is costly. To the extent that private contracts only arise when commitment is not costly, then ratchet effects should not be expected. Perhaps the best example is still government agencies where turnover is common, information poor, and reputations hard to establish, all of which make commitment difficult. In private contracts a stronger incentive exists to curb any of the ratchet incentives and to make commitment more feasible.

This chapter completes our analysis of contract choice. We have shown the strength of the transaction cost approach and the weakness of the standard principal-agent models. In the next two chapters, we analyze different questions that deal with the ownership of assets and the control over stages of production. For the remainder of the book we ignore the role of risk sharing and continue to focus on transaction costs.

III EXTENDING THE FRAMEWORK: FARM ORGANIZATION

In part III of the book (chapters 8 and 9) we extend the analysis of part I to broader organizational issues in farming. In both chapters we introduce seasonality and timeliness costs as forces influencing the gains from specialization and the costs of contracting. In chapter 8 we examine the choice of whether to own or contract for control over assets used in agriculture. We consider the decision to lease land as well as buildings and equipment. We develop a model that focuses on gains from specialization, moral hazard and timeliness costs. Using several different data sets and some historical case studies, we find that farmers tend to own assets when specialization gains are small and when moral hazard and timeliness costs are high.

In chapter 9 we examine farm ownership and vertical integration. Farms, unlike most other modern firms, are still predominantly family businesses, despite the tremendous technological advances that have taken place over the past century. Furthermore, farms almost always control all of the biological stages of production. Farming, we argue, is unique in that nature often limits the gains from specialization in production. Since it takes a year to produce a single crop of wheat, farmers will avoid specializing in any single task involved in wheat production. The failure to generate gains from specialization means that elaborate forms of governance can seldom compete against small family farms due to the transaction costs that arise from the inevitable separation of ownership and control that arises in large-scale corporate firms. When the seasonality of nature can be taken out of production, then farming tends to be organized like most other industries dealing with intermediate goods.

8 Ownership versus Contracting for the Control of Assets

8.1 Introduction

Although our attention has been on the type of contract used to rent land, a more fundamental issue regarding the method of asset control is whether to own assets outright or to contract for their temporary use. For farming, an obvious question is: Who owns the land, the one working the land or someone else? Yet the decision to own or contract can also be examined for other assets like equipment and buildings. It is often argued that farmers, who generally hold large inventories of seldom-used equipment like combines, cultivators, harvesters, and sprayers, own "too much" capital. Many of these expensive assets are used for surprisingly short periods and are simply held in inventory the remainder of the year. Modern combines, for instance, cost well over \$100,000 and are used for as little as two or three weeks a year. Tables 2.8 and 6.8 showed this stark pattern. While land leasing is quite common in both jurisdictions we examine, the leasing of equipment and buildings is rare.[1] At a glance it might seem that it would be better to rent these assets and lower their average costs. In this chapter we develop a model for analyzing the choice of ownership versus contracting and test a set of implications against British Columbia–Louisiana data and against the history of custom combining on the Great Plains.

The rather large literature on contracting and ownership has often focused on the question of "firm" ownership.[2] In this framework, ownership of the firm revolves around which individuals exercise control and have residual claims over all the assets of the firm. Although one can broadly speak of a group of individuals (such as capitalists or laborers) as having control of the firm, in practice the control any party has over different assets varies a great deal across firms. In farming, the dominant ownership form is the family farm, yet within this category some farmers rent all their land and equipment while others own all of these assets. Theories of firm ownership have tended to ignore these details of actual ownership patterns. Of necessity, most theoretical analyses refer only to general contracting problems. Yet, the pattern of ownership within a firm is likely to be determined in part by the incentives *specific* to particular industries and firms, because the transaction costs of owning and contracting always depend on the specific nature of the assets involved. General theories of ownership, then, will never do well in explaining detailed patterns of ownership.

Asset specificity has come to be a dominant theme in the economics of ownership. For example, Milgrom and Roberts (1992) state, "The most important attribute of transactions for studying asset ownership is the asset specificity attribute" (307). Although evidence exists to support the importance of asset specificity in determining the ownership of assets,[3] there seems to have been a tendency to overestimate their importance.[4] In chapter 3 we argued that very few assets on a farm, with the possible exceptions of immovable buildings, fruit trees, and (some) irrigation equipment, are specific to that farm. Land, though potentially specific to an agricultural region, tends not to be specific to any single farmer or landowner. For these reasons, specific assets play a minor role in the analysis in this chapter. We do, however, consider timeliness costs, which might be considered a variant on temporal specificity (Masten, Meehan, and Snyder 1991).

There are, of course, costs associated with contracting and costs associated with ownership. As we have stressed throughout the book, assets are collections of difficult to measure attributes that naturally vary in characteristics and are alterable by people. This makes contracts necessarily incomplete and allows renters opportunities to impose costs on the asset owner. Compared to ownership, all short-term contracts create some form of moral hazard because farmers face lower costs of using attributes that are unspecified and unpriced in a contract. For example, land is rented by the acre but soil quality is not specified. Similarly, many of the quality dimensions of buildings and equipment are not specified. As a result, farmers mine the soil, overload buildings, and generally overutilize the unpriced attributes of the contracted asset (as discussed in chapters 3 and 4).

In this chapter we introduce two costs of ownership. First, when choosing to own rather than contract, the farmer often forgoes the gains from specialization. For example, a farmer can seldom fully exploit the largest tractors, combines, trucks, and other pieces of equipment.[5] Second, ownership has capital costs, not associated with contracting, that can arise when the farmer lacks the wealth to guarantee the purchase of the asset.

In this chapter we also extend our earlier analysis and introduce two new costs of contracting. The first is moral hazard resulting from incomplete control rights over assets. In what we now call *simple contracts* the farmer retains primary control over the physical use of the asset (for example, he operates the leased combine).[6] When the farmer maintains control, he has an incentive to damage or undermaintain the asset because he does not fully own it. *Custom contracts*, however, are contracts in which the asset owner—not the farmer—is the operator and thus retains control over the asset.[7] When the asset owner maintains control, the incentive to harm the asset disappears, but there is now an incentive for moral hazard on the part of the asset owner through the supply of his effort. Thus, there is a trade-off between two types of moral hazard depending on which party controls the asset during the contract period.

The second cost of contracting stems from the imperfect alignment of the contract length and the relevant stage of production. Contract length affects the costs of contracting because of the importance of timeliness in the application of farmer effort. The timing of planting, cultivating, pest application, and harvest are often crucial because it can dramatically reduce farm output and crop quality. If the contract period is shorter than the relevant production stage, the farmer thus incurs timeliness costs.[8] Because the optimal times for important stages are not well known in advance, it is difficult to contract for the precise dates when the asset will be useful. Longer-term contracts can avoid timeliness costs, but longer terms tie up capital longer and increase idle time compared to a short-term contract.

Our focus on capital constraints, moral hazard, specialization gains, and timeliness implies that we necessarily ignore other factors—life cycles, management, risk, taxes—mentioned in the literature on ownership. Our reasons for ignoring these factors are practical. First, since farming is dominated by family farms, issues of managerial shirking and collective decision making are minor. Second, as we showed in chapter 6, there is little evidence that effort to avoid risk plays any role in the organizational design of farms, so throughout our analysis, the farmer and the asset owner are both assumed to be risk neutral. Third, tax incentives, though important in many settings, are not considered here because our data do not allow any observable variation in tax treatment.[9]

We begin section 8.2 by developing a general framework for examining the choice of asset control. We explicitly model the behavior of farmers and asset owners in a number of specific contractual-ownership regimes and derive predictions about the conditions under which ownership will be chosen over contracting. In section 8.3 we empirically confront a number of our predictions with our British Columbia–Louisiana data, and with a detailed case study of custom wheat harvesting on the Great Plains. In our econometric analysis of farm data, we estimate the impacts of economic variables on choice to own or contract for land, equipment, and buildings. Section 8.4 summarizes our findings and concludes the chapter.

8.2   Models of Asset Control

We confine our analysis to three dimensions of asset control: (1) whether the asset is controlled by ownership or contract, (2) if the asset is controlled by contract whether the contract is short- or long-term, and (3) whether the asset owner provides the labor that accompanies the asset. Within this framework are five potential "governance structures," summarized in table 8.1.[10] Case 1, the pure family farm in which the farmer owns the asset and supplies his own labor, is our starting point. Cases 4 and 5, short- and long-term simple leases, are common forms of agricultural contracts and the focus of our econometric analysis in section 8.3. Case 2, the short-term custom lease, is common in harvesting and pesticide application. An important application of this case, custom wheat harvesting, is examined in section 8.3. We ignore case 3, the long-term custom lease, because it is rare in agriculture and we have no direct data to examine it. For each of the four cases we study, we develop a model that incorporates the various incentives—capital costs, moral hazard, specialization, and timeliness—described earlier. Rather than introduce all of these issues at once, we elaborate on them in the cases for which they are relevant.

Table 8.1
Alternative governance structures for asset control

	Own	Short-term contract	Long-term contract
Asset owner provides labor	(1) Pure family farm	(2) Custom contract (e.g., custom harvesting crew)	(3) Custom contract (e.g., year-long pest control contract)
Asset owner does not provide labor	NA	(4) Simple contract (e.g., most equipment leases)	(5) Simple contract (e.g., standard land leases)

Note: NA = not applicable.

The Basic Model

The model in this chapter is a more general version of our model of contract choice. As before, we consider an asset to be a collection of attributes that are both variable and alterable. Typically, just one or a few attributes are priced and the rest remain unpriced and unspecified in a contract. When an attribute is not directly priced moral hazard occurs, the attribute becomes exploited beyond its first-best level, and the moral hazard costs are incorporated into the priced attribute of the asset. For example, when a farmer rents land by the acre, the competitive price per acre reflects the extra nutrients and soil moisture that are expected to be used by the lessor since these margins are not priced directly.[11]

We incorporate this into our basic model by maintaining the original notation, but slightly reinterpreting the variables such that our production function has both a priced and an unpriced attribute of each asset used. The full production and information structure is given by $q = h(e, l, k) + \theta$, where q is the crop output (with price still normalized to 1), e is the amount of *standardized* farmer effort and measured in terms of hours; l is the *priced* or contractually specified standardized attribute of the asset; and k is the *unpriced* or unspecified attribute of the asset. For example, if the asset is land, l would be acres and k might be the soil nutrients; if the asset is a building, l would be square feet and k might be durability. The ratio k/l is a measure of the quality of the asset; the greater the ratio, the higher the quality. Finally, nature's input, θ, is distributed with probability density function $x(\theta)$ and cumulative density function $X(\theta)$. As always, we assume that all marginal products are positive and diminishing, all inputs are independent of one another, and that $E(\theta) = 0$.

Increases in specialization are incorporated into the model as decreases in marginal costs for labor and the asset, which implies that competitive rental markets exist for all inputs. An alternative approach is to introduce specialization effects directly into the production function as we do in chapter 9. Labor specialization occurs when the human capital of the operator increases with the use of the asset; that is, learning by doing occurs as the farmer uses an asset. For many farm labor tasks, the gains from specialization are limited because stages of production tend to be short and require different skills from stage to stage. As a result, farmers tend to be unspecialized "jacks of all trades," as discussed in chapter 9. Farmers, of course, may hire specialized labor to mitigate this cost but they will, in turn, face costs of monitoring the labor and the asset.

We model labor specialization as a fall in its marginal cost (w), assuming that a specialized farmer provides a standardized unit of labor effort at a lower cost than does a nonspecialized farmer. For example, a specialized cutter might cut a field in five hours, while a (nonspecialized) farmer might take ten. The explicit hourly rate of the cutter might be higher, but the effective wage is lower such that the total costs of the cutter are lower. Specialization in the use of the nonlabor assets results when the technology of the asset changes with higher volumes of output. Larger machines often have larger fixed costs, but lower marginal costs of operation such that lower average costs result for large volumes. A farmer who uses a combine for 200 acres will use a different machine than a farmer who combines 2,000 acres.

We model asset specialization as a fall in its marginal cost (r), assuming that a more specialized asset has a lower marginal cost than a nonspecialized one for a standardized unit of l. Specialization in l is not the same as increased quality. Equipment manufacturers might make several different models with different degrees of specialization, yet all could have the same k/l ratio. Similarly, let v be the marginal cost of the nonpriced attribute of the asset. With complete specialization each input is provided at its lowest possible cost, given by w^*, r^*, and v^*, respectively.

The inputs e, l, and k have opportunity costs that depend on the relationship between the asset owner and the asset user. When a farmer supplies his own labor and asset (case 1), we denote the opportunity cost of use as w^o, r^o, and v^o where o means "ownership." When the farmer has a simple contract for the asset, we denote the opportunity cost as w^l, r^l, and v^l, or w^s, r^s and v^s, where l and s mean "long-term" (case 5) and "short-term" (case 4) contracts, respectively. Finally, when there is a custom contract (case 2) the opportunity cost is w^c, r^c, and v^c, where c indicates "custom."

As a benchmark, consider the first-best allocation of effort and asset use. The Coase Theorem implies that, as long as transaction costs are zero, this allocation could be achieved with any of the governance structures shown in figure 8.1.[12] Each input (e, l, k) has a cost of w^*, r^*, and v^* respectively, so wealth is jointly maximized when the input levels of e^*, l^*, and k^* are employed, and the value (net of the costs of the inputs) of the governance structure is $V^*(e^*, l^*, k^*)$. These optimal input levels occur where marginal products equal marginal costs, inputs are fully specialized, and all inputs are delivered at the optimal time. In a second-best world, however, where contracts are incomplete, this outcome is unattainable.

Ownership of Assets

Ownership of all inputs by a single party obviously eliminates the costs of contracting for asset control by eliminating moral hazard and timing costs. Without these costs, asset ownership would dominate contracting, and leasing would not occur. There are two primary reasons why in fact, owning does not always dominate in farming. First, the gains from specialization in effort and in using an asset may be large and not captured by ownership. Second, capital constraints raise the costs of asset use.

Farmer Owns the Asset and Provides Labor (Case 1).   When a farmer provides his own labor, he sacrifices specialization gains because he constantly changes tasks throughout the year, so that $w^o > w^*$. This is, in fact, virtually the definition of a specialist—namely, that he is the low-cost provider of a standardized unit. Similarly, a jack-of-all-trades farmer will likely own an asset that does not fully exploit all technical specialization because the asset's use on a given farm is also likely to be limited, so that $r^o > r^*$. A farmer who owns an asset, however, bears all the costs of that asset—including the costs of the unpriced attribute. Hence, $v^o = v^*$, and there is no moral hazard with respect to the asset. Figure 8.1, top panel, shows the optimal input levels for this case. The optimal input level is simply the intersection of the marginal product curves (h_j, $j = e, l, k$) and the marginal cost curves (i^o, $i = r, v, w$).[13] The figure shows that ownership leads to less effort, ($e^o < e^*$), and less asset use, ($l^o < l^*$), than is first-best. The value of this governance structure is $V(e^o, l^o, k^*)$. Note that $k^o = k^*$, which means that ownership leads to higher quality assets. A farmer might have a smaller combine and use it less often, but it is optimally maintained.

Ownership with Borrowing.   Additional costs of ownership arise because of capital constraints. When borrowing to pay for assets, a farmer may not have enough wealth to guarantee payment in all possible states of the world. With $Q = h(e, l, k) + \theta$, assume the farmer has purchased the asset l with a loan of amount B and promises to repay $(1 + \iota)B$ at the end of the period—where ι is the real rate of interest conditional on a given expectation of bankruptcy. The farmer's income is $Q - (1 + \iota)B$ if output is greater than the loan, but given his limited wealth and limited liability from the protection of bankruptcy his income is zero if $Q \leq (1 + \iota)B$. The farmer's objective is to maximize his expected net income across the possible states.[14] This expectation is not taken over all possible values of θ, but only over those θ that yield a level of income greater than zero ($\theta > (1 + \iota)B - h(e, l, k)$), so with borrowing the owner's input choice problem is

$$\max_{e, l, k} V^{o'} = \int_{(1+\iota)B - h(e,l,k)}^{\infty} [h(e, l, k) + \theta - (1 + \iota)B]x(\theta)d\theta - w^o e - r^o l - v^* k. \qquad (8.1)$$

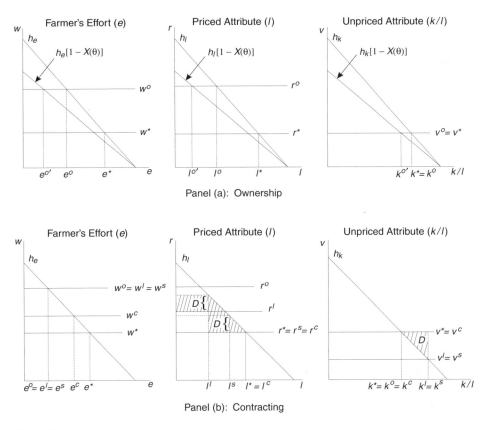

Figure 8.1
Optimal inputs with ownership and contracting

The first-order necessary conditions are

$$h_e[1 - X(\theta)] = w^o \tag{8.2}$$

$$h_l[1 - X(\theta)] = r^o \tag{8.3}$$

$$h_k[1 - X(\theta)] = v^*. \tag{8.4}$$

The right-hand side of each equation is the marginal cost of each input for an (unspecialized) owner of the farm. The left-hand side of each equation is the marginal product faced by the owner who borrows. This marginal product is less than the true marginal product because the term in square brackets is the probability (less than one) that the farmer has a crop that can pay off the loan. Because of the shift in marginal products caused by borrowing, these first-order conditions imply that the farmer uses less effort and fewer units of the asset when the asset is financed through a loan. In effect, the limited liability faced by the farmer means that he farms in a way that lowers the value of the farm in all states of the world. One can imagine a farmer reducing the amount of effort in timing planting and harvesting carefully, for example.

Facing higher costs of ownership from a combination of forgone specialization gains and lower marginal products from the neglect of assets works to lower the value of the ownership governance structure. These results are also shown in the top panel of figure 8.1, where it is clear that input levels are lower than without borrowing: $e^{o'} < e^o < e^*$, $l^{o'} < l^o < l^*$, and $k^{o'} < k^* = k^o$. The value of this governance structure will be $V(e^{o'}, l^{o'}, k^{o'})$.[15]

Contracting for Assets

With contracting the farmer exchanges greater specialization (in effort and asset use) and fewer capital constraints, for the costs of moral hazard (in effort and asset use) and timeliness in the coordination of all inputs. The magnitude of these costs depends on whether the contract is simple or custom, and whether the contract is short- or long-term. In a simple contract, there will be asset moral hazard. In a custom contract there will be no asset moral hazard but there will be effort moral hazard; that is, the operator will shirk. In a short-term contract timeliness costs will be present, but they are absent in long-term contracts. Long-term contracts do not necessarily mean multiple-year contracts because long-term simply means the contract period extends beyond the dates of the relevant season.

Simple Long-Term Contracts (Case 5). With long-term contracts the most efficient size of asset is used and the rental rate falls from r^o to r^l. Still the asset is available for a period at least as long as the season it is required, so there will be periods of unemployment for the asset, and this prevents the marginal cost from equaling the first-best rental rate, r^*. Without a specialized operator for the asset the marginal costs of effort are not minimized, so that $w^o = w^l > w^*$.

Figure 8.1, bottom panel, shows the input choices for this contract. Because the farmer does not own the asset, he faces a lower cost of using the unpriced attribute ($v^l < v^*$), which leads to overuse of the asset ($k^l > k^*$). This causes a deadweight loss per unit of the unpriced attribute equal to area D.[16] With competitive markets for assets, this cost is incorporated in the cost (price) of the priced attribute and drives a wedge of vertical distance D between r^l and h_l, and it creates a full price of $r^l + D$ and a total deadweight cost equal to the hatched area (rectangle plus triangle). The value of this governance structure will be $V^l(e^l, l^l, k^l)$.

Simple Short-Term Contract (Case 4). The advantage of a short-term contract is that an asset may be rented only for the stage(s) it is required, and need not be unemployed on the farm. Since a short-term contract can fully exploit asset specialization and avoid downtime, the marginal cost of the asset's priced attribute (l) is at its lowest level, so that $r^s = r^*$. The cost of exploiting the unpriced attribute (k) remains the same for short and long-term simple leases, so that $k^l = k^s > k^*$. Since the moral hazard on k again creates a per-unit deadweight loss of area D, a wedge is driven between r^s and h_l of distance D, such that the full cost of short-term renting is $r^s + D$. This leads to l^s asset usage where $l^l < l^s < l^*$. Finally, because the farmer is not a specialized operator, the costs of effort are $w^s = w^l > w^*$, which leads to less than the first-best level of effort, or $e^s < e^*$.

A short-term contract also offers the potential for timeliness costs, which have long been recognized in the agricultural literature. For example, in a well-known agricultural finance book, Nelson, Lee, and Murray (1973) state, "One of the most important disadvantages of operating leases, such as custom hiring, is that the machine may not be available when needed. Crop losses arising from delayed harvest can be very costly" (88).[17] There is, for instance, an optimal time to plant a crop, and deviating from it lowers the eventual output, often at an increasing rate. Moreover, the optimal time to employ the controllable inputs is uncertain. Weather, pests, and other natural forces make it nearly impossible to know the optimal time until it is upon the farmer. For example, when deciding when to harvest wheat, farmers test the grain daily for moisture content and pay close attention to weather forecasts. The combination of uncertainty over the optimal time and significant timeliness costs dramatically increases the costs of specifying ex ante the correct delivery date for a contracted input.

Timeliness costs change the production function and can be examined with a simple modification to our production framework. Let d be the date for which e, l, and k are employed during a particular stage (for example, planting) of length L. L indicates the period for which output is positive given an application of effort and asset use. Numerous studies of crop production have shown that output is approximately quadratic in the delivery of all inputs to a particular stage of production (see Nass, Gupta, and Sterling 1973; Kay and Edwards 1994, 416–417). Thus, in a simple quadratic framework, where $q(d) = (d - (d^2/L))[h(e, l, k, \theta)]$, the optimal time is $d^* = L/2$—the midpoint of the stage. The actual date d chosen, however, is constrained by the contract period established ex ante by the two parties for the delivery of l and k.

Figure 8.2 shows the relationship of timeliness to output and shows how timeliness costs may arise with contracting. Ex ante, the farmer and asset owner choose a delivery date of $\bar{d} = (\bar{L} + \bar{d}_0)/2$, where $\bar{L}$ is the expected length of the stage and $\bar{d}_0$ is the expected beginning of the stage. In this case, $\bar{q}$ is the output that would be produced if there were no change in beginning or length of the stage. Even this output, $\bar{q}$, is not first best because of the other incentive and specialization effects discussed above. In general, the entire $q(d)$ function will lie below an unattainable first-best $q(d)$ function. Ex post, however, this particular date may not be optimal given the realized values of d^0 and L.

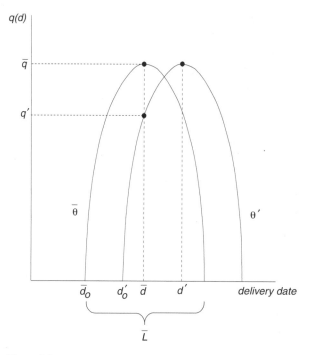

Figure 8.2
Timeliness costs with asset contracting

Figure 8.2 shows the simple case in which the stage length does not differ from its expectation ($L = \bar{L}$) but begins later, at $d_0' > \bar{d}_0$. The optimal time might also change because of changes in the stage length (L), changes in the relationship between output and time ($q = q(d)$), or various combinations of these and changes in the time at which the stage begins. We also ignore the possibility that use of the asset takes place over several days rather than a single day. The ex post optimal delivery time is now $d' > \bar{d}$, which would still generate the optimal output $\bar{q}$. However, because the contract specifies delivery at $\bar{d}$, the output will be reduced to $q' < \bar{q}$. Depending on how sensitive this particular stage is to the timing of asset use, output could be drastically reduced or hardly affected. Figure 8.2 shows a reduction in output by roughly 25 percent from optimal. In the worst case, the entire stage could shift so far that the output, for the contracted time ($\bar{d}$), could be zero. The size of these timeliness costs varies dramatically across crops and across stages for a given crop. Some implications of this variance are examined in our empirical analysis.

With the addition of timeliness costs to the model, first-best input levels require not only specialization and perfect incentives but also optimal timing in their application. Short-term contracting will make such timing quite costly. We assume that timeliness costs do not interact with any other incentive effects, so the value of this governance structure is the expected value of using the input levels (e^s, l^s and k^s) in the presence of timeliness costs:

$$V^s(e^s, l^s, k^s) = \int_\theta x(\theta)[\bar{d} - \bar{d}^2/L][h(e^s, l^s, k^s) + \theta - e^s w^s - l^s r^s - k^s v^s]\, d\theta. \tag{8.5}$$

Custom Short-Term Contract (Case 2). The main alternative to the simple short-term lease is a custom short-term contract. In this contract, the asset owner provides a specialized operator for a period that may not exactly coincide with the crop production stage. Timeliness costs, however, remain. With a specialized asset and operator marginal costs are as low as possible, or $r^c = r^*$, and $v^c = v^*$. Asset moral hazard is eliminated because the farmer cannot exploit the asset with the operator present, so the first-best levels of the priced and unpriced attributes are chosen (l^*, k^* in figure 8.1, bottom panel). The choice of effort is not, however, first-best because the farmer—not the operator—owns the crop causing effort moral hazard. Thus, even though the operator is specialized the farmer must engage in some type of monitoring that makes $w^c > w*$ and effort less than first-best ($e^c < e^*$). The trade-off under a custom contract is clear: Gains from specialized assets and effort must be weighed against effort moral hazard and timeliness costs. The value of the custom contract, $V^c(e^c, l^c, k^c)$, is calculated in the same way as in the simple short-term lease (equation (8.5)), and is given by

$$V^c(e^c, l^c, k^c) = \int_\theta x(\theta)[\bar{d} - \bar{d}^2/L][h(e^c, l^*, k^*) + \theta - e^c w^* - l^* r^* - k^* v^*]\, d\theta. \tag{8.6}$$

Comparative Statics of Asset Control Regimes

Table 8.2 summarizes the incentives inherent in the asset control regimes examined above. As the analysis shows, no single option is globally superior and the first-best output is not possible. Our presumption is that the existing arrangements are chosen to maximize the net value of the farm. This leads to the following general propositions:

PREDICTION 8.1a   The greater the asset moral hazard costs, the more likely ownership and custom operation will be chosen.

PREDICTION 8.1b   When contracting dominates ownership, simple leases are more likely to be chosen as effort moral hazard costs increase, and custom leases are more likely to be chosen as asset moral hazard costs increase.

PREDICTION 8.2a   The greater the gains from labor and asset specialization the more likely contracting will be chosen.

PREDICTION 8.2b   When contracting dominates ownership, custom leases are more likely to be chosen as the gains from effort specialization increase.

Table 8.2
Incentives under various ownership and contracting regimes

	Effort moral hazard	Asset moral hazard	Effort specialization	Asset specialization	Timeliness costs	Capital constraints
Ownership						
Pure family farm	No	No	No	No	No	No
Family farm (borrowing)	No	No	No	No	No	Yes
Contracting						
Short-term custom contract	Yes	No	Yes	Yes	Yes	No
Short-term simple contract	No	Yes	No	Yes	Yes	No
Long-term simple contract	No	Yes	No	Yes	No	No

PREDICTION 8.3a   The greater the timeliness costs, the more likely ownership will be chosen.

PREDICTION 8.3b   When contracting dominates ownership, long-term leases are more likely to be chosen as timeliness costs increase.

PREDICTION 8.4   The greater the capital constraints, the more likely contracting will be chosen.

Because our model in this chapter examines five situations—cases 1 (with two types), 2, 4, and 5—and incorporates several incentive margins, it is not possible to unambiguously rank each of the possible regimes as incentive effects change. This ambiguity arises because it is impossible to compare the magnitudes of various effects without explicit structure on moral hazard costs, specialization gains, timeliness costs, and capital constraints. Instead, we use our general propositions to generate specific empirical predictions. In our applications, reality has narrowed the selection of actual asset control choices, often to simple dichotomies that allow clear comparison of key incentive effects. In particular, in our econometric analysis we examine the choice between owning and leasing assets such as buildings, equipment, and land.

8.3   Empirical Analysis: Owning versus Contracting

In this section we test some of the implications derived from our model of asset control. The costs of contracting and ownership are determined by specific factors like location, crop, and type of contract, which we examine in the context of the model. In the process we identify variables that proxy the key factors in our model: moral hazard losses, specialization gains, timeliness costs, and capital constraints. The list and definitions of variables used in this chapter are provided in table 8.3.

Our empirical analysis has two parts. First, using logit regressions, we use the British Columbia–Louisiana data to estimate the factors that influence the choice between asset ownership and asset contracting.[18] Second, we examine custom combining on the Great Plains using historical and contemporary case study information. Custom combining is the most prevalent type of custom contract in modern agriculture, so its study is important.

With our contract data from British Columbia and Louisiana, we use the following empirical specification, where for any asset i the complete model is

$$A_i^* = X_i \beta_i + \epsilon_i \quad i = 1, \ldots, n; \quad \text{and} \tag{8.7}$$

$$A_i = \begin{cases} 1, & \text{if } A_i^* > 0 \\ 0, & \text{if } A_i^* \le 0, \end{cases} \tag{8.8}$$

where A_i^* is an unobserved farmland ownership response variable; A_i is the observed dichotomous choice of asset ownership for plot i, which is equal to 1 when an asset (land, equipment, or building) is leased and equal to 0 when the asset is owned; X_i is a row vector of exogenous variables including the constant; β_i is a column vector of unknown coefficients; and ϵ_i is a plot-specific error term. We use a logit model to generate maximum likelihood estimates of the model given by equations 8.7 and 8.8 for various contract samples.

Land: Ownership versus Contracting

As we have noted many times, the choice of land control is between ownership and a simple long-term contract. Not all of the incentives identified in table 8.2 are relevant to the decision to own or lease land. In particular, effort moral hazard, asset specialization, and timeliness costs are not likely to be important since there is no specialized operator for land as there is for equipment, and since land is leased for a minimum of a year. Capital constraints, effort specialization, and asset moral hazard are the most important incentives that determine land control.

Increases in capital constraints are predicted to increase the probability of leasing. In our model, capital constraints arise when the farmer does not have the wealth to guarantee the purchase of the asset. In our econometric estimates we measure wealth in two ways. WEALTH is equal to the combined value of land, buildings, and equipment belonging to the farmer. NET WEALTH is the value of buildings and equipment.[19] Effort specialization can influence the ownership versus lease decision for land. The lower the amount of specialized human capital (farming skills), the more likely a landowner will lease out his land. We use a dummy variable, LANDOWNER HUMAN CAPITAL, that identifies landowners who

Table 8.3
Definition of variables

Dependent variables

RENTED BUILDING   = 1 if building was rented; = 0 if owned.
RENTED LAND   = 1 if land was rented; = 0 if owned.
RENTED EQUIPMENT   = 1 if equipment was rented; = 0 if owned.

Independent variables

ACRES   = number of acres covered by contract.
AGE   = farmer's age in years.
BUILDING VALUE   = total value in $1,000s of all owned buildings multiplied by
                              the equity in the farm.
BUILDING AGE   = age in years.
BUILDING SIZE   = square foot of building.
CROP VALUE   = value of crop in dollars.
EDUCATION   = number of years of formal schooling.
EQUIPMENT VALUE   = total value in $1,000s of all owned equipment multiplied by
                              the equity in the farm.
FARM SALES   = gross revenue for 1992 in $100,000 of sales.
GRAINS   = 1 if crop is wheat, barley, oats, or other small grain;
                           = 0 otherwise.
GENERAL BUILDINGS   = 1 if building was a house or garage; 0 otherwise.
HAY   = 1 if a grass crops was the major income producing crop;
                           = 0 otherwise.
IRRIGATED   = 1 if land is irrigated; = 0 if dryland.
LANDOWNER HUMAN CAPITAL   = 1 if not farming, never a farmer, or a widow; = 0 otherwise.
MULTIPLE EQUIPMENT   = 1 if second or third truck or tractor;
                           = 0 if only one piece of equipment.
NET WEALTH   = WEALTH minus the value of either land, equipment, or
                              buildings, depending on the regression.
PASTURE   = 1 if land was used for grazing;
                           = 0 if land not used for grazing.
ROW CROP   = 1 if row crop (corn, sugar beets, sugarcane soybeans,
                              sorghum);
                           = 0 if not a row crop (wheat, oats, barley).
SHARED EQUIPMENT   = 1 if equipment is shared with another farmer;
                           = 0 if not shared.
SPECIALIZED EQUIPMENT   = 1 if harvest, planting, or crop specific equipment;
                           = 0 if equipment is general purpose.
TREES   = 1 if fruit was grown (e.g., apples, pears, etc.);
                           = 0 if no fruit was grown.
WEALTH   = total value of all owned buildings, equipment, and land
                              multiplied by the equity in the farm.
WORKERS   = number of different workers on farm in 1992.

---

have low human capital—that is, when a landowner is either a widow, is not farming, or has never farmed.

As we have argued in the previous chapters, asset moral hazard for land means exploitation of soil, long-lived crops, and irrigation systems. Land leases are designed to mitigate asset moral hazard, but in many cases ownership is a more economical response than detailed contracts with large enforcement costs. Asset moral hazard costs are generally going to be high when a crop has several different dimensions of moral hazard that are not easily handled in a simple contract, and when a specific moral hazard cost is very large.

Multiple moral hazard costs often arise with crops that involve trees and pruning. For example, timber farms, orchards, most nut farms, vineyards, and the like all require the planting of trees that produce output over time. With these crops, pruning is critical for a sustained high-quality harvest. For fruits, output is temporarily higher if no pruning occurs, but eventually the inner part of the tree ceases to produce and the fruit-bearing surface area begins to diminish. To curb this, the leasing agreements tend to be share contracts because they encourage proper pruning.[20] With many fruits, this leads to a second moral hazard cost. A share contract provides an incentive to underreport the quality and quantity of fruit. Unreported fruit can be sold in secondary markets and roadside stands. More important, the farmer may accurately report the volume of fruit but underreport the quality. The low quality sent to the landowner ends up in the canned goods market, while the high-quality fruit kept by the farmer is sold in the more lucrative fresh fruit market. We use the dummy variable TREES to identify these crops.

A second case of multiple asset moral hazard exists for hay crops. These crops have the potential for crop underreporting and for suboptimal crop maintenance. Since hay crops are easily stored, fed to cattle, and sold through various outlets, sharing the crop is seldom feasible. By contracting with cash rent contracts this incentive is eliminated. Compared to a grain crop, a hay crop is a capital asset that requires maintenance over several years. If the crop is not controlled for weeds it loses value and eventually must be replaced. A cash rent contract, of course, creates an incentive for the farmer to exploit the short-term value of the crop by running down the value of the crop capital stock. Our dummy variable HAY identifies those grass crops with multiple asset moral hazard.

Some land assets may not have multiple moral hazard costs, but the single moral hazard cost may be severe. Land used for row crops, such as corn and soybeans, is particularly susceptible to soil exploitation because these crops have large short-term benefits from cultivation and pesticide applications. Irrigated land has more potential for asset exploitation because of the irrigation equipment attached to the land that can be damaged by a leasing farmer who does not face the full costs of using and maintaining the irrigation system. Irrigated land will be more valuable than nonirrigated land, but still there are unpriced attributes such as the maintained quality of the pipes, ditches, wells, and related equipment.

In addition, the farmer could deplete the water resource or may contribute to soil salinization. Pastureland creates an incentive for overgrazing. Overgrazing might be mitigated with a share contract, but sharing live animals is difficult and infrequent given the costs of measuring the livestock characteristics. Pasture is distinct from hay land in that pasture is not cultivated and harvested like alfalfa and other hay crops. We use the dummy variables ROW CROP, PASTURE, and IRRIGATION to identify crops with asset exploitation incentives.

Grain crops generate incentive effects distinct from those mentioned above. Grain crops are less susceptible to moral hazard because limited cultivation reduces the potential for soil exploitation compared to row crops. Also, because grains are sold in markets where third party measurement occurs, there is a reduced potential for crop theft compared to grasses and tree crops. We thus predict that land used for grain crops is more likely leased than land used for nongrain crops. In our regressions we include a dummy variable (GRAINS) that identifies these crops.

Finally, effort specialization can influence the ownership—contract decision for land. The lower the amount of specialized human capital (farming skills), the more likely a landowner will lease out his land. We use a dummy variable—LANDOWNER HUMAN CAPITAL— which identifies landowners that have low human capital.

Table 8.4 presents the logit coefficient estimates from two separate equations. Each of the 1,573 observations is a single plot of land, either leased or owned by the farmer. The variables are organized into those measuring capital constraints, asset moral hazard, effort specialization, and other controls. The coefficients estimates for WEALTH and NET WEALTH are both negative and statistically significant. These estimates provide evidence that capital constraints lead to more leasing of land. The coefficient estimates for IRRIGATED, ROW CROP, HAY, PASTURE, and TREES all have the expected sign and are statistically significant. Land with multiple moral hazard costs or single but severe moral hazard costs is less likely to be leased. The estimated coefficient for LANDOWNER HUMAN CAPITAL is positive and statistically significant, indicating that land leasing is more likely when the landowner lacks specialized farming skills.[21] The estimated coefficient for GRAINS is not significantly different from zero, so we find no support for the prediction that grain crops are more likely to be associated with leased land.

Table 8.4 also shows the coefficient estimates for several control variables. ACRES and CROP VALUE control for the size and value of the farmland plot. The estimated coefficients indicate that the size of the land plot has little impact on the decision to lease or own land. The CROP VALUE estimates, however, indicate that the higher valued crops are more likely to be leased. EDUCATION measures the farmer's formal education. The estimated coefficients indicate that increases in farmer education increase the probability of leasing land. WORKERS indicates the number of laborers on the entire farm. The estimated coefficients indicate that this has no impact on the lease-own decision for land.

Table 8.4
Logit regression estimates of land control choice: British Columbia and Louisiana (1992)
(dependent variable = 1 if land is leased; = 0 if land is owned)

Independent variables			Predicted sign
CONSTANT	−0.684	−0.68	
	(−1.72)	(−1.73)	
Capital constraints			
WEALTH	−0.02		−
	(−1.50)		
NET WEALTH		−0.06	−
		(−1.74)*	
Asset moral hazard			
GRAINS	−0.11	−0.07	+
	(−0.59)	(−0.40)	
HAY	−2.71	−2.69	−
	(−7.14)*	(−7.10)*	
IRRIGATION	−0.327	−0.368	−
	(−2.29)*	(−2.37)*	
PASTURE	−2.60	−2.57	−
	(−4.79)*	(−4.73)*	
ROW CROP	−0.429	−0.42	−
	(−2.14)*	(−2.09)*	
TREES	−3.17	−3.18	−
	(−6.61)*	(−6.67)*	
Effort specialization			
LANDOWNER HUMAN CAPITAL	11.82	11.82	+
	(1.54)	(1.54)	
Controls			
ACRES	0.000	0.000	
	(1.18)	(1.18)	
CROP VALUE	0.001	0.001	
	(1.62)	(1.62)	
EDUCATION	0.04	0.05	
	(1.71)	(1.73)	
WORKERS	0.016	0.02	
	(0.63)	(0.71)	
% correct predictions	77.7	78.1	
Log likelihood	−607	−606.5	
Model χ^2 (df)	961 (13)	962 (13)	
Number of observations	1,573	1,573	

Note: t-statistics in parentheses.
* significant at the 5 percent level (one-tailed test for coefficient with predicted signs).

Equipment: Ownership versus Contracting

For the data we examine, the choice of equipment control regimes is between ownership and a simple long-term contract. When farmers rent equipment such as combines and tractors, they are typically charged by the hour or some other unit of time (for example, day, week, month).[22] Like land, many attributes of leased equipment remain unpriced although the lease typically assigns responsibility for equipment maintenance. Equipment leases are usually written and usually last less than a year. Most long-term (greater than one year) equipment leases have options to buy (Pflueger 1994). As with land, not all of the incentives identified in table 8.2 are relevant for equipment. Asset moral hazard, capital constraints, and timeliness costs are the most important incentives. To a lesser degree, asset specialization is a factor.

Again like land, increases in capital constraints are predicted to increase the probability of leasing. Many pieces of equipment are at least as expensive as a substantial plot of land. For example, a half section (320 acres) of dry wheat land may be worth $128,000 at $400 per acre. Still, a large modern combine or tractor would easily be worth more than $100,000. As with land, we measure wealth using WEALTH (the combined value of land, buildings, and equipment) and NET WEALTH (value of buildings and land).

Timeliness costs are likely to be an important determinant of equipment control in farming. Equipment is seldom rented for an entire season and is often rented for only a particular stage of production. For certain kinds of equipment, during crucial stages, timeliness costs arise because other farmers demand the equipment at the same time. Even in a custom contract, when the equipment owner is in control, he influences the arrival of the equipment and may arrive too early or too late depending on other commitments. Our model implies that increases in timeliness costs will decrease the probability of contracting for assets. In order to test this prediction against our equipment data, we need to distinguish situations with varying levels of timeliness costs. We use three variables, one that measures the number of pieces of similar equipment a farmer owns, one that measures the shared equipment, and one that measures the degree to which a piece of equipment is specialized.

Farmers often use multiple pieces of the same or similar machines (for example, combines, tractors, trucks). Although these pieces of equipment are used on the farm, in terms of timing the first piece is the most important. In other words, it is more important to own one tractor than to own an additional one in order to plant or harvest a crop when Mother Nature's window of opportunity opens. A dummy variable MULTIPLE EQUIPMENT identifies farmers who own additional pieces of the same machine and is predicted to be positively correlated with the probability of leasing. When a farmer shares equipment with a neighbor, the equipment almost certainly has no timing problems because the neighbor faces the same seasonal situation as the farmer. A dummy variable SHARED

EQUIPMENT identifies these types of equipment and is predicted to be positively correlated with the probability of leasing. A farmer may need only two tractors in an average season, but every now and then a bumper crop or severe weather requires additional machines. Equipment that is specialized to a crop (for example, a cherry picker) or to a specific stage (for example, planting, harvest) is more likely to have high timeliness costs with contracting. A dummy variable SPECIALIZED EQUIPMENT identifies planting and harvesting equipment, as well as other equipment that is crop specific, and is used to measure timeliness costs.

Table 8.5 presents the logit coefficient estimates from two separate equations. Each of the 4,961 observations is a single piece of farm equipment (for example, combines, cultivators, sprayers, tractors, trucks), either leased or owned by the farmer. Like the land equations, the dependent variable equals one if the equipment is rented and zero if owned. The independent variables are organized into those measuring capital constraints, asset moral hazard, timeliness costs, and other controls. The coefficient estimates for WEALTH and NET WEALTH are both negative and statistically significant. All of these estimates are consistent with our prediction that equipment leasing is more likely to occur when capital constraints are pressing.

In table 8.5 the estimated coefficients for all measures of timeliness costs support our predictions. The estimated coefficient for MULTIPLE EQUIPMENT is positive and statistically significant, indicating that farmers with additional pieces of a machine are more likely to lease. Likewise, the coefficient for SHARED EQUIPMENT is also positive and statistically significant. The estimated coefficient for SPECIALIZED EQUIPMENT is negative and statistically significant, indicating that specialized machinery is less likely to be leased.[23] More generally, because timeliness costs are not important for land we predict that land leasing will be more prevalent than equipment leasing (even for assets with approximately the same value). Indeed, in our data we find 48 percent of the land plots were leased but only 2 percent of the equipment is leased.

Table 8.5 also shows the coefficient estimates for several control variables. FARM SALES and ACRES control for the size and value of the farm. The estimated coefficients indicate that larger farms are more likely to lease equipment. We also use the value of the equipment in question (EQUIPMENT VALUE) to control for the value of the asset, and find the coefficient estimates are positive and statistically significant. The estimated coefficients for EDUCATION are significantly different from zero, indicating that farmer education has a positive effect on leasing equipment. The estimated coefficients for WORKERS show that farms with more workers are more likely to lease equipment. Unfortunately we have no clear empirical measures of asset moral hazard (for example, exploitation of the machinery by the farmer because of improper use or inattentive maintenance).

Table 8.5
Logit regression estimates of equipment control choice: British Columbia and Louisiana (1992)
(dependent variable = 1 if equipment is leased; = 0 if equipment is owned)

Independent variables			Predicted sign
CONSTANT	−3.99	−3.99	
	(−5.65)*	(−5.65)*	
Capital constraints			
WEALTH	−1.04		−
	(−8.63)*		
NET WEALTH		−1.06	−
		(−6.02)*	
Timeliness costs			
MULTIPLE EQUIPMENT	.81	.82	+
	(3.16)*	(3.18)*	
SPECIALIZED EQUIPMENT	−0.60	−0.61	−
	(−2.22)*	(−2.20)*	
SHARED EQUIPMENT	1.90	1.91	+
	(6.96)*	(6.96)*	
Controls			
ACRES	.000	.000	
	(2.82)*	(2.82)*	
EDUCATION	0.12	0.13	
	(2.82)*	(2.83)*	
EQUIPMENT VALUE	2.08	1.04	
	(6.45)*	(3.35)*	
FARM SALES	0.15	0.16	
	(6.71)*	(6.71)*	
WORKERS	0.18	0.18	
	(6.14)*	(6.14)*	
% correct predictions	98.3	98.3	
Log likelihood	−300	−300	
Model χ^2 (df)	339 (10)	339 (10)	
Number of observations	4,961	4,961	

Note: t-statistics in parentheses.
* significant at the 5 percent level (one-tailed test for coefficient with predicted signs).

Buildings: Ownership versus Contracting

The choice of building control regimes is also a choice between ownership and a simple long-term contract. Buildings are often rented with land and tend to be rented for one year on cash rent terms. Like land and equipment, many attributes of buildings remain unpriced. Again, not all of the incentives identified in table 8.2 are relevant for buildings. Asset moral hazard and capital constraints are the most important incentives. As with land, timeliness costs are not a factor since the typical lease arrangement spans well beyond any seasonal dates.

Like land and equipment, increases in capital constraints are predicted to increase the probability of leasing for buildings. Again, we measure wealth using WEALTH (the combined value of land, buildings, and equipment) and NET WEALTH (value of land and equipment).

For buildings, asset moral hazard means exploitation of the structure because of overuse, improper use, and suboptimal maintenance. We use several variables to measure differences in asset moral hazard costs. First, we use BUILDING AGE because older buildings will be less susceptible to damages by the farmer. Second, we use a dummy GENERAL BUILDING to distinguish those buildings that have a very narrow use. Specialized buildings (for example, storage bins) are seemingly easier to monitor given that the owner of the building would be aware of the depreciation that should normally occur under the specific use. Moral hazard costs with specialized buildings are lower because they tend to be used for single purposes, and it is often very costly to use them for something else. For example, storage bins are uninhabitable.

Unlike our estimates for land and equipment, for buildings we are able to include a variable that measures specific assets. RENTED LAND is a dummy that indicates whether or not the land on which a building sits is rented or owned. When land is owned (rented), we predict that the building is also more (less) likely to be owned because the two assets (land and building) are specific to each other.

Table 8.6 presents the logit coefficient estimates from two separate equations. Each of the 1,938 observations is a single farm building (for example, barn, garage, grainery, machine shop), either leased or owned by the farmer. Like the land and equipment equations, the dependent variable equals one if the buildings is rented and zero if owned. The independent variables are organized into those measuring capital constraints, asset moral hazard, specific assets, and other controls.

The coefficient estimates for WEALTH and NET WEALTH are both negative and statistically significant. These estimates are consistent with our model that equipment leasing is more likely to occur as capital constraints increase. Our model is also strongly supported by the coefficient estimates for the asset moral hazard variables—BUILDING AGE and GENERAL BUILDING. They all have the predicted sign and all are statistically significant.

Table 8.6
Logit regression coefficient estimates of building control choice: British Columbia and Louisiana (1992)
(dependent variable = 1 if building is leased; = 0 if building is owned)

Independent variable			Predicted sign
CONSTANT	−7.14	−7.14	
	(−8.55)*	(−8.55)*	
Capital constraints			
WEALTH	−0.29		−
	(−5.84)*		
NET WEALTH		−0.29	−
		(−5.84)*	
Asset moral hazard			
BUILDING AGE	0.02	0.02	+
	(4.74)*	(4.74)*	
GENERAL BUILDINGS	−0.94	−0.94	−
	(−3.15)*	(−3.15)*	
Specific assets			
RENTED LAND	3.76	3.76	+
	(6.06)*	(6.06)*	
Controls			
BUILDING VALUE	−1.04	−1.33	
	(−2.52)*	(−3.26)*	
BUILDING SIZE	0.04	0.04	
	(4.21)*	(4.21)*	
EDUCATION	0.15	0.15	
	(3.74)*	(3.74)*	
FARM SALES	0.11	0.11	
	(3.41)*	(3.41)*	
WORKERS	0.01	0.01	
	(0.32)	(0.32)	
% correct predictions	93.6	93.6	
Log likelihood	−332.9	−332.9	
Model χ^2 (df)	314 (10)	314 (10)	
Number of observations	1,938	1,938	

Note: t-statistics in parentheses.
* significant at the 5 percent level (one-tailed test for coefficient with predicted signs).

Valuable general-use buildings are less likely to be leased because they are more susceptible to exploitation by the farmer. Older buildings are more likely to be leased. The estimated coefficient for RENTED LAND, which is positive and statistically significant, supports our predictions about the role of specific assets.

Table 8.6 also shows the coefficient estimates for several control variables. FARM SALES controls for the size and value of the farm. The estimated coefficients indicate that farm size is positively related to building leasing. The estimated coefficients for EDUCATION are positive and statistically significant. The estimated coefficient for WORKERS indicates that the number of farm workers has no impact on the probability of leasing buildings. BUILDING SIZE (positively related to leasing) and BUILDING VALUE (negatively related to leasing) are used as controls. BUILDING VALUE might be interpreted as a moral hazard variable. For example, more valuable buildings are more costly to lease because their damage is great.

Summary of Econometric Evidence

Our econometric analysis of leasing versus ownership for buildings, equipment, and land generally supports our model of asset control. All of our estimates support our prediction about the role of capital constraints on the probability of ownership.[24] Variables measuring asset moral hazard are important for buildings and land. For equipment, however, asset moral hazard is less important while estimates of the effects of our measure of timeliness costs support our model. Although these estimates give support to our model, they have two limits. First, most of the variables do not precisely measure incentive effects but rather are reasonable approximations of conditions under which these incentive effects vary. Second, these estimates examined only a subset of the possible asset control regimes, completely ignoring custom contracts that are increasingly common in modern farming. Because of these limits we now turn to a case study examination of custom wheat harvesting.

Custom Combining: A Case Study of Short-Term Custom Leasing

Custom contracting has long been a part of agriculture.[25] Farmers hire custom firms for baling, cultivating, fertilizer and pesticide application, feed grinding, fencing, hauling, land clearing, planting, plowing, and seed cleaning (Strickler, Smith, and Walker 1966). By far, the most historically significant custom contracting is for grain harvesting. And by far the most important custom grain harvesting is the 1,000 mile south-north migration of wheat harvesters that takes place on the Great Plains. A 1971 study by the USDA showed that nearly 3,500 custom cutters harvested 35 percent of the wheat on the Great Plains (Lagrone and Gavett 1975). In 1997, roughly 2,000 custom cutters harvested one-half of the nations wheat crop (DuBow 1999). Overall, however, all custom work comprises just 2 percent of all U.S. farm expenses.[26] Although some cutters work only locally, more than 90 percent make the long interstate journeys. In this section we examine the historical development and modern organization of custom combining on the Great Plains and show that the conditions under which these contracts are used reflect the trade-offs derived in our model.

History and Organization. Custom combiners, also called "custom cutters" and "wheaties," emerged on the Great Plains in the 1920s shortly after the combine replaced binders, reapers, and threshing machines.[27] By cutting and threshing the grain all at once, the combine merged the tasks of several men into one step performed by just one man operating a single machine. The main effect of this was to drastically shorten the length of the harvest season, to as little as two or three weeks for wheat. The old system of reaping and threshing allowed a farmer to cut the grain before it was ripe and thresh it weeks, or even months, later. Effective use of the combine, however, required the grain to be harvested when it was ripe, no sooner and no later. Unripe grain causes heat in storage and could spoil grain or even catch fire. If the grain is too ripe, it becomes brittle and breaks on cutting and is lost. Moreover, standing grain is subject to the potentially devastating threats of hail, rain, and wind. In addition, the combine allowed a farmer to harvest his own grain and had a radical effect on the organization of farms at harvest.[28] In particular, farmers took charge of harvest operations themselves rather than hiring or joining large threshing crews. Even as farmers switched to combines from reapers and threshers, many farmers hired custom combiners from the beginning of their use in the 1920s, but most of these contractors were locals. Outside of custom combining, most custom farm work is now highly localized. In the 1940s, improvements such as rubber tires, self-propulsion, and better roads spurred the modern migration of combines, trucks, and crews north as wheat ripens on the plains.

Since the 1940s custom combiners have begun their migrations by harvesting Texas winter wheat in May and ending with spring wheat in September/October in Montana, North Dakota, or Saskatchewan. The key states where custom cutting is important are Colorado, Kansas, Montana, Nebraska, North Dakota, Oklahoma, South Dakota, and Texas. The vast majority of custom crews have the following basic structure. A custom cutting outfit is a family-based business usually with a husband running the crew, a wife handling cooking, and teenage kids operating some machinery.[29] Invariably other hands are hired to operate machinery, so that a typical crew is comprised of from eight to twelve people. Hired workers are paid monthly wages and have their room and board provided by the crew. The firms are primarily sole proprietorships, but there are some simple partnerships, usually between husbands and wives, fathers and sons, or brothers. The crew has from two to four self-propelled combines (each worth over $150,000), several grain trucks and/or grain carts, a couple of pickup trucks (to carry fuel and other supplies), and a trailer house or two for living and cooking. The crew may travel over 1,000 miles north and harvest more than 15,000 acres of wheat in a season that can last more than five months. Some crews extend this season by harvesting corn later in the fall on the return trip south. The crew will stop at between five and ten farms, working for several weeks at each before packing up and moving north. Cutters often follow the same routes for years, returning again and again to the same farms. Most crews are based in Kansas, Oklahoma, and Texas, but others are based in the northern states and provinces, heading south in May and working their way back home in time for their own harvest.

The contracts between custom combiners and farmers have a structure that dates back to the 1940s when the industry had its first major expansion. Since that time cutters have been paid according to a three-part formula that includes a per-acre fee for cutting, a per-bushel fee for hauling grain to a local storage site, and a per-bushel fee for high-yield crops (usually over 20 bushels per acre). Today the typical contract is "13/13/13" which means: $13 per acre of harvested wheat, 13 cents per bushel hauled, and 13 cents per bushel added to the per-acre charge for high yields.[30] In unusual cases—drought, hail, long hauls, or wind—special harvest rates would be developed to suit both parties.

As with agricultural contracts in general, farmers and cutters rely heavily on verbal agreements, enforced with handshakes and the possibility of renewal. As Isern (1981) notes: The custom cutter who failed to live up to his obligations to a farmer found it hard to obtain work in the locality the next year. Likewise, if a farmer reneged on an agreement, the word spread among custom cutters working the area, and the farmer might be left with no harvesters at all" (92). This discussion is consistent with the earlier analysis of reputation discussed in chapter 3.

Incentives and Implications.   In our framework, custom combining is a classic example of a short-term custom contract (case 2) and thus must be examined in the context of the incentives present in such an arrangement. Foremost among these are specialization gains, moral hazard costs, and timeliness costs. By focusing on these incentives, we are able to show the economic logic of custom combining and indirectly confront some implications of our model. We do this by illustrating how these incentives are manifest in custom combining and by explaining subtle variation in the use and form of custom combining contracts.

The benefit of contracting for custom combining is, of course, derived from intensively using highly specialized equipment with skilled operators. Most wheat farmers only use their own combines for at most twenty days each year. A custom cutter could, however, by moving north with the ripening wheat, use his combines from 100 to 150 days each year. Custom cutters use their combines intensively and buy new machines every two or three years, whereas most farmers keep their own combines for a decade or more. Williams (1953) notes these tremendous gains to specialized equipment: "The economic keynote of the cutters' activities is the ability to get maximum utilization of their expensive and complicated specialized machinery, as they follow the progressive ripening pattern of the south-to-north contour of the wheat belt" (53). The gains from specialized labor are also important. Combine operators and truck drivers repeatedly working long seasons are more specialized than any farmer and his short-term help. These specialized operators are extremely knowledgeable in the use and maintenance of this expensive equipment.[31]

The gains from specialized machines and labor would seem to imply that contracting for harvesting would dominate wheat and grain farming. Timeliness costs for wheat harvest, however, are severe and limiting. For any given wheat farmer, the window for optimal harvest is barely three weeks and standing grain is vulnerable to hail, rain, and wind. The puzzle is how do migratory custom cutters and the farmers who hire them reduce these timeliness costs enough to sustain a viable industry? The answer is found in the geographical (and climatological) contiguousness of the Great Plains. Custom cutters know they can reliably follow the ripening wheat north in order to make intensive use of their expensive equipment. And, similarly, farmers know that cutters will be venturing north each year. Still there remains the problem of getting a cutter to a specific farm at a specific time. The problem is solved, according to Isern and others, by diligent effort on the part of the cutters to contact farmers during the off-season and commit to their harvest. Custom cutters send agents north, ahead of the crew to keep farmers informed on the locations and to relay information back to the cutter on the crop conditions. Furthermore, cutters consistently hop over adjacent farms to avoid timeliness costs. By harvesting one farm every 100 or so miles (south to north), the cutters allow time for adjustments in the optimal harvesting dates in their northward progression. Reputation also appears to play an important part in this commitment, raising the costs of reneging or overbooking by cutters. Isern (1981) summarizes:

The system of verbal agreements held together remarkably well. It was reliable enough that farmers trusted it and custom cutters planned on it, and yet flexible enough to allow for adjustments due to unforeseen circumstances. Sometimes individual farmers or custom cutters acted irresponsibly, and such actions left a bitter taste. The unwritten code of custom combining was a flexible one, but the person who stretched it beyond reason suffered the consequences. (P. 92)

Despite the remarkable stability of contracting in the presence of timeliness costs, there have been occasions—weather driven—when even the strongest reputations could not withstand the pressure. The 1948, 1957, and 1999 harvests are all cases in which unusual weather disrupted the normal northern progression of ripening wheat, leaving northern farmers anxiously awaiting custom cutters who were still not finished with their more southern clients. In each of these years, unusually wet and cool weather in Texas and Oklahoma delayed harvests while unusually warm and dry weather in Kansas and Nebraska advanced harvests. In each case, the northern farmers suffered substantial losses because they were faced with late harvests.[32] Even in these difficult times, cutters make effort to find farmers another cutter when their own commitments are confounded by weather.

Even when the gains from specialization outweigh timeliness costs, moral hazard incentives remain in any custom cutting contract. Moral hazard in the use of the assets (combines and trucks) is significantly reduced by the use of a custom contract rather than a simple lease of equipment to the farmer. Furthermore, most cutting bosses assign an operator to a specific machine for the entire season in order to increase the operator's incentive to properly use and maintain his equipment. The most important moral hazard cost has to do with the effort of the cutting crew and requires monitoring by the farmer. Because the cutter does not own the crop output, and because his compensation does not importantly depend on it, the cutter has an incentive to do less than a first-best job.[33] Cutters may spill grain in the fields, leave isolated fields uncut, and inefficiently thresh the grain.[34]

These incentive effects inherent in custom combining can be summarized. First, the probability that a farmer will choose custom combining (over self-combining) increases as specialization gains increase. Second, the probability that a farmer will choose custom combining (over self-combining) increases as timeliness costs decrease. Third, the probability that a farmer will choose custom combining (over self-combining) increases as moral hazard costs decrease.

Once the basic structure of custom combining is understood it is clear that our model of a trade-off between specialization gains and the costs of timeliness and moral hazard is supported. In addition to the basic structure of the industry, a number of facts about the extent and details of custom combining provide more support.

First, extensive migratory custom combining is not found outside the Great Plains' wheat belt because no other region can match the geographic contiguousness of the Great Plains that substantially reduces timeliness costs.[35] Second, a smaller fraction of wheat is custom harvested on the northern plains (for example, the Dakotas) than is in the central and southern plains (for example, Kansas, Oklahoma). Two reasons seem to explain this differential. Northern farmers are more diversified into other small grains, which extends the length of their overall harvest season, thus allowing them to make more intensive use of their own combines. The northern reaches are also home to spring wheat, which ripens much more unevenly and often needs to be cut by a windrower before being combined. Windrowing has two effects on the use of custom work. It requires cutters to haul pickup "headers" north just for use during the last few weeks of work and it adds a new moral hazard dimension. With windrows cutters can be subjected to unknown hazards, such as small animals, rocks, and wire that can damage their machines.

Third, those Texas wheat farmers who also grow cotton use custom cutters relatively more often. Cotton and wheat require different harvesting machines so the gains from specialized custom cutters is even larger than for a farmer who specializes in wheat. Fourth, custom combiners are more intensively hired by "small" and "large" farmers, but not "middle" size ones.[36] As Isern (1981) notes:

Farmers with only small acreage, perhaps a quarter or half section, employed custom cutters because combines were inordinate investments for them. . . . Big farmers found that harvesting their crops required enormous amounts of capital and troublesome dealings with labor. . . . Big farmers, therefore, chose to employ custom cutters. . . . Farmers with acreage falling in the middle range tended to do more of their own harvesting. They had enough use to justify owning combines, but not so much that they could not find and manage sufficient help for harvest. (Pp. 73–74)

Finally, farmers with lower human capital are more likely to use custom combines, as Isern (1981) also notes: "Part-time farmers especially favored custom cutters because their other work prevented them from supplying the concentrated effort required for the harvest. The same was true for farmers on the verge of retirement" (73).

The annual migration of custom harvesters is, in many ways, a remarkable phenomenon of decentralized market coordination (Hayek 1945) and contracting under highly uncertain conditions.[37] Given the huge gains from specialization in harvesting technology, the limited use of custom cutters gives some indication of the tremendous timeliness costs.[38] Indeed, Ellouise House, executive secretary of the U.S. Custom Harvesters Association, sums up the economic problem: "More and more farmers would hire them (custom harvesters) if there was just some way to guarantee that they could be there at a given time."[39]

8.4 Summary

In this chapter we have developed a model that explains the control of farm assets through ownership and contracting. Both ownership and contracting are costly because of moral hazard, timeliness costs, specialization opportunities, and capital constraints. Our model incorporates these costs and incentives into our analysis, and it further demonstrates the benefits of the transaction cost approach, by slightly modifying the first model developed in chapter 4.

Once again, our empirical work generally supports our model. First, we observe that greater moral hazard costs increase the probability of ownership. This is true for land in the case of crops with soil exploitation and underreporting problems, and true for buildings with complicated uses. Second, we observe that greater specialization gains lead to an increase in contracting. For land, widows, absentee landowners, and inexperienced landowners tended to rent; and for equipment, custom combining is used extensively in the harvest of wheat on the Great Plains. Third, timeliness costs increases the probability of ownership and long-term contracting. For equipment and land contracts, this is important. For land, all contracts are long-term, which mitigate the potentially large timeliness costs between stages of production. For equipment, specialized and necessary pieces of equipment are owned, while redundant and shared equipment is more likely rented. Fourth for all of the assets we examine, a relaxed capital constraint increased the chance of ownership. Finally, the only real evidence of specific assets we find that influences the choice of ownership is that of building on rented land. The ownership of buildings is strongly tied to the ownership of land.

9 Farm Organization and Vertical Control

9.1 Introduction

This chapter explains why farming has remained dominated by small, family-based firms, and why and when the family farm has been occasionally supplanted by large factory-style corporations.[1] We continue to modify our basic model to examine the trade-off between moral hazard incentives and gains from specialization, and we focus on two dimensions of farm organization: the choice of farm ownership and the extent of farm control over successive stages of production. We focus on these two dimensions of firm organization because farms have been and continue to be organized around a well-defined set of production stages.[2]

In chapter 8 we noted that nature plays more than a random role in farm production—namely, a systematic role that restricts the farming production process. In this chapter we analyze this role much more explicitly. Seasonality is the main feature that distinguishes farm organization from industrial organization. Agricultural economists have long recognized this point.[3] Indeed, Holmes (1928) stresses seasonality in discussing the reason for the resilience of the family farm:

> The most fundamental one (reason) is the peculiar seasonal nature of agricultural production and the consequent lack of continuous operations. Almost every line of endeavor on the farm must depend either upon the swing of the seasons or upon the periodic nature of some biological process. There are seed times and harvest times with their specific tasks which, in the main, are of short duration. There is also the case of livestock at the different stages of their development. In no case can a man be put to a single specific task and be kept at it uninterruptedly for a month or a year as is true in the factory. (Pp. 40–41)

Until now, however, agricultural economists have not often connected their insights regarding seasonal production stages, crop cycles, task specialization, and random events to modern theories of the firm. In this chapter we merge these two traditions and incorporate seasonal forces into a model of farm organization.

Nature is incorporated into our model in two different ways: through random shocks to farm output and through seasonal forces such as the length of production stages and the frequency of crop cycles. As always, random production shocks from nature generate opportunities for moral hazard and help explain the dominance of family farms. Second, seasonal parameters (cycles, stages, and so on) limit gains from specialization and create timeliness costs between stages of production. Expanding the size or extent of the farm—by contracting with partners or with firms in adjacent stages—entails increases in moral hazard costs, but expanding the firm has the potential to generate gains from specialization, which, in agriculture, can be severely limited by seasonal factors.

The simplest family farm avoids moral hazard losses because the farmer is the complete residual claimant. The simplest family farm also sacrifices gains from specialized labor available in more complex agricultural firms. Small farm partnerships fall between family farms and large, factory-style corporate farms. The small farm partnership captures some gains from specialization while mitigating moral hazard. By identifying conditions in which these forces vary, we derive testable predictions about the choice of organization and the extent of farm integration. The results are quite striking. Production stages in farming tend to be short and infrequent and often require few distinct tasks, thus limiting the benefits of specialization and making wage labor especially costly to monitor. When farmers are successful in mitigating the effects of seasonality and random shocks to output, farm organizations gravitate toward factory processes, developing the large-scale corporate forms found elsewhere in the economy. We test these predictions using historical industry case studies as well our British Columbia–Louisiana data.

9.2   A Model of Farm Organization

Farm organization can vary from a single owner or simple partnership, where labor is paid by residual claims, to a public corporation with many anonymous owners and specialized wage labor. A pure family farm is the simplest case, in which a single farmer owns the output and controls all farm assets, including all labor assets.[4] Factory-style corporate agriculture is the most complicated case, where many people own the farm and labor is provided by large groups of specialized fixed wage labor. Partnerships are intermediate forms, in which two or three owners share output and capital, and each provides labor.[5]

Agriculture is characterized by several distinct stages of production—planting, cultivation, harvesting, and processing for plant crops; or breeding, husbandry, and slaughter for livestock—largely determined by nature.[6] In principle, there is no reason why a separate farmer could not own and control each stage. It would be possible, for example, for one farmer to prepare the soil, a second farmer to plant, a third farmer to apply pesticides, a fourth to harvest the crop, and so on. Each of these separate "farms" could be connected to the other farms at adjacent stages by market transactions for the output from their particular stage. In reality, however, most farmers control several stages of production, such as soil preparation, planting, cultivation, and harvest. At the same time, differences often exist in the number of firm-controlled stages across different farm products. In many cases, a family farmer harvests and stores his own crop. In other cases, a family farmer may be a member of a cooperative that owns the storage facility. In such a case, the farm is extended from harvest into processing, but the ownership of the "farm" at the two stages is not the same.[7]

Mother Nature: Seasonal and Uncertain Production

To the farmer, a season is a distinct period of the year during which a stage of agriculture (such as planting and harvesting) is optimally undertaken. For example, for spring wheat grown on the northern Great Plains, the month-long planting season usually begins in April and the harvest season is primarily restricted to August. This broad definition of a season, however, hides some important features of nature that directly influence the incentives inherent in agricultural production. To uncover these features, we now model seasonality as a collection of parameters: (1) C, the number of times per year the entire production *cycle* can be completed; (2) S, the number of *stages* in the process; (3) T, the total number of *tasks* in a given stage; and 4) L the *length* of the stages. Crop seasons (stages) are ultimately linked to biological processes (such as birth, planting, flowering, and mating) that depend on such variables as day length, temperature, and rainfall that vary across nature's seasons. Annual crops like wheat and corn have $C = 1$, while irrigated vegetables in Southern California that generate several harvests may have $C = 5$. A continuously harvested or nonseasonal crop would have $C = 365$. Among other things, C indicates how often a stage and its tasks are repeated during the year. Note that tree crops may be annual even though the plant is perennial. Trees for timber represent a case where the crop cycle equals a small fraction.

The first modification of our model is to recognize that farm production is cumulative and to use a stage production function that depends on natural parameters and specialization.[8] Let Q be the final consumer product (such as bacon or bread) derived from a cumulative production process with S discrete stage's of production. The output in each stage is an input into the next stage's production function, so that $Q = Q_s = h(Q_{s-1}(Q_{s-2}(\ldots)))$. Hence, the farmer in our model takes the output from a previous stage as an input into the next stage and makes an optimal effort choice that depends, in part, on what nature did in the prior stage. At each stage the output depends, not only on the previous stage output, but also on farmer effort (e), a capital input (k), and a random stage-specific natural shock (θ) determined by such natural forces as pests and weather. In particular, for the sth stage, the stage-specific random input of nature θ_s is distributed with mean 0 and variance σ_s^2. Consequently, the production function for a single stage is $Q_s = h_s(e_s, k_s; Q_{s-1}) + \theta_s$, where inputs e and k have positive and diminishing marginal productivity, and these marginal products are increasing in Q_{s-1}.

Because there are many tasks within a given stage, we define t_{stn} as the effort (in hours) in the sth stage, on the tth task, performed by the nth worker. Tasks are indexed by $t = 1, \ldots, T$; stages are indexed by $s = 1, \ldots, S$; and workers are indexed by $n = 1, \ldots, N$. Let T be the number of tasks for a given stage and assume that T is exogenous to the farm, determined by nature and technology. Tasks are well-defined jobs that take place during a stage, such as operating a combine or a grain truck during wheat harvest. Tasks may be mostly mental (such as planning and marketing decisions) or mostly physical (such as lifting, shoveling, and operating heavy equipment). Task seasons do not always match stage seasons because a task may not be stage specific. Truck driving may be a task in several stages and have a long season compared to any one stage. A given task may be common to any or all stages of production, like inspecting crops and livestock, or it may be unique to a stage, like operating a combine.

Effort (e), however, does not adequately describe the labor input into farm production. Because workers learn by doing, we define effective labor in stage s for task j as $e_{st} = a_s t_{st}$, where $t_{st} = \sum_{n=1}^{N} t_{stn}$ and $a_s = [N_s L_s / T_s]^\alpha$. The term t_{st} indicates that total task effort is the sum of all of the individual worker's efforts for a given task t in stage s. The effective effort parameter a_s measures the amount of task specialization and is assumed a ratio— the total number of workers multiplied by the length of the stage, and divided by the total number of tasks—raised to $\alpha_s \in (0, 1)$. This means that a worker's marginal productivity increases when he spends more time working at a particular task, which in turn depends on how long a stage is and how many other tasks the worker is performing during the stage. To simplify, we assume that there is only one person working on a task, so $N \leq T$. We assume that workers are identical, which means that gains from specialization do not arise from endowment effects. Instead, gains from specialization arise because, in the words of Becker and Murphy (1992), "The increasing returns from concentrating on a narrower set of tasks raises the productivity of a specialist above that of a jack-of-all-trades" (1139). This formal structure is a more explicit modeling of the same idea first presented in chapter 8.

The parameter α_s indicates the degree to which task specialization can potentially increase output. For some tasks (such as shoveling grain) there may be little to be gained from specialization ($\alpha_s \approx 0$), while for others (such as management decisions or pesticide application) these gains may be great ($\alpha_s \approx 1$). The length of a stage (L) can vary across stages for a single crop and vary across crops for the same stage.[9] Since L is determined by nature and has the same effect on a as changes in N, we initially normalize it to one to minimize notation. This also constrains the value of the effective effort parameter, $a_s \in [0, 1)$.

Specialization effects are at their maximum when $a_s = 1$. This condition could arise for several reasons. First, there may be only one task and one worker ($N = T = 1$). Second, there may be many tasks but the number of workers exactly matches the number of tasks ($T = N > 1$), allowing each worker to completely specialize. Finally, there may simply be no gains from specialization for some stages ($\alpha_i = 0$). Under these assumptions, the full-stage production function becomes

$$Q_s = h_s(a_s t_{s1}, \ldots, a_s t_{sT}, k_s; Q_{s-1}(d)) + \theta_s \quad s = 1, \ldots, S. \tag{9.1}$$

In (9.1) k_s is a stage-specific (physical) capital input, h_s is the stage s production function, and d measures the timing of task effort during the production of the previous stage output.

9.3   The Structure of Farm Ownership

We now use the stage production framework to examine three different farm ownership structures: the family farm, partnerships, and corporate farms. In the first two models the number of workers and the number of owners are the same, so we use N to denote both variables. The marginal cost of capital for all ownership systems is $r = r(N)$, with r decreasing and convex in N and bounded by r^{min}. These costs fall for two reasons as the number of owners and workers increase. First, self-financing is easier with the pooled resources of many owners. Second, capital (such as land and equipment) will be used more intensively and thus more efficiently on a larger farm.[10] This implies that individual family farmers have the highest capital costs, so that $r(N = 1) \equiv r^{max}$. To start, we analyze only one stage ($L = 1$), so we drop the stage subscripts and simply denote the output from the previous stage as q_{-1}. We also normalize stage output prices to one and let w be the opportunity cost of task effort in the labor market. Since all farmers are assumed to be risk neutral and maximize expected profits, farmers choose the ownership structure that maximizes the expected value of the farm.[11]

Family Farms.   The family farmer must make several choices. He must decide how to allocate his farming time across tasks, decide on the level of capital, and decide how much time to spend on and off the farm. The farmer may earn an hourly wage (w) by supplying hours of effort (m) in the labor market. His effort allocation is constrained so that his total time (on-farm and off-farm activities) equals the total time available for the stage (stage length is normalized to 1). The family farm problem is to maximize expected profits (Π^F), written as

$$\max_{t_1,\ldots,t_T,m,k} \Pi^F = h\left\{\left[\frac{1}{T}\right]^\alpha t_1, \ldots, \left[\frac{1}{T}\right]^\alpha t_T, k; q_{-1}(d)\right\} - r^{max}k + wm \qquad (9.2)$$

$$\text{subject to } \sum_{t=1}^{T} t_t + m = L = 1,$$

where $a_t = (1/T)^\alpha$ since $N = 1$ and $L = 1$. The optimal choices (t_t^F, m^F, k^F) solve the following first-order necessary conditions:

$$\left[\frac{1}{T}\right]^{\alpha} \frac{\partial h}{\partial t_j}(t_t^F, m^F, k^F) \equiv w \quad t = 1, \ldots, T; \quad \text{and} \tag{9.3}$$

$$\frac{\partial h}{\partial k}(t_t^F, m^F, k^F) \equiv r^{\max}. \tag{9.4}$$

These solutions have clear implications. Since the family farmer is the complete residual claimant in both activities, there is no moral hazard for task effort. The family farm is, however, hindered by a lack of specialization, which reduces the marginal product of task labor in every given task, as long as there is more than one task ($T > 1$). In addition, though family farms equate marginal costs and benefits for capital, they face higher costs for capital compared to partnerships or corporations, and therefore use less capital, implying a smaller farm with less equipment compared to partnership and factory-corporate farms.

Partnership Farms. Like the family farmer, the partner allocates his time on and off the farm and among the various farming tasks. Because each partner shares farm output but keeps all of his off-farm income, he shifts more effort into off-farm activities than he would if he had no partner. Partners share tasks equally, because partners and tasks are homogeneous. This means that each partner allocates his farm labor over T/N tasks. Furthermore, because the combined resources of the partners exceed that of a single (family) farmer and because of a higher rate of use of those resources, partnerships have lower capital costs than do family farms.[12]

As in our analysis of contract choice, we model the partnership contracting problem in two stages. In the first stage, partners jointly maximize the expected wealth of the farm in choosing capital and partners, subject to the task allocations chosen by each partner. In the second stage, each partner maximizes his expected profits (π^P) by choosing how to allocate his effort over T/N farm tasks and his own nonfarm labor, holding constant the joint choice of capital and the number of partners. Using backward induction, we solve the second stage first, so that for each partner, the problem is

$$\max_{t_1,\ldots,t_{(T/N)},m} \pi^P = \frac{1}{N} h\left\{\left[\frac{N}{T}\right]^{\alpha} t_t; \bar{k}, q_{-1}(d)\right\} + wm \tag{9.5}$$

$$\text{subject to} \sum_{t=1}^{T/N} t_t + m = L = 1,$$

where $\bar{k}$ is a fixed amount of capital owned jointly by the partners, w is the (shadow) wage for the partner, m is each partner's labor market effort, and $a_t = [N/T]^{\alpha}$ is the specialization scalar. Each partner takes $\bar{t}_t$, the task effort of all other partners for the remaining $T(N-1/N)$ tasks, as given. The optimal task effort vector for each partner is $t_t^P(\Phi) = t_t^P(N, T, \alpha, w, L, \bar{t}_n, k, q_{-1}(d))$ and solves the following first-order necessary conditions:

$$\left[\frac{N^{\alpha-1}}{T^\alpha}\right] \frac{\partial h}{\partial t_j}(t_t^P(\Phi)) \equiv w \quad t = 1, \ldots, T/N. \tag{9.6}$$

Equation 9.6 shows that the number of partners does not affect the marginal rate of substitution between tasks on the farm but does affect the amount of each partner's effort on the farm. Thus, as the number of partners increases, each partner spends less time on the farm, and this translates into less time spent on each farm task. Note that when potential specialization gains are greatest ($\alpha = 1$), equation (9.6) reduces to equation (9.3) and the partner's choice of time spent on each task is identical to that of the family farmer because $a = 1/T$ for each task. On the other hand, if specialization has no value ($\alpha = 0$), then equation 9.6 reduces to a classic Marshallian sharecropping first-order condition because $a = 1/N$ for each task, and acts like a tax on task effort. The lesson is that as the potential gains from specialization increase (higher α), the incentives inherent in partnerships become more valuable.

Taking this optimizing behavior into account, the partners' joint problem is to maximize expected profit by choosing the level of capital and the number of partners, subject to each partner's incentive compatibility (*IC*) and individual rationality (*IR*) constraints and the total time constraints of the partners. Because we assume that partners have identical endowments, the effective effort term for each task is $[N/T]^\alpha t$. Similarly, each partner earns off-farm income equal to $wm = w\left[1 - \sum_{t=1}^T t_t\right]$. Substituting this constraint directly into the objective function gives

$$\max_{k,N} \Pi^P = h\left\{\left[\frac{N}{T}\right]^\alpha t_t, k; Q_{-1}(d)\right\} - r(N)k + Nw\left\{1 - \sum_{t=1}^T t_t\right\} \tag{9.7}$$

subject to $(IC_t) \quad t_t = t_t^P(\Phi) = \text{argmax } \pi^P \quad t = 1, \ldots, T$

$\qquad\qquad (IR) \quad \pi^P \geq \bar{V},$

where $\bar{V}$ is the reservation income level for each partner.

The solution to equation (9.7) is derived in appendix B, but the main implications are illustrated graphically in figure 9.1. Simply put, adding a partner yields a return from increased task specialization and lower capital cost. At the same time, adding a partner generates additional costs, in terms of decreased farm effort, from greater moral hazard. The partnership farm will also have greater capital levels than will the family farm (see appendix B). Depending on the relative size of these various effects, a partnership farm may or may not be more valuable than a family farm.

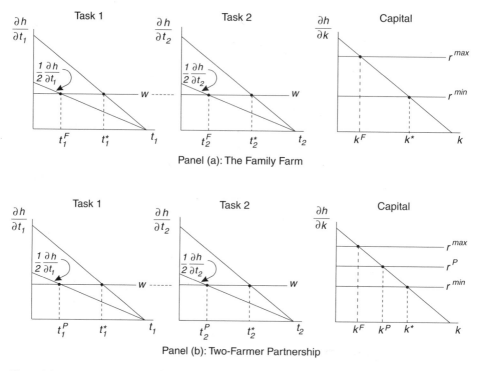

Figure 9.1
The trade-off between specialization and moral hazard

Figure 9.1 shows the trade-off involved in the choice between a family farm and a partnership farm. The figure shows the optimal allocations of effort and capital in each farm organization in the simplest case when (a) there are only two tasks and two partners (so $N = T$ in a partnership); (b) there is one stage-specific type of capital; (c) capital and effort are independent inputs; and (d) $\alpha = 1$. As with all our graphs, we have drawn linear marginal products for added simplicity. For comparison, we show the first-best input levels, denoted by asterisks. Panel (a) shows the case of the family farm. Since there is just one farmer ($N = 1$) and two tasks ($T = 2$), the marginal product rotates downward by one-half, and the optimal task choices are t_1^F and t_2^F. Given the higher cost of capital, the family farm uses k^F units of capital. Panel (b) shows the case of a two-farmer partnership where there are still only two tasks. Under the assumptions used in figure 9.1, the specialization and moral hazard effects exactly offset each other.[13] As a result, allocation of task effort is identical in the two regimes, but because of lower capital costs, the partnership is more valuable. It is easy to see, however, that if the potential gains from specialization decline enough (from smaller values of a or T, or larger values of L), the family farm will become more valuable than the partnership.

Factory-Style Corporate Farms. Finally, consider the large, factory-style corporate farm. In this organization the firm's owners share revenues as well as capital and labor costs, but they do not work themselves. Labor in a factory style corporate organization is provided exclusively by specialized wage employees who are not owners of the firm. With production uncertainty (at each stage), hired workers have incentives to shirk because, unlike family farmers or partners, they are not residual claimants. We capture this in our model by assuming that the corporate farm faces a higher effective wage for its hired workers than does the family or partnership farm; that is, $\bar{w} > w$.[14] We also assume that the corporation faces the lowest possible capital costs. The number of hired workers is determined by the hours of hired task effort through the daily time constraint, where Ω is a constant number of hours each worker can provide in a day. With homogeneous hired labor, the expected value of the corporate farm is given by the solution to

$$\max_{t_t,k} \Pi^{FC} = h \left\{ \left[\frac{N}{T} \right]^\alpha t_t, k; Q_{-1}(d) \right\} - kr^{\min} - \bar{w}_t t_t \quad t_t = 1, \ldots, T \quad (9.8)$$

subject to $\displaystyle\sum_{t=1}^{T} \left(\frac{t_t}{\Omega} \right) = N,$

and N now simply refers to the number of workers hired by the firm.

The solution to equation (9.8) is also derived in appendix B, but the main implications are again straightforward. The factory-corporate farm will tend to use more capital because it faces lower capital costs, but its overall ability to use more farm labor will depend on the potential gains from task specialization and the costs of monitored labor. If, for example, there were no moral hazard in task effort ($\bar{w} = w$), the corporate farm would set the number of workers equal to the number of tasks ($N = T$) and have complete specialization and the lowest capital costs. Under these circumstances, the corporate-factory farm would obviously generate greater net value than all other organizational forms because of its greater task specialization and lower capital costs. In general, the value of the factory-corporate farm will be highest when capital is a relatively important input, when seasonal parameters allow gains from specialization to be high, and when labor monitoring is relatively inexpensive.

Connecting Stages through Firms and Markets

If we consider an adjacent production stage to be simply a collection of additional tasks, then the model of organizational choice for multistage producers is analytically identical to the one-stage model. The decision to keep the next stage of production in the same farm or use the market depends on weighing the gains from specialized stage production against the cost of using the market to connect two firms. In agriculture, a new inter-stage moral hazard problem emerges because of the timeliness costs that arise between stages of production. Our emphasis on timeliness is directly related to the discussion introduced in the last chapter.[15]

As discussed in chapter 8, timeliness costs depend on seasonal parameters and can be examined by letting $q_s = q(d)$, where q_s is the output for stage s and d is the date at which the stage's tasks are completed (such as the date at which planting is completed). As before, we will assume that this timing function is approximately quadratic in d, with a unique optimum, d^*, and that small deviations from d^* (as little as two or three days) for certain crucial stages (planting, irrigating, spraying, and harvesting) can reduce crop output by relatively large amounts, possibly to zero (such as when hail falls before harvest). As in chapter 8 we assume the timing function takes a specific form for the sth stage ($s = 1, \ldots, S$):

$$q(d) = \delta d \left[1 - \frac{d}{L} \right] q, \tag{9.9}$$

where L is the length of stage and δ is a crop-specific response parameter. All of these variables are stage specific even though we suppress the subscripts. The stage length, L, indicates the possible dates for which the task can be undertaken and still generate positive output. The term δ reflects the crop's sensitivity to timing. Increases in δ make deviations from the optimal date more costly.[16] In this specification, the optimal time is exactly in the middle of the stage; that is, $d^* = L/2$.

Timeliness costs create incentive problems, not simply because deviations from d^* reduce output, but because there is temporal variance in d^* that makes it costly to contract across stages. Variance in d^* means that the optimal date for applying task effort cannot be known with certainty prior to the stage; variance in d^* can arise from variance in the length of the stage (L) or simply from variance in the time at which the stage begins. Accordingly, increases in the variance of d^* decrease the probability of firm-to-firm contracting between stages because the farmer in the later stage cannot accurately schedule a specific date. Obviously, increases in d also decrease the probability of firm-to-firm contracting, for any level of variation in d^*, because the firm producing at the earlier stage can impose severe losses on the later stage firm by undertaking tasks at a nonoptimal time.

To focus on timeliness and integration incentives, we assume the organization is constant across two adjacent stages (s and $s - 1$). If the farm is integrated and if stage output has a per-unit value of p_s, then the value of the integrated firm is

$$V^I = p_s \left[h_s(a_s^I t_s, k_s, q_{s-1}(d^*)) + \theta_s \right]. \tag{9.10}$$

In equation (9.10) the superscript I denotes variables specific to the integrated case. Alternatively, two separate, specialized firms could produce the two stages and be connected by a market contract. When separate firms, connected by a market transaction, undertake different stages the value of the market governance structure is:

$$V^M = p_s \left[h_s(a_s^M t_s, k_s, q_{s-1}(d^M)) + \theta_s \right] \tag{9.11}$$

In equation (9.11) the superscript M denotes variables specific to the market connected case.

The trade-off between the values generated in equations 9.10 and 9.11 depends on the relative importance of timing and specialization. The benefit of the integrated regime is the guarantee of optimal timing of task effort at each stage. With integration there is no interstage moral hazard in timing because a single firm controls both stages and applies task effort at the optimal time ($d = d^*$). With market-connected stages, however, the date of task efforts are not optimal ($d^M \neq d^*$) because the incentives of the two farms (or "firms") are not identical. The magnitude of the loss from suboptimal timing will depend on both the impact of timing on output (δ) and the marginal product of last period's output ($\partial h_s / \partial q_{s-1}$).

The cost of the integrated regime is the forgone gain from task specialization. As long as the tasks in the two stages are not identical, there must be a loss of specialization across stages because there are more tasks but the number of farmers is the same. In the simplest case, the number of tasks increases to $T^I = T_s + T_{s-1}$, but this increase is spread over two stages. In general, the effective effort parameter in the market-connected firms will be larger than for integrated firms; that is, $a^M \geq a^I$. This can arise for two reasons since the effort specialization parameter depends on the number of tasks and the length of a stage, $a = [NL/T]^\alpha$. First, there may be more tasks in the integrated case, or $T^I > T^M$. Second, the integrated case may have a shorter stage, or $L^M > L^I$. For example, a specialized firm can perform its tasks over a longer period by contracting with many farms (producing stage $s - 1$) for stage s production as long as the stages for these farms do not perfectly overlap. In this case, the length of stage s for the contracting firm can get large, allowing greater gains from specialization. Finally, it is clear that stages with high values of α are more likely to be contracted for than stages with low values of α.

The Comparative Statics of Farm Organization

To generate predictions about the choice of farm organization we examine how various parameters affect the relative value of the three farm organizations we study. The general model for choosing which farm organization will maximize the expected value of production for any stage is as follows: maximize $V = \max[V^F, V^P, V^{FC}]$, where V^F, V^P, and V^{FC} are the optimal value functions for the family farm (F), the partnership farm (P), and the

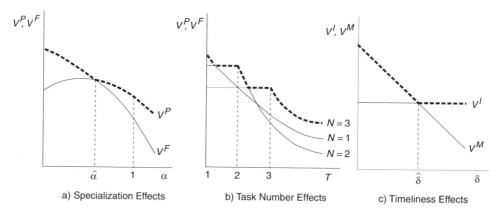

Figure 9.2
Farm organization comparative statics

factory-corporate farm (FC). We can examine the choice of market connection versus cross-stage integration in a similar fashion. We derive value functions by evaluating the firm's objective function at the optimal input levels (see appendix B). Deriving comparative statics predictions requires examining how changes in various parameters ($\alpha, C, \delta, L, \sigma^2, T$) affect the relative values of these indirect objective functions.

Consider the effects of changes in the specialization parameter (α) on the value of the family farm. By the Envelope Theorem, $V_{\alpha}^F < 0$ and $V_{\alpha\alpha}^F > 0$ (see appendix B). This means that the value of a family farm declines as specialization becomes more important. A partnership is just the general case of the family farm where $N \geq 2$ and is allowed to vary. As with V^F, $V_{\alpha}^P < 0$ and $V_{\alpha\alpha}^P > 0$, but the absolute slope of V^P is less than the slope of V^F for low values of α. In addition, the absolute slope of V^P increases as α and N increase. Furthermore, from equations (9.3) and (9.6), when $\alpha = 1$ the task input choices are the same for partnerships and family farms, so when $\alpha = 1$, $V^P > V^F$ by an amount equal to the net savings in capital costs. In the extreme case, when $\alpha = 0$ the family farm makes a first-best task allocation since there are no gains to specialized task effort. The partnership, on the other hand, is penalized because of partner moral hazard. As long as the savings in capital costs are smaller than the moral hazard losses in a partnership, then $V^F > V^P$ when $\alpha = 0$.[17] These value functions, shown in panel (a) of figure 9.2, demonstrate that the optimal number of owners varies with changes in the importance of specialization: Low values of α lead to family farms; high values of α lead to partnerships.

For corporate-factory farms, the slope of V^{FC} is identical to that of the partnership for all values of α for a given N. Since corporate-factory farms have the lowest costs of capital, but the highest labor costs, whether partnership farms or corporate-factory farms emerge depends in part on the net effect of these two costs. Other things equal, corporate-factory farms tend to emerge where large numbers of workers are required and there are many tasks and large gains to specialization. This is because the costs of monitoring hired labor are likely to rise more slowly with T than the moral hazard effect caused by sharing output.[18] This would lead V^{FC} to be higher than V^P and would mean that for large values of α, factory-corporate farms (with specialized wage labor) would tend to dominate.

Another comparative static result arises from changes in the number of tasks (T). Panel (b) of figure 9.2, which assumes that specialization gains are as high as possible ($\alpha = 1$), shows how V^P varies with changes in T for three different values of N. Family farms are the special case, where $N = 1$. Taking into account any differences in the level of task effort for the different size farms, we find that the more partners there are, the lower total task effort is on the farm, which lowers V^P. The value functions are flat as long as $N > T$, because specialization is maximized when $N \geq T$. In the case of a single task ($T = 1$), it must be the case that $V^F > V^P$, unless there is a large capital saving to overwhelm the partnership moral hazard. In addition, the optimal number of owners (N) for a given number of tasks (T) is given by the upper envelope of these curves, which shows that the number of owners is positively related to the number of tasks.

There are similar comparative statics results that explain how timelines costs can determine the extension of the farm into various stages of production. Panel (c) of figure 9.2 shows how the values of the integrated and market farms vary with changes in crop sensitivity (δ). In particular, the relative value of the integrated firm increases in d. Similarly, changes in uncertainty over the stage length (L) also influence the relative values of V^I and V^M. For a given δ, increases in this uncertainty increase the relative value of the integrated farm. When crops have greater timeliness costs, the farm is likely to be integrated over multiple stages. When timeliness is unimportant, the farmer is less likely to control delivery.

Combining these predictions with others derived earlier we can summarize the predictions that we can empirically examine. Below we list these predictions in three categories. In table 9.1 we summarize the basic trade-offs in the model for easier reference.

Choice of Farm Organization

PREDICTION 9.1   As the importance of specialization (α) increases, the family farm becomes less likely and partnerships and factory-corporate farms become more likely.

PREDICTION 9.2   As the number of tasks (T) increases, the family farm becomes less likely.

PREDICTION 9.3   As the length of a stage (L) increases, the family farm becomes less likely.

Table 9.1
Incentives under different organizations

	Effort moral hazard	Effort specialization	Capital constraints	Labor monitoring
Family farm	No	No	Yes	No
Partnership	Some	Yes	Some	No
Corporate farm	Yes	Yes	No	Yes

PREDICTION 9.4   As the number of cycles (C) per year increases (holding constant the number and length of stages), the total amount of time that a single task is undertaken $(L * C)$ increases over a given year, making the family farm less likely.

PREDICTION 9.5   As variance in the stage-specific shock (σ^2) increases, the family farm becomes more likely.

PREDICTION 9.6   As the costs of monitoring labor increase $(\bar{w})$, the family farm and partnership becomes more likely.

Extent of the Farm

PREDICTION 9.7   As crop sensitivity to task timing (δ) increases, the farm is more likely to control adjacent stages.

PREDICTION 9.8   As the variance in the optimal date (d^*) to complete a stage increases, the farm is less likely to control adjacent stages.

PREDICTION 9.9   As the importance of task specialization (α) increases, the farm is more likely to control adjacent stages.

Farm Capital and Farm Size

PREDICTION 9.10   As farm organization shifts from family farms to partnerships and factory-corporate farms, capital stocks (k) per farm increase (see appendix B).

PREDICTION 9.11   As farm organization shifts from family farms to partnerships and factory-corporate farms, farm size and farm output increase.

9.4   Empirical Analysis: Organization and Vertical Control

To test the predictions of our model, we examine industry case studies (historical and contemporary) and analyze econometric evidence from our British Columbia–Louisiana data. The case study data show that family farms tend to dominate when seasonal parameters limit specialization and that large factory-corporate farms tend to dominate when seasonal factors can be mitigated. The case study data also show how changes in seasonal variables (sometimes as the result of technological changes) cause predictable changes in farm organization.

As we noted in chapter 1, we generally ignore the role of government policy, but the issue of farm organization requires a more complete discussion. Federal farm programs and state anticorporate farming statutes may have artificially sustained family farms by preventing the efficient takeover of the industry by the factory-corporate farm. Sumner (1991), however, finds no evidence that federal farm programs generally have subsidized the family farm. Raup (1973), on the other hand, argues that farm policies have subsidized corporate agriculture. More important, our study remains outside this debate for two reasons. First, our historical data predate the implementation of federal and state farm policies. Second, where we examine detailed farm-level data (British Columbia and Louisiana) there are no anticorporate farming statutes (Knoeber 1997).

Typically, the U.S. programs have limited the amount of direct government payments per "person," and this limit could create an incentive to use smaller organizations than otherwise (see Pasour 1990).[19] Many students of agricultural policy have noted, however, that these limitations are relatively easy to skirt. For example, Knutson, Penn, and Flinchbaugh (1998) describe a Mississippi Christmas tree farm in which fifteen corporations (owned by siblings and other relatives) were set up to increase total payments from $50,000 to $1,050,000! Some of the more egregious cases have led to sanctions. For our purposes, we simply ignore these effects because we have no systematic method of incorporating them into the analysis and data.

Historical and Current Case Studies

The family unit has been the dominant organization in farming since the earliest days of agriculture. Family farms were present in ancient Egypt, Israel, and Mesopotamia (Ellickson and DiA. Thorland 1995) and among pre-Columbian American Indians (Cronan 1983). Hayami and Otsuka (1993) report owner-cultivated farm dominance in Asia, Europe, and Latin America as well as in North America. Even in Africa, where land is often owned in common by tribes, farmland is customarily allotted to individual families. Collective farms are a fairly recent political experiment, with typically catastrophic outcomes.[20]

Case studies allow us to examine many of our key predictions in a variety of times and places. After first examining the conditions under which family farming tends to dominate, we study the history of several specific agricultural industries. The first of these histories looks at how the extent of the farm has diminished during the past two centuries. The other histories include an examination of the large Bonanza farms that existed in the Red River Valley at the turn of the century; the impact of the combine on the organization of wheat farms; the technical changes in sugarcane processing on the organization of production; and the emergence of large-scale factory production in the modern livestock industry.

Seasonality and the Dominance of Family Farming. Our model implies that differences in nature's parameters (seasonality and random shocks) explain some differences in agricultural organization. Recall that nature's parameters include the number of cycles (C), the number of stages per year (S), the number of tasks (T) in a stage, the length of the stages (L), and the variance in random production shocks (σ^2). Annual crops with many short stages, few tasks, and many unpredictable natural phenomena dominate farming in North America. These are precisely the conditions for which our model predicts that family farm organization is likely to be chosen. Seasonality in this environment severely limits the gains from specialization and, accordingly, places a premium on a type of organization that serves to squelch moral hazard.

When the number of cycles is low, as with annual grain crops like wheat, the gains from specialization are severely limited (prediction 9.4); the cost of extending a farmer's duties to adjacent stages is lower, because the opportunity to perform repetitive tasks is diminished; and timing between stages is more important. For many North American crops, a low number of cycles is associated with a large number of stages that have few tasks,[21] a condition that limits the gains from specialization (prediction 9.4) and makes labor monitoring costs high (prediction 9.6). Production characterized by few cycles is sensitive to random shocks because hiring workers for a given single task is more expensive because there are more opportunities for shirking. Taken together, these forces imply that a family farm organization is more likely to be optimal when the number of cycles is low. Family units, for example, dominate wheat farms, where there is never more than one crop per year and (on a per-plot basis) sometimes less when arid conditions require fallowing. As of 1997, approximately 80 percent of all wheat farms were family firms, and they were responsible for over 64 percent of all wheat sales. Only 0.025 percent of all wheat farms were nonfamily corporations, responsible for just 0.6 percent of all wheat sales.[22]

When crop production is characterized by many cycles, long stages with many tasks, and few random shocks, our farm organization model predicts that large, factory-corporate farms are more likely. Within the United States, the sole (family) proprietor has been much less common in southern agriculture than in northern agriculture. This is consistent with the key predictions of our model. For example, before the Civil War the South was home to large slave plantations for cotton, rice, and sugarcane. These plantations were large farms that used highly specialized wage labor. As Gray (1941) argues, plantation agriculture thrived because plantations used a "one-crop system permitting the routinizing of operations"; because the crops required "year round employment of labor"; and because the crops required "a large amount of labor on a small amount of land, thus simplifying the problem of supervision" (463).

The famous study of slavery by Fogel and Engermann (1974) also found that slaves were much more important for cotton and sugarcane than for wheat, corn and other grains, even in the antebellum South. For example, they find that the larger the number of residents on a farm (family, hired labor and slaves), the greater the proportion were slaves. Plantation agriculture was designed to exploit a specialized labor force. In the words of Fogel and Engermann:

Specialization and interdependence were the hallmarks of the medium- and large-sized plantations. On family-sized farms, each worker had to fulfill a multiplicity of duties according to a pace and pattern which were quite flexible and largely independent of the activities of others. On plantations, the hands were as rigidly organized as in a factory. Each hand was assigned to a set of tasks which occupied him throughout the year, or at least through particular seasons of the year. There were drivers, plowmen, hoe hands, harrowers, seed sowers, coverers, sorters, ginners, packers, milkmaids, stock minders, carpenters, blacksmiths, nurses, and cooks to give only a partial listing. (P. 203)

This vivid description shows how economic organization exploited task specialization and, more important, shows how the type of crop and seasonal forces shape the potential gains from such specialization.[23]

Compared to grain crops like corn and wheat, plantation crops had a small number of stages that lasted over long periods, allowing great gains from specialization and low cost monitoring. For example, cotton was continually cultivated by hand with hoes, and because the bolls (the seed pod of the cotton plant) ripened so unevenly cotton picking lasted for months (prediction 9.3). Beyond North America, the great exception to family-based agricultural organization is the equatorial plantation (Pryor 1982). Plantation crops, including banana, coffee, and sugarcane, are characterized by relatively long growing stages and a relatively small variance in nature-driven shocks. Indeed, some plantation crops (such as bananas and coffee) may have a continuous year-round harvest. For these crops, large hierarchical organizations with wage labor (or slaves) have dominated (Raup 1973; Pryor 1982).[24]

Temporal Changes in Agriculture: Narrowing the Extent of the Family Farm.   From the colonial period until the mid–nineteenth century, nonplantation farms in the United States were organized as family businesses that controlled nearly the entire production process.[25] Since that time, the growth in the factory method of production has limited the extent of the family farm at both the beginning and the end of the production sequence. As a result, the modern family farm controls a more limited set of production stages.

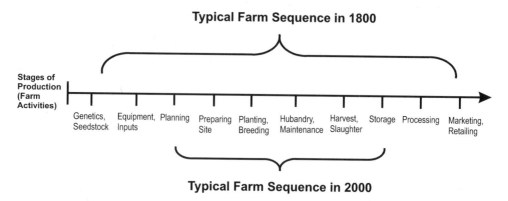

Figure 9.3
The extent of the farm in American history

Until the middle of the nineteenth century, the family farm extended into virtually all stages of farm production, from"farm-making"(clearing land and raising buildings) to processing goods for retail consumption (such as making cheese or sausage). The family had almost no contact with the market for its inputs, except perhaps with a blacksmith. The only contact with the market came when the farmer sold (or bartered) his meat and dairy products directly to consumers (Danhoff 1969). On the prairie, there were sodbusting firms that contracted with family farmers to clear vast stretches of homogeneous grasslands. Sodbusting is a task that has a relatively long season (six months even in the northern reaches of the plains) and almost no timeliness costs. Accordingly, it is not surprising that specialized firms sold this service to farmers, generally per acre of broken prairie.

The main historical exception to selling products directly to consumers was selling grain to gristmills. Gristmills, the first of many firms that specialized in what would otherwise be a single stage of the farm production process, ultimately evolved into large firms that developed factory production techniques. Because grains are easily stored and a mill can be operated continuously, milling grain for flour is almost completely removed from seasonal forces. In this situation the gains from specialization are high: There are no cycles; stages are long; there are many tasks (predictions 9.2, 9.3, 9.5); and timeliness costs are minimal (predictions 9.7, 9.8). All of these factors reduce the value of family production and favor large-scale, factory production.

After the early 1800s dramatic changes in technology led to the rise of separate firms that specialized in single stages of production and year-round operations. New technologies such as refrigeration limited natural forces and allowed otherwise seasonal tasks to be performed throughout the year (prediction 9.3). Overwhelmingly, the new firms engaged in production at either the beginning (equipment, fertilizer, and seed) or the end (marketing, processing, transportation, and storage) of the agricultural production sequence. In the late nineteenth century these firms included flour mills, cheese factories, creameries, early equipment manufacturers (plows, reapers), grain brokers, meatpackers, slaughterhouses, livestock breeders, canneries, and other food processors. This process has continued throughout the twentieth century as advances in biological and chemical technology and new product developments in artificial insemination, feeds, fertilizers, pesticides, and seeds that result in gains from specialization and reduced seasonality for certain stages of production. Accordingly, the family farm has abandoned these stages and now controls only the purely biological growth stages of farm production. Figure 9.3 shows how the extent of a family farm has diminished over time.

Bonanza Farms in the Red River Valley: An Experiment in Factory Farming.   In the last quarter of the nineteenth century, an experiment in farm organization took place on the virgin prairie of the Red River Valley dividing Minnesota and North Dakota. Between 1870 and 1890 a number of extremely large wheat farms were established, some exceeding 50,000 acres (roughly 78 square miles). Even by modern standards these farms were enormous, but their main distinguishing feature was not their size but rather their factory-corporate organization. The owners were typically businessmen with little or no farm experience. These owners raised capital in eastern markets and organized these farms along the lines of contemporary manufacturing firms typically as corporations with professional managers and a specialized wage labor force. The "bonanza farms," as they came to be known, were hailed as the future of agriculture.[26] Yet after only one generation, nearly all the bonanza farms were gone, systematically replaced by family farmers.

Most bonanza farms focused exclusively on wheat production and kept virtually the entire production sequence within the firm: from sodbusting, seed development, machine repair, and hardware supply to blacksmithing, seed cleaning, grain storage, and flour milling. The farms were also highly mechanized and used the latest large-scale equipment. For example, in just the second crop season on the well-known Cass-Cheney Farm, with 4,000 acres of wheat planted, Oliver Dalrymple assembled 26 breaking plows, 40 plows for turning sod, 21 seeders, 60 harrows, 30 self-binding harvesters, 5 steam powered threshers, 80 horses, and 30 wagons.

Labor on bonanza farms was organized in a complex hierarchical system common to industrial manufacturing. Managers were paid a combination of a salary and a commission that depended on farm profits. The farms were broken into 5,000-acre divisions headed by superintendents and 1,200-acre stations headed by foremen. Most of the manual labor force worked out of the stations and were hired in monthly increments and paid a daily wage. Accountants, blacksmiths, mechanics, and hands involved in grain cleaning and storage worked at the farm's headquarters. The labor force varied greatly in size over the seasons, with harvest crews typically twice the size of seeding crews. For instance, in 1877 (for 4,000 acres of wheat) Cass-Cheney had a seeding crew of fifty and a harvest crew of one hundred.

The bonanza farms' combination of modern technology, specialized labor, and professional management practices seemed unstoppable. For example, Bigelow (1880) wrote: "Against the unlimited use of this combination of capital, machinery, and cheap labor the individual farmer, either singly or in communities, cannot successfully contend, and must go under. It is a combination of the most powerful social and economic forces known to man, and all efforts for competition must and will fail so long as the three remain united" (43). Bonanzas, however, began to disappear as early as 1890, and by 1910 they were virtually extinct. There is substantial evidence that the crucial factors in the breakup were the monitoring costs and related inefficiencies associated with large labor forces spread out over great distances. On the Cass-Cheney farm, for example, Oliver Dalrymple managed a harvest crew of 1,000 men and 30 threshing machines spread over 30,000 acres of wheat (roughly 7 miles square if contiguous). Our reading indicates that Dalrymple took great pains to mitigate his moral hazard problems. Managers, superintendents, and foremen were paid by commission. Grain from every field was weighed and recorded so that responsibility could be assigned to foremen and superintendents. Labor was performed in crews one task at a time (such as plowing or seeding) to make supervision easier for the foremen; and rigid rules governed the daily routines of the field hands at work and in the bunkhouse.

The dissolution of the bonanza farms is consistent with the predictions of the model: In highly seasonal crops like wheat, the family farm is predicted to be the organizational structure that maximizes the value of the farm. Recognizing their labor problems early on, many bonanzas began leasing their lands in small units to homesteaders who wanted to expand operations. Later the bonanzas sold their lands in small parcels, typically quarter (160 acres) and half (320 acres) sections, to family farmers. The bonanza era provides a market test of the viability of industrial farming of a highly seasonal crop.[27] Indeed, in 1900 the agricultural economist John Lee Coulter saw the future, writing: "The great estates of the region are doomed to disintegration. The great wheat ranch cannot compete with the small diversified farm."[28]

Wheat Organization and Changes in Harvest Technology.   The history of wheat harvesting provides another test of our model. As we discussed in chapter 8, the geographical and climatological contiguousness of the Great Plains has allowed the development of a thriving custom harvesting industry for wheat. In this section we focus on farmer harvesting and discuss how a major technological change influenced farm organization.

Prior to the invention of a viable combine, harvesting (the cutting, binding, and shocking of the wheat plant) and threshing (separating seed from chaff) of grain were done separately, generally with specialized crews. Farmers would use their own reapers to cut the wheat and then another half dozen men or so would bind (tie in bundles) and shock (stack) the grain. After the wheat had been shocked, it had to be threshed. This was often done in the field (although the binds could also be stored in barns), often by a custom (hired) thresherman and his crew.[29] A key feature of this process was that the grain could remain in the shocked bundles for three or four months until threshing was completed, without serious damage to the grain. This allowed the farmer to cut his wheat over a long time period, independent of the timing of the actual threshing.

The introduction of the "combined harvester thresher," now known simply as the "combine," radically changed wheat harvesting. The combine simultaneously harvests and threshes grain and eliminates the need for rakers, gleaners, shockers, and all of the support crew that go with them. The combine made an obvious and dramatic reduction in the number of tasks (T) during the harvest stage, eliminating the intermediate stages between cutting and threshing (prediction 9.2). After the introduction of tractors with power takeoff, one farmer could complete an entire harvest.[30] The combine took one stage of production that had potentially as many as ten tasks, and reduced them to one. It seems that no other agricultural invention has had as great an impact on a single stage of production. Today approximately 75 percent of all wheat farmers harvest and separate their own grain with combines.

Perhaps even more important than reducing the number of tasks, the combine reduced the length of the harvest stage (L) by compressing two long stages (binding and threshing) into a single short stage (prediction 9.3). In the process, the combine created substantial timeliness costs (δ, var (d^*)) (predictions 9.7 and 9.8). With combines the cutting and threshing of grain is done simultaneously, and the grain left standing in the field is exposed to natural elements such as hail, rain, or wind that can knock it down or dampen it. Furthermore, a combine requires grain to be ripe before cutting so that the threshing within the machine can be done properly. According to Isern (1990), "Harvesting with the combine began seven to ten days later than harvesting with the binder. During this time a hailstorm might level the crop, insect pests might attack it, lodging might occur, or the grain might bleach out. In addition, wheat that stood until dead ripe was more likely to shatter at the cutter bar" (192). Our model predicts that all of these changes in tasks, skills, and timing encouraged family farm harvests.

Another test of our model arises from differences in spring and winter wheat. On the Great Plains, winter wheat is grown in the south, roughly from Texas to South Dakota, and harvested earlier than the spring wheat grown farther north in the Dakotas, Montana, and Canada. Spring wheat has greater timeliness costs (larger d and var(d^*)) than winter wheat (predictions 9.7 and 9.8). Spring wheat is more susceptible to weeds (which increase water content and cause mold), has shorter harvesting seasons, does not ripen evenly on the northern prairies, and has more morning dew, which can often delay combining until the afternoon. All of these features lowered the value of the combine for spring wheat compared to winter wheat.

Consistent with these facts, combines were adopted in the winter wheat regions of the Great Plains, just after World War I, but they were not used in the spring wheat areas until the late 1920s, when the swather was invented. The swather cuts and lays the grain down on the stubble, suspended above the ground and exposed to the air, allowing it to dry and ripen quickly. After the grain dries in the "windrow," it can be picked up by the combine and threshed. The swather reduced the timeliness costs endemic to the combine, and within a few years the combine was a fixture on the northern plains as well as on the southern plains.

The combine also reduced the gains from specialized skills (α) (prediction 9.1). Threshing crews had been large—usually more than a dozen men. Some of the threshing jobs required different skills from general farming. The engineer, who maintained the steam engine and kept it running, and the separator man, who acted as his assistant and supervised the crew feeding the machine, were highly skilled relative to the other laborers and the farmer. Both had mechanical knowledge that was of little use in other farming stages where steam was not used. The combine and the gasoline tractor eliminated the need for these skills.

The organization of the turn-of-the-century custom threshing industry is consonant with the predictions of our model. During the late nineteenth and early twentieth centuries, threshing crews were separate firms that in the aggregate employed hundreds of thousands of men. In essence, they were highly specialized "factory farms" that focused on a single production stage. There were great gains from specialization of tasks in this stage and relatively low monitoring costs for hired labor. In this environment, factory-style threshing firms could thrive. Threshing was a long stage, but since the wheat yield was not sensitive to the time of threshing, binding and threshing could be cheaply connected through the market. Although the farmer had to pay close attention to the timing of reaping and binding so that severe weather would not damage the wheat, he could be flexible about threshing because the shocked bundles of wheat could remain unharvested for several months without damage. The combine extended the growing operation into the harvest stage because it generated timeliness costs during harvest. When the number of tasks fell to one, eliminating the gains from specialization, the appropriate farm organization was the family farm.

Sugarcane in Louisiana: Reducing the Extent of the Farm.   The growing and processing of sugarcane provides another example of how seasonality and changes in technology can influence the extent of the farm. Cane was first commercially grown in Louisiana at the end of the eighteenth century. At that time the ground was plowed, planted, and cultivated with the same basic tools for corn and other row crops. At harvest, the cane would be cut by hand and hauled by oxcart to a sugarhouse. There it would be crushed by rollers powered by oxen, and the juice would drain over time into a series of vats. The juice would be brought to a boil and defecated with lime. As the vats progressed, the juice would become a thick syrup and finally would be crystallized in a cool room. There, gravity would be used over a period of two to three weeks to separate the molasses (the dark brown syrup) from the raw sugar.

In this setting the sugarhouse was owned by the farmer and several features constrained its size. First, once sugarcane is cut the valuable complex sugar (sucrose) begins to breakdown into less valuable simple sugars (fructose), making it important to process the raw cane within a few days.[31] This required the sugarhouse to be located close to the fields, given the speed of oxcarts and the lack of railroads. This also meant that the cane, unlike the raw sugar, could not be stored for any length of time. Without coordination between farmers, each essentially had to mill his own cane. Second, the boiling required great amounts of fuel. Heitman (1987) states that "[w]ith the exception of the cost of the cane itself, cordwood to fuel the furnaces was the most expensive cost element of the sugar-making process."

Several innovations took place during the nineteenth century that altered these constraints. First, the introduction of steam-driven mills, like the steam-driven threshers, allowed larger volumes of cane to be processed in one day. Second, rail allowed access to larger supplies of cane and better access to large fuel supplies. Third, many mill technical advances like centrifugals and chemical instruments increased large mill performance. All of these made for huge changes in the optimal size of a sugar mill. Galloway (1989, 140) notes that whereas the old plant could process 1.25 tons of cane per hour, a modern plant can process 227 tons per hour.

Given the labor-intensive cultivation of sugarcane, there was no way a single farmer could provide or even monitor enough wage labor to supply a large modern mill. Farmers entered into long-term contracts with mill owners, or even became part owners of large mills, in order to coordinate the harvest and keep the mill running continuously (predictions 9.7 and 9.8). This coordination was crucial because cut cane cannot be stored. Prior to the changes in milling technology, the family farm was the dominant organization at both the growing and processing stage. Once the new mill technology emerged, however, the family unit only survived at the growing stage.[32] Again, timeliness costs, in this case caused by the rapid deterioration of the cane, influence the choice of organization. The distinction with grains, which are storable after harvest, is striking. As table 1.7 shows, grain production and processing are nearly always segregated by markets, while in sugarcane production and processing are intimately linked through long-term contracts or ownership.[33]

Industrialization of Livestock Production: Reducing the Role of Nature. Nowhere in agriculture has there been more reorganization toward factory-corporate farming than in livestock. This has been especially true for broilers, feedlot cattle, and hogs, where in the past fifty years large factory-corporate firms have come to dominate what were once family farms with small numbers of livestock (Kilman 1994; McBride 1997). For instance, from 1969 to 1992, there was rising concentration in all livestock industries except cow-calf farms (McBride 1997).

The general trend has been to remove stock from an open environment and rear them in climate-controlled barns. In terms of our model, new technologies—in disease control, handling, nutrition, and transportation—have reduced seasonality by increasing the number of cycles per year (prediction 9.4) and reduced the importance and variability of random shocks from nature (prediction 9.5). Compared to field crops, livestock production allows for greater reduction of natural forces because stocks are mobile during growing stages and can often be reared indoors.

The most striking example of factory-corporate livestock production is in feedlot cattle. In the first half of this century "farmer-feeders," located primarily in the Corn Belt, supplied the overwhelming majority of finished cattle to slaughterhouses (Martin 1979, Thompson and O'Mary 1983). These farmers typically had less than 1,000 head of cattle that were purchased in late summer or fall and fattened during the late fall and winter (an off-season for grain farming). During the last forty years, the fed cattle industry has been almost completely transformed into one dominated by large corporate firms that employ highly specialized wage labor. The typical commercial feedlot produces fat cattle in a manner similar to how Ford or GM produces cars: 500- to 600-pound feeder calves are converted into finished cattle after four to five months of feeding and sold to slaughterhouses when they are roughly 1,200 pounds. Production is largely removed from seasonal forces: Young cattle are brought in and fat cattle are sold on a weekly and sometimes daily basis. Labor is highly specialized and includes accountants, feed buyers, cattle buyers, veterinarians, and engineers, as well as less skilled laborers who operate feed mills, load and unload cattle from trucks, and clean feeding pens. The *1997 Census of Agriculture* shows that huge firms dominated the fed cattle industry; 640 firms with average sales of 31,909 head per year accounted for over 75 percent of all fed cattle sold.[34] The 1997 Census also reports that just over one-half of all cattle sold and receipts generated come from feedlots organized as corporations. Many of the cattle on commercial feedlots are actually owned by producers who pay the feedlots for "custom feeding" (see Uvaceck 1983).

The cow-calf industry, which supplies young feeder cattle to commercial feedlots, could not be more different. In the cow-calf system, beef brood cows produce a single calf (twins are rare) each year. This calf is weaned after seven to eight months (weighing 500–600 pounds) and sold to feedlots. Firms in this industry average only 48 head per farm and are dominated by small, family organizations.[35] The industry is strikingly unconcentrated; less than 1 percent of farms have more than 500 head. The 1997 Census also shows the limited presence of corporations: only 2.9 percent of all farms are corporations and just 18.7 percent of the cow inventory is held by corporations.[36] The operation of a cow-calf operation is highly subject to nature, especially seasonal forces (Martin 1979). Although there are regional differences that allow feedlots to operate year round, it is typical for operators in the northern regions to breed cows in the fall, calve in the early spring, pasture the animals during the summer, and wean and sell feeder calves in the fall. Compared to the routine, factory processes in feedlot operations, running a cow-calf farm comprises relatively unpredictable short stages (such as calving) that occur only once a year and require on-the-spot decision making (prediction 9.3).

Like feedlots, the broiler industry has its roots in small farms. In fact, the industrialization of chicken production preceded that in cattle feedlots. Prior to the 1930s, most chickens were raised in relatively small flocks on family farms. During this period eggs, not meat, were the primary products and most chickens were slaughtered in the spring. The reorganization of the poultry industry began in the 1930s, and today virtually all broilers (2- to 3-pound chickens) are produced by large, factory-corporate firms.[37] The introduction of antibiotics and other drugs have allowed poultry to be bred, hatched, and grown in highly controlled indoor environments in which disease, climate, food, water, and vitamins and other inputs are regulated to the point where poultry barns are virtual assembly lines. At the various stages of production, broiler companies employ wage laborers who undertake specialized but routine tasks such as cleaning, feeding, and immunizing.

Modern broiler production begins in a company-owned breeding farm where eggs are laid. The eggs are typically delivered to a hatchery firm, which more closely resembles a hospital than a farm. After eggs are incubated and the chicks are hatched, the broiler organization takes on an old form. Even with modern technology, the critical "grow-out" period of a chicken's life is subject to random forces of disease and weather. Thus the large companies routinely contract out growing services to small, family-based "growers" and compensate them as partial residual claimants of the growth of the broilers in size and value.[38] Growers feed and care for the chickens for a six-week period until they become large enough for processing. Once chicks have matured, they return to the company for processing in large assembly-line facilities that employ hundreds of workers.

In the last two decades, the hog industry has followed the path of the broiler industry.[39] Hog production is increasingly dominated by large, factory-corporate firms that breed and farrow (birthing) pigs in confinement in huge indoor facilities. Like the broiler industry, the hog companies routinely contract with small firms for the grow-out period and later do the processing in assembly-line fashion in company-owned facilities with company labor.[40]

Table 9.2
Definition of variables

Dependent variables	
CAPITAL	= total capital assets (buildings, land and equipment) in $100,000.
FAMILY FARM	= 1 if the farm is owned and operated by the family farmer.
FARM ACRES	= number of acres on the farm.
Independent variables	
AGE	= farmer's age in years.
BC	= 1 if the farm is located in British Columbia; = 0 if located in Louisiana.
BEEF	= 1 if farm livestock are beef cattle; = 0 if no beef cattle.
CYCLES > 1	= fraction of farmland in crops that have more than one cycle; = 0 otherwise.
CYCLES < 1	= fraction of farmland in crops that have fewer than one cycle; = 0 otherwise.
DAIRY	= 1 if farm livestock are dairy cattle; = 0 if no dairy cattle.
EDUCATION	= number of years of formal schooling.
FAMILY FARM	= 1 if the farm is owned and operated by the family farmer;
	= 0 if not a family farm.
IRRIGATION	= fraction of land plot that is irrigated.
RENTED LAND	= 1 if land was rented; = 0 if owned.

The contrast between industrial livestock and grain farming, which could hardly be more dramatic, results from the elimination of seasonal parameters and the reduction of random forces (θ and σ^2) in their production (predictions 9.3 and 9.5). The driving force in modern livestock production is to reduce the role of nature by bringing production indoors to control climate and disease. As a result, except for cow-calf operations, the livestock industry is perhaps the most specialized of any farm commodity, and the most dominated by companies organized in the corporate-factory form.[41]

Evidence from Contemporary Farms in Louisiana and British Columbia

The evidence from the historical and aggregate data provides support for our model, but it does not allow us to conduct any formal econometric hypothesis tests. In this section we use our farm-level data to test some specific predictions. This analysis comes in two parts. First, we estimate the determinants of farm organization; that is, the determinants of the choice between family and larger nonfamily organizations. Second, we estimate the effect of the choice of farm organization on the size of the farm, both in terms of the value of capital and the acreage controlled by the farm. The variables used in the regressions are listed and defined in table 9.2. For the first exercise we use a dummy variable FAMILY FARM to identify family farms.[42] For the second exercise we use CAPITAL and FARM ACRES as our dependent variables.

The Choice of Farm Organization.   Prediction 9.4 says that as the number of cycles increases, we predict that family farming will be less common. One important element of seasonality that can be defined empirically is the number of cycles per year for a given crop in a given location. We classify the crops in our sample into three categories using the variable CYCLES: crops that potentially have more than one cycle per year; crops that always have just one cycle per year; and crops that may have fewer than one cycle per year.[43] In the equations reported in table 9.1, we include the variables CYCLES > 1 and CYCLES < 1, leaving CYCLES = 1 out of the equations.[44] The distinction between beef and dairy cattle can also be used to test some predictions of our model. Dairy animals are kept close to their barns so that they can be milked twice a day, while beef animals usually range in open pastures. Daily milk production is easier to measure than beef production, and dairy processors engage in exceptional forms of measurement to ensure that the farmer does not carelessly handle or tamper with the milk.[45] Finally, there are more routine day-to-day tasks with dairy production than cow-calf beef operations. None of the beef operations in our sample are large feedlots with similarly routine daily tasks. All of these factors reduce monitoring costs on dairy farms. In terms of our model, dairy farms have more cycles and fewer stages than beef operations. Hence, the use of farm managers and partners is more viable on dairy farms than beef farms. Since the gains from specialization are greater with more tasks, our model predicts that the probability of family farm organization will be higher for beef operations (positive coefficient on BEEF) than for dairy operations (negative coefficient on DAIRY). The omitted category consists of farms with either no stock or noncattle stock.

Prediction 9.5 says that as the natural stage uncertainty (σ^2) diminishes, the farm is less likely to be a family farm. Irrigation can control the effect of nature by reducing variance in output. In terms of the model, irrigation reduces σ^2. The coefficient on the variable IRRIGATION (percent of farmland irrigated) is predicted to have a negative sign. The estimated equation also included numerous control variables including the percentage of rented farmland (RENTED LAND), farmer's age (AGE, AGE2), farmer's education (EDUCATION, EDUCATION^2), and a dummy for British Columbia (BC).

We use the British Columbia-Louisiana data to estimate the determinants of farm organization choice and test some specific predictions from our model. The empirical specification, for the complete model is

$$F_i^* = X_i \beta_i + \epsilon_i \quad i = 1, \ldots, n; \quad \text{and} \tag{9.12}$$

$$F_i = \begin{cases} 1, & \text{if } F_i^* > 0 \\ 0, & \text{if } F_i^* \leq 0, \end{cases} \tag{9.13}$$

where F_i^* is an unobserved farm organization response variable; F_i is the observed dichoto-mous choice of farm organization for farm i, which is equal to 1 for family farms and equal to 0 for nonfamily farms; X_i is a row vector of exogenous variables including the constant; β_i is a column vector of unknown coefficients; and ϵ_i is a farm-specific error term. We use a logit model to generate maximum likelihood estimates of the model given by equations (9.12) and (9.13).

The first column in table 9.3 shows the logit coefficient estimates for the model given by equations (9.12) and (9.13) for a sample of 959 farms. Prediction 9.6 implies that the estimated coefficient on CYCLES > 1 should be negative and the estimated coefficient on CYCLES < 1 should be positive. In table 9.3, both estimated coefficients for the CYCLES variable have the predicted signs and are statistically significant. Prediction 9.6 also implies that the estimated coefficient for BEEF and DAIRY should be positive and negative, respectively. Table 9.3 shows that the coefficient estimates BEEF and DAIRY have the predicted signs and the estimates are statistically significant. Prediction 9.5 implies that the estimated coefficient for IRRIGATION (percent of farmland irrigated) should be negative. Indeed, the estimated coefficients for IRRIGATION are negative, although the estimates fall just short of being statistically significant. The estimated coefficients on the control variables AGE, AGE^2, EDUCATION, and $EDUCATION^2$ (listed as farmer variables in the table) have no predicted coefficient signs. The estimates show, however, that older and more educated farmers are more likely to organize their operations as family farms.

The Level of Capital across Farm Organizations. Prediction 9.10 states that the level of capital will be lowest for family farmers who face the highest costs of capital and largest for corporate farms that face the lowest cost of capital. Simple farm-level averages from the British Columbia–Louisiana data confirm this prediction. In these data, the average value of capital, across all crops, for family farms is $75,474; for partnerships the average is $122,583, for family corporations the average is $191,692, and for nonfamily corporate farms the average is $281,205. The differences in these means are all statistically signifi-cant.

We can more precisely test this prediction by estimating the level of capital per farm (k_i) using the following empirical model:

$$k_i = F_i \gamma_i + X_i \xi_i + \epsilon_i \quad i = 1, \ldots, n, \tag{9.14}$$

where F_i is a farm organization choice dummy variable; γ_i is the corresponding coefficient; X_i is a row vector of exogenous variables including the constant; ξ_i is a column vector of unknown coefficients; and ϵ_i is a farm-specific error term.

Table 9.3
Regression estimates on farm organization and farm capital: British Columbia and Louisiana (1992)

	Farm organization	Farm capital	Farm acreage
Dependent variable	FAMILY FARM	CAPITAL	FARM ACRES
Model	Logit	OLS	OLS
Independent variables			
CONSTANT	−1.92	−1.92	−15.75
	(−1.31)	(−2.78)*	(−0.03)
Crop variables			
CYCLES> 1	−1.17	.65	19.61
	(−5.18)*	(1.42)	(0.25)
CYCLES< 1	1.03	−0.60	−163.36
	(2.43)*	(−0.99)	(−1.53)
BEEF	0.83	−0.86	25.41
	(3.56)*	(−2.17)*	(.38)
DAIRY	−1.39	4.18	−347.46
	(−2.59)*	(3.93)*	(−1.86)
Farm variables			
BC	−0.20	1.36	−270.15
	(−0.34)	(3.79)*	(−4.62)*
IRRIGATION	−0.01	0.06	−6.10
	(−1.15)	(4.49)*	(−2.58)*
RENTED LAND	−0.35	−0.20	
	(−1.90)	(−0.55)	
FAMILY FARM		−2.54	−431.96
		(−7.22)*	(−7.45)*
Farmer variables			
AGE	0.07	0.10	13.53
	(1.48)	(1.23)	(0.97)
AGE^2	−40.006	−0.008	−0.14
	(−1.53)	(−1.09)	(−1.01)
EDUCATION	0.34	0.52	84.95
	(2.21)*	(1.79)	(1.68)
EDUCATION^2	−0.01	−0.02	−2.19
	(−2.44)*	(−1.81)	(−1.13)
Observations	959	859	959
% correct	74.77%	NA	NA
Log likelihood	550.3	NA	NA
Model χ^2 (df)	78.08(12)	NA	NA
$\bar{R}^2$	NA	0.171	0.129
F (df)	NA	16.68 (12,846)	13.95 (12,946)

Note: t-statistics in parentheses. NA = not applicable.
* significant at the 5 percent level (one-tailed test for coefficient with predicted signs).

We estimate equation (9.14) using OLS for a sample of 859 farms. This sample is slightly smaller than that used to estimate the farm organization model because of missing data for the CAPITAL variable.[46] The second column in table 9.3 shows the OLS coefficient estimates for the model. Prediction 9.10 implies the hypothesis that the coefficient on F_i (measured with the variable FAMILY FARM) is *negative*; that is, $\gamma_i < 0$ because a family farm will have the highest capital costs among the farm organizations we examine. As predicted, the estimated coefficient is negative and statistically significant. In the OLS estimate of CAPITAL we use the same set of exogenous variables (X) used in the farm organization estimates. In general, the estimated coefficients for these variables are statistically significant. These estimates are also, in many cases, consistent with human capital theory. For example, older and more educated farmers tend to have greater capital stocks, but the effects of education and experience tend to have diminishing returns. The estimates also show that dairy farms use more capital than nondairy farms and that farms with irrigated land are more capital intense.[47]

In addition to using the dollar level of capital as a measure of a farm's capital intensity, we also estimate equation 9.14 by substituting farm acreage for capital (prediction 9.11). Because farm acreage includes rented land, the variable RENTED LAND is omitted from the FARM ACRES equation. The results shown in the third column of table 9.3 support prediction 9.11 and further confirm the capital stock regression. Not only do family farms have less capital, they also utilize less land. Our estimates show that, ceteris paribus, family farms use roughly 400 fewer acres of land than nonfamily farms.

9.5 Summary

Although the organization of industry has generally followed a transition from family firms to large factory-style corporations, farming remains a last bastion of family production.[48] Production stages in farming tend to be short and infrequent and require few distinct tasks, thus limiting the benefits of specialization and making wage labor especially costly to monitor. Only when farmers can control the effects of nature by mitigating the effects of seasonality and random shocks to output does farm organization gravitate toward factory processes, developing into the large-scale corporate forms found elsewhere in the economy.

Our model explains both important historical trends in agriculture and more subtle differences in farm organization. As our model predicts, family-controlled farm production has narrowed to those stages that include the most biologically based aspects of farming. Factory farming has failed in highly seasonal crops. Changes in wheat harvesting technology, which shortened stages and increased the severity of timing problems, have altered the structure of farm organization by extending the family farm into the harvest stage. Changes in livestock technology, which largely eliminated nature, have allowed factory-corporate production to dominate in feedlot cattle, hogs, and poultry. Our model also correctly predicts impacts on farm organization in British Columbia and Louisiana due to crop cycles and monitoring costs. Finally, our model correctly predicts the differences in capital levels and farm acreage observed in different farm organizations.

EW Notably, our focus on the trade-off between moral hazard incentives and the gains from specialization in a large organization often generates predictions at odds with those based on risk sharing. Our model says that family farms will emerge especially in the most risky situations—large variance in season dates, large variance in stage specific random shocks, and so on—because these situations are filled with tremendous potential for moral hazard. The risk-sharing approach, however, would imply that large-scale organizations would emerge to spread this risk around. Yet as the world has shown us time and time again, the family farm dominates agriculture whenever Mother Nature remains unchecked.

Although there is compelling support for our approach, we have made a number of simplifications. First, we limited the discussion of hired labor to the corporate farm. Although this is where hired labor is most important, it remains true that nearly all farms hire some part-time labor and often use family labor. Second, we did not examine interstage complementarity and changing farm ownership over different stages. These important features of organization are left for future research. Third, we have ignored the role of economies of scale. It is possible, for example, that farms become large factory-corporate firms when the extent of the market increases enough for firms to capture scale economies. The economies-of-scale argument would imply that for commodities like corn and wheat, actively traded in world markets, farms should be large corporate firms. Certainly, an extensive market is a necessary condition for large-scale production, but it is not sufficient. Only when seasonal forces are limited can economies of scale be realized, as for example, in milling grain into flour. It simply would not pay to invest in highly specialized, large-scale capital unless seasonal forces were so lacking that highly specialized wage labor could effectively be employed. In this regard, our findings are consistent with Becker and Murphy (1992) who note: "The efficient division of labor is then limited by coordination costs, not by market size" (1142).

Should we worry about the end of family farming? Will family farms be with us in the twenty-first century? No, and yes. Although the organization of industry has generally followed a transition from family firms to large factory-style corporations, most farming remains a family production activity. Short infrequent production stages in farming limit the benefits of specialization and create moral hazard. Farm organization will gravitate toward factory processes only when farmers can control the seasonal and random shock effects of nature. When this occurs, farms develop into the large-scale corporate businesses found elsewhere in the economy. If wheat could be grown indoors, wheat farming would begin to look like automobile manufacturing or broiler production. Massive factory production in grains, however, seems unlikely. To be sure, farms will continue to get larger in acreage and output, and there will be fewer farm families. But this does not imply a fundamental change in firm structure. This is neither good nor bad, just evidence of the invisible hand at work in the organization of an industry.

10 Conclusion

Most of the six acres of land we had bought with the house was planted with vines, and these had been looked after for years under the traditional system of metayage: the owner of the land pays the capital costs of new vine stock and fertilizer, while the farmer does the work of spraying, cropping and pruning. At the end of the season, the farmer takes two-thirds of the profits and the owner one-third.
—Peter Mayle, *A Year in Provence*

The excerpt from Mayle's famous travelogue through the south of France describes the simple structure of typical cropshare contracts and generates a number of interesting questions. One wonders how long the contracts are, and whether they are written? How often are they renewed, and why does the owner pay for fertilizer but not for spraying and pruning? Are the terms similar for other crops? As powerful as neoclassical economics is, it can only address issues related to prices and volumes of trade—it is silent on how trade is organized. The transaction cost paradigm, however, is intended to answer and capable of answering these questions.

A telling example of the distinction between transaction cost and neoclassical economics is illustrated on a recent back cover of the *Journal of Political Economy* (*JPE*) addressing Mayle's observation. The *JPE* regularly features excerpts from literary sources on its back cover, accompanied by titles that cleverly link economic theory to the subject at hand. In its December 2000 issue the *JPE* reprinted Mayle's quote with the neoclassical title "Cobb and Douglas Visit the South of France." The reference to a constant-returns-to-scale production function with coefficients on labor of two-thirds and on capital of one-third was too much to resist. This seemingly trivial example shows how a purely neoclassical approach is incapable of explaining contracts and organization. As Coase pointed out over sixty years ago, the nature of the firm hinges on transaction costs. A pure neoclassical model has nothing to say about organizational issues. The allocation of resources is independent of all distributions of property rights in the neoclassical model.

The Transaction Cost Approach

The transaction cost approach is related to other economic models of organization.[1] For example, models found in modern contract theory or agency theory routinely contain transaction cost elements, either explicitly or implicitly. These models often start with unobservable effort, actions, or types. In fact, the recent work by Baker, Gibbs, and Holström (1994), Holmström and Milgrom (1994), Lazear (1995), and Prendergast (2002)—with its focus on empirical phenomenon, abstraction from risk sharing, and analysis of multiple incentives—is hard to distinguish from transaction cost economics.[2] Likewise, the work of Hart (1995) and the recent work in the economics of property law and contract law (for example, Ellickson 1991; Hansmann 1996) use models of organization related to the transaction cost model described here. What then makes the transaction cost approach any different, if at all?

Perhaps it is a matter of emphasis, but in our view there are several points that distinguish the transaction cost approach to contracts and organization. First, transaction cost economics has an empirical focus on real social phenomenon, such as actual contracts, firms, law, regulations, and so on. It is important that economists explain observable phenomena. In contrast to this, many purely theoretical models explain stylized facts that often have little correspondence with the world. In this respect, transaction cost economics is "applied economics." Second, transaction cost economics emphasizes testable hypotheses and not simply the generation of logical explanations. Telling a story, no matter how difficult, is valuable, but ultimately the test is how well that story fares against real data. These first two points are important if we feel the goal of economics is the empirical understanding of human behavior.

Third, transaction cost economics recognizes and emphasizes that assets are complex collections of attributes, and that a full understanding of economic organization must explain the details of the ownership and control of these attributes. Although many contract models are based on hidden actions, these models often have single dimensions over which these actions take place. For example, in these models a manager may be constrained to shirking only over hours of effort. It seems likely, however, that the real problem with controlling managers happens on margins other than effort levels in terms of hours worked.[3] Fourth, transaction cost economics abstracts from risk aversion and risk avoidance and, instead, focuses on pure incentive trade-offs. As we have mentioned in many places, the inclusion of risk sharing adds complications without adding empirical tractability, and the transaction cost approach avoids this line of reasoning. Finally, transaction cost economics assumes that organizations are chosen to maximize the total value net of transaction costs. Whether it is a farmer and a landowner, a worker and a capitalist, or a lawyer and a client, the transaction cost approach argues that the structure of organization is governed by the pursuit of wealth and the specific transaction costs that arise in that context.

Ultimately, the value of the transaction cost paradigm comes down to the importance one places on the role of transaction costs. On this point, again we side with Coase. In both his work on the firm and on social cost, Coase pointed out that transaction costs were necessary and sufficient for an explanation of organization. This follows from the Coase Theorem, which states that contracts and organizations do not have an impact on the efficient allocation of resources when transaction costs are zero. When transaction costs are positive, then the allocation of property rights matters and different organizational forms yield different levels of wealth. Hence, the most important aspect of Coase's work relates to what he said about positive transaction costs. It is ironic that so few know of Coase's work beyond the simple zero transaction cost understanding of the Coase Theorem. As Coase (1988) himself said: "The world of zero transaction cost has often been described as a Coasian world. Nothing could be further from the truth. It is the world of modern economic theory, one which I was hoping to persuade economists to leave" (174).

An Empirical Understanding of Agricultural Organization

Transaction cost economics has a long-standing tradition of successful empirical analysis. This has been our focus too, and in working with the data from the four regions we have examined, we have found some robust results. Without simply repeating the empirical details, we wish to summarize several dominant findings. We make this summary with the understanding that our results are far from universal and many types of agriculture were ignored.

First, when farmers and landowners contract for land, the contracts are simple in the sense that they are mostly oral and short term. They tend to be policed through the market via reputation, and the common law assists in providing default rules to simplify the structure of contracts. Specific assets are often absent as well, providing further rationale for simple contracts. In many rural farm settings, where individuals know one another well, expect to have repeated dealings with each other, and can observe individual behaviors, then reputations can sustain optimal behavior. This does not work for all farming activities, but as we have noted, it is sufficient for blatantly observable cheating. In those less common cases where specific assets are present, contracts become more formal, more detailed, and longer lasting.

Second, contract structures are used to police behavior that is difficult to verify by a third party. This behavior, which is costly to observe, is present when individuals are not full residual claimants, and it is strongly influenced by enforcement and measurement costs. We were often able to link these costs to specific characteristics of the crops and land. In particular, crop type was an important factor in determining the type of contract that governs its production because different crops present different opportunities for farmer moral hazard. We also found some evidence for the presence of capital constraints leading to more share contracting. Individual characteristics related to education or family relationships with other contracting parties are not large or robust explanatory variables of contract choice. Nor did we find support for the traditional agricultural ladder theory of farm organization. Wealth levels were found to be important in questions of asset ownership. One of the strongest categories of evidence we found for the transaction cost approach was our discovery of the input sharing dichotomy that depended on the costs of measuring inputs.

Third, the classic trade-off between risk and incentives does not explain the choice of contracts or organizations in agriculture, nor elsewhere as the recent agency literature has shown. Our empirical results show two things: The basic risk predictions are refuted, and the estimated risk parameters are relatively small. In particular, the classic prediction that more risky crops should be shared is debunked by our data. A decade ago this failure to find support for the risk-incentive trade-off would have been somewhat surprising, but in recent years the evidence has been accumulating and agency theory has responded as well.

Fourth, we found that farming is dominated by family production when the random and systematic effects of nature cannot be controlled. Mother Nature not only provides an opportunity for moral hazard but also limits the possibilities of specialization. Generally speaking, farm production provides many opportunities for moral hazard and few for exploiting economies of size. Thus farming is fertile ground for family production. In those cases where nature's seasons and uncertainty can be controlled, agricultural production tends to be organized as large-scale corporate firms as in much of the modern economy. Our findings here offer support for the ideas of many early-twentieth-century agricultural economists (for example, Brewster 1950, Ellickson and Brewster 1947; Holmes 1928) and even those of some classical economists (for example, Mill 1965 [1871]).

Beyond agriculture, empirical work in transaction cost economics has been a success story, particularly in our understanding of property rights (Alston, Libecap, and Mueller 2000; Libecap 1989) and modern business organization (Masten 1996; Masten and Williamson 1999). To this body of literature our study adds a detailed industry-wide analysis across space and time. Though this study may add more depth than breadth, it shows how a consistent analytical framework can be used to generate a myriad of testable hypotheses.

Limits of the Transaction Cost Approach

Again, it is a question of emphasis, but there are three limitations common to this paradigm. First, a detailed knowledge and data is required for an accurate understanding of contracts and organization. How can one start with the assertion that contracts are designed to mitigate transaction costs if one has no idea how these costs arise? Sitting in an office, one can imagine shirking behavior and outright theft, but often the realistic threats and actual behaviors are more subtle. Likewise, knowledge about an asset's attributes and their relative importance often requires some firsthand experience or frontline knowledge. If economists are really going to understand firm behavior, then they have to become aware of the details of firms and production.

Second, empirical work in transaction cost economics often, but not always suffers from data limitations. With transaction cost economics, there are no directly observable or measurable variables to gauge transaction costs. In farming, there is no input called a "transaction cost," nor is there any perfect signal of such a variable. If there was, then the contracting parties themselves would know what it was, and there would be no transaction costs. Generally speaking, this problem has contributed to an almost "second-class" stature for transaction cost economics within the profession. Although using proxy variables is a second-best alternative, we feel that some proxies are better than others. We have attempted two things to alleviate this problem. First, we have sought predictions from our models that did not require a measurement of transaction costs. For example, in our prediction regarding the input-output sharing dichotomy, nothing in the prediction requires such a variable, even though the prediction falls from a transaction cost model. The input and output shares are completely observable. Second, we have sought to find practical and effective proxies. In the empirical risk-sharing literature, the proxies for risk are often self-reported indices of risk preferences or ad hoc dummy variables (for example, gender). We have never relied on survey data over preferences. All of our data come from questions regarding the facts of the farm, and our measures of risk (exogenous variability) come from the actual output data from the region.

Finally, perhaps because of the empirical focus, transaction cost economics often suffers from a lack of a generally accepted, well-defined body of theory. Even the very definition of transaction costs is still not generally accepted. Many economists simply view it as "the cost of trading" or the "costs of a market transaction." With such definitions it is easy to see that the Coase Theorem has little relevance to the study of organization.[4] This limited formal theory is perhaps another reason for the second-class status of transaction cost economics, but even this shortcoming is changing over time. As mentioned above, much of modern contract theory is adopting the transaction cost approach, and there is a movement away from the simplistic view of transaction costs just mentioned. This book, with our explicit definition, consistent modeling, and empirical focus is simply another step forward in the formal development of transaction cost economics.

Final Remarks

We have found that the pattern of contracts and organization in modern and historical agriculture is consistent with an effort to mitigate transaction costs. These costs, in turn, arise from attempts to establish and maintain property rights to complex assets, such as land, equipment, crop and livestock output, and human capital. Ownership of assets and tasks and output is ideal in terms of incentives but forgoes the potential gains from specialization. Thus people contract with each other and transaction costs ensue. Although our book has focused on several specific transaction cost issues on the farm, we hope that it has become obvious that the number of such related issues in agriculture is virtually endless. Whether the issue is how farmers and custom operators control moral hazard in the presence of great timeliness costs, or how land rental creates potential for soil exploitation by renting farmers, transaction costs are ubiquitous.

The theory of organizations has developed a great deal over the past thirty years, and we want to suggest that agricultural economists, with their knowledge of farming, are well positioned to take advantage of the fertile ground of economic organization. A number of interesting issues in the economics of contracts and organization could be examined in agriculture. How important are share-fixed fee combination contracts such as those in franchising? How important is reputation in enforcing contracts? What types of transaction cost problems arise from dynamic changes in contract terms and renegotiation? Perhaps one of the most pressing problems is what best explains the recent and dramatic increase in the use of production contracts. One advantage of having agricultural economists interested in organization is that the demand for data would increase. Data collection is crucial, but currently the census bureaus in Canada and United States do not gather much organizational and contract data. This no doubt reflects the dominance of the neoclassical economists in agricultural circles. Finally, it should be noted that interest in organizational issues would mean a return to the historic roots of agricultural economics, back to the ideas of those who first pondered the nature of the farm.

Appendix A: Data

A.1   Description of Data Sets

1986 Nebraska and South Dakota Data

The data from Nebraska and South Dakota come from the *1986 Nebraska and South Dakota Leasing Survey*. The leasing survey was conducted by Professor Bruce Johnson of the University of Nebraska and Professor Larry Jannsen of South Dakota State University (Johnson et al. 1988). The survey was funded by the Economic Research Service of the United States Department of Agriculture. A summary of the study and the survey procedures can be found in Bruce Johnson, Larry Jannsen, Michael Lundeen, and J. David Aitken, *Agricultural Land Leasing and Rental Market Characteristics: A Case Study of South Dakota and Nebraska* (report prepared for the Economic Research Service of the United States Department of Agriculture, 1988).

Johnson and Jannsen obtained a list of landowners and farmers (from the Agricultural Stabilization and Conservation Service List of Producers) in each county in Nebraska and South Dakota that participated in, or was eligible to participate in, federal commodity programs. (According to Steven Munk, USDA Extension Agent for Minnehaha County in Sioux Fall, SD, essentially all farmers in these two states were eligible for federal programs.) From the farmer-landowner list, a random sample of names was chosen; the survey was sent to 6,347 individuals in Nebraska and 4,111 in South Dakota. The response rate was 32 percent in Nebraska and 35 percent in South Dakota. The number of usable responses was 1,615 for Nebraska and 1,155 for South Dakota. Each observation represents a single farmer or landowner for the 1986 crop season. For most of our tests we reorganized the data so that each observation is a single farmland contract between a farmer and a landowner. Because many individuals had more than one contract, this increased the sample size by 20 percent and resulted in 2,101 observations for Nebraska and 1,331 for South Dakota.

The *Leasing Survey* data contain information on the general attributes of the farmer and landowner, the number of acres owned and leased, the type of contract, the shares and cash rent, the type of crop grown, and other similar information. The data set has no information on the levels of inputs used in farming. There are several questions on pasture/range leases, but due to differences in the type of questions, the pasture lease data are not comparable to that for the cropshare or cash rent contracts. There are relatively few pasture leases as well. The *Leasing Survey* data were combined with county level data on population per square mile (the DENSITY variable) taken from the *County and City Data Book 1987*, published by the Bureau of the Census (U.S. Department of Commerce, Bureau of the Census 1989a).

1979 British Columbia Contract Data

Data for the 1979 British Columbia landowner-farmer contracts come from the *British Columbia Ministry of Agriculture Lease Survey*. This survey was conducted by the Farm Management group in the Vernon, British Columbia, office of the ministry. The survey was done by telephone and included farmers from throughout the province; however, farmers in the Okanagan Region were oversampled. The number of usable responses was 378. This survey asked few questions and thus has fewer variables.

1992 British Columbia and Louisiana Contract Data

A single survey questionnaire was used to collect information for both of these data sets. Al Ortego, USDA Extension Economist at Louisiana State University, and Howard Joynt, British Columbia Ministry of Agriculture, both provided help in designing the 1992 survey and collecting related data. Funding for the data collection was provided by the Social Sciences and Humanities Research Council of Canada.

Data for the landowner-farmer cropshare contracts come from the *1992 British Columbia Farmland Ownership and Leasing Survey*, which we conducted in January 1993. The survey was sent to a random sample of 3,000 British Columbia farm operators. The number of usable responses was 460. Data for the landowner-farmer cropshare contracts come from the *1992 Louisiana Farmland Ownership and Leasing Survey*, which we conducted in January 1993. The survey was sent to a random sample (chosen by the parish USDA County Agents) of 5,000 Louisiana farm operators. The number of usable responses was 530. Unlike the Nebraska–South Dakota data, these data do not have detailed information on landowners or input sharing. The survey does have information on ownership

Table A.1
Definition of dependent variables

Dependent variables	
ADJUSTMENT	= 1 if cash rent contract contained a clause adjusting rent for high yields.
ANNUAL	= 1 if an annual contract, = 0 if a multiyear contract.
CAPITAL	= total capital assets (buildings, land and equipment) in $100,000.
CHEMICAL APPLICATION	= 1 if farmer pays 100% of chemical application cost;
	= 0 if the farmer pays the same portion as his cropshare.
CONTRACT	= 1 if contract was a cropshare contract; = 0 if a cash rent contract.
DRYING	= 1 if farmer pays 100% of crop drying cost;
	= 0 if the farmer pays the same portion as his cropshare.
ENERGY	= 1 if farmer pays 100% of the irrigation energy cost;
	= 0 if the farmer pays the same portion as his cropshare.
FAMILY FARM	= 1 if the farm is owned and operated by the family farmer;
	= 0 if not.
FARM ACRES	= number of acres on the farm.
FERTILIZER	= 1 if farmer pays 100% of the fertilizer cost;
	= 0 if the farmer pays the same portion as his cropshare.
HARVEST	= 1 if farmer pays 100% of the harvesting cost;
	= 0 if the farmer pays the same portion as his cropshare.
HERBICIDE	= 1 if farmer pays 100% of the herbicide cost;
	= 0 if the farmer pays the same portion as his cropshare.
INSECTICIDE	= 1 if farmer pays 100% of the insecticide cost;
	= 0 if the farmer pays the same portion as his cropshare.
ORAL	= 1 if an oral contract; = 0 if a written contract.
QSHARE	= 1 if farmer pays all input costs;
	= 0 if farmer pays input costs equal to his output share.
RENTED BUILDING	= 1 if building was rented; = 0 if owned.
RENTED LAND	= 1 if land was rented; = 0 if owned.
RENTED EQUIPMENT	= 1 if equipment was rented; = 0 if owned.
SEED	= 1 if farmer pays 100% of the seed cost;
	= 0 if the farmer pays the same fraction as his cropshare.
SHARE	= percent of crop to the farmer.
SHARE-UP	= 1 if share to farmer increased in past 5 years; = 0 if not.
SHARE-DOWN	= 1 if share to farmer decreased in past 5 years; = 0 of not.

of land and other assets and farm organization. The 1,004 different farms that make up the British Columbia–Louisiana sample are often arranged in various ways to create different data sets. A data set may be organized around a farm, a plot of land, equipment, or buildings, the sample size varies depending on the choice of the question to be examined. All of the variables used in the book are defined in tables A.1 and A.2. Their means and standard deviations are provided in tables A.3, A.4, and A.5.

A.2 Contract Data Compared to State and Provincial Averages

For selected variables we compared our sample means to those taken from statewide census data for *1987 Census of Agriculture,* the most recent census (U.S. Department of Commerce, Bureau of the Census 1989b, c). The comparisons are shown in table A.6. In many cases the means are nearly identical; in all cases they are within one standard deviation of each other. We conclude that our samples are quite representative of agriculture in British Columbia, Louisiana, Nebraska, and South Dakota.

A.3   Crop Yield Variability Data

Data on yield variability come from state and provincial agricultural statistical offices. We collected a times series (1975–1991) of per-acre yields for each crop at the county and parish level for Louisiana, Nebraska, and South Dakota. The precise number of years varied across crops because of data availability. The most common unit of measure is bushels and tons, although these vary by crop and jurisdiction. For Nebraska and South Dakota, the same data were collected for "regions," which from five to ten counties and their compositions were drawn from the respective state department of agriculture crop reporting systems. Regional data was unavailable for Louisiana crops. For British Columbia, yield data are only available for each of the eight "Census Agricultural Regions" most of which are larger and more heterogeneous than the American states, were used in the study. As a result, these regions are of little use for the risk tests that we used for the U.S. data. Table A.7 shows the variable means for the crop yield data, while table A.7 shows the distribution of yield variability (measured both by coefficient of variation and by standard deviation) for some of the major widespread crops in the four jurisdictions.

OLS Estimation of Cropsharing at the State-Province Level

Table A.9 shows OLS estimation of three separate equations for each state or province. The dependent variables in these equations are the fraction of cropshare contracts, the fraction of cropshare acres among leased acres, and the fraction of cropshare acres among all acres farmed. These represent three different measures of what it might mean to increase sharing when a crop becomes more uncertain. Overall, the regression estimates fail to reject the null hypothesis that CV does not influence contract choice; in other words, we find no support for the hypothesis that higher yield variability leads to more cropsharing. We also pooled the data and obtained the OLS estimates found in table A.10, where absolute t-statistics are in parentheses, the adjusted $R^2 = 0.42$, and the overall F-value = 4.97. FRACTION CROPSHARE = the fraction of all land in cropshare contracts, while the other independent variables are state-provincial dummies for four of the five samples.

Price-Yield Correlations

In chapter 6 we discussed the possibility that prices and yields might be negatively correlated. Table A.11 shows the price-yield correlations for various crops and across various regions. In general, the table shows no statistically significant correlation.

Additional Risk Regressions

In chapter 6 we estimated many regressions to test the relationship between crop yield variation and contract choice. We also estimated several different specifications using this microlevel data, which are shown in table A.12. The dependent variable in our estimated equation, CONTRACT, is dichotomous (1 if cropshare contract, 0 if cash rent), so we use logit regression. Data limitations prevent us from using CVs for each crop for state- and province-level samples, so we instead use crop dummy variables to estimate the effects of exogenous variability on contract choice.

   In table A.12, equations (1)–(6) show that crop riskiness does not successfully explain the use of share contracts among Nebraska, South Dakota, British Columbia, and Louisiana farmers. Of the twenty-eight estimated crop dummy coefficients in equations (1)–(5), only four are consistent with risk sharing. In all equations the left-out crop dummy is WHEAT. Each equation includes a dummy variable OTHER CROPS whose parameter estimates are not reported because the crops included in this dummy vary across regions: In Nebraska it might be rye or sunflowers, while in Louisiana it might be sweet potatoes. As such, comparisons of it with WHEAT have little meaning. Testing the risk-sharing hypothesis requires ranking crops by CV for the appropriate state or province. Because the crops and the CV rankings vary across these jurisdictions, it is not possible to visually compare the

Table A.2
Definition of independent variables

Independent variables

ABSENT	= 1 if landowner lived in county different than contracted land; = 0 otherwise.
ACRES	= number of acres covered by contract.
ACRES OWNED	= percentage of farmed acres that are owned by the farmer.
AGE	= farmer's age in years (categorical for Nebraska and South Dakota).
BEEF	= 1 if farm livestock are beef cattle; = 0 if no beef cattle.
BC	= 1 if the farm is located in British Columbia; = 0 if located in Louisiana.
BUILDING VALUE	= total value in $1,000s of all owned buildings multiplied by the equity in the farm.
BUILDING AGE	= age in years.
BUILDING SIZE	= square foot of building.
CAPITAL	= total capital assets (buildings, land and equipment) in $100,000.
CORN[a]	= 1 if corn was the major income producing crop; = 0 if not.
CHANGED PARTIES	= 1 if contracting parties have changed in past five years;
	= 0 if they have not changed.
COUNTY CV	= coefficient of variation for crop yield in a county.
COUNTY MEAN	= mean crop yield in a county.
COUNTY STD	= standard deviation of crop yield in a county.
CROP VALUE	= value of crop in dollars.
CYCLES > 1	= fraction of farmland in crops that have more than one cycle.
CYCLES < 1	= fraction of farmland in crops that have fewer than one cycle.
DAIRY	= 1 if farm livestock are dairy cattle; = 0 if no dairy cattle.
DENSITY	= population per square mile in the county of farm operation.
EDUCATION	= years of formal schooling.
EQUIPMENT VALUE	= total value in $1,000s of all owned equipment multiplied by the equity in the farm.
FAMILY	= 1 if landowner and farmer were related.
FAMILY FARM	= 1 if the farm is owned and operated by the family farmer;
	= 0 if not a family farm.
FARM INCOME	= 1 if less than 30% of total income comes from farming,
	= 2 if between 30% and 49%,
	= 3 if between 50% and 80%,
	= 4 if more than 80%.
FARM SALES	= gross revenue for 1992 in $100,000 of sales.
FULLTIME	= 1 if the operator is a full-time farmer; = 0 if not a full-time farmer.
FUTURES MARKET	= 1 if there is an organized futures market for the crop (barley, canola, cotton, corn, oats, rice, soybeans, sugar, wheat);
	= 0 if there is no futures market.
GENERAL BUILDINGS	= 1 if building was a house or garage; = 0 if not.
GRAINS	= 1 if crop is wheat, barley, oats, or other small grain; = 0 otherwise.
GRASS	= 1 if alfalfa, brome, or native hay; = 0 otherwise.
HAY	= 1 if hay or other grass crops were the major income-producing crops;
	= 0 otherwise.
HIGHVALUE	= 1 if crops were irrigated or were row crops; = 0 otherwise.
INPUTS CHANGED	= 1 if share of inputs changed in past five years;
	= 0 if there was no change.
INPUTS	= the number of inputs where the farmer pays all costs.
INFORMATION	= 1 if parties knew each other prior to lease; = 0 parties are new.
IRRIGATED	= 1 if land is irrigated; = 0 if dryland.
IRRIGATION	= fraction of land plot that is irrigated.
INSTITUTION	= 1 if the landowner is an institution (available only for Nebraska and South Dakota farmer samples);
	= 0 if landowner is an individual.

Table A.2 (continued)

Independent Variables

LAND VALUE	=	total value in $1,000s of all owned land multiplied by the equity in the farm.
LANDOWNER		
HUMAN CAPITAL	=	1 if landowner is not farming, never was farmer, or is widow;
	=	0 otherwise.
LEASED ACRES	=	the fraction of the farmer's total farming acreage in the current lease.
LIVE ON FARM	=	1 if farmer lives on his farm.
MARKET	=	1 if the input is seed, fertilizer, herbicide, or insecticide;
	=	0 if another input.
MILES	=	number of miles land plot is from homebase.
MULTIPLE EQUIPMENT	=	1 if second or third truck or tractor;
	=	0 if there is just one piece of equipment.
NET WEALTH	=	WEALTH minus the value of either land, equipment or buildings, depending on the regression.
NEW FARMER	=	1 if farmer is new within five years;
	=	0 if farmer has not changed.
NEW LAND OWNER	=	1 if land owner is new within five years;
	=	0 if landowner has not changed.
NUMBER OF EQUIPMENT	=	the total number of pieces of equipment on the farm.
NUMBER INPUTS		
CHANGED	=	1 if more inputs were shared in past five years; = 0 if not.
PASTURE	=	1 if land was used for grazing.
REGIONAL CV	=	coefficient of variation for crop yield in a region.
REGIONAL MEAN	=	mean crop yield in a region.
REGIONAL STD	=	standard deviation of crop yield in a region.
ROW CROP	=	1 if row crop (corn, sugar beets, sugarcane soybeans, sorghum);
	=	0 if not a row crop (wheat, oats, barley).
ROW*HAY	=	ROW × HAY.
SHARED EQUIPMENT	=	1 if equipment is shared with another farmer;
	=	0 if it is not shared.
SIZE	=	average size of farm in county of lease.
SPECIALIZED		
EQUIPMENT	=	1 if harvest, planting, or crop specific equipment;
	=	0 if equipment is general.
STATE CV	=	coefficient of variation for crop yield in a state or province.
TREES	=	1 if fruit was grown (e.g., apples, pears, etc.);
	=	0 if no fruit was grown.
VALUE	=	average per-acre dollar value of farmland in county of lease.
WEALTH	=	total value (in dollars) of all owned buildings, equipment, and land multiplied by the equity in the farm.
WIDOW	=	1 if the farmland owner is a farm widow; = 0 if not a widow.
WORKERS	=	number of different workers on farm in 1992.
YEARS DURATION	=	number of years contract has been in place.

[a] There are many crops that have similar dummy variables. For example, WHEAT = 1 if wheat is the major income producing crop, and so on.

Table A.3
Summary statistics for leased farmland Louisiana and British Columbia

	Louisiana (1992)		British Columbia (1992)		British Columbia (1992)	
Variable	Mean	Standard deviation	Mean	Standard deviation	Mean	Standard deviation
CONTRACT	0.67	0.47	0.29	0.46	0.39	0.49
SHARE	77.4	6.8	75.07	11.1	73	11.4
ACRES	2,989	369	281.8	100	111.3	1,204
AGE	47	13	47.6	11.4	40.9	12.5
EDUCATION	13.2	2.3	12.5	2.5	11.05	3.14
FARM INCOME	3.06	1.17	2.6	1.2	NA	NA
FULLTIME	0.93	0.26	0.75	0.44	NA	NA
FUTURES	0.78	0.41	0.18	0.39	0.12	0.33
IRRIGATED	26.2	42.01	35	46	0.54	0.49
LIVE-FARM	0.74	0.44	0.86	0.35	NA	NA
MILES	5.36	8.34	3.18	6.03	NA	NA
WIDOW	0.02	0.13	0.01	0.09	NA	NA
BUILDINGS	71,970	71,964	139,650	147,309	NA	NA
EQUIPMENT	142,907	162,513	79,334	91,408	NA	NA
LAND	173,022	442,614	153,770	326,906	NA	NA
WEALTH	243,530	298,190	288,100	305,800	NA	NA

Note: NA = not available.

results across the six equations. In general, risk sharing implies that crops with CVs greater (less) than the WHEAT CV should have positive (negative) coefficient estimates. The crop CVs can be ranked by referring to table A.12.

Consider South Dakota where WHEAT has the largest CV, so that the risk-sharing prediction is that the coefficient estimates for all crop dummies should be negative. As table A.12 shows, none of the estimates are consistent with this prediction. Only two estimates have a negative sign, and none of the estimates are significantly different from zero. For Nebraska, WHEAT has the lowest CV (of the dryland crops), so all coefficient estimates are predicted to be positive. Inspection shows that estimates for OATS and SORGHUM are positive and significant but that the estimate for CORN is negative and significant and the estimate for BARLEY is insignificantly different from zero. For British Columbia and Louisiana, the comparisons require separating crops into two categories using table 6.1: CV greater than WHEAT and CV less than WHEAT. For British Columbia, ALFALFA and HAY are low CV crops, so their coefficient estimates should be negative; the estimates for all other crops should be positive. Only the estimate for BARLEY in the 1992 sample is consistent with these predictions. In the 1979 sample only the ALFALFA estimate is consistent with risk sharing. Most of the parameter estimates are insignificantly different from zero but many have signs that are the direct opposite of those predicted by risk sharing. Finally, for Louisiana, CORN and RICE have CVs greater than WHEAT, so their estimated coefficients should be positive and the other estimates should all be negative. None of the estimates support the risk-sharing thesis for the Louisiana data, and some estimates (for example, COTTON) directly refute the prediction.

Control Variables Used in Chapter 6

Throughout chapter 6, we reported coefficient estimates only for those variables explicitly cited in the theoretical predictions. For table 6.5, the Nebraska–South Dakota equations included ACRES, AGE, DENSITY, and FAMILY. For the 1992 British Columbia–Louisiana equations the controls included ACRES, AGE, EDUCATION, FARM INCOME, FULLTIME, INSTITUTION, IRRIGATED, LIVE-FARM, and MILES. The 1979 British Columbia equation included ACRES, AGE, EDUCATION, IRRIGATED, and LAND VALUE.

Table A.4
Summary statistics of farmland contracts: Nebraska and South Dakota (1986)

Dependent variables	Mean	Standard deviation
ADJUSTMENT	0.10	0.32
ANNUAL	0.65	0.48
CROPSHARE	0.59	0.09
CHEMICAL APPLICATION [a]	0.71	0.45
CHEMICAL APPLICATION [b]	0.75	0.43
CONTRACT	0.71	0.46
DRYING [a]	0.62	0.48
DRYING [b]	0.57	0.50
ENERGY [a]	0.81	0.39
ENERGY [b]	0.78	0.41
FERTILIZER [a]	0.18	0.38
FERTILIZER [b]	0.15	0.36
HARVEST [a]	0.91	0.28
HARVEST [b]	0.92	0.28
HERBICIDE [a]	0.42	0.49
HERBICIDE [b]	0.39	0.49
INSECTICIDE [a]	0.45	0.50
INSECTICIDE [b]	0.43	0.49
ORAL	0.58	0.49
QSHARE [a]	0.71	0.67
QSHARE [b]	0.60	0.49
SEED [a]	0.76	0.43
SEED [b]	0.74	0.44

[a] Based on the full sample.
[b] Based on the farmer sample.

In table 6.6 the control variables (ACRES, AGE, EDUCATION, FAMILY, IRRIGATED) are not reported in the tables. Where we use standard deviation in crop yield instead of coefficient of variation, we use mean yield as a control variable in the equations. For Louisiana there is not enough data to estimate the equation for sorghum and wheat. For tests in section 6.3 we used FARM INCOME and INSTITUTION. In table 6.7 the control variables included ACRES, AGE, EDUCATION, FARM INCOME, FULLTIME, INSTITUTION, IRRIGATED, LIVE-FARM, and MILES as well as individual crop dummies.

Table A.5
Summary statistics of farmland contracts: Nebraska and South Dakota (1986)

Independent variables	Mean	Standard deviation
ACRES	445.9	980.8
AGE	4.26	1.68
AGE^2	21.25	12.18
CHANGE	0.13	0.34
CAPITAL [a]	30	40
CORN	0.70	0.46
DENSITY	30.2	93.9
FAMILY	0.44	0.50
FARM INCOME [a]	2.69	1.37
HIGHVALUE	0.90	0.03
INFORMATION	0.97	0.18
INPUTS	4.70	2.17
INSTITUTION [a]	0.10	0.29
IRRIGATED	0.36	0.48
LEASEDACRES	62.10	34.57
MARKET	0.49	0.50
OATS	0.16	0.37
ROW CROP	0.84	0.365
SIZE	946.10	793.30
SOYBEANS	0.49	0.50
VALUE	535.40	257.80
WHEAT	0.45	0.50
YEARS	11.56	10.42

[a] Based on the farmer sample.

Table A.6
Comparison of contract data with state/province averages

British Columbia

Farm size in acres	1979 Survey		1992 Survey	
	Mean	Standard deviation	Mean	Standard deviation
BARLEY	725	841	1,631	2,857
OATS	1,212	1110	1,704	3,309
WHEAT	783	431	1,887	3,434
CORN	117	75	184	166
APPLES	21.8	34	20	38

Louisiana

Owned land in acres	1987 Census	1997 Census	1992 Survey	
	Mean	Mean	Mean	Standard deviation
STATE-WIDE	293	331	321	511
MILO	278	NA	152	410
WHEAT	137	158	229	197
RICE	183	337	241	252
SOYBEANS	220	344	248	395
COTTON	307	408	303	439
SUGARCANE	396	561	703	803
Value of equipment	$38,323	$59,330	$120,814	$144,408
Value of land and buildings	$268,630	$380,871	$249,564	$447,780

Nebraska and South Dakota

Farm size in acres	1987 Census	1997 Census	1986 Survey	
	Mean	Mean	Mean	Standard deviation
Nebraska	749	885	571	2041
South Dakota	1,214	1,418	1,350	1,322

Note: NA = not available.

Table A.7
Variable means for crop yield data

1986 Nebraska–South Dakota Crop Samples

Variable	Dryland corn	Irrigated corn	Dryland soybeans	Irrigated soybeans	Dryland sorghum	Irrigated sorghum	Barley	Oats	Wheat
REGIONAL CV	0.24 (0.04)	0.09 (0.04)	0.18 (0.02)	0.10 (0.02)	0.19 (0.04)	0.09 (0.01)	0.24 (0.03)	0.24 (0.06)	0.22 (0.07)
COUNTY CV	0.26 (0.05)	0.12 (0.03)	0.20 (0.03)	0.11 (0.02)	0.20 (00.04)	0.11 (0.02)	0.29 (0.06)	0.24 (0.06)	0.21 (0.07)
REGIONAL STD	17.61 (4.54)	11.79 (5.08)	5.19 (0.46)	3.93 (0.67)	11.15 (0.88)	8.37 (1.15)	9.05 (0.76)	10.86 (2.49)	6.47 (1.58)
COUNTY STD	19.33 (4.58)	14.88 (4.35)	5.71 (.84)	4.54 (.79)	12.98 (1.79)	9.79 (1.67)	10.88 (1.92)	10.99 (2.37)	6.35 (1.42)
REGIONAL MEAN	73.29 (12.65)	127.31 (6.01)	29.40 (1.99)	40.51 (1.44)	62.53 (13.13)	90.71 (4.92)	38.87 (4.52)	45.98 (4.77)	31.11 (4.51)
COUNTY MEAN	74.29 (12.08)	125.56 (8.61)	29.44 (2.92)	40.51 (2.39)	67.27 (10.58)	90.06 (5.61)	37.80 (4.73)	46.73 (6.72)	31.07 (5.06)

1992 Louisiana Crop Samples

Variable	Cotton	Corn	Rice	Sorghum	Soybeans	Sugarcane	Wheat
PARISH CV	0.19 (0.05)	0.34 (0.13)	0.15 (0.04)	0.33 (0.11)	0.24 (0.08)	0.18 (0.04)	0.23 (0.04)
PARISH STD	136.70 (31.23)	26.19 (9.95)	6.09 (1.52)	14.71 (2.99)	5.85 (0.92)	5.11 (0.97)	7.77 (1.40)
PARISH MEAN	697.74 (82.48)	77.76 (12.14)	40.42 (4.47)	45.46 (6.03)	25.85 (5.01)	29.00 (1.46)	33.27 (1.89)

Note: Standard errors in parentheses.

Table A.8
Distribution of crop yield variability

	Louisiana Corn (bushels/acre)		British Columbia Apples (1.000 tons/acre)	
	SD	CV	SD	CV
Minimum	6.05	0.14	89.33	0.02
Maximum	50.38	0.76	9494.32	0.56
Mean	23.46	0.3	2658.12	0.27
Standard deviation	9.21	0.12	3568.52	0.20
Observations	33	33	66	66

	Louisiana Wheat (bushels/acre)		Louisiana Rice (tons/acre)	
	SD	CV	SD	CV
Minimum	3.3	0.1	2.44	0.06
Maximum	11.82	0.35	20.73	0.39
Mean	7.37	0.22	7.07	0.16
Standard deviation	2.12	0.07	4.2	0.08
Observations	37	37	29	29

	Nebraska Corn (bushels/acre)		South Dakota Corn (bushels/acre)	
	SD	CV	SD	CV
Minimum	9.83	0.21	6.16	0.10
Maximum	28.08	0.75	19.41	0.40
Mean	17.53	0.28	13.14	0.23
Standard deviation	4.43	0.06	3.20	0.07
Observations	89	89	38	38

	Wheat (bushels/acre)		Wheat (bushels/acre)	
	SD	CV	SD	CV
Minimum	3.03	0.09	4.33	0.14
Maximum	11.39	0.44	10.15	0.38
Mean	5.71	0.17	7.15	0.28
Standard deviation	1.53	0.05	1.32	0.06
Observations	89	89	65	65

	Oats (bushels/acre)		Oats (tons/acre)	
	SD	CV	SD	CV
Minimum	4.99	0.1	4.81	0.17
Maximum	12.55	0.29	18.18	0.42
Mean	9.31	0.2	12.13	0.29
Standard deviation	1.65	0.03	2.49	0.06
Observations	88	88	66	66

Note: Data for corn, oats, and wheat excludes irrigated acreage. Observations are counties for Nebraska and South Dakota, parishes for Louisiana, and provincial regions for British Columbia.

Table A.9
OLS estimation: Cropsharing and crop variability

Dependent variable: Fraction cropshare contracts

	British Columbia 1979	1992	Louisiana 1992	Nebraska 1986	South Dakota 1986
CONSTANT	0.481	0.221	0.786	0.605	0.637
	(1.04)	(0.45)	(11.92)	(7.23)	(10.27)
STATE CV	−0.246	1.176	−0.583	1.128	−0.168
	(−0.108)	(0.468)	(−1.54)	(1.85)	(−0.493)
R^2	0.002	0.042	0.28	0.300	0.046
F-value	0.012	0.219	2.39	3.429	0.243
Observations	8	8	9	10	7

Dependent variable: Fraction of leased acres under cropshare contracts

	British Columbia 1979	1992	Louisiana 1992
CONSTANT	0.107	0.231	0.920
	(0.28)	(0.40)	(7.58)
STATE CV	0.183	.84	−1.19
	(−1.00)	(0.30)	(−1.86)
R^2	0.14	0.01	0.76
F-value	1.00	0.09	3.47
Observations	8	8	9

Dependent variable: Fraction of all acres under cropshare contracts

	British Columbia 1979	1992
CONSTANT	0.173	0.56
	(0.80)	(4.12)
STATE CV	−0.35	−.40
	(−.329)	(−.55)
R^2	0.017	0.04
F-value	1.00	0.09
Observations	8	9

Note: t-statistics in parentheses.

Table A.10
OLS estimation: Cropsharing and crop variability

FRACTION CROPSHARE	=	(0.43)*CONSTANT − (3.82)	(0.08)*CV + (0.17)	(0.02)*BC79 + (0.24)	(0.28)*LA (3.13)
	+	(0.19)*SD + (2.08)	(0.33)*NE (3.64)		

Table A.11
Price-yield correlations for various crops at the state or province level

CROP	British Columbia	Louisiana	Nebraska	South Dakota
Alfalfa	NA	NA	0.220	NA
Apples	−0.009	NA	NA	NA
Barley	0.025	NA	0.060	−0.588*
Corn (Irrigated)	NA	NA	−0.449	−0.578
Corn (Dryland)	NA	NA	−0.411	−0.665
Corn (All)	NA	−0.239	NA	NA
Cotton	NA	−0.288	NA	NA
Hay	NA	0.267	NA	NA
Oats	133	NA	−0.709*	−0.727*
Canola	0.568	NA	NA	NA
Sorghum (Irrigated)	NA	NA	−0.470	NA
Sorghum (Dryland)	NA	NA	−0.576*	NA
Sorghum (All)	NA	−0.266	NA	−0.407
Sugarcane	NA	−0.026	NA	NA
Soybeans (Irrigated)	NA	NA	−0.172	NA
Soybeans (Dryland)	NA	NA	−0.414	NA
Soybeans (All)	NA	NA	0.135	−0.404
Rice	0.275	−0.652*	NA	NA
Wheat	NA	0.208	−0.235	−0.278

Note: NA = not available.
* significant at the 5 percent level.
Sources: Nebraska Agricultural Statistical Service, U.S. Department of Agriculture, report prepared for Dean Lueck. "Historic Estimates, Principal Crops, South Dakota" (no other information on this available). South Dakota Agricultural Statistical Service, U.S. Department of Agriculture. "Agricultural Statistics & Prices for Louisiana 1985–1991," Hector Zapata and David Frank, Louisiana Agricultural Statistics Service. "Agricultural Statistics & Prices for Louisiana 1986–1992," Hector Zapata, Louisiana Agricultural Statistics Service. British Columbia Ministry of Agriculture, internal statistics, 1994.

Table A.12
Logit regression coefficients: Contract choice and crop type
(dependent variable = 1 if cropshare contract; 0 if cash rent)

Contract Sample

Independent variables	All crops British Columbia 1979	1992	All crops Louisiana 1992	Dryland crops Nebraska 1986	Dryland crops South Dakota 1986	Dryland crops Nebraska and South Dakota 1986
CONSTANT	1.03	0.43	5.58	−1.30	−1.98	−1.51
	(0.91)	(0.20)	(0.41)	(4.55)*	(−3.95)*	(−6.61)*
ALFALFA	−2.42	−1.74				
	(−1.91)*	(−1.04)				
APPLES	−0.24	0.80				
	(−0.24)	(0.52)				
BARLEY	−1.35	1.74		5.33	−0.08	0.46
	(−0.98)	(1.72)*		(0.28)	(−0.16)	(0.84)
CANOLA	−0.75	1.11				
	(−0.55)	(0.71)				
COTTON			−0.93			
			(−1.70)*			
CORN	−5.21	−0.41	−0.58	−2.95	1.33	−1.77
	(−3.17)*	(−0.29)	(−0.98)	(4.64)*	(1.68)*	(−4.18)*
HAY	−0.51	−0.97	−4.43			
	(−0.51)	(−0.65)	(−0.33)			
OATS	−1.42	1.10	4.21	2.44	−0.53	0.81
	(−0.73)	(0.98)	(0.31)	(2.22)*	(−0.83)	(1.89)
RICE			0.05			
			(0.07)			
SORGHUM				2.10	0.61	2.16
				(5.53)*	(0.57)	(6.03)*
SUGARCANE			0.51			
			(0.87)			
FUTURES	1.78	−1.07	−4.34	5.23	4.15	4.69
MARKET	(1.13)	(−0.62)	(−0.32)	(8.15)*	(5.69)*	(11.11)*
Correct predictions	71%	76%	71%	93%	91%	93%
Model χ^2	115.66	47.05	95.86	370.60	168.62	552.25
Observations	506	210	825	855	226	1081

Notes: t-statistics in parentheses. WHEAT is the left-out crop dummy variable in all equations.
* significant at the 5 percent level for a one-tailed t-test.

Appendix B: Mathematical

B.1 The Solution to the Partnership Problem

Assuming the first-order approach is satisfied, noting that $h = h(e, k, q_{-1})$ and $e = at$, the following two first-order necessary conditions define the solution to equation (9.5):

$$\left[\frac{\partial h}{\partial k} - r(N)\right] + N\left[\frac{\partial h}{\partial e_t}\left(\frac{N}{T}\right)^\alpha - w\right]\left[\sum_{t=1}^{T}\frac{\partial t_t^P}{\partial k}\right] = 0 \tag{B.1}$$

$$\left[\frac{\partial h(\alpha)}{\partial e_t}\left(\frac{N^{\alpha-1}}{T}\right)^\alpha - w\right]\left[\sum_{t=1}^{T}\right] + N\left[\frac{\partial h}{\partial e_t}\left(\frac{N}{T}\right)^\alpha - w\right]\left[\sum_{t=1}^{T}\frac{\partial t_t^P}{\partial N}\right] + \left[w - \left(\frac{\partial r}{\partial N}\right)k\right] = 0 \tag{B.2}$$

Equations (B.1) and (B.2) illustrate the trade-offs in a partnership farm. Equation (B.1) defines the conditions for the optimal level of capital and can be discussed as two parts. In part 1, the first bracketed term is simply the net marginal product of capital. Part 2 is the total indirect effect of capital choices on task effort and comprises three terms. The last bracketed term is the effect of a change in capital stock on task effort, summed over all tasks, while the first bracketed term is the size of the distortion in effort. The sign of $(\partial t_t/\partial k)$ depends on whether capital and task effort are complements or substitutes (see section B.2). Term 3 multiplies all of this by the number of partners (N) to get a total effect. Equation (B.2) defines the conditions for the optimal number of partners. The marginal benefit of adding another partner comprises an increase in task specialization (part 1) and a fall in marginal capital costs (part 3). The marginal cost is the total indirect effect of reduced farm task effort that results from an increase in the number of residual claimants (part 2).

Part 1 comprises two terms. The first term in brackets is the specialization effect of changing the number of partners (holding the number of tasks constant), which is then summed over all the tasks in the stage (term 2). Part 3 comprises two independent terms, the direct effect on capital costs and the addition of off-farm income. Part 2 parallels the second part in equation (B.1) and, accordingly, comprises three terms. The only difference is that the distortion on effort is multiplied by the effect of partnership size on task effort. This effect can be shown to be nonpositive (see section B.3); the effect is negative except in the case in which specialization effects are at their maximum ($\alpha = 1$), thus eliminating the effect altogether.

B.2 Effect of Partnership Capital on a Farm Partner's Task Effort

We want to evaluate the partial derivative $\partial t_t^P/\partial k$, so first create an identity from equation (9.6), assuming homogeneous partners, to get

$$\left(\frac{N^{\alpha-1}}{T_\alpha}\right)\frac{\partial h}{\partial t_t}(t_t^P(\Phi)) \equiv w. \tag{B.3}$$

Differentiate equation (B.3) with respect to k and solve to get

$$\frac{\partial t_t^P}{\partial k} = \frac{-\left(\frac{\partial^2 h}{\partial t_t \partial k}\right)}{\left(\frac{\partial^2 h}{\partial t_t^2}\right)}. \tag{B.4}$$

The denominator in equation (B.4) is negative by assumption, but the sign of the numerator depends on whether capital and effort are substitutes or complements (or independent). Thus, sign of $\partial t_t^P/\partial k$ is positive (negative) if k and t are complements (substitutes).

B.3   Effect of Partnership Size on a Farm Partner's Task Effort

To evaluate the partial derivative $\partial t_t^P / \partial N$, differentiate equation (B.3) with respect to N and solve to get

$$\frac{\partial t_t^P}{\partial N} = \left(\frac{-(\alpha - 1)}{N} \right) \frac{\left(\frac{\partial^2 h}{\partial t_t \partial N} \right)}{\left(\frac{\partial^2 h}{\partial t_t^2} \right)} \leq 0. \tag{B.5}$$

The sign of the second term on the right-hand size is negative, but the sign of the first term depends on the value of $\alpha \in (0, 1)$. If $\alpha = 1$ (maximum specialization potential), then changes in the number of partners (N) have no effect on task effort (t). However, if $0 \leq \alpha < 1$, then an increase in the number of partners will decrease task effort.

B.4   The Solution to the Factory-Corporate Farm Problem

The solution to equation (9.7) is given by the optimal input choices t_t^{FC} and k^{FC} that solves the following first-order necessary conditions:

$$\left[t_t \left(\frac{(\alpha / \Omega)(N^h)^{\alpha - 1}}{T} \right) + \left(\frac{N}{T^\alpha} \right)^\alpha \right] \frac{\partial h}{\partial t_t} (t_t^{FC}, k^{FC}) \equiv \bar{w} \quad t = 1, \ldots, T \tag{B.6}$$

$$\frac{\partial h}{\partial k} (t_t^C, k^C) \equiv r^{min} \tag{B.7}$$

B.5   The Relationship between Farm Capital and Farm Organization

Prediction 9.10 states that family farms will employ less capital than partnerships and that partnership will employ less capital than corporate farms. Although it appears to be a straightforward implication of our assumption that the capital costs function, $r = r(N)$, is decreasing and convex in N, the prediction also depends on the relationship between task effort (t) and capital (k) and on the specialization coefficient (a). Consider a move from a family farm to a partnership, which means that N increases. The main prediction is that, ceteris paribus, k must increase, but an increase in N (inherent in a shift from a family farm to a partnership) must decrease the level of task effort (t). When N increases, the marginal product of effort shifts outward because of specialization gains. The marginal product also shifts inward because of shirking. Under our maintained assumptions—$\alpha \in (0, 1)$ and $N \leq T$—the outward shift (specialization gains) can never be larger than the inward shift (moral hazard losses). In general, the inward shift will be larger so that an increase in N will reduce t. Only when $\alpha = 1$ do the two effects exactly offset each other. To see this, note that a worker's full marginal product depends on (a) his ownership share of the output, or $1/N$; and (b) the specialization coefficient, $a = (N/T)^\alpha$. Now define Ψ to be the marginal product shifter where

$$\Psi = \left(\frac{1}{N} \right) \left(\frac{N}{T} \right)^\alpha = \left(\frac{N^{\alpha-1}}{T^\alpha} \right). \tag{B.8}$$

It is easy to see from equation (B.8) that $\Psi \in (0, 1)$, which means that an increase in the number of owners (N) can never increase task effort (t). Given that t must decline from an increase in N, there are three possible cases to consider in order to determine the final choice of capital.

1. Capital (k) and effort (t) are independent $(h_{tk} = 0)$.

In this case an increase in N unambiguously leads to an increase in k because the decrease in from the change in N has no effect on the marginal product of k.

2. Capital (k) and effort (t) are substitutes ($h_{tk} < 0$).

In this case an increase in N unambiguously leads to an increase in k because the decrease in t from the change in N shifts out the marginal product of capital, thus adding to the effect of lower capital costs.

3. Capital (k) and effort (t) are complements ($h_{tk} > 0$).

In this case an increase in N can possibly lead to a decrease in k because the decrease in t from the change in N shifts in the marginal product of capital, thus countering the effect of lower capital costs. Only if the complement effect is strong enough to exceed the effect of reduced capital costs, $r'(N)$, can a partnership optimally employ less capital than a family farm. When this is the case, however, the value of the family farm will always exceed the value of the partnership because the deadweight loss (compared to first-best) for the partnership will be greatest since the partnership cannot attain greater efficiency in task effort and is less efficient in capital employment. Thus, even though it is possible for the model to generate a partnership with less capital than a family farm, such a partnership will never be the wealth-maximizing choice of farm organization. The same analysis holds for the comparison between corporate and family or partnership farms, although a sufficiently low effective wage ($\tilde{w}$) could, in principle, lead to greater task effort under corporate organization.

B.6   Comparative Statics of Farm Organizations

The value function for the family farm is

$$V^F = h\left(\left[\frac{1}{T}\right]^{\alpha} t_1^f, \ldots \left[\frac{1}{T}\right]^{\alpha} t_T^f, k^f; q_{-1}(d)\right) - r^{\max} k^f + wm^f. \tag{B.9}$$

The value function for the partnership farm is

$$V^P = h\left(\left[\frac{N^P}{T}\right]^{\alpha} t_1^P, \ldots \left[\frac{N^P}{T}\right]^{\alpha} t_T^P, k^P; q_{-1}(d)\right) - r(N^P)k^P + wm^P. \tag{B.10}$$

Changes in α

1. $V_\alpha^F = (1/T)^\alpha ln(1/T) \sum_{t=1}^{T} \partial h/\partial t_t(\cdot) t_t < 0$

2. $V_{\alpha\alpha}^F = (1/T)^\alpha [ln(1/T)]^2 \sum_{t=1}^{T} \partial h/\partial t_t(\cdot) t_t > 0$

3. $V_\alpha^P = (N/T)^\alpha ln(N/T) \sum_{j=1}^{T} \partial h/\partial t_j(\cdot) t_t$

So when α is close to zero the first term approaches one, and the derivative is smaller in absolute terms than V_α^F. As α increases in size, however, the first term also decreases, but more slowly than for V_α^F. Hence, the whole derivative can be larger than V_α^F in absolute terms.

Changes in T (assuming that $\alpha = 1$)

1. $V_T^F = (-1/T) \sum_{t=1}^{T} \partial h/\partial t_t(\cdot) t_t < 0$

2. $V_{TT}^F = (1/T^2) \sum_{t=1}^{T} \partial h/\partial t_t(\cdot) t_t > 0$

Table B.1
Definitions of theoretical variables

Variable		
a	=	amount of task specialization.
c	=	cost of nonland and nonlabor inputs.
d	=	date when inputs are used.
e	=	farmer inputs, including effort.
h	=	crop production function.
k	=	nonland and nonlabor inputs: chapters 4, 5.
	=	unpriced attributes of land, equipment and buildings: chapter 8.
	=	capital: chapter 9.
l	=	land attributes: chapters 4, 5.
	=	priced attributes of land, equipment or buildings: chapter 8.
m	=	hours of market work: chapter 9.
	=	input measurement costs: chapter 5.
q	=	input share paid by the farmer.
r	=	actual opportunity cost of land inputs.
r'	=	cost of land attributes to the farmer renting land.
s	=	farmer's share of output.
t	=	task effort.
v	=	cost of the unpriced attributes of land, equipment and buildings.
w	=	opportunity cost of effort.
C	=	number of crop cyles per year.
C^c	=	fixed contract cost of a cash rent contract.
C^s	=	fixed contract cost of a cropshare contract.
L	=	length of stage of production.
Q	=	observable crop output.
R	=	farmer's coefficient of absolute risk aversion.
T	=	number of tasks in a given stage.
U	=	farmer's utility function.
V	=	value of the contract or organization.
Y	=	farmer's income from the land contract.
α	=	degree to which specialization matters.
β	=	cash side payment made by the farmer.
θ	=	nature's random input.
ι	=	interest rate.
μ	=	fixed cost of output measurement: chapter 4.
	=	mean of prices: chapter 6.
Ω	=	constant number of hours each worker can provide in a day.

Notes

Chapter 1: Introduction

1. Legally speaking, a farmland contract is a lease since it falls under property law, not contract law. In this book, however, we use the terms interchangeably.

2. Studies of sharecropping are nearly as common as the contracts themselves. Since the original efficiency rationale for sharecropping (Cheung 1969), early studies have included Allen (1985), Allen and Lueck (1992b, 1993a), Alston, Datta, and Nugent (1984), Eswaran and Kotwal (1985), Hallagan (1978), Lucas (1979), Newberry and Stiglitz (1979), Shaban (1987), Stiglitz (1974), while more recent studies include Ghatak and Pandey (2000), Ackerberg and Botticini (2000), and Ray (1999). See Hayami and Otsuka (1993) or Taslim (1992) for the most recent surveys of this literature. Cheung (1969) surveys the literature from Smith to his time.

3. Some of this literature is discussed later in this chapter.

4. Most readers are no doubt aware of the connection between Coase's two most famous papers. For a discussion, see Barzel and Kochin (1992).

5. Cheung solved this problem by incorporating explicitly what has come to be known as an "individual rationality" constraint in contracting optimization problems.

6. Neihans (1987).

7. See Allen (2000) for a complete discussion of the history and use of the term "transaction costs."

8. Ironically, when Demsetz (1968) discusses property rights, he uses this definition, even though he maintains his separate definition of transaction costs.

9. Barzel (1985) is devoted almost entirely to defending this point.

10. The empirical successes of the transaction cost literature are also important and discussed below on specific topics.

11. This approach is also implicit in Coase (1960). See Milgrom and Roberts (1992) for a critique.

12. This approach also renders suspect the literature on "Marshallian efficiency," which purports to test whether or not share contracts are efficient (Nabi 1986, Shaban 1987). If contracts are chosen to maximize expected joint value, then little insight is gained when examining efficiency by focusing on the use of a single input or output. In this paradigm, all contracts will generate a different set of inputs and output choices.

13. This approach has its origins in measurement and monitoring costs (Barzel 1982a; Lazear 1986). It is also related to the multitask literature begun with Holmstrom and Milgrom (1991).

14. Although, interestingly, J. S. Mill and early agricultural economists of the twentieth century were keenly aware of it.

15. Barzel (1997, chap. 3) discusses these issues.

16. This has also been the dominant theoretical approach among economists studying nonagricultural business contracts.

17. See, for instance, Chavas and Holt (1990), Pope and Just (1991), and Young and Burke (2001).

18. See Allen and Lueck (1995, 1999b) and Prendergast (1999, 2002) on this literature, and Masten and Saussier (2000) for a comparison of the empirical results for agency models with risk aversion compared to transaction cost models. Masten and Saussier (2000) conclude that transaction cost models have been "far more successful both at generating testable hypotheses and in explaining actual contracting practices" (215).

19. Most empirical contract studies outside of agriculture (Crocker and Masten 1988, Joskow 1987) have focused on incentives such as enforcement costs, moral hazard, and specific assets. Other empirical studies have focused on risk sharing (Garen 1994; Kawasaki and McMillan 1987; Lang and Gordon 1995; and Gaynor and Gertler 1995). For a survey, see Shelanski and Klein (1995). A few studies in this literature have examined U.S. farm contracts (Allen and Lueck 1992a, 1993a,b; Alston and Higgs 1982; Alston, Datta, and Nugent 1984).

20. See Grossman and Hart (1983), Harris and Raviv (1979), Holmström (1979, 1982), Ross (1973), Hart and Holmström (1987), Sappington (1991), Shavell (1979), and Stiglitz (1974) for classic analyses using the risk-sharing/incentive trade-off. The multitask literature is usually developed in a similar framework, even though

risk aversion is not required to explain contract choice in the presence of multiple tasks (Allen and Lueck 1998; Prendergast 2000).

21. Recent studies, including Allen and Lueck (1992b, 1993a), Crocker and Masten (1988), Eswaran and Kotwal (1985), Joskow (1987), Lazear (1986), and Leffler and Rucker (1991), have examined contracts without resorting to risk-averse preferences. Shelanski and Klein (1995) summarize this large and growing literature.

22. In the franchising literature, for example, key predictions have turned on unverifiable claims about whether franchisors or franchisees are more risk averse (Lafontaine 1992).

23. The details of these empirical difficulties are examined in chapter 6.

24. For our understanding of agricultural policy in the United States and Canada, we rely on Gardner (1981), Knutson, Penn, and Flinchbaugh (1998), Pasour (1990), Orden, Paarlberg, and Roe (1999), Rausser (1992), and Schmitz, Furtan, and Baylis (2002).

25. An overriding rhetorical goal of farm policy has been to provide farmers with "parity" prices for their agricultural products approaching the level (in real terms) of 1910–1914, which tended to be near all-time highs.

26. This is a bit of a simplification because the government "loan rate" acts as a price floor, so payments are actually the difference between the target price and the higher of the loan rate and the market price.

27. Marketing orders avoid antitrust liability under the Capper-Volstad Act of 1922 and the Agricultural Marketing Adjustment Act of 1937.

28. See Orden, Paarlberg, and Roe (1999) or Schmitz, Furtan, and Baylis (2002) for a discussion of the 1996 legislation.

29. For example, there are and have been programs for honey, peanuts, tobacco, and wool.

30. See Schmitz Furtan, and Baylis (2002) for a discussion.

31. Barley and oats have been included during some years.

32. Available online at http://www.usda.gov/agency/obpa/Budget-Summary/2002/2002budsum.htm (accessed on November 5, 2001).

33. Schmitz Furtan, and Baylis (2002, Table 8.6) show that farm payments as a share of net farm income are substantially lower for farmers in the provinces of Alberta, Manitoba, Ontario, and Saskatchewan than for the farmers in the neighboring states of Minnesota, Montana, and North Dakota.

34. It is worth noting here, however, that farmland contracts routinely mention and assign ownership of the government payment (see the sample contract in figure 3.1), thus affecting the rental rates of these leases.

35. Overall, however, our sentiments are similar to Hansmann (1996), when he states: "To be sure taxes, subsidies, regulation and organizational law all differ from one society to another in various ways for various industries, and these clearly have importance for the patterns of ownership that we observe. But they are generally not so strong as to swamp the basic costs of market contracting and of ownership" (295).

36. For example, the works of Brewster (1950), Ellickson and Brewster (1947), Holmes (1928), (1929), and Johnson (1944) all consider questions that are discussed in this book.

37. See, for example, Johnson (1950), Schickele (1941), or Taylor (1910).

38. Even this may be changing. Hennessy and Lawrence (1999) have recently called for more emphasis on "the economics of transaction costs and contractual relationships" (65) in the agricultural literature.

39. The classic summary of this development literature is found in Otsuka and Hayami (1988).

40. Important works in economic history include Ackerberg and Botticini (2000), Alston and Higgs (1982), Carmona and Simpson (1999), Luporini and Parigi (1996), and Pudney, Galassi and Mealli (1998).

Chapter 2: Farming in North America

1. This is similar to definitions found in the agricultural literature. For example, Scolville (1947) defines the farmer as one who "makes most of the managerial decisions, participates regularly in farm work, and on which his role

as employer of labor is minor relative to his other functions" (518). In the U.S. Census a farmer is called an "operator." An operator is "a person [who] operates a farm/ranch, either doing the work or making day-to-day decisions about such items as planting, harvesting, feeding, and marketing. The operator may be the owner, a member of the owner's household, a salaried manager, or a tenant." See U.S. department of Commerce, Bureau of the Census (1999), 1997 Census of Agriculture, Vol. 3: Agricultural Economics and Land Ownership Survey (AELOS) (1999), Appendix A, p. 3.

2. In the United States, 1997 is the most recent census year, while in Canada the most recent census year is 1996.

3. U.S. Department of Commerce, Bureau of the Census, (1999), Table 47, p. 63. The most recent agricultural census available is 1997. The census definition of a farm is "any place from which $1,000 or more of agricultural products were produced and sold or normally would have been sold during the census year." The U.S. Census uses the following categories: (a) individual or family, (b) partnership, (c) corporation (family held or nonfamily held), and (d) other (trusts, municipalities, and so on).

4. U.S. Department of Agriculture (1920), Table 229, p. 701. In 1860 there were just over 2 million farms in the United States comprising about 400 million acres (less than half the current farm acreage). Not until 1950 did tractors outnumber draft horses and mules on U.S. farms.

5. U.S. Bureau of the Census Department of Commerce, (1976), Part 1, pp. 457–62 and U.S. Department of Agriculture, Agricultural Statistics (1994), Table 536 p. 330.

6. U.S. Department of Agriculture, Bureau of the Census (1999), Table 13, p. 22.

7. This underestimates the change, of course, given the changes in quality of fertilizers over time.

8. See Kislev and Peterson (1982) for an analysis of the economics of farm technology.

9. See table 2.3. In both states, farms tend to be larger in the western counties where the land is less valuable. Since 1986, the year for our Great Plains data, average farm size in the United States has increased by about 10 percent.

10. All figures from U.S. Department of Commerce, Bureau of the Census, Table 9.

11. This information is not available for British Columbia.

12. Smith (1776), Book 3, Chapter 2.

13. As noted at the beginning of this chapter, farmers are defined as individuals with control over production, and who make farming decisions over several margins. Still, at some level these distinctions become blurry. For instance, Alston and Higgs (1982) made a distinction between "sharecroppers" and "share tenants." Croppers are farm laborers without capital who are paid with a share of the crop. Tenants are farmers who own capital and lease land by paying a share of the crop. By their definition, we consider only share tenants. As we show in chapter 9, true farmers tend not to be hired on a fixed wage basis because of the severe incentive problems that would arise if the farmer's wealth did not depend directly on the value of the harvested crop. Having said all this, is a custom harvester hired on a wage basis a farmer? Probably, but for the our purposes we will call him a hired worker.

14. U.S. Department of Commerce, Bureau of the Census, Chapter 1, Table 16, p. 24.

15. The idea that share contracts are a primitive form of organization in agriculture is found in Bardhan and Srinivasan (1971), Deininger and Feder (2001), Eswaran and Kotwal (1985), Newberry and Stiglitz (1979), and Otsuka and Hayami (1988). Eswaran and Kotwal argued: "As markets develop, . . . sharecropping will give way to fixed rental contracts. . . . Sharecropping would dominate when markets are either absent or undeveloped and the class structure is polarized" (360). The conventional wisdom of the extinction of the cropshare contract probably stems from Day (1967), who presented evidence from the Mississippi Delta cotton belt. Day's study was of sharecroppers, along the lines of Alston and Higgs (1982), who owned little capital and lived on the landowner's farm; they were ultimately replaced by seasonal wage laborers. Still, there is some evidence that the frequency of cash renting is on the rise. In Iowa, Pieper and Harl (2000) find 48.8 percent of leased acres under cash renting in 1987, and 57.1 percent of acres under cash renting in 1997 (23, Table 5.1). They also find that nonresidents are more likely to use cropshare contracts (26, table 5.10).

16. The Great Plains region extends from Texas to Montana and North Dakota and north into the Canadian provinces of Alberta, Saskatchewan, and Manitoba.

17. Only a small fraction of land contracts are combinations of cash and share arrangements. For example, the aggregate U.S. data show just over 10 percent of all land lease contracts not categorized as cash or share because

they include adjustable cost leases, cash-share combinations, and other nonstandard agreements (U.S. Department of Commerce, Bureau of the Census 1999). This represents a slight increase (from 6%) from 1988 (AELOS 1988).

18. In British Columbia the Ministry of Agriculture divides the province into several large regions for statistical purposes that tend to be much larger than American counties, hence, it is more likely the landowner lives in the same municipality as the rented land, but they still could be quite distant and not monitor farmers closely.

19. Newberry and Stiglitz (1979) forcefully argue this point and have influenced later writers, such as F. Allen (1985) and Hurwicz and Shapiro (1978). Eswaran and Kotwal (1985) develop a model that explains why fifty-fifty is common, but also questioned the validity of the claim for only fifty-fifty sharing.

20. Share contracts come in two dominant forms: those that simply share the output, with the farmer paying for all of the inputs; and those that share both the output and the input costs other than the land and labor. Chapter 5 is entirely devoted to the issue of input sharing.

21. Roy (1963) gives an early account of contracting practices in agriculture. See Perry et al. (1997) for a recent overview. They find that in 1993 such contracts covered almost one-third of the value of U.S. farm production, on $47 billion.

22. U.S. Department of Commerce, Bureau of the Census, (1993), Table 848, p. 531.

23. U.S. Department of Commerce, Bureau of the Census (1993), Table 47, p. 63.

24. These changes include the introduction of railroads, refrigeration, chemical fertilizers, tractors, and combines to name a few.

25. Mighell and Jones (1963) were the first to carefully document the extent of vertical coordination across agricultural products.

26. In chapter 6 we also use data on landowner-farmer contracts from British Columbia during the 1979 crop year. These data were collected by telephone survey and provide information on 378 contracts and have fewer variables than the other data we use.

27. There exist large numbers of very small farms in both Canada and the United States. In terms of total output, these farms produce very little. The presence of small farms lowers the average size and average value of farms, while at the same time it increases the total number of farms.

Chapter 3: The Simplicity of Agricultural Contracts

1. The analysis in this chapter draws on Allen and Lueck (1992a).

2. This finding is quite common. In Illinois, Sotomayer Ellinger, and Barry (2000) also find 54 percent of contracts are oral. In Kansas, Tsoodle and Wilson (2000) find that over 85 percent of the contracts for nonirrigated crops are oral. In Oklahoma, Burkhart (1991) finds that the majority of contracts are oral.

3. And, as we note in chapter 1, the allocation of government payments is often specified as it is in the contract in figure 3.1.

4. To simplify the analysis, we examine the issues of complexity and structure independently. In practice, of course, the distinction is not always clear. The structure of a contract can be used to provide incentives on margins that could otherwise be observed by a third party and enforced by a market or court. Likewise, measurement could be used as a substitute for structure of margins that are difficult to observe.

5. Unlike in the other chapters, we do not develop a formal model but instead rely on an extensive literature.

6. The literature on specific assets and their role in contracts and vertical integration is large, with substantial empirical support (for example, Joskow 1987; Masten 1985). Hart's (1995) property rights theory of the firm is one of the more recent works that relies heavily on the presence of specific assets to explain ownership. Indeed, without specific assets, ownership has no effect in his model. Recently the most famous case study of this theory, Fisher Body and General Motors, has come under attack. Coase (2000) and others in the same issue argue that specific assets were not a major factor in explaining the merger of the two firms. Hansmann (1996) and Holmström and Roberts (1998) also put less emphasis on specific assets as a factor determining ownership.

7. Nearly all farms are vertically integrated to a certain degree. Most farmers own some land and buildings. The potentially capturable quasi-rents would be huge for a farmstead located on another's land.

8. Interestingly, Klein, Crawford, and Alchian (1978) briefly discussed orchards near the end of their classic paper.

9. In fact, the mean duration of the contract relationship in our Nebraska–South Dakota data is 11.5 years. In their Illinois data, Sotomayer Ellinger, and Barry (2000) find a mean duration of 14.4 years. Similarly, in their Kansas data, Tsoodle and Wilson (2000) find a mean duration of 16 years.

10. Learning over time could create dynamic incentive problems and lead to "ratchet effects," which are examined in chapter 7.

11. It may appear that a farmer caught cheating will suffer only in terms of price—higher cash rents or lower shares—but this is not the case. Abusing the land is suboptimal and so a poor farmer will never be able to pay enough to compensate for the damage done. Hence, just as shirking workers are fired and do not have their wages lowered, cheating farmers are also "fired."

12. Hamilton (1990) agrees: "The general view in U.S. common law is that an implied covenant of good husbandry does exist in the lease of farmland" (234). Hamilton (1990, 1993) and Harl (1998) discuss the details of the good husbandry covenant.

13. 255 Iowa 30, 120 N.W. 2d 451 (Supreme Court of Iowa, 1963).

14. Once again, orchard regions may be unique because of the great variability in elevation, aspect (slope direction), and soil quality in a relatively small region.

15. See Harl (1998), and Meyer et al. (1985) for detailed reports on the common law related to farm leases. In addition to disputes over farming operations, disputes have arisen over termination notice, government payments, taxes, subletting, and building maintenance. In the early 1990s, J. David Aiken, agricultural law specialist at the University of Nebraska, informed us that the last farmland lease case in Nebraska was in 1987 and involved termination notice, not husbandry. Aiken was aware of only one other Nebraska case in the 1980s; it too was a dispute over notice of termination. In private correspondence, Theodore A. Fietshans, agricultural law specialist at North Carolina State University, also notes that leasing disputes are seldom litigated (January 3, 2002).

16. Note that AGE is measured differently in our data. In the Nebraska–South Dakota data the AGE variable is categorical, but in the British Columbia–Louisiana data AGE is in actual years.

17. In Nebraska and South Dakota, for instance, if the beginning and ending dates of the lease are not mentioned, they are typically set by default at December 1 to December 1.

18. The Statute of Frauds was first codified in England in 1677 and is now found in the Uniform Commercial Code and in state statutes. See *Neb Rev Stat* §§111.205 and 111.210 and *SD Comp Laws Ann* §43-32-5. Although the original English law referred only to leases lasting more than three years, most U.S. states require writing for leases lasting more than one year. See Harl (1998) for a discussion of the Statute of Frauds in farm leasing.

19. The practice of resolving disputes in the shadow of the law is discussed in great length by Ellickson (1991). There he analyzes how farmers and ranchers resolve tresspassing disputes in Shasta County, California. He found that individuals often resolved their disputes without the least attention to the law. Some legal writers criticize farmers for not putting contracts in writing more often and tend to attribute this to "tradition" rather than an alternative enforcement regime. Harl (1998), however, notes that oral leases are common and that the Statute of Frauds is routinely ignored. Harl also notes that some jurisdictions treat oral contracts as legitimate "tenancy at will" leases meaning that no definite time period is required.

20. We do not have data on the age of the landowner, nor do we have any reason to think they would correlate strongly.

21. Sotomayer Ellinger, and Barry (2000, 22) also find that oral contracts are more likely for (a) older farmers, (b) larger plots of land, and (c) among family members. They did not have data to estimate the effect of specific assets.

22. In their detailed analysis of viticulture in eighteenth and nineteenth century Catalonia, Carmona and Simpson (1999) find that share contracts were long term, reflecting the long-lived vine crops. The contracts were also automatically renewed as long as the farmer replanted vines appropriately. In fact, the contracts were called *rabassa morta*, which means "dead root." The contracts would only be terminated when more than two-thirds of the vines were dead or had not been replanted.

23. These farms and their demise are described and discussed in detail in chapter 9. Drache (1964) gives the most detailed history.

24. Our information comes from an examination of a set of land contracts for the Amenia and Sharon Land Company, which operated in Cass County, North Dakota. We examined these contracts in the archives at the North Dakota State University library.

25. Institute for Regional Studies, North Dakota State University, Archives of the Amenia and Sharon Land Co. Mss 134/Box 27 "Farm Contracts"/Folders 1–4.

26. North Dakota did not gain statehood until 1889 (along with the surrounding states of South Dakota and Montana) and immigration rates were high.

Chapter 4: Choosing between Cropshare and Cash Rent Contracts

1. The analysis in this chapter draws on Allen and Lueck (1992b).

2. Otsuka and Hayami (1988), found empirical work done only for the Third World, historical Europe, and the postbellum South. There are surprisingly few empirical studies of modern Western agricultural contracts (Allen and Lueck 1992a, 1992b, 1993a; Brown and Atkinson 1981; Canjels 1996; Sotomayer, Ellinger, and Barry 2000; and Young and Burke 2001).

3. There are very few explanations of cropsharing based solely on risk sharing, and Cheung (1969) and Stiglitz (1974) actually have elements of both transaction costs and risk aversion in their theories of share tenancy. Interestingly, Cheung later focused on transaction costs and Stiglitz on risk. In addition, there are also the screening theories of F. Allen (1985) and Hallagan (1978).

4. See, for example, Ackerberg and Botticini (2000), Carmona and Simpson (1999), Galassi (1992), and Hoffman (1984).

5. This holds because of the optimal share conditions that are derived explicitly in chapter 5.

6. For studies that ignored risk-sharing see Alston, Datta, and Nugent (1984), Eswaran and Kotwal (1985), Lucas (1979), and Reid (1977).

7. Schickele (1941) also noted the incentive to overuse the land in a short-term lease.

8. Hamilton (1990) notes these incentives too. He states: "Cash rental [can] provide an incentive for tenants to maximize production . . . and thus may lead to heavier use or purchased inputs of fertilizer and chemicals" (242). He also notes that cash rent contracts "may promote the planting of cash crop monocultures . . . rather than the use of crop rotations" (242).

9. Eswaran and Kotwal (1985) also recognize this feature of cropsharing and write: "We view sharecropping as a partnership in which both agents have incentives to self-monitor" (353).

10. We recognize that double moral hazard may be important for other types of farmland. Indeed, in chapter 8 we incorporate double moral hazard when considering contracting for equipment. Barzel (1997) uses a double moral hazard framework to analyze farm contract choice, as do Carmona and Simpson (1999) in the context of share contracts in Catalan viticulture. In retail franchise contracts double moral hazard is certainly important; see Lafontaine (1992), Bhattacharyya and Lafontaine (1995), and Arruñada, Garicano, and Vázquez (2001).

11. This seemingly obvious cost of sharing is ignored by most writers, although three exceptions are Barzel (1997), Lazear (1986), and Umbeck (1977).

12. There are some cases, however, in which a lessee's cattle are weighed at the beginning and the end of the season, and the pasture owner is paid a share of the herd's weight gain. More common, though less so than straight cash renting, is the case in which a landowner also owns cattle and leases them both to a rancher who retains a share of the annual calf crop.

13. Since we assume it is prohibitive for the landowner to measure inputs by simply observing the output, landowners are unable to entice optimal resource allocation using repeated contracts. Because the landowner can only rely on the incentive structure of the contract, our one-period model is appropriate.

14. As we noted in the introduction to this chapter, we assume the inputs are independent for several reasons. An additional reason is that this assumption yields testable predictions supported by the available data (Friedman 1953).

15. Because $\theta \sim (0, \sigma^2)$ and because risk neutral parties maximized expected profits, the error term, θ, vanishes from all first-order conditions.

16. Occasionally cash rent is paid in two or three installments during the growing season. This payment is a sunk cost and thus does not influence the farmer's choice of e or l.

17. Although we use a single period model to address soil exploitation, recent studies have used intertemporal and dynamic models (Dubois 2002; Ray 1999). Consider a simple intertemporal framework in which L is labor effort and $F(L)$ is the current output with $F' > 0$, $V(L)$ is the forgone future output with $V' < 0$, and $C(L)$ is the cost of effort with $C' > 0$. The first best effort level (L^*) must satisfy $F' + V' = C'$, however, a short term cash rent contract generates $F' = C'$ and effort $L^s > L^*$. This framework incorporates our land exploitation incentive but does not account for effort moral hazard or output monitoring.

18. This assumption and its implications are inconsistent with our data set. Dollars are rarely shared, and inputs are not always shared in the same proportion. Eswaran and Kotwal (1985) assume that net revenue is shared, which implies that input costs are shared in the same proportion as the output and that the costs of output division are zero. See chapter 5 for a complete discussion on variations in output shares and the relationship between input and output shares.

19. Underreporting the quality and quantity of crops and livestock in share contracts is an ancient problem. In the Old Testament, Genesis 30:37-43 records how Jacob became "exceedingly prosperous" at the expense of his partner and father-in-law, Laban, by manipulating the breeding stock in such a way that he always received a higher-quality share of the animals.

20. As noted in chapter 1, we assume that competition among farmers and landowners is strong enough that only the most valuable contract is chosen. Contracts that failed to maximize joint wealth would simply not survive.

21. AGE, ACRES OWNED, and INSTITUTION are only available from surveys of farmers; ABSENT is only available from surveys of landowners.

22. DENSITY is only used in the U.S. samples because the regions in British Columbia are too large to be meaningful measures of urbanization.

23. We do this because the Nebraska–South Dakota data leave open the possibility for the ROW CROP and HAY variables to have a slight overlap. In the British Columbia–Louisiana data, this design problem does not exist and so the variable is excluded from estimates in table 4.4.

24. Many farmers now own semi-tractor trailers that allow them to haul grain hundreds of miles to large central locations. This change will likely increase measurement costs of output and reduce the attraction of cropshare contracts.

25. Hay is often used as a livestock feed by the leasing farmer, making third party measurement even more difficult.

26. Irrigation for rice in Louisiana, however, does not fit this description, since it is for pest control rather than to supplement soil moisture.

27. Indeed, for hay crops, the farmer's ability to deplete the soil by excessive tilling is minimal, because the soil is seldom manipulated; the crop is simply harvested periodically.

28. The irrigation variable could also be explained by risk sharing. Irrigated crops are less variable and hence are more likely to be cash rented under the assumption of risk aversion. In chapter 6 our data refute this interpretation.

29. The finding in the farmer sample might be interpreted as a refutation of risk sharing because it indicates that farmers who are more specialized in agriculture choose contracts (cash rent) that put more residual ownership on their actions (Allen and Lueck 1992b).

30. Few row crops are grown in British Columbia, so this finding is not surprising.

31. As we note later in our discussion of European agriculture, cropshare contracts have a centuries-old tradition in vines and trees.

32. As noted previously, we devote chapter 6 to exhaustively testing risk-sharing predictions.

33. See Eswaran and Kotwal (1985).

34. Later in chapter 6, in the context of testing for evidence of risk sharing in contract choice, we use data that focus on farmer wealth rather than just acres owned. The results there are consistent with those here that there is some modest evidence that capital constraints have an impact on contract choice, even though this effect is small when compared to the effect of the other transaction cost variables. In chapter 8 we explicitly model capital constraints in the context of asset ownership. For the decision to own or lease an asset, the effect of capital constraints is much larger.

35. Sotomayer, Ellinger, and Barry (2000) find support for this prediction in their Illinois contract data, using net worth to measure financial constraint. One difficulty with our data and the data used by Sotomayer, Ellinger, and Barry is that there is no information on the presence of multiple payments in cash rent contracts that would reduce attraction of cash rent contracts in avoiding capital constraints.

36. One bit of evidence in favor of family acting as a trust or information variable is that absentee landowners are more likely to contract with family members.

37. Hoffman (1984), in an examination of 83 contracts from Lyonnais, found that landowners with vines "found sharecropping preferable to renting" (316). He reports that "highly commercial crops were often raised by croppers: not just wine in the Lyonnais, but also mulberry trees for the silk trade farther south" (319). In a discussion of Hoffman's earlier work, Sella (1982) states: "Sharecropping was best suited to labor intensive farming involving a variety of arable and tree crops leases involving fixed rent, on the other hand, were preferred where either livestock or monoculture predominated" (162).

38. See Carmona and Simpson (1999) for a detailed discussion of historical share contracts for grapes in Spain.

Chapter 5: Sharing Inputs and Outputs

1. The analysis in this chapter draws on Allen and Lueck (1993a).

2. In particular, we assume that the partial derivatives of the production function have the signs $h_i > 0$, $h_{ii} < 0$, and $h_{ij} = 0$ for $i, j = e, l$, and k—implying that the inputs are independent.

3. As noted in chapter 4, we maximize expected profits so the optimality conditions do not contain information about θ or its distribution.

4. It may seem possible that $l^s < l^*$ obtains, but this cannot occur because it would imply such a small output share (s) to the farmer that the input distortions would not be minimized. See figure 5.1.

5. The terms $e_s(h_e - w) > 0$, $l_s(h_l - r) < 0$, and $k_s(h_k - c) \geq 0$ are the marginal distortions resulting from using e^s, l^s, and k^s rather than e^*, l^*, and k^*. The positively signed partial derivatives e_s, l_s, and k_s indicate the effect of a change in the output share on the farmer's input use. Equation (5.3) requires that the marginal cost of an increase in the farmer's share of the crop—shown by the positive terms $e_s(h_e - w)$ and $k_s(h_k - c)$—equal the marginal gain from the increased share, as shown by the negative term $l_s(h_l - r)$. Equation (5.4) has an analogous interpretation for changes in the input shares.

6. The assumption of lump-sum input measurement costs seems reasonable for a single farmland contract. In particular, there is no reason to think these costs would depend on s or q.

7. This solution was first offered by Heady (1947). Heady did not, however, consider input enforcement costs, and as a result he did not derive the second optimal sharing rule. Berry (1962) and Schickele (1941) also discuss the effects of sharing input costs.

8. Note that if $l^s < l^*$, this condition cannot be satisfied.

9. This prediction is consistent with a pure neoclassical model. If the farmer's contribution is higher, his return should be too.

10. Braverman and Stiglitz (1986) compare cost-sharing contracts with those "fixed input contracts" that specify input levels in the contracts. In the data we examine, this type of contract is not observed.

11. We do not report the huge χ^2 statistics from the cross-tabs of input and output shares.

12. Similarly, Carmona and Simpson (1999) find that when Catalan vineyard share contracts introduced input cost sharing, the farmer's share declined. Taylor (1910) found widespread use of share contracts in Wisconsin during the late 1800s and early 1900s; he noted that typical cropshares were one-third to landowners, but were 50-50 when input costs were also shared.

13. Although it is true that these "nonmarket" inputs can occasionally be purchased in the market, they are generally provided by the farmer.

14. The obvious exception is seed. Later we address this apparent anomaly.

15. In separate equations, we used a dummy variable that measured whether or not the inputs had long-term effects on the land by increasing the value of the land beyond the production of the current crop. If the input enhances the value of the land, then the landowner is more likely to share the costs in order to maximize the contract value of the land lease. As expected, this variable had a negative effect on the probability of the farmer's paying all input costs. Because nearly all of these long-term inputs are market inputs, the MARKET coefficient also captures this effect.

16. Because we include those few cases where the input share does not equal 100 percent of the cropshare, our sample size for these equations is slightly larger than for the logit estimates of contract choice in table 5.9.

17. This reputation effect is consistent with our findings in chapter 3.

18. This discreteness has also been found in Kansas (Tsoodle and Wilson 2000) where the most common share is 67-33 (65–70%) with 60-40 and 50-50 each accounting for about 15 percent of the contract. Less than 5 percent of the cropshare contract in their sample have terms outside these parameters.

19. *The 1995 Cooperative Extension Service Farm Leasing Survey,* Department of Agricultural and Consumer Economics, University of Illinois, 1996.

20. Corn makes such a practice simple, but it would be impossible with wheat which is not harvested by the row and is subject to great losses if left standing in the field during the harvest season (see chapters 8 and 9). Even in corn, larger modern equipment that harvests more than two rows at a time will increase the cost of this practice. Professor Joseph Atwood (private conversation with the authors, June 3, 2002) notes this corn harvest practice is still common in Nebraska.

21. Recent studies in Illinois (Young and Burke 2001) and Kansas (Tsoodle and Wilson 2000) also show a similar input sharing dichotomy in their Illinois contract data. Since the 50-50 cropshare is more common in Illinois, the data also show that 50-50 inputs sharing is also common. It should be noted that neither of these papers attempt to explain the relationship between input and output sharing.

Chapter 6: Risk Sharing and the Choice of Contract

1. The analysis in this chapter draws on Allen and Lueck (1995, 1999a).

2. It is a moot point where the theory of contract choice based on risk aversion and incentives begins. Three early papers certainly were Cheung (1969), Stiglitz (1974), and Harris and Raviv (1979).

3. See Chiappori and Salanié (2000) and Prendergast (1999, 2000, 2002).

4. As noted in chapter 1, Masten and Saussier (2000), draw similar conclusions.

5. Even though there have been studies of agricultural contracts that ignore differences in attitudes toward risk (for example, Allen and Lueck 1992a, 1993a; Alston and Higgs 1982; Alston, Datta, and Nugent 1984, Eswaran and Kotwal 1985; Laffont and Matoussi 1995), the risk-sharing model is still the standard.

6. Hayami and Otsuka (1993) note these first two points.

7. Technically, the farmer need only be more risk averse than the landowner. We follow the standard convention and assume the landowner is risk neutral.

8. Most of these predictions have been derived elsewhere—including Hirshleifer and Riley (1992), Kawasaki and McMillan (1987), Leland (1978), and Stiglitz (1974)—and are conveniently summarized in Hayami and Otsuka (1993).

9. For example, see Laffont and Matoussi (1995), or Hayami and Otsuka (1993) for agricultural cases, and Garen (1994) or Kawasaki and McMillan (1987) for business cases.

10. The linear mean-variance utility function is routinely used, especially in agriculture (Chavas and Holt 1990, Pope and Just 1991).

11. Kawasaki and McMillan (1987) derive a similar optimal sharing parameter in their model of sales compensation.

12. This prediction is not unique to the risk-sharing model.

13. We do this because in North America land contract shares tend not to be continuous, as shown in chapter 5.

14. Cheung (1969) first suggested this distinction in costs between cash and share contracts.

15. Predictions 6.5 and 6.6 assume that neither $V^c > V^s$ nor $V^s > V^c$ hold for all parameter values.

16. Even when data on prices is relevant, it is not clear that historical price variability data are an appropriate measure of a farmer's forward-looking price variability because of continual changes in market conditions. Historical measures of yield variability are more reliable because they are mostly determined by long-term natural forces such as weather and pest populations.

17. The possibility of a negative correlation between yield and price might suggest that sharing output can actually mitigate risk. However, because all of the farmers in our sample operate in competitive world markets, this is highly unlikely. Indeed, calculations of price-yield correlations at the state or province level indicate that negative relationships are not common (see table A.11). More important, because our tests exploit regional and county (or parish) yield variability, even negative statewide price-yield correlations are not relevant.

18. Alternatively, one could, in principle, test the model with data on individual risk preferences. Ordinarily such data would seem impossible to obtain, although some (Gaynor and Gertler 1995) use self-reported risk preference measures.

19. For instance, a recent study of executive compensation contracts by Garen (1994) notes the "endogeneity problem," but then uses industry-wide R&D expenditures as a measure of the exogenous variability, claiming that "settings in which R&D is important should display a greater variance in returns in investment opportunities." Kawasaki and McMillan (1987) and Lafontaine (1992) use proxy variables that are endogenous to firm behavior as well. Sotomayer, Ellinger, and Barry (2000) use farm yield that also depends on farmer behavior. Interestingly, in their recent survey Chiappori and Salanié (2000) do not mention the empirical difficulty of obtaining exogenous risk measures.

20. Rosenzweig and Binswanger (1993), confirming many studies, find that the timeliness of monsoons is an important variable in explaining crop yields in India but that rainfall amounts are not good explanatory variables. In chapters 8 and 9, timeliness costs are an an important issue in farm organization and ownership.

21. This requires that the total output of the region be bounded. This model assumes the covariance between effort e and natural parameters θ is zero, which is consistent with the standard production technology assumed in the principal-agent literature.

22. For other types of agriculture, heterogeneous regions may generate enough idiosyncratic risk that performing this test may not be possible. Lafontaine and Bhattacharyya (1995) argue that such heterogeneities plague franchising studies of risk sharing. On the other hand, if regions were perfectly homogeneous, one might expect relative performance contracts for farm production. Such contracts are never observed in our data set but are found in chicken production where (homogeneous) technology and inputs are provided by a single supplier to many growers (Knoeber 1989).

23. Some of these data are not available for British Columbia because its regions tend to encompass the entire provincial production for the crops we examine (see table A.7). Also, our measures of crop yield variability are not consistent between British Columbia and the other three states because of data limitations. In particular, British Columbia yield data are not available for smaller, county-like areas.

24. Higgs (1973) conducts a similar exercise using aggregate data from eleven Southern states for 1910. Considering only two crops (corn and cotton) he finds a positive effect on CV but notes the U.S. Census data does not distinguish between "sharecroppers" or unskilled laborers without capital, with "share farmers" who provide their own capital.

25. The two states are not clones though. Nebraska has a greater fraction of land similar to the Corn Belt and South Dakota has more land similar to the High Plains. Also, climate and soil tend to improve as one travels from north to south. Because the statewide crop CV rankings differed between the two states, the coefficient estimates from the pooled sample could not be used to directly test the effects of crop riskiness mentioned earlier.

26. Unfortunately, data limitations in calculating yield variability prevent us from estimating these effects in British Columbia using the specification that follows.

27. At the same time, because these farmers all face essentially the same market prices, there is no variation in prices across our sample of contracts.

28. We also use MEAN as a control variable when STD is used to approximate σ_{ij}^2.

29. The size of some Louisiana crop samples (mostly sorghum and wheat) were further restricted because we were not able to identify the parish for some farmers. Regional yield statistics are not available in British Columbia, so this test could not be performed. The samples (n_j) were generally smaller for COUNTY CV and STD, compared to REGIONAL CV and REGIONAL STD, because the states do not calculate yields for counties when total output is below a threshold; therefore COUNTY CV and COUNTY STD were not always available even when REGIONAL CV and REGIONAL STD were available.

30. We are unable to estimate a wheat equation for Louisiana because of the small number of observations.

31. We use other methods to test the robustness of these estimates. First, we estimated OLS regressions using $ln(s/1-s)$ as the dependent variable. We also estimated the same 46 equations by expanding the sample to include cash rent contracts and counting them as 100 percent share contracts. For each cash contract, we set $s = 0.999$ in order to insure that the dependent variable, $ln(s/1-s)$, is defined for all contract observations. Next we estimated the 46 equations without control variables, using only the CV or STD variables, and with a smaller set of control variables than used in table 6.6. Finally, we used Heckman's two-step estimation method in order to control for the contract choice selection problem. None of these alternative specifications change the findings reported in table 6.6 in any significant way.

32. Stiglitz (1974) is one of the earliest papers to make the point about risk-sharing and futures markets.

33. It is possible that futures markets have arisen for those crops that have highly variable yields, although this seems unlikely. Simple inspection of our data shows that futures markets are found for nearly all widely traded and storable crops. Furthermore, Pirrong (1995) and Williams (1987), argue that futures markets exist to reduce the transaction costs of measurement and trading commodities.

34. These coefficients, along with the ones mentioned in the next paragraph in the text, are not reported.

35. This is hardly surprising, however, since we also found that rice land is nearly always cropshared (table 6.3).

36. Prendergast (2002) develops a similar model in which greater output variability lowers the returns to input-based contracts, thus increasing the use of output-based contracts.

37. Additional evidence across crops is found in appendix A (table A.12).

38. Risk preference assumptions are also crucial in franchising models (Lafontaine 1992). In the standard model— the franchisee is risk averse but the franchisor is risk neutral—risk-sharing implies that greater exogenous variability will result in more fixed payment contracts (hired managers). If, as some have argued, risk preferences are reversed (Martin 1988), the contract choice prediction is reversed.

39. Demsetz and Lehn (1985) develop a similar argument in their study of outside shareholders in a corporation. Greater uncertainty makes the risk cost of concentrated shareholding (less diversification) greater, and this is the effect that most focus on. Demsetz and Lehn argue that more uncertainty increases the value of shareholder monitoring of the manager, and so increases the benefit of concentrated shareholding. They also present evidence that this monitoring effect dominates. Greater uncertainty is linked to greater concentration of outsider shareholding.

40. It should be noted that it was not possible for us to directly test risk-sharing predictions against those from our transaction cost model because of the different data requirement for each test. The clearest tests of the risk-sharing model used contract data for specific crops. The transaction cost predictions, however, required that we use contracts for land with differing crops to account for differences in soil exploitation and output measurement costs.

Chapter 7: Ratchet Effects in Agricultural Contracts

1. The analysis in this chapter draws on Allen and Lueck (1999b).

2. See Berliner (1957) for a Soviet application, and Weitzman (1980), and Baron and Besanko (1984) for early formal analyses.

3. Methods of commitment may take different forms, including long-term agreements, reputation, and specific investments. Kanemoto and MacLeod (1992) show how competition from older workers can ameliorate the ratchet effect under some circumstances.

4. The landowner is made better off from the new knowledge; hence, the fixed side payment made by the farmer to the landowner must also increase with the incentives in the contract.

5. Refutable implications arising from dynamic models, like the ratchet effect, are rare. This may explain the common use of adjectives like "celebrated" (Salanié 1997, 158) in discussions of the ratchet effect.

6. In a standard principal-agent model, lower standards over time are not possible. This is because the informed farmer would never accept the initial contract if it contained performance standards that were too high and violated his individual rationality constraint.

7. Much of the ratchet literature still examines Soviet-style organizations. More recently, however, the applications have expanded to include the U.S. military (Ickes and Samuelson 1987), private ownership (Olsen and Torsvik 1993), and labor markets (Kanemoto and MacLeod 1992). The analysis of ratchet effects is now found in theoretical texts like Milgrom and Roberts (1992), Laffont and Tirole (1993), and Salanié (1997).

8. This model is similar to the one in Milgrom and Roberts (1992).

9. Although the ratchet effect is often discussed in the context of risk-averse farmers, it does not depend on any of the classical principal-agent assumptions. In particular, risk aversion is not necessary. A ratchet effect can exist in more complicated multiple moral hazard models and models of adverse selection without the assumption of risk aversion. For an example of a ratchet effect model with moral hazard and no risk aversion, see Meyer and Vickers (1997).

10. This is a reasonable assumption in our context, given the demographic similarity of farmers and landowners on the Great Plains (see chapters 2 and 6). Also, the use of tractors and other types of farm machinery tends to equalize the ability to farm, since sheer physical strength is less of a factor. We recognize that farmers are not truly identical and that the landowner will learn about specific farmers.

11. The ratchet effect appears to grind against the old ladder hypothesis (Spillman 1919) that implies young farmers start with cropshare contracts, move on to cash rent contracts, and eventually have sole ownership of the farm. However, they are not necessarily at odds. With models that incorporate the ratchet effect, a new tenant farmer is not the same as a young tenant farmer.

12. This simple production function allows us to focus on the ratchet effect. See Meyer and Vickers (1997) for a similar setup.

13. This simple specification of the correlation in random inputs can easily apply to agriculture where the effect of nature is often relatively straightforward. For example, a particular hay field may have poor drainage or slope, which leads to poor drying conditions and reduced hay output. Knowledge of this learned in the first period helps the landowner better estimate the drying contribution of nature in the second period.

14. In order for there to be a ratchet effect, $\gamma > 0$ because otherwise the landowner would be ignoring the first-period information.

15. Because we focus on gross income, the $C(e)$ term is gone. This simplifies the analysis without altering the predictions.

16. The benefit of the acquired information is the reduction in the variance in the landowner's estimate of the value of random input; that is, $Var(\theta_2 - \hat{\theta}_2) < Var(\theta_2)$. When the landowner has a better measure of the random input, he has a more accurate picture of the farmer's contribution as well and can better alter the contract to increase his returns. Although the share to the farmer increases, the side payment to the landowner also increases, making the landowner better off.

17. We assume, for simplicity, that the inputs k_i are observable. This leads to a strong prediction about input shares over time. This prediction, however, is not found elsewhere in the ratchet literature, and does not hold if inputs are assumed unobservable. Our purpose here is to focus on output shares.

18. The British Columbia–Louisiana data do not have the required information to test these predictions.

19. As we noted in chapter 2, cropshare contracts usually do not contain a side payment. We can still use these data to test the ratchet effect model, however, because inputs are shared and adjustments can be made to input shares that are equivalent to adjusting fixed payments. The analysis of case II demonstrated how easily the model can be adjusted along these lines.

20. In chapter 5 we found a strong positive relationship between the number of inputs shared and the output share, as well as a strong positive relationship between the size of the input cost share and the output share.

21. We use the log of the odds ratio to create a nonlimited dependent variable, since the share is naturally bounded from 0 to 1.

22. This estimated equation has an unusually high number of correct predictions. This occurs simply because there are very few positive responses. For most contracts, the terms of trade remain relatively stable over time.

23. In both chapters 4 and 5, the ROW CROP dummy was an important variable explaining the choice of contract.

24. For example, if we could identify situations where there was a new technology shock or a new crop produced on the land, we could better isolate the effect of landowner information on the land.

Chapter 8: Ownership versus Contracting for the Control of Assets

1. Irwin and Smith (1972) note that relatively little equipment is leased in agriculture compared to nonagricultural industries where leasing of automobiles, trucks, and large-scale equipment is routine. In recent years, however, year-long leasing of tractors has become more common.

2. Indeed, Hansmann (1996) devoted his book to analyzing when capitalists, workers, or consumers own the firm and did not explicitly consider the variation of control within firms. Other theories of ownership have been developed by Barzel (1997), Grossman and Hart (1986), Henderson and Ioannides (1983), Hart and Moore (1990), and Wiggins (1990).

3. Joskow (1987) provides evidence for the importance of specific assets in coal production. Nickerson and Silverman (2002) examine the choice between owner-operator trucking firms and hired truckers. See Shelanski and Klein (1995) for a survey of this empirical literature.

4. This point is also noted by Hansmann (1996), who argues that specific assets are overrated as a foundation for explaining ownership. Holmström and Roberts (1998) are also skeptical of the general applicability. As we noted in chapter 3, Coase and others have challenged the classic specific assets story of General Motors and Fisher Body (see Coase 2000).

5. See Becker and Murphy (1992) for a general analysis of specialization and Allen and Lueck (1998) for an application to agriculture. Barzel (1997) explicitly introduces the lack of specialization as an important cost of sole ownership and also discusses the trade-off between this and moral hazard.

6. Reality, of course, is more complicated. Landowners, for instance, may provide other farming inputs, and often share input costs. Landowners tend not to closely monitor the farmer and often live a long distance from their land. Similarly, equipment lessors often take care of repairs and large-scale maintenance. In our framework, "control" is an economic, not a legal, term.

7. The term "custom," used by farmers and contractors, refers to the case where the owner of the equipment also supplies the labor. For example, "Custom work entails the hiring of person and machines to perform specified tasks" (Montana Cooperative Extension Service 1990, 1). It does not mean that the work is somehow customized to the specific farm.

8. Edwards and Boehle (1980) define timeliness costs as "the indirect cost of lower crop yields that occur because planting and harvesting are not completed during the optimal time periods" (810). See also Short and Gitu (1991).

9. Pasour (1990) has argued that the U.S. tax code may alter the incentives for the lease-own decision by allowing farm capital owners to depreciate capital at a faster rate than owners of nonfarm capital. Ford and Musser (1994) stress tax rates and capital rationing in their model of the lease-purchase decision. Hansmann (1991) shows that federal tax law has long provided a net subsidy to owner-occupied housing. There is also a large literature in urban economics that tends to focus on life cycles and taxes (Henderson and Ioannides 1983).

10. A sixth arrangement, in the lower left-hand cell in table 8.1, is left blank because it makes no sense to consider the case in which the farmer does not use his labor (which includes family, hired labor, and slaves).

11. See Barzel (1997, chap. 3) for a discussion of the indirect pricing of exploited attributes.

12. For simplicity and ease of reading, the graphs are again drawn with straight lines, and we set $w^* = r^* = v^*$.

13. The lower marginal product curves given by $h_j[1 - X(\theta)]$, $j = e, l, k$ are not relevant for this case and can be ignored.

14. This model is fashioned after Barzel and Suen (1994). Sengupta (1997) has a model with limited liability as well as moral hazard in technique and effort that generates similar implications. In chapter 4 we empirically considered some implications of capital constraints for the choice of share and cash land contracts.

15. Consider the case in which an asset owner supplies labor, effectively becoming a farmer. If the asset owner decides to farm with the asset directly, his human capital input may be so low that w^o is extremely high, and this lowers the value of the governance structure. For a number of reasons (for example, the asset owner lives far from the farm, is too old to farm, is an aged widow, or lacks the knowledge or the physical ability to farm), this fall in value may be drastic. We examine this case in our empirical work on land where we have information on the landowner.

16. The area is equivalent to the vertical distance because the two graphs plot different values.

17. See chapter 9 for more detail on the role of nature and timeliness in farming.

18. This is not the only econometric approach to this problem. For example, in the absence of contract data Nickerson and Silverman (2002) estimate the fraction of output governed by various control regimes for a sample of firms.

19. We do this because WEALTH is partially determined by the value of the asset owned and may be correlated with the error term. Estimates using these variables are virtually identical.

20. Asset ownership may also be separated to mitigate this incentive. For example, in Catalonian grapes, the farmer owned the vines but leased the land (Carmona and Simpson 1999). As we noted in chapter 3, these share contracts were automatically renewed as long as the farmer replaced the dead vines.

21. The estimates for NET WEALTH and LANDOWNER HUMAN CAPITAL are only significant at the 10 percent level in a one-tailed test.

22. Tractor prices vary with the horsepower, so rates are often discussed in terms of "horsepower hours." See Edwards and Meyer (1986) and Pflueger (1994) for some details on modern farm equipment leasing.

23. Barry, Hopkin, and Baker (1988) note the following in their book on farm finance: "The greatest success for operating leases is with general purpose items, which have user demands spread over various time periods" (298).

24. In terms of risk sharing, an increase in wealth might lower risk aversion under DARA and lead to more ownership if asset ownership is riskier than leasing. We had little evidence in support of this effect in our chapter 6 analysis of farmland contracts.

25. This section is based primarily on the fascinating work of Isern (1981), a farm boy turned historian and a keen observer of farm organization. The USDA study by Lagrone and Gavett (1975) is another important source.

26. See U.S. Department of Commerce, Bureau of the Census (1999), Table 3, "farm production expenses." The census does not collect data on specific custom services.

27. Prior to the introduction of the combine—a machine that combined harvesting and threshing—small grain harvests were mostly done by large crews in two separate stages. Crews cut and bundled the grain, which would then be stacked or stored until a second crew came along and threshed the grain (separated the grain from the chaff).

28. See chapter 9 for a discussion of how the extent of the farm has changed.

29. Isern (1981) reports that many cutters have been in the business for two or three generations.

30. According to Isern, this formula was typically 3/3/3 when it first emerged in the early 1940s. The high yield payment compensates the cutter for slower progress (in terms of acres) with higher yields and greater wear and tear on the machines.

31. Isern (1981) also notes that it is costly for farmers to hire reliable and experienced short-term labor.

32. See Isern (1981) for 1948 and 1957. For 1999, see the AP article "Custom Cutters: Kansas Farmers Watch Wheat Quality Decline while Waiting for Harvesting Crews to Arrive," *Bozeman Daily Chronicle*, Sunday, July 11, 1999.

33. It is somewhat of a puzzle why cutter payments do not depend directly on the crop yield. Perhaps the answer is that such yield payments would not adequately compensate the farmer because the yield contribution of the cutter could not be easily separated from that of the farmer during the growing season.

34. For example, DuBow (1999) reports how cutters flatten "any strips of missed wheat with the grain cart's monster treads" (37). This "trick," used to "make the cutting look more precise," implicitly lowers the crew's cost of completing a job.

35. This contiguousness does not hold for wheat planting and pesticide application, partly because spring wheat dominates in the north and winter wheat dominates in the south. As a result, we do not observe migratory custom planting or pesticide application for wheat. We do find custom harvesting in Germany, where custom cutters follow the ripening grain up certain river valleys as elevation changes lead to different, but contiguous, harvesting times.

36. In an Iowa Extension Services bulletin prepared for farmers, Edwards and Meyer (1986) note: "Custom hiring is particularly useful for specialized machines that are expensive to purchase and used only seasonally. This method is also attractive for beginning farm operators with limited capital resources and labor, for other farm operators who are expanding and have other uses for available capital, and for small scale farmers."

37. Government intervention is limited. States regulate vehicles and often discriminate against out-of-state combine crews with taxes and license fees. States also require that cutters clean machines before crossing state borders in order to limit the transportation of noxious weeds.

38. Over the past decade, locations for hauling grains have become more centralized and hauling distances have increased. As a result, there has been a dramatic increase in the optimal size of grain trucks. Hauling grain, however, is not subject to any timeliness problems. As our model predicts, farmers are abandoning their hauling roles with small five-ton trucks to rent hauling services from operators with semi-tractor trailer units.

39. House is quoted in Stephanie Sorenson, "From Texas to Montana: Tracking Shorty's Crew on the Custom Harvest Trail," *Prairie Grains* (September 1997): 3.

Chapter 9: Farm Organization and Vertical Control

1. The analysis in this chapter draws on Allen and Lueck (1998).

2. Binswanger and Rosenzweig (1986), Johnson and Ruttan (1994), Nerlove (1996), and Royer and Rodgers (1998) are among the studies that examine organizational issues beyond sharecropping in undeveloped countries. Important recent studies of agriculture by Bardhan (1989), Hayami and Otsuka (1993), and Hoff, Braverman, and Stiglitz (1993) focus on land and labor contracts and ignore broad organizational questions. Roumasset (1995) is a recent paper with a similar focus to this chapter.

3. See, for example, Brewster (1950), Castle and Becker (1962), Ellickson and Brewster (1947), Heady (1952), Holmes (1928), and Schultz (1954).

4. We ignore intrafamily incentives and consider a husband-and-wife team (and their juvenile children) as a single agent. While this assumption ignores intrafamily shirking, this is unlikely to be serious as long as families are bound by intergenerational contracts. We also ignore the distinction made in chapter 8 between control of assets through ownership and contracting.

5. We include "family-held corporations" within "partnerships" because such corporations are often established under "subchapter S" of the Internal Revenue Service code and are more like small partnerships than large-scale corporations. For the issues we study, this distinction is not important.

6. Eleven stages of growth, from planting to ripening, exist in "Feeke's Scale of Wheat Development." See *The Wheat Grower* (September 1994): WF-8.

7. Recognizing that ownership is not constant across stages of production points out the ambiguity of questions like "How big is the farm?" A farm may be 1,000 acres at planting but harvesting may be done by another "farm" over 80,000 acres.

8. Ellickson and Brewster (1947) also recognize the common cumulative feature of agriculture: "For the number of simultaneous operations in agriculture varies little with either the size of farm or the 'state of the industrial arts.' It makes little difference, for example, whether a corn-hog farm covers the whole state of Iowa or on 160 acres, or whether farming is done with oxen, flails, and sickles or with high-powered tractors and combines; the number of production steps that can be done at the same time on such farms remains substantially unchanged" (841).

9. For example, the harvest season for spring wheat might be three weeks but can be several months for sugarcane. In the simple case of homogeneous stages, $L = 365/(C * S)$ so that if just one stage requires a year to complete the process, then $L = 365$ days.

10. In making this assumption, we assert that the reduction in capital costs outweighs the moral hazard problems that might arise with multiple owners or users of capital. Compared to labor effort, capital levels are easily observed and often assigned to a specific partner or hired worker.

11. Once again, the random input (θ) and its variance (σ^2) play no direct role in the objective function or the optimality conditions. None of the organizations we discuss are first-best: this requires full specialization ($a = 1, r = r^{\min}$), no moral hazard, and optimal timing.

12. Our model of partnership is distinct from recent studies by Gaynor and Gertler (1995) and Lang and Gordon (1995) that emphasize risk sharing as the motivation for partnerships.

13. This is because $a = 1/2$ in both cases.

14. We recognize that a firm with a corps of hired labor is likely to have hired managers as well. Our model simply lumps together the adverse selection and moral hazard problems of managers with the moral hazard of workers. Analysis of these issues can be found in the burgeoning literature on the internal workings of the firm (Baker, Gibbs, and Hölstrom 1994; Lazear 1995).

15. Mighell and Jones (1963) also discuss "interstage" incentives. More recently, Hennessy (1996) develops a model in which intermediate product quality is costly to measure, thus creating incentives for vertical coordination. This justification has the same impact as our timelines argument.

16. In practice, the importance of timing can vary greatly across crops and stages. Harvest timing, for example, is crucial (δ is large) in spring wheat, where delays can result in large losses from hail, rain, or wind. Once wheat is threshed, however, there is almost no timing problem associated with milling the wheat into flour ($\delta \approx 0$). Sugarcane, on the other hand, must be processed into raw sugar within 24 hours after cutting or the cane's sugar content will decline dramatically (again δ is large).

17. This is most likely to hold for small partnerships (for example, if $N = 2$) and when capital is relatively unimportant because the marginal deadweight losses from moral hazard fall with an increase in partners while the marginal benefits of capital cost savings increase with the number of partners.

18. This holds because increases in the number of partners lead to approximately quadratic increases in moral hazard losses. This relationship is essentially that derived from the analysis of the deadweight losses from commodity taxation.

19. A $50,000 limit per person was created in 1981. "Persons" include individuals, partnerships, estates, and corporations.

20. The crop failures and famines in China and the Soviet Union are the most obvious cases, but other important examples abound. See Nerlove (1996) and Pryor (1992). Closer to home, farming on Indian reservations in the western United States has been tremendously unproductive because typical land tenure institutions do not allow

individual farmers to control land and other assets (Anderson and Lueck 1992). Raup (1973) shows that history is littered with examples of factory farming outdone by small family farms.

21. Production agriculture has many complementary tasks across stages that also reduce the effective number of tasks. For example, many tasks, like on-the-spot decision making, are performed jointly, so the skills for one task transfer easily to other tasks. Successful farming depends on making many small decisions, often immediate, and often regarding the timing of actions. Timing and-on-the spot decisions are highly complementary and common across many tasks within a stage. Being a good judge of weather for planting is complementary to judging the weather for harvest. Also, if a family farm controls planting, it is likely to control other stages that require the same inputs. For example, cultivation and harvest require the use of tractors and general farming knowledge, and are thus likely to be controlled by family farms. On the other hand, because processing crops usually calls for large and different forms of capital, the farm that grows the crop is unlikely to process it. Farming is characterized by a host of complementary tasks, both at a given stage, and across stages.

22. See U.S. Department of Commerce, Bureau of the Census (1999), United States Data, Table 47, Summary by Type of Organization.

23. Fogel and Engermann (1974), however, attribute this organization to economies of scale, but this claim ignores the source of such economies in the slave owner's ability to monitor repetitive tasks relatively cheaply over long stages of production.

24. The general issue that farming is not subject to great gains from specialization, and therefore small farms are at no great disadvantage, was noted very early by J. S. Mill (1965 [1871]):

> the operations of agriculture are little susceptible of benefit from the division of labour. . . . There is no particular advantage in setting a great number of people to work together in ploughing or digging or sowing the same field, or even in mowing or reaping it unless time presses. A single family can generally supply all the combination of labour necessary for these purposes. (P. 144)

25. For historical data, we rely on Bidwell and Falconer (1925), Danhoff (1969), Gray (1941), and Schlebecker (1973).

26. Our most important source is Drache (1964). See also Briggs (1932) and Bigelow (1880). Drache and others use "bonanza" for farms over 3,000 acres, although the most prominent of these tended to be between 20,000 and 50,000 acres. Drache finds 91 farms of this size in the region in 1880. He also finds 15 farms that had at least 20,000 acres. This compares to an average farm size of little more than 200 acres during this time. The *1997 Census of Agriculture* (U.S. Department of Commerce, Bureau of the Census 1999) reports that the average farm size in the relevant North Dakota counties was roughly 1,000 acres.

27. The bonanza farms should not, however, be considered a systematic business failure. The stockholders of the Northern Pacific and entrepreneurs like Oliver Dalrymple profited from introducing wheat and its technology to an uncultivated territory. The bonanza farmers capitalized on increasing land values that depended on their own efforts. For instance, land bought in 1875 for $1.00 per acre was sold in 1885 for as much as $25.00 per acre, yielding an annualized nominal return of 38 percent during a period in which price levels fell nearly 20 percent. Drache (1964) shows that bonanza farmers learned quickly that they could do better by abandoning the factory system and leasing or selling their land to local homesteaders. Because they could break soil all summer without having to establish homes for families, it is also likely that the bonanzas were able to exploit specialization gains in sod busting.

28. Coulter is cited in Drache (1964, 213).

29. According to Isern (1990): "In pure custom threshing the thresherman provided not only the machinery, the engineer, and the separator man but also the full crew of men required to do the threshing. . . . the farmer was responsible only for hauling away the grain as it fell from the spout of the separator. The pure custom thresherman provided board for his crew, usually by maintaining a mobile cook shack and hiring a cook" (75).

30. One-man "pull-type" combines (pulled by tractors) were available by 1926, and by the 1940s self-propelled combines were on the market. Although the combine was invented in 1838, it was used sparingly (mainly in California) before the gasoline engine was perfected. Combines required an enormous amount of power that made them unwieldy in the fields when powered by horses or mules (Isern 1990). Data from the USDA show the adoption

of the combine was swift and decisive. In 1920 there were only 4,000 combines, but by 1930 there were 61,000, by 1940 there were 190,000, and by 1950 there were 714,000. See U.S. Department of Agriculture, *Agricultural Statistics 1957*, (1958), Table 639, p. 532.

31. Hotter weather tends to increase decay as does freezing. Also, modern growers burn cane fields prior to cutting as a cheap disposal method for waste leaves. Burning, which began during World War II, makes the cane even more susceptible to tissue decay. See Alexander (1973) on "post harvest quality decline" (577–581).

32. In their study of technology and structure of agriculture, Ellickson and Brewster (1947) note the establishment of vertical control in instances where timeliness costs were crucial. "There are, for example, instances of full owner operators ceasing to be family farmers because they have so bargained away their control over farm operations . . . Such instances are found most frequently in cases of extremely perishable crops, where 'timing' is of the essence and where alternative market outlets are not available" (844).

33. Sugar has another interesting feature: Though the cane is fragile to store, the raw sugar is extremely robust. Once the raw sugar is further processed into refined sugar, it again becomes fragile and easily deteriorates. As a result, raw sugar is processed close to the point of production but is then shipped all over the world, where it is refined near the point of consumption.

34. U.S. Department of Commerce, Bureau of the Census (1999), United States Data, Table 25, Cattle and Calves-Sales. The trend toward larger firms continues. The NASS "Cattle on Feed" report for February 14, 1997, shows the 45 largest firms with an average inventory of 54,689 head and an average annual sales of 124,578 head.

35. U.S. Department of Commerce, Bureau of Census (1993), Table 18, p. 25. McBride (1997) shows that this average of 40 heads per farm has remained stable as far back as 1969.

36. U.S. Department of Commerce, Bureau of the Census (1999) United States Data, Table 47, Summary by Type of Organization.

37. See Knoeber (1989) or Vukina (2001) for detailed discussions of the poultry industry changes during the twentieth century.

38. Although the chickens are grown indoors, weather influences output through large shocks. Power outages, as well as cold or hot outside temperatures can lead to small changes in inside temperatures that can be disastrous in the crowded barns. Hence it is important to have a residual claimant on site. As these barns become more insulated over time to outside factors, the barns begin to be run by wage employees. Knoeber (1989) analyzes the details of the tournament-based grower compensation contracts.

39. Royer and Rogers (1998, part III) have edited several chapters detailing the changes in the hog industry.

40. Kliebenstein and Lawrence (1995) argue that contracting in the hog industry is because of risk sharing. Huffman (2001), however, notes the importance of task specialization and the constraints imposed by biological production. What he calls "phases" are roughly equivalent to our "stages":

> Livestock production is relatively free of constraints due to seasonal or spatial attributes. Production can be organized in sequential phases where all phases from birth to finishing occur on one farm or where different farms specialize in different phases. Advances in animal health products, animal feeding, housing and equipment, and management have made it technically possible to speed up the growing and finishing phases by using large confined animal production systems which greatly increase animal densities and populations. To further reduce disease problems in large confined animal systems, animals of different ages can be separated and raised apart in "all-in, all-out" systems. With the growing and finishing of animals and birds in a facility in phased groups, livestock production becomes similar to production of industrial goods where workers have the opportunity to specialize in a particular phase of production. (P. 4)

41. Timber is another agricultural product whose organization relies on factory-corporate form rather than the family firm. Large corporations own commercial timberland, and timber production is accordingly undertaken by highly specialized wage employees of these corporations. These firms typically extend from planning and harvesting through processing and marketing to retail outlets, so there are, for example, tree planting crews, timber thinning crews, timber harvesting crews, truck drivers, as well as specialized employees who work inside processing facilities. Again, the nature-driven incentives explain the organizational form. Trees have long lives that are not affected by seasons in the way grains and other crops are. Trees can be planted, husbanded, and harvested

over extended seasons (often year round). This means that a large landowner can move specialized labor from plot to plot. The fact that each stage has a great length means that there are large gains from specialization by learning and intensive capital use. Similarly, the monitoring of labor under well-defined routine conditions is relatively cheap, so moral hazard losses are smaller.

42. The survey asked the respondents to classify their farms as a family farm, partnership, corporate farm, or family corporation. If a family corporation used no hired labor and contained only one family as a residual claimant, this farm was also classified as a family farm (using other information on the survey).

43. For example, hay crops usually have three cycles per year, perhaps more under irrigation. Many nurseries and greenhouses have almost continuous production during the year. Although fruit trees provide only one crop per year, we classify them differently from grains because it takes several years for a tree to bear fruit and as the tree ages radical pruning may prevent a crop in the following year. Hence, on average a fruit tree has less than one cycle per year. We do not know, however, the number of cycles being used by the respondents to our survey.

44. Included in CYCLES > 1 are hay crops, pasture, nursery crops, vegetables, and sugarcane (planted only once every 3–5 years); included in CYCLES = 1 are annual grain and row crops such as barley, rice, soybeans, and wheat; and included in CYCLES < 1 are tree fruits, nuts, and timber.

45. Milk tanks must be cleaned by the farmer who might exploit this by adding water, stones (or other bulky items), or milk from other farms to increase the reading on the outside of the tank in order to cheat the milk processor. The processors test the milk constantly for foreign particles to police this, and thus simultaneously monitor workers on the dairy farm.

46. The variable CAPITAL is not adjusted for the equity position of the farmer. Thus it is not the same as the variable WEALTH used in chapter 8.

47. It may seem that equations (9.12 to 9.14) represent a simultaneous system but it is appropriate to estimate 9.14 using OLS because the equations are actually a recursive system in which capital levels depend only on farm choice. As a check, we also estimated 9.14 using a two-stage method in which F_i was replaced by the predicted value of the farm organization (from the logit model); this did not appreciably change the coefficient estimates.

48. This basic fact not only grinds against popular culture, which confuses the reduction in farmers with a reduction in family farming, but is also inconsistent with an old prediction made by O. R. Johnson (1944). He argued that "industrialization" of farming is inevitable except for livestock. In particular, he wrote: "Industrial techniques are difficult to apply to this phase of agriculture [livestock production]" (535).

Chapter 10: Conclusion

1. As we noted in chapter 1, what we have been calling the transaction cost approach is related to what many are recently calling "the New Institutional Economics."

2. A similar sentiment is expressed by Gibbons (1998), who argues that agency theory "should become better integrated with Coase-Williamson literature" (129).

3. Wing Suen has made this point to us. In Hong Kong many executives are called "7-11's" because they work eleven hours a day, seven days a week. No doubt there is an agency problem with the executives, but it certainly is not with the hours of work they put in.

4. Most of the criticisms that are directed at the Coase Theorem stem from this incomplete definition of transaction costs. Using this definition, Usher (1998) easily shows that the Coase Theorem is "tautological, incoherent or wrong."

References

Ackerberg, Daniel, and Maristella Botticini. "The Choice of Agrarian Contracts in Early Renaissance Tuscany: Risk Sharing, Moral Hazard, or Capital Market Imperfections?" *Explorations in Economic History* 37 (2000): 241–57.

Ackerberg, Daniel, and Maristella Botticini. "Endogenous Matching and the Empirical Determinants of Contract Form." *Journal of Political Economy* 110 (2002): 564–591.

Alchian, Armen A. "Uncertainty, Evolution and Economic Theory." *Journal of Political Economy* 58 (1950): 211–221.

Alchian, Armen A., and Harold Demsetz. "Production, Information Costs and Economic Organization" *American Economic Review* 62 (1972): 777–795.

Alexander, A. G. *Sugarcane Physiology*. New York: Elsevier, 1973.

Allen, Douglas W. "What Are Transaction Costs?" *Research in Law and Economics* 14 (1991): 1–18.

Allen, Douglas W. "Transaction Costs." In Boudewijn Bouckaert and Gerrit DeGeest, eds., *Encyclopedia of Law and Economics*, Vol. 1, 893–926. Cheltenham, UK: Edward Elgar Press, 2000.

Allen, Douglas W., and Dean Lueck. "Contract Choice in Modern Agriculture: Cash Rent vs. Cropshare." *Journal of Law and Economics* 35 (1992a): 397–426.

Allen, Douglas W., and Dean Lueck. "The Back-Forty on a Handshake: Specific Assets, Reputation, and the Structure of Farmland Contracts." *Journal of Law, Economics, and Organization* 8 (1992b): 366–377.

Allen, Douglas W., and Dean Lueck. "Transaction Costs and the Design of Cropshare Contracts." *RAND Journal of Economics* 24 (1993a): 78–100.

Allen, Douglas W., and Dean Lueck. *The 1992 British Columbia Farmland Ownership and Leasing Survey.* Burnaby, BC: Simon Fraser University, 1993b.

Allen, Douglas W., and Dean Lueck. *The 1992 Louisiana Farmland Ownership and Leasing Survey.* Baton Rouge: Louisiana State University, 1993c.

Allen, Douglas W., and Dean Lueck. "Risk Preferences and the Economics of Contracts." *American Economic Review* 85 (1995): 447–451.

Allen, Douglas W., and Dean Lueck. "The Nature of the Farm." *Journal of Law and Economics* 41 (1998): 343–386.

Allen, Douglas W. and Dean Lueck. "The Role of Risk in Contract Choice." *Journal of Law, Economics, and Organization* 15 (1999a): 704–736.

Allen, Douglas W., and Dean Lueck. "Searching for Ratchet Effects on Agricultural Contracts." *Journal of Agricultural and Resource Economics* 24 (1999b): 536–552.

Allen, Franklin. "On the Fixed Nature of Sharecropping Contracts." *The Economic Journal* 95 (March 1985): 30–48.

Alston, Lee J., and Robert Higgs. "Contractual Mix in Southern Agriculture since the Civil War." *Journal of Economic History* 42 (1982): 327–353.

Alston, Lee J., Samar Datta, and Jeffrey Nugent. "Tenancy Choice in a Competitive Framework with Transaction Costs." *Journal of Political Economy* 92 (1984): 1121–1133.

Alston Lee J., Gary D. Libecap, and Bernardo Mueller. *Title, Conflict and Land Use.* Ann Arbor: University of Michigan Press, 2000.

Anderson, Terry L., and Dean Lueck. "Land Tenure and Agricultural Productivity on Indian Reservations." *Journal of Law and Economics* 35 (1992):427–454.

Arruñada, Benito, Luis Garicano, and Luis Vázquez. "Asymmetric Completion, Non-Linear Incentives and Last-Resort Termination in Automobile Franchise Contracts." *Journal of Law, Economics, and Organization* 17 (2001): 257–284.

Baker, George, Michael Gibbs, and Bengt Holmström. "The Internal Economics of the Firm: Evidence from Personnel Data." *Quarterly Journal of Economics* 109 (1994): 881–919.

Bardhan, Pranab K., ed. *The Economic Theory of Agrarian Institutions.* Oxford: Clarendon Press, 1989.

Bardhan, Pranab K., and N. Singh. "On Moral Hazard and Cost Sharing Under Sharecropping." *American Journal of Agricultural Economics* 69 (1987): 382–383.

Bardhan, Pranab K., and T. N. Srinivasan. "Cropsharing Tenancy in Agriculture: A Theoretical and Empirical Analysis." *American Economic Review* 61(1) (1971): 48–64.

Baron, David, and David Besanko. "Regulation and Information in a Continuing Relationship." *Information Economics and Policy* 1 (1984): 267–302.

Barry, P., J. Hopkin, and C. Baker. *Financial Management in Agriculture.* Danville: Interstate Printers and Publishers, 1988.

Barzel, Yoram. "Transaction Costs: Are They Just Costs?" *Journal of Institutional and Theoretical Economics* 141 (1985): 4–16.

Barzel, Yoram. *Economic Analysis of Property Rights*, 2d ed. Cambridge: Cambridge University Press, 1997.

Barzel, Yoram. "Measurement Cost and the Organization of Markets." *Journal of Law and Economics* 25 (1982a): 27–48.

Barzel, Yoram. "The Testability of the Law of Demand." In William F. Sharpe and Cathryn M. Cootner, eds., *Financial Economics: Essays in Honor of Paul Cootner,* 233–245. New York: Prentice Hall, 1982b.

Barzel, Yoram, and Levis Kochin. "Ronald Coase on the Nature of Social Cost as a Key to the Problem of the Firm." *Scandinavian Journal of Economics* 94 (1992): 19–31.

Barzel, Yoram, and Wing Suen. "Equity As a Guarantee." Working Paper, University of Washington, 1994.

Becker, Gary S., and Kevin M. Murphy. "The Division of Labor, Coordination Costs, and Knowledge." *Quarterly Journal of Economics* 107 (1992): 1137–1160.

Berliner, Joseph S. *Factory and Manager in the Soviet Union.* Cambridge: The MIT Press, 1957.

Berry, Russell L. "Cost Sharing as a Means of Improving the Share Rent Lease." *Journal of Farm Economics* 44 (1962): 796–807.

Bhattacharyya, Sugato, and Francine Lafontaine. "Double-Sided Moral Hazard and the Nature of Share Contracts." *RAND Journal of Economics* 26 (1995): 761–781.

Bidwell, Percy Wells, and John I. Falconer. *History of Agriculture in the Northern United States, 1620–1860.* Washington, DC: Carnegie Institution, 1925.

Bigelow, Poultney. "The Bonanza Farms of the West." *The Atlantic Monthly* 45 (1880): 33–44.

Binswanger, Hans, and Mark R. Rosenzweig. "Behavioral and Material Determinants of Production Relations in Agriculture." *Journal of Development Studies* 22 (1986): 503–539.

Braverman, Avishay and Joseph E. Stiglitz. "Sharecropping and the Interlinking of Agrarian Markets." *American Economic Review* 72 (1982): 695–715.

Braverman, Avishay and Joseph E. Stiglitz. "Cost-Sharing Arrangements under Sharecropping: Moral Hazard, Incentive Flexibility, and Risk." *American Journal of Agricultural Economics* 68 (1986): 642–652.

Brewster, John M. "The Machine Process in Agriculture and Industry." *Journal of Farm Economics* 32 (1950): 69–81.

Briggs, Harold E. "Early Bonanza Farming in the Red River Valley of the North." *Agricultural History* 6 (1932): 26–37.

Brown, D. J., and J. H. Atkinson. "Cash and Share Renting: An Empirical Test of the Link between Entrepreneurial Ability and Contractual Choice." *Bell Journal of Economics* 12 (1981): 296–299.

Burke, Mary A., and H. Peyton Young. "The Terms of Agriculgtural Contracts: Theory and Evidence." Working Paper No. 16, Center on Social and Economic Dynamics, The Brookings Institution and Johns Hopkins University, 2000.

Burkhart, Barry G. "Leases: Farmland Lease Provisions in Oklahoma," *Oklahoma Law Review* 44 (1991): 461–491.

Canjels, Eugene. "Risk and Incentives in Sharecropping: Evidence from Modern U.S. Agriculture." Working Paper, New School University, December 1996.

Carmona, Juan, and James Simpson. "'Rabassa Morta' in Catalan Viticulture: The Rise and Decline of a Long-Term Sharecropping Contract, 1670s–1920s." *Journal of Economic History* 59 (1999): 290–315.

Castle, Emery N., and Manning H. Becker. *Farm Business Management.* New York: Macmillan, 1962.

Chavas, Jean-Paul, and Matthew T. Holt. "Acreage Decisions under Risk: The Case of Corn and Soybeans." *American Journal of Agricultural Economics* 72 (1990): 529–538.

Cheung, Steven N. S. *The Theory of Share Tenancy* Chicago: University of Chicago Press, 1969.

Chiappori, Pierre Andre. and Bernard Salanié. "Testing Contract Theory: A Survey of Some Recent Work." Invited Lecture, World Congress of the Econometric Society Seattle, August 2000.

Coase, Ronald H. "The Nature of the Firm." *Economica* 4 (1937): 386–405.

Coase, Ronald H. "The Problem of Social Cost." *Journal of Law and Economics* 3 (1960): 1–4.

Coase, Ronald H. "The Acquisition of Fisher Body by General Motors." *Journal of Law and Economics* 43 (2000): 15–32.

Coase, Ronald H. *The Firm, the Market, and the Law.* Chicago: University of Chicago Press, 1988.

Crocker, Keith J., and Scott E. Masten. "Mitigating Contractual Hazards: Unilateral Options and Contract Length." *RAND Journal of Economics* 19 (1988): 327–343.

Cronan, William. *Changes in the Land.* New York: Hill and Wang, 1983.

Danhoff, Clarence H. *Changes in Agriculture: The Northern United States, 1820–1870.* Cambridge: Harvard University Press, 1969.

Day, Richard H. "The Economics of Technological Change and the Demise of the Sharecropper." *American Economic Review* 51 (1967): 427–449.

Deininger, Klaus, and Gershon Feder. "Land Institution and Land Markets." In B. L. Gardner and G. C. Rausser, eds., *Handbook of Agricultural Economics*, Vol. 1B. Amsterdam: Elsevier Science, 2001.

Demsetz, Harold. "The Cost of Transacting." *Quarterly Journal of Economics* 82 (1968): 33–53.

Demsetz, Harold, and Kenneth Lehn. "The Structure of Corporate Ownership: Causes and Consequences." *Journal of Political Economy* 93 (1985): 1155–1177.

Drache, Hiram. *The Day of the Bonanza.* Fargo: North Dakota Institute for Regional Studies, 1964.

Dubois, Pierre. "Moral Hazard, Land Fertility and Sharecropping in a Rural Area of the Philippines." Forthcoming in *Journal of Development Economics* (2002).

DuBow, Shane. "Wheaties: Chasing the Ripening Harvest across America's Great Plains." *Harper's Magazine* (August 1999): 33–44.

Edwards, William, and Michael Boehle. "Machinery Selection Considering Timeliness Losses." *Transactions of the American Society of Agricultural Engineers* (1980): 810–821.

Edwards, William, and V. Meyer. "Acquiring Farm Machinery Services: Ownership, Custom Hire, Rental, Lease." Cooperative Extension Service of Iowa State University, Ames, 1986.

Ellickson, John C., and John M. Brewster. "Technological Advance and the Structure of American Agriculture." *Journal of Farm Economics* 29 (1947): 827–847.

Ellickson, Robert C. *Order Without Law.* Cambridge: Harvard University Press, 1991.

Ellickson, Robert C., and Charles DiA. Thorland. "Ancient Land Law: Mesopotamia, Egypt, Israel." *Chicago-Kent Law Review* 71 (1995): 321–411.

Eswaran, Mukesh, and Ashok Kotwal. "A Theory of Contractual Structure in Agriculture." *American Economic Review* 75 (1985): 352–367.

Fogel, Robert William, and Stanley L. Engermann. *Time on the Cross.* Boston: Little, Brown, 1974.

Ford, S., and W. Musser. "The Lease-Purchase Decision for Agricultural Assets." *American Journal of Agricultural Economics* 76 (1994): 277–285.

Frank, Stuart D., and Dennis R. Henderson. "Transaction Costs as Determinants of Vertical Coordination in the U.S. Food Industries."*American Journal of Agricultural Economics* 74 (1992): 943–950.

Friedman, Milton. "The Methodology of Positive Economics." In *Essays in Positive Economics Chicago*, 3–47. Chicago: The University of Chicago Press, 1953.

Freixas Xavier, Roger Guesnerie, and Jean Tirole. "Planning under Incomplete Information and the Ratchet Effect." *Review of Economic Studies* 52 (1985): 173–191.

Galassi, Francesco. "Tuscans and Their Farms: The Economics of Share Tenancy in Fifteenth Century Florence." *Rivista di storia economica* 9 (1992): 77–94.

Galloway, J. H. *The Sugar Cane Industry: An Historical Geography from Its Origins to 1914*. Cambridge: Cambridge University Press, 1989.

Gardner, Bruce L. *The Governing of Agriculture*. Lawrence: University of Kansas Press, 1981.

Garen, John E. "Executive Compensation and Principal-Agent Theory." *Journal of Political Economy* 102 (1994): 1175–1199.

Gaynor, Martin, and Paul J. Gertler. "Moral Hazard and Risk Spreading in Partnership." *RAND Journal of Economics* 26 (1995): 591–613.

Ghatak, Maitreesh, and Priyank Pandey. "Contract Choice in Agriculture with Joint Moral Hazard in Effort and Risk." *Journal of Development Economics* 63 (2000): 303–326.

Gibbons, Robert. "Incentives in Organizations." *Journal of Economic Perspectives* 12 (1998): 115–132.

Goldberg, Victor P. "Aversion to Risk Aversion in the New Institutional Economics." *Journal of Institutional and Theoretical Economics* 146 (1990): 216–222.

Gray, L. C. *History of Agriculture in the Southern United States to 1860, Vols. I and II*. New York: Peter Smith, 1941. (Reprinted with the permission of the Carnegie Institution of Washington.)

Gray, L. C., Charles Stewart, Howard Turner, J. T. Sanders, and W. J. Spillman. "Farm Ownership and Tenancy." *Yearbook of the Department of Agriculture, 1923*. Washington, DC: U.S. Printing Office, 1924.

Grossman, Sanford J., and Oliver D. Hart. "An Analysis of the Principal-Agent Problem." *Econometrica* 51 (1983): 7–45.

Grossman, Sanford J., and Oliver D. Hart. "The Costs and Benefits of Ownership: A Theory of Vertical and Lateral Integration." *Journal of Political Economy* 94 (1986): 691–719.

Hallagan, William. "Self-Selection by Contractual Choice and the Theory of Sharecropping." *Bell Journal of Economics* 9 (1978): 344–354.

Hamilton, Neil D. "Adjusting Farm Tenancy Practices to Support Sustainable Agriculture." *Journal of Agricultural Taxation and Law* 12 (1990): 226–252.

Hamilton, Neil D. "Feeding Our Future: Six Philosophical Issues Shaping Agricultural Law." *Nebraska Law Review* 72 (1993): 210.

Hansmann, Henry. "Condominium and Cooperative Housing: Transaction Efficiency, Tax Subsidies, and Tenure Choice." *Journal of Legal Studies* 20 (1991): 25–71.

Hansmann, Henry. *The Ownership of Enterprise*. Cambridge: Harvard University Press, 1996.

Harl, Neil E. *Agricultural Law*. New York: Matthew Bender, 1998. (Chapter 121, "Farm Leases," in vol. 13, prepared by Philip E. Harris and Alan C. Schroeder.)

Harris, Milton, and Artur Raviv. "Optimal Incentive Contracts with Imperfect Information." *Journal of Economic Theory* 2 (1979): 231–259.

Hart, Oliver. *Firms Contracts and Financial Structure*. Oxford: Clarendon Press, 1995.

Hart, Oliver D., and Bengt Holmström. "The Theory of Contracts." In T. F. Bewley, ed., *Advances in Economic Theory: Fifth World Congress*, 71–155. Cambridge: Cambridge University Press, 1987.

Hart, Oliver D., and John Moore. "Property Rights and the Nature of the Firm." *Journal of Political Economy* 98 (1990): 1119–1158.

Hayami, Yuruiro, and Keijiro Otsuka. *Economics of Contract Choice: An Agrarian Perspective.* Oxford: Oxford University Press, 1993.

Hayek, Friedrich A. "The Uses of Knowledge in Society." *American Economic Review* 35 (1945): 519–530.

Heady, E. O. "Economics of Farm Leasing Systems." *Journal of Farm Economics* 29 (1947): 659–678.

Heady, E. O. *Economics of Agricultural Production and Resource Use.* New York: Prentice Hall, 1952.

Heitman, J. *The Modernization of the Louisiana Sugar Industry: 1830–1910.* Baton Rouge: Louisiana State University Press, 1987.

Helmberger, Peter G., Gerald R. Campbell, and William D. Dobson. "Organization and Performance of Agricultural Markets." In *A Survey of Agricultural Economics Literature*, Vol. 3, ed., Lee R. Martin, 503–653. Minneapolis: University of Minnesota Press, 1981.

Henderson, J. Vernon, and Yannis Ioannides. "A Model of Housing Tenure Choice." *American Economic Review* 73 (1983): 98–113.

Hennessy, David A. "Information Asymmetry as a Reason for Food Industry Vertical Integration." *American Journal of Agricultural Economics* 78 (1996): 1034–1043.

Hennessy, David A., and John D. Lawrence "Contractual Relations, Control and Quality in the Hog Sector." *Review of Agricultural Economics* 21 (1999): 52–67.

Higgs, Robert. "Race, Tenure, and Resource Allocation in Southern Agriculture, 1910." *Journal of Economic History* 33 (1973): 149–169.

Hirshliefer, Jack, and John G. Riley. *The Analytics of Uncertainty and Information.* Cambridge: Cambridge University Press, 1992.

Hoff, Karla, Avishnay Braverman, and Joseph Stiglitz, eds. *The Economics of Rural Organization: Theory, Practice, and Policy.* Oxford: Oxford University Press, 1993.

Holmes, C. L. *Economics of Farm Organization and Management.* Boston: D.C. Heath, 1928.

Holmes, C. L. "Prospective Displacement of the Independent Family Farm by Large Farms of Estate Management and the Socio-Economic Consequences." *Journal of Farm Economics* 11 (1929): 227–247.

Hoffman, Phillip T. "The Economic Theory of Sharecropping in Early Modern France." *Journal of Economic History* 44 (1984): 309–319.

Holmström, Bengt. "Moral Hazard and Observability." *Bell Journal of Economics* 10 (1979): 74–91.

Holmström, Bengt, "Moral Hazard and Teams." *Bell Journal of Economics* 13 (1982): 324–340.

Holmström, Bengt, and Paul Milgrom. "Multi-Task Principal-Agent Analyses: Incentive Contracts, Asset Ownership, and Job Design." *Journal of Law, Economics, and Organization* 7 (1991): 24–25.

Holmström, Bengt, and Paul Milgrom. "The Firm as an Incentive System." *American Economic Review* 84 (1994): 972–991.

Holmström, Bengt, and John Roberts. "The Boundaries of the Firm Revisited." *Journal of Economic Perspectives* 12 (1998): 73–94.

Hopkin, J. "Leasing versus Buying of Machinery." *Journal of American Society of Farm Managers and Rural Appraisers* (1971): 17–23.

Hueth, Brent, and Ethan Ligon. "Producer Price Risk and Quality Measurement." *American Journal of Agricultural Economics* 81 (1999): 512–524.

Huffman, Wallace E. "Human Capital: Education and Agriculture." In B. L. Gardner and G. C. Rausser, eds., *Handbook of Agricultural Economics*, Vol. 1A. Amsterdam: Elsevier Science, 2001.

Hurwicz, Leonid, and Leonard Shapiro. "Incentive Structures Maximizing Residual Gain under Incomplete Information." *Bell Journal of Economics* 9 (1978): 180–191.

Ickes, Barry, and Larry Samuelson. "Job Transfers and Incentives in Complex Organizations: Thwarting the Ratchet Effect." *RAND Journal of Economics* 18 (1987): 275–286.

Irwin, George D., and Lawrence N. Smith. "Machinery Leasing: Perspective and Prospects." *Agricultural Finance Review* 33 (1972): 42–47.

Isern, Thomas D. *Bull Threshers and Bindlestiffs: Harvesting and Threshing on the North American Plains.* Lawrence: University of Kansas Press, 1990.

Isern, Thomas D. *Custom Combining on the Great Plains.* Norman: University of Oklahoma Press, 1981.

Johnson, Bruce, Larry Janssen, Michael Lundeen, and J. David Aitken. "Agricultural Land Leasing and Rental Market Characteristics: A Case Study of South Dakota and Nebraska." Report prepared for the Economic Research Service of the United States Department of Agriculture, Washington, DC, 1988.

Johnson, D. Gale. "Resource Allocation Under Share Contracts." *Journal of Political Economy* 58 (1950): 111–123.

Johnson, Nancy L., and Vernon W. Ruttan. "Why Are Farms So Small?" *World Development* 22 (1994): 691–706.

Johnson, O. R. "The Family Farm." *Journal of Farm Economics* 26 (1944): 529–548.

Joskow, Paul L. "Contract Duration and Relationship-Specific Investments: Empirical Evidence from Coal Markets." *American Economic Review* 77 (1987): 168–185.

Kanemoto, Yoshitsugu, and W. Bentley MacLeod. "The Ratchet Effect and the Market for Secondhand Workers." *Journal of Labor Economics* 10 (1992): 85–98.

Kawasaki, Sehchi, and John McMillan. "The Design of Contracts: Evidence from Japanese Subcontracting." *Journal of the Japanese and International Economies* 1 (1987): 327–349.

Kay, Ronald D., and William Edward. *Farm Management,* 3d ed. New York: McGraw-Hill, 1994.

Kilman, Scott. "Power Pork: Corporations Begin to Turn Hog Business into an Assembly Line." *Wall Street Journal,* March 28, 1994, p. 1.

Kislev, Yoav, and Willis Peterson. "Prices, Technology, and Farm Size." *Journal of Political Economy* 90 (1982): 578–595.

Klein, Benjamin, and Keith B. Leffler. "The Role of Market Forces in Assuring Contractual Performance." *Journal of Political Economy* 89 (1981): 615–641.

Klein, Benjamin, Robert G. Crawford, and Armen A. Alchian. "Vertical Integration, Appropriable Rents, and the Competitive Contracting Process." *Journal of Law and Economics* 21 (1978): 297–326.

Kliebenstein, James B., and John D. Lawrence. "Contracting and Vertical Coordination in the United States Pork Industry." *American Journal of Agricultural Economics* 77 (1995): 1213–1218.

Knoeber, Charles R. "A Real Game of Chicken: Contracts, Tournaments, and the Production of Broilers." *Journal of Law, Economics, and Organization* 5 (1989): 271–292.

Knoeber, Charles R. "Explaining State Bans on Corporate Farming." *Economic Inquiry* 35 (1997): 151–166.

Knoeber, Charles R. "Land and Livestock Contracting in Agriculture: A Principal-Agent Perspective." In Boudewijn Bouckaert and Gerrit De Geest, eds., *The Encyclopedia of Law and Economics*, Vol. 3, 1133–1153. Cheltenham, UK: Edward Elgar Press, 2000.

Knoeber, Charles R., and Walter N. Thurman. "Testing the Theory of Tournaments: An Empirical Analysis of Broiler Production." *Journal of Labor Economics* 12 (1994): 155–179.

Knutson, Ronald D., J. B. Penn, and Barry L. Flinchbaugh. *Agricultural and Food Policy,* 4th ed. Upper Saddle River, NJ: Prentice-Hall, 1998.

Kohn, Meir. "A Finance Approach to Understanding Patterns of Land Tenure." Dartmouth College Working Paper 01-12, 2001.

Kreps, David. "Corporate Culture and Economic Theory." In J. E. Alt and K. A. Shepsle, eds., *Perspectives on Positive Political Economy*. Cambridge: Cambridge University Press, 1990.

Laffont, Jean-Jacques, and Mohamed Salah Matoussi. "Moral Hazard, Financial Constraints and Sharecropping in El Oulja." *Review of Economic Studies* 62 (1995): 381–400.

Laffont, Jean-Jacques, and Jean Tirole. *A Theory of Incentives in Procurement and Regulation.* Cambridge: The MIT Press, 1993.

Lafontaine, Francine. "Agency Theory and Franchising: Some Empirical Results." *RAND Journal of Economics* 23 (1992): 263–283.

Lafontaine, Francine, and Sugato Bhattacharyya. "The Role of Risk in Franchising." *Journal of Corporate Finance* 2 (1995): 39–74.

Lagrone, William F., and Earle E. Gavett. *Interstate Custom Combining in the Great Plains in 1971.* Economic Research Service Paper no. 563. Washington, DC: U.S. Department of Agriculture, 1975.

Lang, Kevin, and Peter-John Gordon. "Partnerships as Insurance Devices: Theory and Evidence." *RAND Journal of Economics* 26 (1995): 614–629.

Lazear, Edward P. "Salaries and Piece Rates." *Journal of Business* 59 (1986): 405–431.

Lazear, Edward P. *Personnel Economics.* Cambridge: The MIT Press, 1995.

Leffler, Keith B., and Randall R. Rucker. "Transactions Costs and the Efficient Organization of Production: A Study of Timber-Harvesting Contracts." *Journal of Political Economy* 99 (1991): 1060–1087.

Leland, Hayne "Optimal Risk-Sharing and the Leasing of Natural Resources with Application to Oil and Gas Leasing on the OSC." *Quarterly Journal of Economics* 92 (1978): 413–437.

Libecap, Gary D. *Contracting for Property Rights.* Cambridge: Cambridge University Press, 1989.

Louisiana Agricultural Statistics Service. *Louisiana Agricultural Statistics.* Baton Rouge: Louisiana Department of Agriculture, 1975–1991.

Lucas, Robert E. B. "Sharing, Monitoring, and Incentives: Marshallian Misallocation Reassessed." *Journal of Political Economy* 87 (1979): 501–521.

Luporini, Annalisa, and Bruno Parigi. "Multi-Task Sharecropping Contracts: The Italian Mezzadria." *Economica* 63 (1996): 445–457.

Lyon, Thomas P., and Steven C. Hackett. "Bottlenecks and Governance Structures: Open Access and Long-Term Contracting in Natural Gas." *Journal of Law, Economics, and Organization* 9 (1993): 380–398.

Marion, Bruce W. *The Organizational Performance of the U.S. Food System.* Lexington, MA: Lexington Books, 1986.

Martin, J. Rod. "Beef." In Lyle P. Schertz and Others, *Another Revolution in U.S. Farming?* Washington, DC: U.S. Department of Agriculture, 1979.

Martin, Robert. "Risk Sharing and Franchising." *American Economic Review* 78 (1988): 954–968.

Masten, Scott E. "The Organization of Production: Evidence from the Aerospace Industry." *Journal of Law and Economics* 27 (1985): 403–418.

Masten, Scott E., ed. *Case Studies in Contracting and Organization.* Oxford: Oxford University Press, 1996.

Masten, Scott E., and Oliver E. Williamson, eds. *The Economics of Transaction Costs.* Cheltenham, UK: Edward Elgar Press, 1999.

Masten, Scott E., and Stéphane Saussier. "Econometrics of Contracts: An Assessment of Developments in the Empirical Literature on Contracting." *Revue-d'Economie Industrielle* 92 (2000): 215–236.

Masten, Scott E., James Meehan, and Edward Snyder. "The Costs of Organization." *Journal of Law, Economics, and Organization* 7 (1991): 1–26.

McBride, William D. "Changes in U.S. Livestock Production 19690-92." *Economic Research Service Report #754.* Washington, DC: U.S. Government Printing Office, 1997.

Meyer, Keith C., Donald B. Pedersen, Norman W. Thorson, and John H. Davidson Jr. *Agricultural Law: Cases and Materials.* St. Paul: West Publishing, 1985.

Meyer, Margaret, and John Vickers. "Performance Comparisons and Dynamic Incentives." *Journal of Political Economy* 105 (1997): 547–581.

Mighell, R., and L. Jones. "Vertical Coordination in Agriculture." *Agricultural Economics Report* no. 19, February 1963.

Milgrom, Paul, and John Roberts. *Economics, Organization and Management.* Englewood Cliffs: Prentice Hall, 1992.

Mill, John S. *Principles of Political Economy.* Sir W. J. Ashley, ed. New York: Kelley, [1871] 1965.

Montana Cooperative Extension Service. "Summary of the Montana 1990 Custom Rate Lease Agreement Survey." Montana State University, 1990.

Mulherin, J. Harold. "Complexity in Long Term Contracts: An Analysis of Natural Gas Contractual Provisions." *Journal of Law, Economics, and Organization* 2 (1986): 105–118.

Nabi, Ijaz. "Contracts, Resource Use and Productivity in Sharecropping." *Journal of Development Studies* 22 (1986): 429–442.

Nass, H. G., U. Gupta, and J. Sterling. "Effects of Seeding Date, Seed Treatment and Folair Sprays on Yield and Other Agronomic Characteristics of Wheat, Oats, and Barley." *Canadian Journal of Plant Science* 55 (1973): 451–460.

Niehans, Jurg. "Transaction Costs." In John Eatwell, Murray Milgate, and Peter Newman, eds., *The New Palgrave: A Dictionary of Economics*, Vol. 4, 676–679. New York: Macmillan, 1987.

Nebraska Agricultural Statistical Service. *1987 Nebraska Agricultural Statistics*, various years.

Nelson, A., W. Lee, and W. Murray. *Agricultural Finance*, 6th ed. Ames: Iowa State University Press, 1973.

Nerlove, Marc L. "Reflections on the Economic Organization of Agriculture: Traditional, Modern, and Transitional." In David Martimort, ed., *Agricultural Markets: Mechanisms, Failures, and Regulations*, 9–30. Amsterdam: North-Holland Press, 1996.

Newberry, David, and Joseph Stiglitz. "Sharecropping, Risk-Sharing, and the Importance of Imperfect Information." In James A. Roumasset, Jean-Marc Boussard, and Inderjit Singh, eds., *Risk, Uncertainty and Agricultural Development*. Berkeley: University of California Press, 1979.

Nickerson, Jack A., and Brian S. Silverman. "Why Aren't All Truck Drivers Owner-Operators? Asset Ownership and the Employment Relation in Interstate For-Hire Trucking." Forthcoming in *Journal of Economics, Management and Strategy* (2002).

The 1995 Cooperative Extension Service Farm Leasing Survey. Department of Agricultural and Consumer Economics, University of Illinois, 1996.

Olsen, Trond E., and Gaute Torsvik. "The Ratchet Effect in Common Agency: Implications for Regulation and Privatization." *Journal of Law, Economics, and Organization* 9 (1993): 136–158.

Orden, David, Robert Paarlberg, and Terry Roe. *Policy Reform in American Agriculture: Analysis and Prognosis.* Chicago: University of Chicago Press, 1999.

Otsuka, Keijiro, and Yujiro Hayami. "Theories of Share Tenancy: A Critical Survey." *Economic Development and Cultural Change* 36 (1988): 31–68.

Otsuka, Keijiro, Hiroyuki Chuma, and Yujiro Hayami. "Land and Labor Contracts in Agrarian Economies: Theories and Facts." *Journal of Economic Literature* 30 (1992): 1965–2018.

Pasour, E. C., Jr. *Agriculture and the State.* San Francisco: The Independent Institute, 1990.

Perry, Janet, Mitch Morehart, David Banker, and Jim Johnson. "Contracting: A Business Option for Many Farmers." *Agricultural Outlook* (May 1997): 2–5.

Pflueger, Burton W. "Farm Machinery Costs: Own, Lease, or Custom Hire." Cooperative Extension Service of South Dakota State University, January 1994.

Pieper, Charles A., and Neil E. Harl. "Iowa Farmland Ownership and Tenure 1982–1997: A Fifteen-Year Perspective," Iowa State University Extension, Pub. EDC 198, January 2000.

Pirrong, Stephen Craig. "The Efficient Scope of Private Transactions-Cost-Reducing Institutions: The Successes and Failures of Commodity Exchanges." *Journal of Legal Studies* 24 (1995): 229–255.

Pope, Rulon D., and Richard E. Just. "On Testing the Structure of Risk Preferences in Agricultural Supply Analysis." *American Journal of Agricultural Economics* 73 (1991): 743–748.

Pratt, J. W. "Risk Aversion in the Small and in the Large." *Econometrica* 32 (1964): 122–136.

Prendergast, Canice. "The Provision of Incentives in Firms." *Journal of Economic Literature* 37 (1999): 7–63.

Prendergast, Canice. "What Trade-off of Risk and Incentives?" *American Economic Review* 90 (2000): 421–425.

Prendergast, Canice. "The Tenuous Trade-off between Risk and Incentives." Forthcoming in *Journal of Political Economy* (2002).

Pryor, Frederic L. "The Plantation Economy as an Economic System—A Review Article." *Journal of Comparative Economics* 6 (1982): 288–317.

Pryor, Frederic L. *The Red and the Green*. Princeton: Princeton University Press, 1992.

Pudney, Stephen, Francesco Galassi, and Fabrizia Mealli. "An Econometric Model of Farm Tenures in Fifteenth Century Florence." *Economica* 65 (1998): 535–556.

Rao, C. H. Hanumatha. "Uncertainty, Entrepreneurship, and Sharecropping In India." *Journal of Political Economy* 79 (1971): 578–595.

Raup, Philip M. "Corporate Farming in the United States." *Journal of Economic History* 33 (1973): 274–290.

Rausser, Gordon C. "Predatory versus Productive Government: The Case of U.S. Agricultural Policies." *Journal of Economic Perspectives* 6 (1992): 133–157.

Ray, Tridip. "Share Tenancy as Strategic Delegation," *Journal of Development Economics* 58 (1999): 45–60.

Reid, Joseph D., Jr. "The Theory of Share Tenancy Revisited—Again." *Journal of Political Economy* 85 (1977): 403–407.

Rosenzweig, Mark R., and Hans P. Binswanger. "Wealth, Weather Risk and the Composition and Profitability of Agricultural Investments." *Economic Journal* 103 (1993): 56–78.

Ross, Steven A. "The Economic Theory of Agency: The Principal's Problem." *American Economic Review* 63 (1973): 134–139.

Roumasset, James. "The Economic Nature of the Agricultural Firm." *Journal of Economic Behavior and Organization* 26 (1995): 161–177.

Roy, Ewell Paul. *Contract Farming, U.S.A.* Danville, IL: Interstate Printers and Publishers, 1963.

Royer, J. S., and R. Rogers, eds. *The Industrialization of Agriculture: Vertical Coordination in the U.S. Food System.* Aldershot, UK: Ashgate Publishing, 1998.

Salanié, Bernard. *The Economics of Contracts.* Cambridge: The MIT Press, 1997.

Sappington, David E. M. "Incentives in Principal-Agent Relationships." *Journal of Economic Perspectives* 5 (1991): 45–66.

Schickele, Rainer. "Effect of Tenure Systems on Agricultural Efficiency." *Journal of Farm Economics* 23 (1941): 185–207.

Schlebecker, John T. *Whereby We Thrive: A History of American Farming, 1607–1972.* Ames: Iowa State University Press, 1973.

Schmitz, Andrew, W. Hartley Furtan, and Katherine R. Baylis. *Agricultural Policy, Agribusiness, and Rent-Seeking Behavior.* Toronto: University of Toronto Press, 2002.

Schultz, Theodore W. *The Economic Organization of Agriculture.* New York: McGraw-Hill, 1954.

Scolville, Orlin J. "Measuring the Family Farm." *Journal of Farm Economics* 29 (1947): 506–519.

Sella, Domenico. "Discussion." *Journal of Economic History* 42 (1982): 161–162.

Sengupta, Kunal. "Limited Liability, Moral Hazard, and Share Tenancy." *Journal of Development Economics* 52 (1997): 393–407.

Serfes, Konstantinos. "Risk-sharing versus Incentives: Contract Design under Two-Sided Heterogeneity." SUNY-Stony Brook Working Paper, October 2001.

Sexton, Richard J., and Nathalie Lavoie. "Food Processing and Distribution: An Industrial Organization Approach." In Bruce L. Gardner and Gordon C. Rausser, eds., *Handbook of Agricultural Economics*, Vol. 1B. Amsterdam: Elsevier Science, 2001.

Shaban, Radwan Ali. "Testing between Competing Models of Sharecropping." *Journal of Political Economy* 95 (1987): 893–920.

Shapiro, Carl. "Premiums for High Quality Products as Returns to Reputation." *Quarterly Journal of Economics* 98 (1983): 659–680.

Shavell, Steven. "Risk Sharing and Incentives in the Principal and Agent Relationship." *Bell Journal of Economics* 10 (1979): 55–73.

Shelanski, Howard A., and Peter G. Klein. "Empirical Research in Transaction Cost Economics: A Review and Assessment." *Journal of Law, Economics, and Organization* 11 (1995): 335–361.

Short, Cameron, and Kangethe W. Gitu. "Timeliness Costs for Machinery Selection." *Canadian Journal of Agricultural Economics* 39 (1991): 457–462.

Smith, Adam. *The Wealth of Nations*, ed. Kathryn Sutherland. Oxford: Oxford University Press, [1776] 1992.

Sotomayer, Narda L., Paul N. Ellinger, and Peter J. Barry. "Choice among Leasing Contracts in Farm Real Estate." *Agricultural Finance Review* 60 (2000):71–84.

South Dakota Agricultural Statistical Service. *South Dakota Agriculture*, various years.

Spillman, W. J. "The Agricultural Ladder." *American Economic Review* 9 (1919): 170–179.

Statistics Canada. *Census Overview of Canadian Agriculture, 1971–1991.* Ottawa: Queen's Printer, 1992.

Stiglitz, Joseph. "Incentives and Risk-Sharing in Sharecropping." *Review of Economic Studies* 41 (1974): 219–55.

Stiglitz, Joseph. "Sharecropping." In John Eatwell, Murray Milgate, and Peter Newman, eds., *The New Palgrave: A Dictionary of Economics,* 320–323. New York: Macmillan, 1987.

Strickler, Paul E., Helen V. Smith, and Wilbert H. Walker. *Uses of Agricultural Machinery in 1974.* Economic Research Service, Statistical Bulletin No, 377. Washington, DC: U.S. Department of Agriculture, 1966.

Sumner, Daniel A. "Targeting Farm Programs." *Contemporary Policy Issues* 9 (1991): 93–106.

Taslim, M. A. "A Survey of Theories of Cropshare Tenancy." *Economic Record* 68 (1992): 254–275.

Taylor, H. C. "Methods of Renting Farm Lands in Wisconsin." Bulletin No. 198. Madison: The University of Wisconsin Agricultural Experiment Station. July 1910.

Tsoulouhas, Theofanis, and Tomislav Vukina. "Processor Contracts with Many Agents and Bankruptcy." *American Journal of Agricultural Economics* 81 (1999): 61–74.

Thompson, G. B., and Clayton C. O'Mary, eds. *The Feedlot*, 3d ed. Philadelphia: Lea and Febiger, 1983.

Townsend, Robert M. "Risk and Insurance in Village India." *Econometrica* 62 (1994): 539–91.

Tsoodle, Leah J., and Christine A. Wilson. "Nonirrigated Crop-Share Leasing Arrangements in Kansas." Staff Paper no. 01-02. Kansas State University Department of Agricultural Economics, August 2000.

Umbeck, John. "A Theory of Contract Choice And the California Gold Rush." *Journal of Law and Economics* 20 (1977): 421–437.

U.S. Department of Agriculture. *Agricultural Statistics 1986.* Washington, DC: U.S. Government Printing Office, 1987.

U.S. Department of Agriculture. *ASCS Commodity Fact Sheet*, various issues. Washington, DC: U.S. Government Printing Office, 1988.

U. S. Department of Commerce, Bureau of the Census. *Historical Statistics of the United States: Colonial Times to 1970.* Washington, DC: U.S. Government Printing Office, 1976.

U.S. Department of Commerce, Bureau of the Census. *County and City Data Book 1987*. Washington, DC: U.S. Government Printing Office, 1989a.

U.S. Department of Commerce, Bureau of the Census. *1987 Census of Agriculture*, Vol. 1, Pt. 27, Nebraska. Washington, DC: U.S. Government Printing Office, 1989b.

U.S. Department of Commerce, Bureau of the Census. *1987 Census of Agriculture*, Vol. 1, Pt. 41, South Dakota. Washington, DC: U.S. Government Printing Office, 1989c.

U.S. Department of Commerce, Bureau of the Census. *1987 Census of Agriculture, Vol. 3: 1988 Agricultural Economics and Ownership Survey*. Washington, DC: U.S. Government Printing Office, 1989d.

U.S. Department of Commerce, Bureau of the Census. *Statistical Abstract of the United States 1993*. Washington, DC: U.S. Government Printing Office, 1993.

U.S. Department of Commerce, Bureau of the Census. *1977 Census of Agriculture, Vol 3: Agricultural Economics and Land Ownership Survey*. Washington, DC: U.S. Government Printing Office, 1999.

Usher, Daniel. "The Coase Theorem is Tautological, Incoherent or Wrong." *Economic Letters* 61 (1998): 3–11.

Uvaceck, Edward, Jr. "Economics of Feedlots and Financing." Chapter 2 in G. B. Thompson and Clayton C. O'Mary, eds., *The Feedlot*, 3d ed. Philadelphia: Lea and Febiger, 1983.

Vercammen, James, and Andrew Schmitz. "Marketing and Distribution: Theory and Statistical Measurement." In Bruce L. Gardner and Gordon C. Rausser, eds., *Handbook of Agricultural Economics*. Amsterdam: Elsevier Science, 2001.

Vukina, Tomislav. "Vertical Integration and Contracting in the U.S. Poultry Sector." *Journal of Food Distribution Research* 32 (2001): 29–38.

Weitzman, Martin. "The Ratchet Principle and Performance Incentives." *Bell Journal of Economics* 11 (1980): 302–308.

Wiggins, Steven. "The Comparative Advantage of Long-Term Contracts and Firms." *Journal of Law, Economics, and Organization* 6 (1990): 155–170.

Williams, Charles M. "Enterprise on the Prairies." *Harvard Business Review* 31 (1953): 97–102.

Williams, Jeffrey. "Futures Markets: A Consequence of Risk Aversion or Transactions Costs?" *Journal of Political Economy* 95 (1987): 1000–1023.

Williamson, O. E. "Transaction-Cost Economics: The Governance of Contractual Relations." *Journal of Law and Economics* 22 (1979): 233–261.

Williamson, O. E. "The New Institutional Economics: Taking Stock, Looking Ahead." *Journal of Economic Literature* 38 (2000): 595–613.

Young, H. Peyton, and Mary A. Burke. "Competition and Custom in Economic Contracts: A Case Study of Illinois Agriculture." *American Economic Review* 91 (2001): 559–573.

Index